D0812207

1408711

PS
3231
A554
1962
c.2

Walt Whitman Handbook

By

GAY WILSON ALLEN
New York University

DISCARDED

MY 30 '89

HENDRICKS HOUSE, INC.

NEW YORK, 1962

COPYRIGHT, 1946

HENDRICKS HOUSE, INC.

PUBLISHED, 1957

HENDRICKS HOUSE, INC.

*All rights reserved. No part of this book may be re-
produced in any form, by mimeograph or any other
means, without written permission from the publisher.*

Reprinted, 1962

Printed in the U.S.A.

To

EVE AND EVELYN

*in gratitude
and affection*

CONTENTS

PREFACE

I

The Crofts series of excellent *Handbooks* for the major British poets has long been useful to students and teachers of English literature, but for various reasons similar guides have not been published for American writers. Yet—without in any way attempting to compare the importance of American authors with such giants as Chaucer, Shakespeare, Milton, or Spenser—I think anyone acquainted with the vast body of scholarship and critical interpretation already accumulated around such American poets as Walt Whitman will agree that "Handbook" guides are almost as seriously needed for the American as for the major English poets.

But though the fecundity of scholarship in the field of American Literature is today comparable to the similar activities in other literary fields, the problems which have confronted me in preparing this *Walt Whitman Handbook* have been in many ways unique to the subject. For one thing, Whitman biography, despite the scores of published books, continues in a state of flux. Even some of the basic facts are still a matter of dispute. And when we come to the interpretation of Whitman's poetry, the diversity of opinion and the controversies still far from dead are little short of bewildering.

As I worked on this *Handbook,* therefore, it gradually and necessarily became more ambitious. My task has been not only to summarize the vast scholarship in the field but also to select and evaluate the significant contributions. Furthermore, despite abundance of publications, certain phases of Whitman's thought and art—especially his sources and his influences—have been insufficiently investigated, and I have had to fill in some of the gaps (notably in Chapters III and VI) in order to give a well-rounded account of the poet and his work. Thus here some new interpretations appear in print for the first time, but I believe they are in harmony with the latest and best Whitman scholarship—of Canby, Furness, Matthiessen, Schyberg, and the others whom I mention throughout the book.

Possibly in a few years from now this *Handbook* might have been easier to write, but at the present time there is no indication as to when, if ever, Whitman scholarship will reach an equilibrium, and meanwhile the book is needed. If the field continues to develop at the present rate, the book may be out of date in a few years; but I hope that it will prove sufficiently useful in the meantime to justify future editions—and that the faults of this edition may be largely overcome in future revisions. To this end I invite suggestions and corrections.

II

I am, of course, already indebted to the many authors of articles and books about Walt Whitman, especially to Holloway, Catel, Schyberg, and Canby. In order to acknowledge this tremendous debt and to make it easy for students to find their way around in the maze of Whitman publications, I have used many quotations and footnotes. In the absence of both a published Whitman concordance and a complete bibliography, these should be doubly useful.

My debt to several friends and scholars is so great that I must mention them specifically. In addition to many other personal favors, Dr. Clifton Joseph Furness has read Chapter I and supplied me with many facts and criticisms. The Whitman dealer, Mr. Alfred Goldsmith, and the well-known bibliographical scholar, Mr. Rollo G. Silver, have read and criticized Chapter II. Professor Oscar Cargill, the historian of modern ideas, has read Chapters III, IV, and V and offered many helpful suggestions. Dr. Oreste Pucciani kindly lent me his personal copy of his Harvard Dissertation on *French Criticism of Walt Whitman* and has permitted me to quote from his unpublished work. And I am similarily indebted to Dr. Dorothy Frederica Mercer for the use of her University of California dissertation on *Leaves of Grass and the Bhagavad Gita: A Comparative Study*. Mr. Fernando Alegria, of the University of California, has generously permitted me to use his unpublished studies of Whitman in Latin America. Dr. Horst Frenz of Indiana University, who is investigating relationships between American and European literatures, has supplied me with bibliographical data and has read the Germanic part of Chapter VI. The Danish biographer and critic, Dr. Frederik Schyberg, first aroused my interest in Whitman's relations to World Literature, and up until the German invasion of Denmark generously sent me books and information. I have also had the good luck to have several talks with Dr. Henry Seidel Canby on this subject and am indebted to him for encouragement and advice. My colleague, Dr. Emerson Shuck, has also offered helpful criticisms of

Chapters I and II, and Dr. Cecil L. Rew has assisted me in reading proof on Chapter VI. To all these men and women I am deeply grateful, and to others who have helped in various ways, such as President Frank J. Prout, who lightened my teaching load in order that I might make more rapid progress on this book; to Mrs. Evelyn Simmons Hart, who has verified quotations and footnotes and often challenged me to prove my statements; and to my wife, Evie Allison Allen, who has aided the work in more ways than I can specify. Professor Walter Hendricks, the publisher, has given unceasingly of his time, effort, and interest to make the book a success.

Several libraries have courteously made their resources available to me, including Newberry in Chicago, Library of Congress, Yale Library, New York Public, Toledo Public, Oberlin College Library, and both the Public and the University Library at Bowling Green.

III

For permission to quote from copyrighted publications, I am indebted to the following persons and firms:

Jay B. Hubbell, editor of *American Literature;* Ralph Tyler Flewelling, editor of *The Personalist;* Horatio Smith, editor of *Romanic Review;* the University of Chicago Press, publisher of *Ethics;* Emory Holloway, author of *Whitman, An Interpretation in Narrative* and editor of *Pictures;* George Allen and Unwin, Ltd.; American Book Co.; Chapman and Grimes (formerly Richard Badger); Cornell University Press; Doubleday, Doran and Co.; E. P. Dutton and Co.; Alexander Gardner, Ltd.; Harper and Brothers; Harvard University Press; Harcourt, Brace and Co.; Houghton, Mifflin Co.; Little, Brown and Co.; Longmans, Green and Co.; The Macmillan Co.; David McKay Co.; Methuen and Co., Ltd.; Oxford University Press; Philosophical Library; G. P. Putnam's Sons; Grant Richards, Ltd.; George Routledge and Sons, Ltd.; Charles Scribner's Sons; Martin Secker and Marburg, Ltd.; Peter Smith; University of Michigan Press; University of Pennsylvania Press; and Writers' Editions. Authors and publishers are listed wherever quotations from copyrighted articles and books are used.

G. W. A.

Bowling Green, Ohio

CHRONOLOGICAL TABLE

[Note: Some of the dates for the events in Walt Whitman's life, especially the early years, are extremely difficult to establish. His own statements are often contradictory, and the earlier biographers added to the confusion. Clifton Joseph Furness has sifted all available data for his forthcoming factual biography and he has generously checked and corrected the following table. The complete evidence, too complicated for brief summary, will be given in Mr. Furness's biography.]

SIGNIFICANT EVENTS IN WHITMAN'S LIFE

1819   Born May 31 at West Hills, Huntington Township, Long Island.

1823   Family moved to Brooklyn.

1825   LaFayette visited Brooklyn, July 4—one of the poet's most cherished memories.

1825–30   Attended public school in Brooklyn. Family frequently shifted residence in city.

1830–31   Office boy in lawyer's office, then doctor's; probably quit school at this time.

1831–32   Worked in printing offices, began to learn the trade. Printer's apprentice on *Long Island Patriot.*

1832   Summer. Worked at Worthington's printing establishment.

1832   Fall—to May 12, 1835 worked as compositor on *Long Island Star.*

1833   The Whitman family moved back to the country.

1835   May 12th—till May, 1836, worked in printing offices in New York City.

1836–38 Taught in various schools on Long Island. Participated in debating societies.

1838   Spring—Spring, 1839. Edited *Long Islander* in Huntington.

1839–41 Returned to teaching on Long Island.

1840   Fall. Campaigned for Van Buren.

1841   May. Went to New York and worked as compositor for *The New World.*

1842   Edited for a few months *The Aurora* and *The Tatler.*

1843   Spring. Edited *The Statesman.*

1844   Summer. Edited *The New York Democrat.*

1844   October. Worked on *The New York Mirror.*

1841–48 Contributed to several prominent New York journals: *Democratic Review, Broadway Journal, American Review, New York Sun, Columbian Magazine.*

1846–47 Edited the Brooklyn *Daily Eagle.*

1848   Quit (or was discharged from) editorship of *Eagle* in January. February 11 left, with brother Jeff for New Orleans to take up editorial position on the *Crescent.* First number of *Crescent,* published March 5, contained Whitman's poem "Sailing the Mississippi at Midnight." May 24 resigned position, sailed to St. Louis May 27. Arrived home June 15. Back in Brooklyn, became editor of the *Brooklyn Freeman,* first number issued Sept. 9, 1848.

1849   In spring the *Freeman* became a daily. In April Whitman was also conducting a printing office and bookstore on Myrtle Avenue—still listed in the *Brooklyn Directory* for 1851.

Resigned editorship Sept. 11, Free-Soilers having joined regular party.

1851–54 Followed carpentering trade in Brooklyn—exact details of this period are scanty.
Addressed Brooklyn Art Museum, March 31, 1851.

1855 First edition of *Leaves of Grass* published by the author, on or near July 4; Father died soon after, probably July 11. Fowler and Wells were agents for the book. Conway first to visit the poet. Emerson wrote his "greetings" July 21.

1856 Second edition of *Leaves of Grass,* published sometime between Aug. 16 and Sept. 12, Fowler and Wells again acting as agents. In November Alcott and Thoreau visited the poet—Emerson the following year.

1857-59 Edited Brooklyn *Times;* unemployed by summer of 1859. Frequented Pfaff's Restaurant, a Bohemian gathering place.

1860 Third edition of *Leaves of Grass* published in Boston by Thayer and Eldridge, preceded by famous discussion with Emerson over sex poems.

1861 Thayer and Eldridge failed and the plates for the third edition were secured by a dishonest publisher, who printed and sold pirated copies for a number of years. Soon after the bombardment of Fort Sumter, April 18, Whitman recorded in his diary a moral and physical dedication. About this time deserted Pfaff's and Bohemian friends.

1862 Dec. 14 read brother George's name in list of wounded and went immediately to the war front in Virginia to find him. Became an unofficial nurse.

1863–64 Worked in field and army hospitals. Beginning of
friendship with O'Connor and Burroughs.
Health broke down in mid-summer of '64 and he returned to his mother's home in Brooklyn for six months.

1865-66 In January 1865 appointed clerk in Indian Bureau of
the Department of the Interior, discharged by James
Harlan on June 30, but in July became clerk in Attorney General's office. *Drum Taps* issued in 1865;
Drum Taps with annex called *Sequel to Drum Taps*
published in 1866, containing "When Lilacs Last in
the Dooryard Bloom'd and Other Pieces." After Whitman's discharge from clerkship, O'Connor began writing his "vindication", published in 1866 as *The Good
Gray Poet*.

1867   Fourth edition of *Leaves of Grass*. Reviewed by
William Rossetti. Burroughs published first biography,
Notes on Walt Whitman as Poet and Person.

1868   Rossetti edited *Selections* from *Leaves of Grass;* well
received in England. O'Connor published *The Carpenter*, presenting in thin disguise Whitman as a
modern Christ.

1869   Mrs. Anne Gilchrist became acquainted with Whitman's poetry.

1870   Mrs. Gilchrist published "An English-woman's Estimate of Walt Whitman" in the Boston *Radical Review*.
First edition of *Democratic Vistas*, incorporating essays
published in the *Galaxy* during 1867-68.

1871   Fifth edition of *Leaves of Grass*.
Delivered "After All, Not to Create Only" ["Song
of the Exposition"] at opening of American Institute
in New York.

Swinburne greeted Whitman in *Songs Before Sunrise;* Tennyson wrote fraternal letters; Rudolf Schmidt translated *Democratic Vistas* into Danish.

Mrs. Gilchrist wrote a proposal of marriage and Whitman diplomatically declined in letter of November 3.

1872   Delivered "As a Strong Bird on Pinions Free" ["Thou Mother with thy Equal Brood" in 1882 ed.] at Dartmouth College commencement. Thérèse Bentzon (Mme. Blanc) published critical article in *Revue des Deux Mondes,* June 1.

Quarrel with O'Connor over Negro suffrage, and perhaps personal matters.

1873   Paralysis in February after preliminary spells of dizziness for over a year.

Mother died May 23.

1874   "The Song of the Universal" read at Tufts College commencement by proxy.

Discharged during midsummer from position in Washington, which had been filled by a substitute since Feb. 1873. In "Prayer of Columbus" the poet identified himself with the "battered, wrecked old man."

1875   Spent summer at Timber Creek, Stafford Farm. In November sufficiently recovered to visit Washington with Burroughs; they attended reburial of Poe in Baltimore.

1876   Wrangle in United States over Whitman's neglect started by article published in Jan. 26 *West Jersey Press,* which Robert Buchanan quoted in London *Daily News,* March 13.

Spring to autumn spent at Timber Creek.

Sixth edition of *Leaves of Grass,* in two volumes (I. *Leaves of Grass;* II. *Two Rivulets,* including "Passage to India" and miscellaneous prose). Rossetti and Mrs. Gilchrist sold many copies in England; the money and recognition aided poet's recovery.

In September Mrs. Gilchrist arrived in Philadelphia and rented a house, which Whitman visited frequently.

1877   January, spoke in Philadelphia on Tom Paine's anniversary.

February, New York friends gave a reception and lionized the poet. Visited Burroughs on the Hudson. In May, Edward Carpenter arrived from England. Dr. R. M. Bucke, recently appointed head of asylum at London, Ontario, visited Whitman and became close friend.

Burroughs published "The Flight of the Eagle" in *Birds and Poets*—passages contributed by Whitman himself.

1878   Health better. Repeated excursion up Hudson.

1879   April 14 gave Lincoln lecture in New York (given each year for thirteen years).

Sept. 10 started trip West—visited St. Louis (where favorite brother, Jeff, lived), Topeka, Rockies, Denver, Utah, Nevada.

1880   Returned from western trip in January.

April, delivered the Lincoln Memorial Address in Boston.

June, went to Canada to visit Dr. Bucke. Took boat trip up St. Lawrence.

1881   Second Boston edition of *Leaves of Grass,* published in November by Osgood (title-page bears 1881-82).

1882   February, the Society for the Suppression of Vice claimed the Osgood edition immoral. May 17 Osgood ceased publication, gave plates to Whitman. After his own "Author's Edition" in Camden, Whitman found a new publisher in Rees Welsh and Company, Philadelphia (soon succeeded by David McKay). Edition of 3,000 copies sold in one day. *Leaves of Grass* now practically complete, subsequent editions being mainly reprints.

Pearsall Smith, wealthy Philadelphia glass merchant and prominent Quaker, became friend.

Specimen Days and Collect published in autumn.

1883   Dr. Bucke published his biography—approved and supervised by Whitman.

1884   Sale of the Philadelphia edition enabled Whitman to buy a house in Mickle Street, Camden, New Jersey; March 26 moved in, remained until his death.

June, Edward Carpenter made a second visit.

New friends: Traubel, Harned, Talcott Williams, Donaldson, Ingersoll, others.

1885   Sun stroke in July. Walking became difficult and many friends, headed by Donaldson, bought a horse and phaeton for Whitman.

1886   Royalties from 1881 edition dwindled. *Pall Mall Gazette* promoted fund which resulted in a New Year's present of eighty pounds. Boston friends made up a purse of $800 for a cottage on Timber Creek (never built).

1887   The Lincoln lecture at Madison Square Theatre attended by many notables—took in $600. Poet sculptured by Morse and St. Gaudens, painted by Herbert Gilchrist and Thomas Eakins.

1888   Another paralytic stroke, early in June.

Continued trying to finish *November Boughs*.

1889   "House-tied."

1891   Last birthday dinner in Mickle Street home. Dec. 17, chilled, took pneumonia.

1892   Managed to publish tenth edition of *Leaves of Grass*, which the literary executors (Traubel, Harned, Bucke) were "authorized" to perpetuate.
        Died March 26, buried in prepared tomb in Harleigh Cemetery, Camden.

CHAPTER I

THE GROWTH OF WALT WHITMAN BIOGRAPHY

When I read the book, the biography famous,
And is this then (said I) what the author calls a man's life?
And so will some one when I am dead and gone write my
   life?
(As if any man really knew aught of my life,
Why even I myself I often think know little or nothing
   of my real life,
Only a few hints, a few diffused faint clews and indirections
   I seek for my own use to trace out here.)[1]

INTRODUCTION

"Perhaps no man contributing to world literature," declared Charles N. Elliot in 1915, "has been the subject of so many books, magazine articles and pamphlets as Walt Whitman. Certainly no American has. Even at the time of his death the number of critical studies of his work, favorable or adverse, often bitterly so, constituted a formidable array. Each year since, the list has grown by at least one book devoted wholly or in part to the subject of Whitman's life and work."[2]

---

[1] *When I Read the Book,* one of the eight new poems in the 1867 edition of LEAVES OF GRASS.
[2] Charles N. Elliot, *Walt Whitman as Man, Poet and Friend,* (Boston: Richard G. Badger, 1915), p. 9.

1

In the last quarter century Whitman biography and criticism have shown no sign of decreasing in volume,[3] and both at home and abroad he has become a favorite subject for scholarly research. Not even the now almost universal recognition of the poet's genius and his increasing importance as a major force in world literature wholly explain this ever-continuing flood of writing about his life and work. One explanation is that from the first publication, LEAVES OF GRASS has been a "problem" to critics, friendly and unfriendly alike; and the poet succeeded so thoroughly in identifying himself with his book that every reader has felt impelled to search out the secrets of life concealed in the images, ideas, and even the forms of the poems. That is the way Walt Whitman affects his readers—like Shakespeare in his sonnets.

Unlike Shakespeare, however, the major facts of Whitman's life are fairly well known (for the convenience of the reader, they have been summarized in this *Handbook* in a "Chronological Table," p. xi). Of course, there are a few blind or partly obscure spots in his chronology (such as the years immediately preceding the first and third editions of LEAVES OF GRASS), though the later biographers have gradually added to the factual information contained in the lives written by his inner circle of friends. But for a poet, and especially for so subjective a poet as Walt Whitman, the inner life is more important than the external one, and it is his inner life which has always challenged his biographers and prevented the achievement of a "definitive" life.

---

[3] See G. W. Allen's *Twenty-five Years of Walt Whitman Bibliography: 1918-1942*, (Boston, F. W. Faxon Co., 1943).

poet's life in the confessions of his poems—and this is the secret of his perennial fascination. But LEAVES OF GRASS, however autobiographical it may be, is also a work of art, which is to say the product of creative imagination, and to search for biographical fact in its pages is to write literary criticism rather than the history of a man's life. Thus, it is not possible, even less than with most poets, to separate the criticism of his work from the biography of his life.

Walt Whitman biography has grown, therefore, not by the simple accumulation of newly discovered and more exact information concerning his daily goings and comings, but by new and fresh insight into his motives, wider knowledge of the intellectual world in which he lived and moved, clearer understanding of the meanings which his poetry and prose have had for himself and for the many critics who have interpreted him. Moreover, his biography is no longer simply the story of Walt Whitman, or of a remarkable book which he wrote. He has become a legend, a national symbol, even a pivotal figure in an international literary movement. To tell the story of his biographical growth is also to tell much of the story of the growth of modern literature and thought. For this reason, what critics and biographers have thought of Walt Whitman and the theories on which they have based their interpretations of him, is fully as important as the literal facts of his life. After discovering when and why the various interpretations arose, however, the student of Whitman should be better able to sift fact from legend. Furthermore, if definite trends are discovered in the evolution of these biographies, perhaps future stages of Whitman scholarship may be anticipated—even aided and hastened.

THE TESTIMONY OF FRIENDS:
O'CONNOR, BURROUGHS, BUCKE

The circumstances under which Walt Whitman's friends began to write about his life profoundly affected the course and development of his biography. On June 30, 1865, he was dismissed from his government clerkship by the Secretary of the Interior, Mr. James Harlan, who had discovered that his employee was the author of LEAVES OF GRASS, a book which Mr. Harlan thought to be "full of indecent passages," meaning of course the sex poems (*Enfans d'Adam* and *Calamus* in the 1860 edition). One of the poet's devoted friends, William Douglas O'Connor, a government clerk, several months later published a bitter denunciation of Harlan and "a vindication" of Whitman which he called *The Good Gray Poet*.[4] Though hardly to be called a biography, this pamphlet laid the foundation for the first legends in Whitman biography and influenced many succeeding interpretations in Europe as well as America. The personality described by O'Connor sprang from the poet's avowed purposes in LEAVES OF GRASS fully as much as from O'Connor's personal love and admiration. This personality, familiar to "thousands of people in New York, in Brooklyn, in Boston, in New Orleans, and latterly in Washington [is] . . . a man of striking masculine beauty—a poet—powerful and venerable in appearance; large, calm, superbly formed; oftenest clad in the careless, rough, and

---

[4] *The Good Gray Poet: A Vindication* was first published for O'Connor in pamphlet form by Bunce and Huntington, New York, 1866, but was reprinted in Richard Maurice Bucke's *Walt Whitman* (Philadelphia: David McKay, 1883), pp. 99-130. References in this chapter are made to the original pamphlet, but since the essay is short it should not be difficult for the reader to locate the quotations in Bucke.

always picturesque costume of the common people".[5]
There is something almost mythical in the description of
the "head, majestic, large, Homeric, and set upon his
strong shoulders with the grandeur of ancient sculpture".
Reverently O'Connor continues:

> I marked the countenance, serene, proud, cheerful,
> florid, grave; the brow seamed with noble wrinkles;
> the features, massive and handsome, with firm blue
> eyes; the eyebrows and eyelids especially showing that
> fulness of arch seldom seen save in the antique busts;
> the flowing hair and fleecy beard, both very gray, and
> tempering with a look of age the youthful aspect of
> one who is but forty-five; the simplicity and purity of
> his dress, cheap and plain, but spotless, from snowy
> falling collar to burnished boot, and exhaling faint
> fragrance; the whole form surrounded with manliness,
> as with a nimbus, and breathing, in its perfect health
> and vigor, the august charm of the strong.[6]

Almost everyone who knew Walt Whitman intimately
was conquered by his magnetic presence, and there is no
reason whatever to doubt the sincerity of O'Connor's en-
thusiatic description; nevertheless, we have here the first
of the superman legends. "We who have looked upon
this figure, or listened to that clear, cheerful, vibrating
voice, might thrill to think, could we but transcend our
age, that we had been thus near to one of the greatest
of the sons of men."[7]

O'Connor is also the first source for some of the typical
anecdotes. "I hold it the surest proof of Thoreau's insight,
that after a conversation, seeing how he incarnated the im-

---

[5] O'Connor, op.cit., 3.   [7] Ibid.
[6] Ibid., 4.

mense and new spirit of the age, and was the compend of America, he came away to speak the electric sentence, 'He is Democracy!' "[8] The names of Whitman and Lincoln are linked by the story of the President's seeing the poet walk by the White House, inquiring who he was, and remarking thoughtfully, "Well, *he* looks like a MAN!"[9] The anecdote of LaFayette's passing through Brooklyn and by chance holding the future poet in his arms[10] sounds like an omen of his future destiny. And at the time he wrote the essay, O'Connor could say of Whitman, as of a Modern Christ:

> He has been a visitor of prisons; a protector of fugitive slaves; a constant voluntary nurse, night and day, at the hospitals, from the beginning of the war to the present time; a brother and friend through life to the neglected and the forgotten, the poor, the degraded, the criminal, the outcast; turning away from no man for his guilt, nor woman for her vileness.[11]

On the theory that Whitman's poems grew out of the "great goodness, the great chastity of spiritual strength and sanity"[12] of this saintly life, no vileness can possibly be found even in the frankest of them, though O'Connor admits that in all some eighty lines in the entire book might be objectionable to the ultra-prudish and squeamish. But he maintains that if these were expurgated, far greater portions of the Bible, the *Iliad* and the *Odyssey*, Shakespeare, Dante, and other masterpieces in world literature would also have to be rejected.

On the one hand LEAVES OF GRASS is elevated to an

---

[8] *Ibid.*, 5.
[9] *Ibid.*
[10] *Ibid.*, 6.

[11] *Ibid.*, 7.
[12] *Ibid.*, 6

eminent position in the greatest literature of all time, and on the other hand it is praised as "a work purely and entirely American, autochthonic, sprung from our own soil; no savor of Europe nor of the past, nor of any other literature in it".[13] Such of course was the poet's own ideal, and we have here the first glorified confirmation of Walt Whitman's literary fame on his own grounds.

John Burroughs, a friend of the same period, no less ardent but with more reserved emotions and intellect, published his first book on Whitman two years later, 1867. *Notes on Walt Whitman as Poet and Person* was a collaboration, for parts of it were actually written by Whitman himself and he freely edited the whole manuscript.[14] Both Burroughs and Whitman have been severely blamed by some commentators for this fact, but John Burroughs was then a young man taking his first steps in writing, more or less under Whitman's tutelage, and he doubtless thought that the poet's help made the book more accurate and authoritative. Nevertheless, Burroughs's *Notes* presented interpretations which must have been thoroughly congenial to Whitman himself and should be considered, like Burroughs's later studies and Bucke's more systematic account, as semi-autobiography.

The *Notes* is divided into two parts: the first a study and interpretation of LEAVES OF GRASS, including a defense of the author's theory and expression of Beauty and Personality; and the second, a personal biographical

---

[13] *Ibid.*, 26.

[14] John Burroughs, *Notes on Walt Whitman as Poet and Person*, (New York: American News Co., 1867.) A second revised and enlarged edition was published in New York by J. S. Redfield, 1871, but references in this chapter are given to the 1867 edition. For proof that Whitman wrote the earlier chapters of this book see F. P. Hier, Jr., "End of a Literary Mystery", *American Mercury*, I, 471-478 (April, 1924).

sketch, followed by a criticism of *Drum-Taps*. The book is, therefore, mainly an exegesis, more or less "official", although the manner in which the author exploits his own country origin gives it an informal, personal tone which sounds completely original. But considering the origin of the *Notes,* it is significant that Burroughs confesses: "I am not able, nor is it necessary, to give the particulars of the poet's youthful life."[15] In fact, he is convinced that the "long foreground" mentioned in Emerson's famous "greeting" letter of 1855, "that vast previous, ante-dating requirement of physical, moral, and emotional experiences, will forever remain untold."[16] However, the LaFayette episode is given, and we are also told that "From the immediate mother of the poet come, I think, his chief traits."[17] Here is the basis, but not yet the elaboration, of the theory soon to be developed by Bucke and Whitman himself that the poet's genius was a product of his ancestry and environment.

The mythical account given of his travels may have been due either to Whitman's vagueness concerning his New Orleans period or to Burroughs's drawing erroneous factual conclusions from the literary theory that the poet must first absorb his country, sounding every experience, before expressing it in verse. At any rate, the reader is told that in 1849 Whitman began travelling, and is given the impression that he spent one year in New Orleans (actually only a little over two months) and another wandering around in the West. "He saw Western and Northwestern nature and character in all their phases, and probably took there and then the decided inspiration

[15] *Ibid.,* 79.
[16] *Ibid.,* 83.
[17] *Ibid.,* 79.

of his future poetry. After some two years, returning to
Brooklyn . . ."[18] It is an ironical commentary that when
Whitman actually did visit the West in 1879—exactly
thirty years later!—he re-announced in *Specimen Days:*
"I have found the law of my own poems." Already in
Burroughs's *Notes* biographical fact and poetic imagination have become almost inseparably inter-grown, perhaps for the very reason that the poet, "Like Egypt's lord
. . . builds against his form's annihilation . . . Strange immortality! For in this book Walt Whitman, even in his
habit as he lived, and ever gathering hearts of young and
old, is to surely walk, untouched by death, down through
the long succession of all the future ages of America."[19]

The *Notes* contains also the theory on which all the
early friends of LEAVES OF GRASS were to justify and explain the style which most of the first readers found obscure: "The poet, like Nature, seems best pleased when
his meaning is well folded up, put away, and surrounded
by a curious array of diverting attributes and objects."[20]

The first complete life of the author of LEAVES OF
GRASS was Dr. Richard Maurice Bucke's *Walt Whitman,*
1883. Whitman told Edward Carpenter that he himself
"wrote the account of my birthplace and antecedents which
occupies the first twenty-four pages of the book".[21] So
highly did he think of this collaborated biography that in
1888 he asked Bucke not to revise it but to "*let it stand
just as it is*",[22] and on his seventy-second birthday he de-

---

[18] *Ibid.*, 82.
[19] *Ibid.*, 73.
[20] *Ibid.*, 43.
[21] Edward Carpenter, *Days with Walt Whitman,* (London: George
Allen, 1906), 37.
[22] Horace Traubel, *In Re Walt Whitman,* (Philadelphia: David McKay,
1893), v.

fended this work as the final word on his life: "I thoroughly accept Dr. Bucke's book."[23]

The poet who had announced at thirty-seven:

My tongue, every atom of my blood, form'd from this soil, this air,
Born here of parents born here from parents the same, and their parents the same.[24]

and who prided himself that,

Before I was born out of my mother generations guided me,
My embryo has never been torpid, nothing could overlay it.[25]

has now had time to investigate his genealogy and to draw definite conclusions regarding his ancestry. With the aid of Savage's *Genealogical Dictionary* he thought he could trace his lineage back to Abijah Whitman in sixteenth century England, whose son, the Rev. Zechariah Whitman, came to America in the *True-Love* in 1640, or "soon after".[26]

Though the ancestry is presented as sound on both sides, the Whitmans as "a solid, tall, strong-framed, long-lived race of men" and the Van Velsors as "a warm-hearted and sympathetic" people, we read that

There is no doubt that both Walt Whitman's personality and writings are to be credited very largely to

---

[23] *Ibid.,* 311.
[24] *Song of Myself,* Sec. 1.
[25] *Ibid.,* Sec. 44.
[26] Cf. *Specimen Days* (David McKay imprint, n.d.), 9. Dr. Bucke, p. 13, says 1635, but there is no evidence for this date. As a matter of fact, the Rev. Zechariah Whitman had no children, as Bliss Perry discovered—see his *Walt Whitman: His Life and Works* (Boston: Houghton Mifflin, 1906), 2, note 2.

their Holland origin through his mother's side. A faithful and subtle investigation (and a very curious one it would be) might trace far back many of the elements of LEAVES OF GRASS, long before their author was born. From his mother also he derived his extraordinary affective nature, spirituality and human sympathy. From his father chiefly must have come his passion for freedom, and the firmness of character which has enabled him to persevere for a lifetime in what he has called "carrying out his own ideal."[27]

But to Louisa Van Velsor is given chief credit: "Walt Whitman could say with perhaps a better right than almost any man for such a boast, that he was

'Well-begotten and rais'd by a perfect mother'."[28]

The environment, however, is found to be no less perfect: "Perhaps, indeed, there are few regions on the face of the earth better fitted for the concrete background of such a book as LEAVES OF GRASS."[29] The poems have achieved the purpose announced in the '55 Preface, for it is now said that, "In their amplitude, richness, unflagging movement and gay color, LEAVES OF GRASS . . . are but the putting in poetic statements of the Manhattan Island and Brooklyn of those years [poet's youth], and of today".[30]

The mythical travels encountered in Burroughs's *Notes* are continued:

The fifteen years from 1840 to 1855 were the gestation or formative periods of LEAVES OF GRASS not only in Brooklyn and New York, but from several extensive

[27] Bucke, *op. cit.*, 17.
[28] *Ibid.*, 18.
[29] *Ibid.*
[30] *Ibid.*, 20.

jaunts through the States . . . Large parts of the poems, and several of them wholly, were incarnated on those jaunts or amid these scenes. Out of such experiences came the physiology of LEAVES OF GRASS, in my opinion the main part. The psychology of the book is a deeper problem; it is doubtful whether the latter element can be traced. It is, perhaps, only to be studied out in the poems themselves, and is a hard study there.[31]

These "extensive jaunts through the States" are puzzling not only because later biographers have found no record of them, but also because in *Specimen Days,* published one year before Bucke's biography, Whitman gives an accurate, though general, account of his New Orleans trip. In a newspaper article, reprinted in *Specimen Days,* he does make a statement which, for lack of punctuation, could have been misunderstood by Bucke: "I enjoy'd my journey and Louisiana life much. Returning to Brooklyn [,] a year or two afterward I started the 'Freeman' . . ."[32] But surely in his close coöperation—or collaboration—with Dr. Bucke on the biography Whitman would have corrected the mistaken belief that he returned to Brooklyn *a year or two after* the New Orleans trip. One must conclude that the poet had no objection to such imaginative interpretations of the origin of his poems.

The point is that Dr. Bucke accepted in the most literal sense Whitman's literary claim that his poems were the expression of the life which he had absorbed. On such grounds the admirer of LEAVES OF GRASS feels himself compelled to idealize the poet's whole life and background. Thus his education in printing offices, contact with people, and private study were not only adequate but "the

---

[31] *Ibid.,* 136.   [32] *Specimen Days,* 196.

most comprehensive equipment ever attained by a human being."[33] One wonders whether Taine's theory of "race, surroundings, epoch"[34] could have influenced both the poet and the biographer in their belief that the creator of literature must be the product of perfect ancestry, perfect environment, and perfect training or experience. On the romantic doctrine of "absorbing" and "expressing" the life of a nation, they thought the poet's meager formal education was more than compensated by his contact with "things" and "humanity"; hence that "reading did not go for so very much" in his education.[35]

Bucke's *Walt Whitman* does not attempt to solve one of the greatest problems in the biography of the poet, the almost miraculous contrast between Whitman's writings before and after 1855. But it was the personal contact with Whitman and the study of his writings that later led Dr. Bucke, the psychiatrist, to study the phenomenon of mysticism, which the doctor called "cosmic consciousness."[36] The double nature of the poet, a profound spirituality mingled with an exuberant animality, remains a paradox in the biography—though it is not treated as such—, but Dr. Bucke's later book helps to explain this puzzle, for it is a familiar paradox among mystics. In defense of the animal side of Whitman's disposition, Bucke claims in his biography that the *Children of Adam* poems have established "the purity, holiness and perfect

---

[33] Bucke, *op. cit.,* 19.

[34] Hippolyte Adolphe Taine expressed this doctrine in the famous introduction to his *L'Histoire de la littérature anglaise* (1864), translated into English by H. Van Laun in 1873.

[35] Bucke *op. cit.,* 21.

[36] Richard Maurice Bucke, *Cosmic Consciousness,* A Study in the Evolution of the Human Mind (Philadelphia: Innes and Sons, 1901). Fourth edition, New York: E. P. Dutton, 1923.

sanity of the sexual relation,"[37] while *Calamus* presents "an exalted friendship, a love into which sex does not enter as an element."[38] Not the slightest taint of abnormality is seen in either of these groups. And as for Whitman's illness in the summer of 1864 and his paralysis in 1873, these are attributed simply to the contraction of "hospital malaria" and overwork as a war-nurse.

O'Connor's interpretation of Whitman as a modern prophet is strongly confirmed by Bucke: "LEAVES OF GRASS belongs to a religious era not yet reached, of which it is the revealer and herald . . . What the Vedas were to Brahmanism, the Law and the Prophets to Judaism . . . the Gospels and Pauline writings to Christianity . . . will LEAVES OF GRASS be to the future of American civilization." It is "the bible of Democracy."[39]

The great value of Dr. Bucke's biography is that it conveys the remarkable personality of Walt Whitman. And others have confirmed the testimony which he gave after the poet's death: "To the last [his face] had no lines of care or worry—he lived in an upper spiritual stratum—above all mean thoughts, sordid feelings, earthly harassments."[40] Such observations led this devoted friend to study the lives of other mystics and to write a forerunner of William James's analysis of the psychology of mysticism in *The Varieties of Religious Experience*.

FIRST BRITISH INTERPRETATIONS: ROSSETTI TO SYMONDS

Before continuing the story of Whitman biography in America, we need to observe his reception and growing

---

[37] Bucke's *Whitman*, 166.
[38] *Ibid.*
[39] *Ibid.*, 183-185.
[40] "A Personal Note on the Good Gray Poet," Elliot, *op. cit.*, 50.

reputation abroad—especially in England—, for what the foreign critics said about him had, sooner or later, considerable influence on American evaluations. Professor Harold Blodgett has already ably told the story of Walt Whitman in England[41] and it need not be repeated here in detail, but it is important to know that the first edition of LEAVES OF GRASS reached the British several months after its appearance in America, and that by the 1860's Whitman had many prominent admirers there, including William Michael Rossetti, John A. Symonds, Moncure Conway, Mrs. Anne Gilchrist, Swinburne (who later renounced Whitman), and others.

In 1866 Conway published an account[42]—later denounced by Whitman as fanciful[43]—of a visit to the poet in which he found him lying on his back on the parched earth in a blazing sun of nearly 100°, "one of his favourite places and attitudes for composing 'poems'."[44] The following year William Michael Rossetti published a sane and discriminating article on Whitman in the London *Chronicle*.[45] This led, Rossetti says, to an opportunity to edit the poems, and the edition was published in 1868.

This edition, called *Poems by Walt Whitman,*[46] was both a selection and an expurgation, for the only reason for not reprinting the complete fourth edition of LEAVES OF GRASS was the desire of Rossetti and the publisher to

---

[41] Harold Blodgett, *Walt Whitman in England,* (Cornell University Press, 1934).

[42] Moncure D. Conway, "Walt Whitman", *The Fortnightly Review,* VI, 538-548 (October 15, 1866).

[43] See William Sloane Kennedy, *Reminiscences of Walt Whitman* (Paisley and London: Alexander Gardner, 1896), 51-74.

[44] Conway, *op. cit.* In his *Autobiography* (Boston, 1905) Conway omits this fantastic statement—see vol. I, 218.

[45] "Walt Whitman's Poems", *The London Chronicle,* July 6, 1867.

[46] *Poems by Walt Whitman* (London: John Camden Hotten, 1868).

eliminate the "objectionable" poems, and Whitman would not agree to outright expurgation of the complete collection.[47] Rossetti's "Prefatory Notice"—mainly the *Chronicle* article—is reserved and admits the poet's faults (as Rossetti saw them) as freely as his virtues. The faults: "he speaks on occasion of gross things in gross, crude, and plain terms"; he uses "absurd or ill-constructed" words; his style is sometimes "obscure, fragmentary, and agglomerative"; and "his self-assertion is boundless"[48]—though partly forgivable as being vicarious. But these are balanced by the poet's great distinctions, "his absolute and entire originality," and his comprehension and intensity in both subject-matter and expression, which Rossetti thinks great enough to enlarge the canon of poetic art. The volume contains about half the poems of the 1867 edition of the LEAVES and the original preface. The selections are well chosen and proved a fortunate introduction of Walt Whitman to England. But it is significant to observe that the British were spared the poems which had so shocked America and that even Whitman's friendly editor found objectionable crudities in the style of LEAVES OF GRASS, as have most British critics since then.

As a result of Rossetti's edition one of the most remarkable episodes in Whitman's life and literary influence took place. Mrs. Anne Gilchrist, the brilliant widow of the great biographer of Blake, read Rossetti's *Selections,* then the complete LEAVES OF GRASS, and came to feel that the American poet's message was a personal plea for love which she could answer. The strange story of this one-sided and pathetic courtship is well known and has been

---

[47] Cf. Blodgett, *op. cit.,* 25-30.   [48] Rossetti, *Poems, op. cit.,* 4.

sympathetically told by Holloway.[49] Whitman fully appreciated her tender feeling for his poems but was unable to return a personal emotion, even after she had come to America and he had been hospitably received in her Philadelphia home. Of special interest to the growth of his reputation, however, is the essay, "An Englishwoman's Estimate of Walt Whitman," published in the Boston *Radical Review*, May, 1870.[50] Here for the first time a woman, and one widely known in artistic and literary circles, defended in print the sanity and purity of the infamous sex poems. The article was doubly reassuring to Whitman after Rossetti's reserved critical introduction.

After Rossetti and Mrs. Gilchrist's championship of Whitman came Edward Dowden. In his essay on "The Poetry of Democracy: Walt Whitman"[51] he shows considerably more enthusiasm than Rossetti. Like Burroughs and Bucke he interprets Whitman as the product and representative of American environment and life. He thinks that the American poet is "not shaped out of old-world clay . . . and [is] hard to name by any old-world name." As the spokesman for "a great democratic world, as yet but half-fashioned"[52] he is not terrified by the fear of vulgarity, and "selection seems forbidden to him"[53]; all words are eligible for his poetry, and he does not have to sacrifice directness and vividness to propriety. Here we have a new twist to Whitman's own theory, an application not possible for his American biographers, and yet

---

[49] Emory Holloway, *Walt Whitman*, (New York: Alfred A. Knopf, 1926), 257-264.
[50] Reprinted in *In Re, op. cit.*, 41-55.
[51] *The Westminster Review*, XCVI, 33-68 (July, 1871); reprinted in *Studies in Literature* (London, 1878).
[52] *Studies in Literature*, 473.
[53] *Ibid.*, 476.

given with admiring approval, just as the sex poems are declared to be the product of "a robust, vigorous, clean man, enamored of living, unashamed of body as he is unashamed of soul, absolutely free from pruriency of imagination, absolutely inexperienced in the artificial excitements and enchancements of jaded lusts."[54]

In 1886 Ernest Rhys edited a new selection of LEAVES OF GRASS.[55] The complete work was still too strong for British tastes, despite the fact that the book was far more widely appreciated in England than in America. Rhys's introduction adds nothing new to Whitman's biography or criticism, merely echoing the poet's old-age conclusion that his function is "initiative, rather than a consummation in poetry" and that his "poetic vision [is] fearlessly equal to the far range of later science,"[56] a claim later amplified by an Australian scientist, William Gay.[57]

One of the keenest and most competent students of Whitman's life and art in the nineteenth century was the brilliant classical scholar, John Addington Symonds. Admitting that at the age of twenty-five LEAVES OF GRASS was a revelation to him, influencing him more than any other book except possibly the Bible, and that, "It is impossible for me to speak critically of what has so deeply entered into the fibre and marrow of my being,"[58] he nevertheless was actually the first critic to raise certain embarrassing questions which have agitated biographers ever since.

---

[54] *Ibid.,* 505.
[55] Published in the Canterbury Poets Series (London: Walter Scott, 1886).
[56] *Ibid.,* x-xi.
[57] William Gay, *Walt Whitman: His Relation to Science and Philosophy,* (Melbourne: Firth and M'Cutcheon, 1895).
[58] John Addington Symonds, *Walt Whitman: A Study,* (London: George Routledge, New York: E. P. Dutton, 1893), 41.

In the strictly biographical part of his book Symonds
agrees with Bucke and Burroughs that, "Walt inherited
on both sides a sound constitution, untainted blood, come-
liness of person, well-balanced emotions, and excellent
moral principles,"[59] and gives a sketch of the biographical
facts which differs from the previous accounts only in the
more restrained and discriminating language. But in the
"Study" of LEAVES OF GRASS we encounter the first attack on O'Connor's "modern Christ" interpretation: "the
ways [Whitman] chose for pushing his gospel and ad-
vertising his philosophy, put a severe strain on patience.
Were Buddha, Socrates, Christ, so interested in the dust
stirred up around them by second-rate persons, in third-
rate cities, and in more than fifth-rate literature?"[60]

As a student of "Greek friendship" and Renaissance
homosexuality among artists, Symonds recognized in the
Calamus poems symptoms of emotional abnormality in
the poet. Finally he wrote Whitman a frank letter asking
for information. The reply, dated August 19, 1890 has
become famous:

> My life, young manhood, mid-age, times South, &c.,
> have been jolly, bodily, and doubtless open to criticism.
> Though unmarried I have had six children—two are
> dead—one living Southern grandchild, fine boy, writes
> to me occasionally — circumstances (connected with
> their fortune and benefit) have separated me from inti-
> mate relations.[61]

Symonds did not publish this letter, and it was not made
public until Edward Carpenter quoted it in 1906, but it

---

[59] *Ibid.*, 11-12.
[60] *Ibid.*, 38.
[61] Quoted by Edward Carpenter, *op. cit.*, 142-143.

had an important influence on Symonds's own thinking. In fact, he seems to have been so convinced by it that he was reassured about *Calamus*. He decided that what the poet called "the 'adhesiveness' of comradeship is meant to have no interblending with the 'amativeness' of sexual love . . . it is undeniable that Whitman possessed a specially keen sense of the fine restraint and continence, the cleanliness and chastity, that are inseparable from the perfectly virile and physically complete nature of healthy manhood."[62] And yet he must admit that "those unenviable mortals who are the inheritors of sexual anomalies, will recognize their own emotions in Whitman's 'superb friendship . . . latent in all men'." Symonds is still "not certain whether [Whitman's] own feelings upon this delicate topic may not have altered since the time when *Calamus* was first composed."[63]

Like all the English critics, Symonds is bothered by Whitman's "form," or rather lack of conventional form. "Speaking about him," he says, "is like speaking about the universe . . . Not merely because he is large and comprehensive, but because he is intangible, elusive, at first sight self-contradictory, and in some sense formless, does Whitman resemble the universe and defy critical analysis."[64] Such a justification would, of course, have pleased the poet who declared,

I am large, I contain multitudes.[65]

Despite all his misgivings and reservations, however, Symonds renders homage to the man who helped him to strip his own soul of social prejudices, and he gratefully recommends LEAVES OF GRASS to others.

---

[62] Symonds, *op. cit.*, 92-93.
[63] *Ibid.*, 93.
[64] *Ibid.*, 33-34.
[65] *Song of Myself*, Sec. 51.

THE AMERICAN APOTHEOSIS:
TRAUBEL, KENNEDY, DONALDSON, BURROUGHS

Whitman's death in 1892 stimulated his personal friends in America to renewed activity in spreading his fame, an activity which long ago had become a "cause," an almost religious as well as a literary crusade. One of the first acts of his literary executors, Horace L. Traubel, Dr. R. M. Bucke, and Thomas B. Harned, was to publish a memorial volume called *In Re Walt Whitman*.[66] In addition to the tributes of friends and admirers, this book contains translations of the most important criticisms which had appeared in France, Germany, and Denmark. Here we find abundant proof that the American poet had already attained considerable international reputation and influence (a subject to be treated later in this *Handbook*).[67]

In Re is also the first of the Boswellian publications of the inner circle. Traubel, especially, had long been recording indiscriminately the poet's old-age garrulity and had now begun to question his family and acquaintances. His record of conversations with Walt's brother George,[68] however, opens up new biographical possibilities. Here we get a glimpse of the Whitman family. It is revealing to see their literary ignorance, their indifference and even antagonism to the young poet's ambitions because he showed so little desire for making money; we are not surprised that Walt was never known to fall in love, in fact, seemed completely indifferent to girls, and they to him. Whether or not Walt was as "clean in his habits" as George thought he was, we nevertheless get in these

---

[66] See note 22.   [68] *In Re*, 33-40.
[67] See Chap. VI.

notes a convincing picture of uneventful, commonplace, though not uncongenial family background. Walt Whitman's family did not lack affection for him, but it was as unaware of his genius as were his literary enemies. George's testimony helps to explain the loneliness, discouragement and despair so evident in the third edition of LEAVES OF GRASS.

Another contributor to the *In Re* volume was William Sloane Kennedy, a devoted friend of the poet in his Camden period, who in two essays discussed the "Dutch" and the "Quaker Traits of Walt Whitman."[69] These interpretations Kennedy amplified in his *Reminiscences of Walt Whitman*, published in 1896. There was nothing new in emphasizing these traits in which the poet himself took considerable pride, but Kennedy contributed to the subject a richer fund of information and a more vigorous gusto than previous biographers had displayed. Kennedy himself could be Quixotic as any of the "hot little prophets," to use Bliss Perry's phrase, but he brought to his Whitman idolatry an alert and cultivated mind. Reporting a conversation with the poet in 1880, Kennedy remarks, "I can't tell how it was, but the large personality of the man so vivified the few words he spoke that all the majesty of Greece—especially her sculpturesque art-idea—seemed to loom up before me as never before in my life, although the study of Greek literature had been a specialty of my collegiate and post-collegiate years."[70]

Reminiscences includes a good deal of biographical material, "Memories, Letters, Etc.," and some valuable sympathetic criticism of LEAVES OF GRASS. The second part of the book, "Drift and Cumulus," is still useful to a

[69] *Ibid.*, 195-199; 213-214.   [70] Kennedy, *op. cit.*, 1.

Whitman student for its analyses of the meaning of individual poems; and the third part, "The Style of Leaves of Grass," contains the first adequate explanation of the "organic principle" which Whitman had borrowed or inherited indirectly from German romanticism. The poet himself had insisted that the analogy of his rhythm was to be found in Nature, but Kennedy made the first real start in rationalizing his prosodic theory and practice. His *Fight of a Book for the World*, 1926, which might be called the first Whitman handbook, continues the interpretations of Kennedy's earlier publication and is of considerable value to the Whitman bibliographer.

The year 1896 also saw the publication of a second book by one of Walt Whitman's personal friends, Thomas Donaldson.[71] His *Walt Whitman, the Man* was based on first-hand knowledge of the poet during two periods, Washington from 1862-73 and Camden 1873-1892, but it contains meager biographical details. "No man tells the public the whole story of his life," says Mr. Donaldson. "Mr. Whitman never told the public the story of his life. I do not now propose to tell it for him."[72] Perhaps this is negative evidence that Whitman told his friends little about his early life. But Donaldson's book made one positive contribution which was later to be extensively amplified. He indicated plainly that Whitman's poems celebrating "love of comrades" were written not out of actual experience but as a compensation for his own loneliness. He put into his poems the "passionate love of comrades" for which he found no human recipient. If Donaldson had developed this interpretation he would

---

[71] Thomas Donaldson, *Walt Whitman, the Man*, (New York: Harper, 1896).
[72] *Ibid.*, 17.

have been the first psychological biographer of Whitman. The book remains best known, however, for its testimony to the way the poet affected his intimate associates. "I never met a man of such standing who possessed as little personal egotism, or rather who made it less manifest in contact with him."[73]

The third friend to publish a book in 1896 was John Burroughs, who called his new biography *Walt Whitman, A Study*. He plead guilty to the same sort of "one-sided enthusiasm" found in all the publications of the personal friends: Bucke, Kennedy, Traubel and Donaldson. When Burroughs met Whitman in the fall of 1863 "he was so sound and sweet and gentle and attractive as a man, and withal so wise and tolerant" that Burroughs soon trusted the book as he trusted the man, for he "saw that the work and the man were one, and that the former must be good as the latter was good."[74] If Whitman could have had the same hand in this book that he had had in the *Notes*, the work could not have been more favorable.

Although John Burroughs knew Whitman over a longer period than most of the friends who wrote about him, the theory which he held—following the author's own clues —of the origin of LEAVES OF GRASS was not likely to lead him to question, examine, or discover new biographical information. "What apprenticeship he served, or with whom he served it, we get no hint,"[75] he is content to say. Of course the apprenticeship and the days of doubt and uncertainty were nearly or entirely over by the time Burroughs made Whitman's acquaintance in Washington;

---

[73] *Ibid.*, 77.
[74] John Burroughs, *Walt Whitman, A Study*, (Boston: Houghton Mifflin, 1896), 4.
[75] *Ibid.*, 72.

hence he can truthfully testify: "We never see him doubtful or hesitating; we never see him battling for his territory, and uncertain whether or not he is upon his own
ground."[76] All these interpretations are based on the
theory that Whitman himself cultivated: "Leaves of Grass
is an utterance out of the depths of primordial, aboriginal
human nature. It embodies and exploits a character not
rendered anaemic by civilization, but preserving a sweet
and sane savagery, indebted to culture only as a means to
escape culture, reaching back always, through books, art,
civilization, to fresh, unsophisticated nature, and drawing
his strength from thence."[77] This theory would not en-
courage Burroughs to undertake biographical research.

He made another interpretation, however, which might
have—and in recent years has—led to literary investigation. "We must look for the origins of Whitman," he says,
". . . in the deep world-currents that have been shaping the
destinies of the race for the past hundred years or more;
in the universal loosening, freeing, and removing obstruc-
tions; in the emancipation of the people . . .; in the
triumph of democracy and of science; . . . the sentiment
of realism and positivism, the religious hunger that flees
the churches . . . etc."[78]

Although Burroughs finally became impatient with
Whitman's senile pleasure in the fawning of the Camden
and Philadelphia clique, he never modified the conviction
which he expressed in "The Flight of the Eagle," published in *Birds and Poets,* 1877: "to tell me that Whitman
is not a large, fine, fresh, magnetic personality, making
you love him, and want always to be with him, were to

---

[76] *Ibid.*   [78] *Ibid.,* 231.
[77] *Ibid.,* 76.

tell me that my whole past life is a deception, and all the impression of my perceptives a fraud."[79] Clara Barrus's valuable book on *Whitman and Burroughs, Comrades* was later (1931) to document this friendship with the publication of many interesting letters, which reveal Burroughs as a more intelligent partisan than most of the inner circle, but one who, until the end of his life, was unwavering in his loyalty and devotion to Whitman. This record of one of the most important friendships in the poet's life is itself a distinguished contribution to scholarship, containing much new material on Whitman's reputation at home and abroad, and sound, intelligent critical judgments.

The publication of the ten-volume deluxe edition of Whitman's works in 1902[80] may be taken as a convenient termination of the first stage of his biography. Two intimate admirers (Trowbridge and Edward Carpenter—to be discussed presently) were to publish important testimony after this date, but the first cycle had practically run its course. The biographical "Introduction" to the Camden Edition, written by the literary executors Bucke, Harned, and Traubel, adds only a few meager details. But since this Introduction is based on the publications of Burroughs, Bucke, Donaldson, Kennedy and the favorable criticism of friends and admirers in Europe, a précis of the essay will serve to emphasize the state of Whitman biography in 1902.

The sketch begins by stressing the antiquity and typical

---

[79] *Birds and Poets* (Boston: Houghton Mifflin Co., 1877, 1895), 188.

[80] *The Complete Writings of Walt Whitman,* issued under the editorial supervision of his Literary Executors, Richard Maurice Bucke, Thomas B. Harned, and Horace L. Traubel; with additional bibliographical and critical material by Oscar Lovell Triggs, New York and London: G. P. Putnam's Sons, 1902). (See bibliography at end of Chap. II in this *Handbook*.)

Americanism of the poet's ancestry. These "working people, possessed of little or no formal culture, and with no
marked artistic tastes in any direction," had large families,
were long-lived, and passed on to Walt their virile moral
and physical energy. "There was no positive trace of degeneracy anywhere in the breed."[81] Little seems to be
known about Walter Whitman Senior; the brothers are
vaguely described as of "solid, strong frame, fond of animals, and addicted to the wholesome labors and pleasures
of the open air";[82] but the simple, almost illiterate, mother
is represented as sweet, spiritual, ideal, and the poet's
most important ancestor.[83]

Whitman's "long foreground" is interpreted as mainly
his boyhood environment, the outdoor scenes and activities on Long Island and his contact with all sorts of people, especially unlettered folk. This "study of life" is said
to have provided a better education for the future poet
than the schools could possibly have done. Although his
reading of Shakespeare, Homer, and the Bible is emphasized, these biographers agree that books were less important in his "apprenticeship" than outdoor experiences,
urban life, and such amusements as the opera, concerts,
theatrical performances, and fairs and museums.[84]

The New Orleans trip is thought to have been significant in the poet's development, but "There was an atmosphere of mysteriousness unconsciously thrown about
the episode."[85] The only known reason for Whitman's
leaving was Jeff's poor health. No precise information is
given for his inability to hold any job more than a few
weeks or months.

---

[81] *Ibid.*, I, xviii.
[82] *Ibid.*, xxi.
[83] *Ibid.*, xxii.

[84] *Ibid.*, xxvi-xxviii.
[85] *Ibid.*, xxxv.

In the publication of the first edition of LEAVES OF GRASS the "hidden purpose of his life was suddenly revealed."[86] The gestation, experimentation—in short, the sources—of this work are unknown to these biographers. Since they believe that the book is "cosmic and baffles all adequate account,"[87] they are not predisposed to exert much effort to find the "hidden purpose." From this time on they make the story of the book the story of Walt Whitman. Everything is grist for the mill; any effort to spread the "new gospel" is laudable, even writing anonymous reviews and self-advertizing; the poet's life and personality are observed to grow more Christ-like each day. The sex poems express the divine order of paternal and fraternal love; the poet sacrificed his health in his overly-zealous hospital ministrations; all persecutors and depreciators of the man or his book are properly condemned. But through all suffering, disappointments, and misunderstanding Walt Whitman grows daily more serene, lovable, and triumphant over the world and the flesh. Such was the apotheosis of Walt Whitman in 1902, ten years after his calm death in Camden.

FIRST STEPS IN A RE-EVALUATION: TROWBRIDGE, EDWARD CARPENTER

The process of re-evaluation had already begun in 1903. Although John Townsend Trowbridge was one of Walt Whitman's Boston friends, his autobiography, *My Own Story: with Recollections of Noted Persons,* shows plainly the new epoch dawning in Whitman's biographical and critical interpretation. Ever since O'Connor's partisan de-

---

[86] *Ibid.,* xxxvii.   [87] *Ibid.*

fence of the "Good Gray Poet," Whitman's indebtedness to Emerson had become a problem in criticism and biography. After addressing Emerson as "master" in the impulsive open-letter of the second edition of LEAVES OF GRASS, Whitman finally in a letter to Kennedy in 1887 denied flatly that he had read the master before beginning his own book.[88] Burroughs, whose youthful enthusiasm for Emerson first led him to read Whitman, was always divided on the question. The Camden circle tried to deny any influence whatever. Of considerable value, therefore, is Trowbridge's testimony that when the poet visited Boston in 1860 to see his ill-fated third edition through the press he confessed to having read Emerson's *Essays* in 1854. "He freely admitted that he could never have written his poems if he had not first 'come to himself,' and that Emerson helped him to 'find himself' . . . 'I was simmering, simmering, simmering; Emerson brought me to a boil'."[89]

Traubel, Harned, and Bucke, were always inclined to accept every utterance of the poet as gospel truth, but Trowbridge expresses the opinion that Whitman's long invalidism affected his memory.[90] For example, it is obviously not true that without the Civil War years "and the experience they gave, LEAVES OF GRASS would not now be existing,"[91] for the third edition was published in 1860. Furthermore, Trowbridge is convinced that "in matters of taste and judgment he was extremely fallible, and ca-

---

[88] See Kennedy, *op. cit.*, 76.

[89] John Townsend Trowbridge, *My Story: With Recollections of Noted Persons*, (Boston: Houghton Mifflin Co., 1903), 366-367.

[90] Cf. the testimony of Whitman's friends on his "unconscious fabrication" regarding the mysterious "children"—Clara Barrus, *Whitman and Burroughs: Comrades*, (Boston: Houghton Mifflin Co. 1931), 336-338.

[91] Trowbridge, *op. cit.*, 398.

pable of doing unwise and wayward things for the sake of a theory or a caprice."[92] He can foresee the time when "some future tilter at windmills will attempt to prove that the man we know as Walt Whitman was an uncultured impostor," but Trowbridge sensibly concludes that "after all deductions it remains to be unequivocally affirmed that Whitman stands as a great original force in our literature."[93]

At this point we might note the corroborating evidence and opinion of the British disciple, Edward Carpenter—though at the moment we are violating strict chronology, for *Days with Walt Whitman* appeared in 1906, after important books by Binns, Perry, and Bertz. Edward Carpenter was a young, impressionable English poet who visited Whitman for the first time in 1877 and thereafter joined the band of followers, even to the extent of trying to adopt the thought and style of LEAVES OF GRASS in his own poetry. But when he came to write his book, Carpenter perceived clearly that the inner circle of American friends was "more concerned to present an ideal personality than a real portrait."[94] Without in the least minimizing his admiration or personal indebtedness, Carpenter tried to give a "real portrait," and thereby succeeded in making a valuable contribution to the growth of Whitman biography.

Carpenter's most sensational revelation is Whitman's letter to Symonds in 1890 regarding the illegitimate children.[95] As we have already seen, this letter seems to have

---

[92] *Ibid.*, 397.

[93] *Ibid.*, 400. (For a partial fulfillment of the "impostor" conjecture see discussion of Shephard, p. 73.)

[94] Edward Carpenter, *op. cit.*, 52.

[95] *Ibid.*, 142-143.

allayed Symonds's worst suspicions about the origin of the
Calamus emotions, but Carpenter can see that there is
more to the subject than has yet been revealed. Remembering Doyle's testimony that he had never known "a case
of Walt's being bothered up by a woman,"[96] George's
word that Walt had always been indifferent to girls,[97] and
Burroughs's statement that the poet's "intimacies with men
were much more numerous and close than with women,"[98]
Carpenter concluded that there must have been "a great
tragic element in his nature"[99] which prevented happiness
in love affairs. And yet he knows that Love ruled Whitman's life, "that he gave his life for love." The implications are plain that the poems are a sublimation of this
love.

Walt Whitman's "double nature" had been hinted before, but Carpenter offers fresh evidence of this paradoxical disposition. He records his impression of the
poet's "contradictory, self-willed, tenacious, obstinate
character, strong and even extreme moods, united with
infinite tenderness, wistful love, and studied tolerance . . ."[100] Carpenter reports a most revealing confession that Whitman made to him: "There is something in
my nature *furtive* like an old hen! . . . That is how I felt
in writing 'Leaves of Grass.' Sloane Kennedy calls me
'artful'—which about hits the mark."[101] And then Whitman added a sentence which deserves to be italicized:
"I think there are truths which it is necessary to envelop

[96] See Preface to *Calamus* [Whitman's letters to Peter Doyle], edited by
R. M. Bucke, (Boston: Laurens Maynard, 1897). Also in *Complete
Writings, op. cit.,* VIII, 7.
[97] *In Re,* 34.
[98] Quoted by E. Carpenter, *op. cit.,* 150.
[99] *Ibid.,* 47.
[100] *Ibid.,* 38.
[101] *Ibid.,* 43.

or wrap up." Carpenter left for later biographers the
pastime of guessing what these "truths" were, but he fully
appreciated the importance of the confessed "furtive" sensation which the poet experienced in writing LEAVES OF
GRASS (meaning how many editions?). In the summer
of 1886 Whitman demonstrated his own understanding of
the psychological significance of these revelations in a self-
analysis for Carpenter: "The *Democratic Review* essays
and tales came from the surface of the mind, and had no
connection with what lay below—a great deal of which
indeed was below consciousness. At last came the time
when the concealed growth had to come to light . . ."[102]

Carpenter no less than Bucke thought Whitman's cosmic consciousness his strongest faculty. For this reason
both believed he was a new type of man. But Carpenter
did not see him with the distorted perspective of the "hot
little prophets" who would like to worship at the shrine
of a new Messiah: "while [Whitman] does not claim to
deliver a new Gospel, he seems to claim to take his place
in the line of those who have handed down a world-old
treasure of redemption for mankind."[103] In *To Him that
was Crucified* we have not a successor of Christ but a con-
tinuer of a world-wide and age-long tradition.[104] In an
appendix called "Whitman as Prophet" Carpenter cites
parallels to LEAVES OF GRASS from the Upanishads. This
emphasis on religious tradition and literary analogies for
LEAVES OF GRASS links Edward Carpenter with the first
of the critical biographers, though his first-hand information and his literary discipleship classify him as one of the
apostles—even if at times a doubting Thomas.

[102] *Ibid.,* 73.
[103] *Ibid.,* 75.
[104] *Ibid.,* 76.

CRITICAL BIOGRAPHY AT LAST:
BINNS, BERTZ

We have already seen how arbitrary classifications of the biographers can be. Although on the whole Burroughs wrote as much under the spell of Whitman's personal influence as anyone, at times he could be acutely objective and critical. And both Symonds and Edward Carpenter, who eagerly confessed their profound indebtedness to the American poet, did much to bring about a complete re-evaluation of Walt Whitman in biography; while Henry Bryan Binns, an Englishman whose *Life of Walt Whitman* (1905) is the first complete, factual, and exhaustive biography, was as tenderly sympathetic with the poet as his most intimate friends had been.

Binns did his job so thoroughly that his book is still, nearly forty years later, one of the most reliable accounts of Walt Whitman's life. Not content with reading all available Whitman literature, Mr. Binns came to the United States and observed the scenes which had exerted the greatest influence on the life of his subject. For example, when Sculley Bradley visited Timber Creek and made an exhaustive study of the place where Whitman one summer regained the use of his limbs after a spell of invalidism, he found that only Binns had given an accurate description of the place.[105] Such accuracy was certainly new in Whitman biography, though in his Preface Binns disclaims any intention of writing a "critical" or "definitive" life.

---

[105] Sculley Bradley, "Walt Whitman on Timber Creek," *American Literature*, V, 235-246 (November, 1933). [In conversations with the author of this Handbook Professor Bradley amplified this opinion of Binns.]

Nevertheless, after a factual account of Whitman's youth and early manhood, Binns originates the most colorful of all the conjectures about the poet's mysterious New Orleans period. In the attempt to account for the marked change which seems to have come over Whitman after this trip, he creates a New Orleans romance.

It seems that about this time Walt formed an intimate relationship with some woman of higher social rank than his own—a lady of the South where social rank is of the first consideration—that she became the mother of his child, perhaps, in after years, of his children; and that he was prevented by some obstacle, presumably of family prejudice, from marriage or the acknowledgment of his paternity.[106]

As evidence for this conjecture Binns cites the letter to Symonds, Whitman's old-age remarks to Traubel, and the emotional awakening and poetic power which is evident in LEAVES OF GRASS a few years after this trip. The awakening and the power are acknowledged by all the biographers, but Binns was the first to create so bold a theory: "Who emancipated him? May we not suppose it was a passionate and noble woman who opened the gates for him and showed him himself in the divine mirror of her love?"[107] Future biographers were slow to relinquish so romantic a picture as the warm-blooded, dark-skinned Southern lady of high-born Creole caste.

This theory works best for the *Children of Adam* poems. The *Calamus* group is explained by Binns as not the product of experience but of frustrated love: "he who

---

[106] Henry Bryan Binns, *A Life of Walt Whitman*, (London: Methuen and Co., 1905), 51.
[107] *Ibid.*, 52.

knew and loved so many men and women, seems to have
carried forward with him no equal friendship from the
years of his youth . . . He longed for Great Companions,
but he did not meet them at this time upon the open road
of daily intercourse."[108]

Despite Binns's avowed purpose not to indulge in
critical interpretations, he was the first biographer or critic
to attempt a close reading of the subjective meaning of
Whitman's poems as they developed through the many
editions. For example, *Drum-Taps* "is a Song of the
Broad-Axe, not a scream of the war-eagle."[109] The poet
who had formerly expressed his awakened sensibility and
his frustrated longing for human companionship learned,
through the War and the hospital, social solidarity and a
"sense of citizenship."

Binns also uses effectively the comparative method to
clarify Whitman's relations to his age and to other writers.
Like Triggs,[110] he finds revealing parallels in the thought
of Whitman and Browning. Tolstoi, with his "Oriental
tendency toward pessimism and asceticism,"[111] serves
mainly as a contrast. Whitman's mysticism is thought to
be indirectly indebted to George Fox, and his individualism directly influenced by Mill's *Principles of Economy*.[112]
A very interesting parallel is Proudhon, "the peasant, who
. . . looked forward to voluntaryism as the final form of
society."[113]

In a calm, reasonable manner Binns accepts Whitman

---

[108] *Ibid.,* 163.
[109] *Ibid.,* 209.
[110] Oscar L. Triggs, *Browning and Whitman: A Study in Democracy,*
(University of Chicago, 1893).
[111] Binns, *op. cit.,* 295.
[112] *Ibid.,* 298, 308.
[113] *Ibid.,* 309.

as a modern prophet. "To be an American poet-prophet, to make the American people a book which should be like the Bible in spiritual appeal and moral fervour, but a book of the New World and of the new spirit—such seems to have been the first and the last of Whitman's day-dreams."[114] But whereas, "Other men have given themselves out to be a Christ, or a John the Baptist, or an Elijah; Whitman without their fanaticism, but with a profound knowledge of himself, recognized in a peasant-born son of Mannahatta, an average American artisan, the incarnation of America herself."[115]

The story of the rise and growth of the Whitman cult in Germany belongs to the history of LEAVES OF GRASS in World Literature more than to the growth of biography, and will therefore be treated in Chapter VI, but the publication of Eduard Bertz's *Der Yankee-Heiland* in 1905 marks an important turn in Whitman biography because this was the first outright attempt to destroy completely the "Yankee-Saint" legend. Whitman's works were discussed in Germany as early as 1868 by Ferdinand Freiligrath, and soon after Knortz-Rolleston's translation in 1889 the American poet was practically worshiped in the Rhineland[116] much as Shakespeare had been in the eighteenth century. But most German critics merely elaborated the "official" portrait created by Whitman and his acolytes, though more fanatically than even the most ardent American friends. Especially is this true in the writings of Johannes Schlaf.[117]

[114] *Ibid.,* 55.
[115] *Ibid.,* 335.
[116] Cf. Chap. VI, 508.
[117] Schlaf's best known work is probably his monograph *Walt Whitman,* 1904, published as vol. XVIII of *Die Dichtung.*

Bertz first read LEAVES OF GRASS in 1882 while he was living in his "woodland retreat" in Tennessee. After returning to Germany he sent Whitman in 1889 an appreciative article which he had published in the *Deutsche Presse* to celebrate the poet's seventieth birthday. In response Whitman showered Bertz with favorable reviews and self-advertizing, and the German admirer could not reconcile this action with his idealization of the saintly-prophet. Bertz, still and always, regarded Whitman as one of the major lyric poets of the world,[118] but from this time on he became suspicious and critical of Whitman's life and character.

These suspicions led to a study of Walt Whitman's sex pathology, published as "Walt Whitman, ein Charakterbild" in the *Jahrbuch für sexuelle Zwischenstufen,* 1905. Here Bertz argued that Whitman belonged to the "intermediate sex", to use Edward Carpenter's term, or "Uranians".[119] This psychopathic interpretation dominates Bertz's attempt to unmask the poet in *Der Yankee-Heiland.*

The feminine and even hysterical *Grundton* of his being is obvious to any observant reader, in the emotional, impassioned character of his world-outlook. No one familiar with modern psychology and sex-pathology is in the slightest doubt that the erotic friendship,

---

[118] Eduard Bertz, *Der Yankee-Heiland: Ein Beitrag zur Modernen Religionsgeschichte,* (Dresden: Verlag von Carl Reissner, 1906), 100.

[119] W. C. Rivers, in *Walt Whitman's Anomaly* (London, 1913) makes a similar classification: "If Walt Whitman was homosexual, then, to what variety of male inversion did he belong? Essentially the *passive* kind, as one might expect from his pronouncedly feminine nature," p. 64. Edward Carpenter, in *Some Friends of Walt Whitman: A Study in Sex-psychology* (London, 1924) accuses Rivers of having accentuated "the petty or pathological marks," p. 14. Carpenter thinks that Nature may be evolving a new form of humanity, "inclusive of male and female."

which is found in the poetry and life of our wonderful prophet, is to be explained in any other way than by his constitutional deviation from the masculine norm.[120]

This interpretation casts a new light on many phases of Whitman's life. His love for the young soldiers suffering in the hospitals was "fundamentally sexual",[121] though sublimated and ennobled. His "abundant joy" was another myth; actually "his life was filled with the intense agony of a confused soul. His love was unrequited; it was a renunciation and so he placed it beyond the grave."[122] Even his "supposedly universal sympathy . . . [was] rooted not so much in his heart as in his phantasy" and turns out to be only a "formal, artistic theory."[123] In the same manner, Whitman's paralysis is thought to have been the result of some hereditary taint; the breakdown due to the hospital strain was a myth, like the similar myth about Nietzsche's hospital work.[124]

Bertz's attempt to destroy the "prophet myth" results also in an attack upon Whitman's pretensions as a thinker and a philosopher. Though he claimed to be the poet of science and progress, he was "at heart opposed to Darwinism but afraid to say so openly."[125] His "new religion" actually came far more from the Hebrew prophets than from scientific thought, though he fooled himself into thinking that he had reconciled the two through some sort of Hegelian sophistry. His chiliasm and theodicy[126]

---

[120] Bertz, *op. cit.*, 228-229.
[121] *Ibid.*, 205.
[122] *Ibid.*, 212.
[123] *Ibid.*, 203.
[124] *Ibid.*, 30.
[125] *Ibid.*, 127.
[126] Bertz finds striking parallels between Novalis and Whitman's doctrine that "there is really no evil in the world," *Ibid.*, 146-147.

were intuitive and romantic and irreconcilable with empirical rationalism.

> . . . if he had wished to be nothing except a lyricist his poetic greatness would certainly be uncontested. But unfortunately he wanted above all to be a prophet and . . . the founder of a tenable scientific religion with a definitely philosophic world outlook, and this point of view conflicted with his spiritual nature; his purely lyrical talent was not sufficient for that.[127]

Scholarly Biography in America: Perry and George Rice Carpenter

The beginnings of Whitman scholarship—the attempt to discover and tell the whole truth—might be dated from Binns, but before Bliss Perry's *Whitman* in 1906 at least no one in America had even attempted to tell the poet's life completely and impartially. Perry did not have access to many of the private notebooks and unpublished manuscripts which have since been collected and edited by Holloway and Furness, but he made the most of the sources available.

In his biography Perry traces down the known facts of Whitman's ancestry, which he finds to be undistinguished but respectable. The events of his youth and early manhood are recited calmly and without bias. Not even the New Orleans trip provokes any fanciful guesses or romantic interpretations. Where the facts are inadequate or missing altogether, Perry freely admits the lacunae. He rejects the pathological interpretations of the *Calamus* poems, though agreeing with Burroughs that there was a good deal of the woman as well as the man in Walt

---

[127] *Ibid.*, 100.

Whitman.[128] He agrees also with Burroughs that there is "abundant evidence that from 1862 onward his life was stainless so far as sexual relations were concerned,"[129] yet frankly admits that the evidence for earlier years is scanty. The first LEAVES OF GRASS was "a child of passion" and "sexual emotion" helped to generate it. "Its roots are deep down in a young man's body and soul," but it is "a clean, sensuous body and a soul untroubled as yet by the darker mysteries."[130] In the poems of joy Perry finds "the spirit of blissful vagrancy which dominated his early manhood."[131] Perry travels a road separate from that of the later psychological biographers.

Without denying or minimizing Walt Whitman's affectations of dress and manner, a sympathetic interpretation is placed on them by the observation that "the flannel shirt and slouch hat are as clearly symbolical as George Fox's leathern breeches, or the peasant dress of Count Tolstoi."[132] Whitman's letters to his mother and friends give the reader a clear, eye-witness account of the War and the hospital experiences. With kindly detachment Perry chronicles the poet's dismissal from his clerkship in Washington and O'Connor's feud not only with the puritanical Harlan but also with all British literature and European influences. Even the Camden period—with "its *vates sacer*, . . . the band of disciples, the travel-stained pilgrims and ultimately the famous tomb"[133] is neither satirized nor sentimentalized.

But probably Perry's greatest service for Whitman biography and criticism, and for American literature, was his interpretation of LEAVES OF GRASS in terms of inter-

---

[128] Perry, *op. cit.*, 64.
[129] *Ibid.*, 46.
[130] *Ibid.*, 47.

[131] *Ibid.*, 21.
[132] *Ibid.*, 74.
[133] *Ibid.*, 214.

national literary and artistic developments. "A generation trained to the enjoyment of Monet's landscapes, Rodin's sculptures, and the music of Richard Strauss will not be repelled from Whitman merely because he wrote in an unfamiliar form."[134] Perry also helped to lessen the shock for readers by calling attention to the parallels between LEAVES OF GRASS and Oriental poetry (so much admired by the American Transcendentalists) and the familiar English version of the poetry of the Bible.[135]

Whitman's faults and literary lapses are also freely admitted. In a left-handed manner the "physiological passages" are defended as usually bearing "the mark, not so much of his imaginative energy as of his automatic describing."[136] Like Burroughs, Perry finds absent in Whitman love of man for woman and a sense of family, home, and social cooperation. "Beyond the unit he knows nothing more definite than his vague 'divine average' until he comes to 'these States' and finds himself on sure ground again."[137] But most objectionable to the Camden disciples was such a criticism as this: "Monist as he was in philosophy, he was polytheist in practice: he dropped on his knees anywhere, before stick or stone, flesh or spirit, and swore that each in turn was divine."[138] Nevertheless, Walt Whitman, "in spite of the alloy which lessens the purely poetic quality and hence the permanence of his verse, is sure . . . to be somewhere among the immortals."[139]

The condition in which Perry left Whitman biography after the publication of his book may be summed up in his own conclusion:

---

[134] *Ibid.*, 282-283.   [137] *Ibid.*, 293.
[135] *Ibid.*, 276.   [138] *Ibid.*, 294.
[136] *Ibid.*, 289.   [139] *Ibid.*, 307.

No Whitman myth, favorable or unfavorable, can forever withstand the accumulated evidence as to Whitman's actual character . . . The 'wild buffalo strength' myth, which he himself loved to cultivate, has gone; the Sir Galahad myth, so touchingly cherished by O'Connor, has gone, too; and Dr. Bucke's 'Superman' myth is fast going. We have in their place something very much better; a man earthy, incoherent, arrogant, but elemental and alive.[140]

It is not in the least surprising that Perry's biography should have, as Kennedy put it, "excited . . . much protest from Whitmanites"[141] and he, himself, was no exception. The Whitmanites could not bear any qualification of their hero and were quick to attribute any reservations either to prudery or the stultifying influence of "culture". Kennedy thought the book was "written with an eye on Mrs. Grundy", by an author who lived in the stuffy air of libraries and the class-room. He is a spokesman of the genteel, conforming, half-baked middle-class . . ."[142]

A work more to the taste of the "Whitmanites" was Horace Traubel's *With Walt Whitman* in Camden, the first volume of which appeared in 1906. Two more volumes were published, and Traubel had material for a fourth volume which has never been completed.[143] From March 28, 1888 Traubel kept daily notes of his conversations with Whitman, and in these books he reports them with a fullness that puts Boswell to shame—though unfortunately Traubel had Boswell's industry without his

---

[140] *Ibid.*, 291.
[141] William Sloane Kennedy, *The Fight of A Book for the World*, (West Yarmouth, Mass.: Stonecroft Press, 1926), 93.
[142] *Ibid.*, 94.
[143] See bibliographical description on p. 101.

genius. Because the books do provide many minute details of the poet's last years that would not otherwise have
survived, they have some value for the student of his
ideas; but they also do Whitman a disservice by em-
balming his trivial, garrulous, and often foggy thoughts
in the final years of pain, failing memory, and perhaps at
times of outright delusion.[144] Only limitless veneration
and uncritical judgment could have enabled anyone to
accumulate such a mass of commonplace manuscript—
though he did preserve valuable letters.

The new epoch of scholarly biographies in America was
continued, however, with George Rice Carpenter's *Walt
Whitman,* published in the "English Men of Letters"
series in 1909. This book, like others in the series, is not
particularly original or distinguished, though it summarizes the facts accurately and coherently. It might be
described as a concise version of Bucke (for facts) and
Perry (for interpretation). Bucke's account of Whitman's
sound ancestry is retained in chastened rhetoric, Binns's
New Orleans romance is passed over in silence, and the
story of the illegitimate children is unquestioningly
accepted. "We know (and wish to know) nothing more
than that he had at times been lured by the pleasures of
the flesh, like many a poet before him, and that he had
known the deep and abiding love of woman".[145] (Later
biographers were to lack such well-bred reticence.) In the
next to the last paragraph of the biography Carpenter
mentions literary relationships but quickly asserts that
these are "not of great importance in Whitman's case. He

---

[144] Cf. Note 90.
[145] George Rice Carpenter, *Walt Whitman,* (New York: The Macmillan Co., 1909), 64 note.

was little influenced by books,"[146] and apparently was thought not to have influenced others—as of course he had not in America before 1906, though he had in Europe.

FRENCH AND BRITISH CRITICS: BAZALGETTE, DE SELINCOURT, LAWRENCE, BULLETT

In 1908 Léon Bazalgette, in his *Walt Whitman: L'-Homme et son Oeuvre*—still known in the United States mainly in a bowdlerized translation[147]—revived the idealized interpretations of Burroughs and Bucke with a critical enthusiasm and lack of reserve possible only to a master of the French language. Like the earliest biographers, he believes that the man cannot be separated from the book, and therefore frequently "evoke[s] the work to explain the man."[148] As a matter of fact, he deliberately carries on the work of the Bucke school, for he announces in the preface the intention of building, "to the measure of my strength, a French dwelling for the American bard."[149] And his sources are Whitman's personal friends, rather than later biographies: "I efface myself as much as possible, in the humility of a compiler, behind those who were in personal contact with him and caught him on the spot."[150]

---

[146] *Ibid.*, 171.

[147] *Walt Whitman: the Man and His Work*, translated from the French by Ellen Fitzgerald, (Garden City: Doubleday, Page and Co., 1920). The translator states: ". . . I have felt justified in abridging M. Bazalgette's treatment of the New Orleans episode, not that it may not be true but that it is a mystery which neither H. B. Binns nor he can clear by elaborate guess work; I have also as much as is consistent with the unity of the book lightened his emphasis on the *Leaves of Grass* conflict," viii. The warm description of Whitman's supposed first sexual ecstasies are freely deleted.

[148] *Ibid.*, 5.

[149] *Ibid.*, xvii.

[150] *Ibid.*, 4.

Once more the poet's ancestry shines in resplendent glory. From the Whitmans, "the most vigorous British element in one section" of the isle, and the Van Velsors, "typical representatives of the old Americanized Dutch," Walt Whitman inherited, from the one, "firmness of character, verging almost upon hardness," and from the other, "abundant vitality and joviality."[151] Little Walt "found in his cradle the enormous strength and health accumulated by his family, nowise diminished like the family fortune, but increased each generation."[152] The "centuries of silent labour close to the earth and to the sea, centuries of robustness and open air"[153] had prepared the way for him.

Bazalgette idealizes Whitman's youth and apprenticeship years with a more vivid imagination than either Burroughs or Bucke possessed. "The memory of this happy period remained dear as ever to the poet, past the period of his virility . . . What animal strength and what largeness these intervals of life, wild, exultant, diffusive of unconscious joy, near the sea and on it, were preparing for the individual!"[154] And then when he comes to the young man's sexual awakening, which again is believed to have been the New Orleans period, Bazalgette displays an exuberance which evidently shocked the American translator, for she thought it necessary to leave whole paragraphs unrevealed in sober English.[155]

It is not easy in a few words to explain Bazalgette's exact interpretations of the New Orleans period, for it is both subtle and French. He is quite aware that Walt Whitman did not conduct himself like a typical Anglo-

---

[151]*Ibid.*, 12, 13.
[152] *Ibid.*, 23.
[153] *Ibid.*, 94.

[154] *Ibid.*, 35.
[155] See note 147 above.

Saxon young man in love, but Bazalgette is sure that he was not abnormal. Whitman merely appeared to be cold because he did not abandon himself to flirtations and pretty speeches. And he may not have been sexually aroused until his brief sojourn in the South:

Il est possible, toutefois, que, jusqu'à son séjour à la Nouvelle-Orléans, l'amour n'ait été pour lui qu'une expérience concrète parmi mille autres expériences et qu'il n'ait pas eu encore la révélation totale de la femme, âme et corps, la sensation despotique et toute-puissante de son être entier, aimant et aimé.[156]

But the hypothetical romance first created by Binns, "dans son livre si nourri, si pieux, si chaleureux,"[157] seems to Bazalgette to exaggerate the importance of this education in love. The future poet tore himself away and returned to his home in the North because "he could not endure that a woman should hold a place in his life which might fatally lessen the domain of his liberty."[158] Still, "Walt had plunged into the heart of the continent and, undoubtedly, into the heart of woman."[159]

Although other biographers admit the scarcity of exact information concerning Whitman's life between the New Orleans trip and the first edition of LEAVES OF GRASS, Bazalgette asserts confidently that at thirty "the perfect concordance between the interior Walt and his physical appearance is a genuine subject of astonishment."

---

[156] Léon Bazalgette, *Walt Whitman L'Homme et son Oeuvre,* (Paris: Mercure de France, 1908), 92. Quotations from these passages which Miss Fitzgerald so discreetly omitted are kept in the original in order to avoid any confusion between the French and American versions of Bazalgette's biography.

[157] *Ibid.,* 94.

[158] Fitzgerald translation, 84.

[159] *Ibid.,* 86.

In fact, "however magnificent, however eternal may be for us his book, Walt, the man in the flesh who is about to put it forth, is at least its peer at this moment."[160] Perhaps such enthusiastic statements were intended to be understood in a symbolical manner, for Bazalgette goes on to say that Walt Whitman "was more a Whitman man than his father or his brother George, more a Van Velsor than his mother or his brother Jeff . . ."[161] When so little is known about either family, this super-inheritance must be mystical rather than biological. And the same is true in Bazalgette's treatment of the *Calamus* motif in LEAVES OF GRASS. He admits the "impassioned character" of some of Whitman's "attachments of man to man,"[162] but thinks Schlaf[163] has successfully replied to the psychopaths who had seen in these friendships "a sexual anomaly":

> In any case, it is not the searchers for anomalies who will ever find the key. Perhaps he who shall describe the exact nature of the attachment which united the Apostle of Galilee [*sic*] to his disciple John will be able to clear the mystery of love which is concealed in the tender comradeships of the Good Gray Poet.[164]

After this point, to summarize the rest of Bazalgette's book would be an anti-climax in this account of the growth of Whitman biography, not because the French biographer falters or weakens, but because from here on the point of view is thoroughly familiar to us. With gusto

---

[160] *Ibid.*, 91.
[161] *Ibid.*, 97.
[162] *Ibid.*, 220.
[163] Cf. Note 117 above. Johannes Schlaf also wrote *Walt Whitman Homosexueller, Kritische Revision einer Whitman-Abhandlung von Dr. Eduard Bertz*, (Minden: Bruns' Verlag, 1906).
[164] Fitzgerald translation of Bazalgette, 220-221.

Bazalgette dilates on "Walt Whitman, a Cosmos," with vicarious pleasure he exults in O'Connor's avenging the Harlan "insult," shares the pride of the intimate friends over the poet's victories in the British Isles, and finally with loving tenderness describes the calm death "while the rain gently fell," and the "pagan funeral" which intrusted the last remains to the elements. No biographer has written Walt Whitman's life with more genuine emotion.

Basil De Selincourt's English biography shares a good deal in spirit and point of view with the French biography of Bazalgette and was no doubt influenced by it. Both are, strictly speaking, critics rather than biographers, for they are interested less in discovering facts and establishing new evidences for their interpretations than in reading the text sympathetically; and at times their reading is so sympathetic that they too become myth-makers.

De Selincourt does, however, give a new twist to the New Orleans hypothesis started by Binns: "There can be no doubt that his trip South was taken with conscious intention, that his new job attracted him because of the new contexts it would afford to his daily dreams and meditations."[165] Not even Burroughs and Bucke assumed that the poet thus consciously planned and controlled his destiny. Accepting Binns's theory completely that Whitman first experienced love in the romantic South, De Selincourt discovers a pregnant symbolism: "This visit to the South, always associated in his mind with the ecstatic and desolating history of his loves, became typical to him of the

[165] Basil De Selincourt, *Walt Whitman: A Critical Study,* (London: Martin Secker, 1914), 18.

fusion of the Northern and Southern States into a nation, and seemed to give him the right to speak as representative of the whole."¹⁶⁶

Although he insists that Whitman "was not the type to sow wild oats," De Selincourt nevertheless accepts completely the story of the six illegitimate children and the romance with the New Orleans lady of "gentle birth," but

> his six children were not all the offspring of one mother, their father convincing himself, under the influence partly of his feelings, partly of confused theory, that, as an exceptional man, loved now by this woman and now by that, he could find and give an adequate conjugal love in more than one relationship . . . pledged already to transcendental union with his country, [he] may have felt that the serene confiding joys of domesticity and its complete personal surrender must not be his.¹⁶⁷

Such promiscuity on principle certainly reaches a new high, or a new low, of some sort in Whitman biography! De Selincourt asserts that *Out of the Cradle Endlessly Rocking,* which he conveniently dates back to "one of the all but earliest *Leaves,*" is "the song virtually of a husband mourning for the death of one who was in all but name his wife,"¹⁶⁸ *i.e.,* the New Orleans woman of gentle birth, while *Once I Pass'd through a Populous City* may refer to a "humble mother."

De Selincourt admits an inconsistency in Whitman's pretending to despise culture yet trying to write poetry. "He was without the discipline of education and under-

---

¹⁶⁶ *Ibid.,* 18-19.   ¹⁶⁸ *Ibid.,* 23-24.
¹⁶⁷ *Ibid.,* 20-22.

rated or ignored its value."[169] And another paradox is found in the war poems: although Whitman "regarded himself and we regard him as peculiarly the poet of the war; yet . . . the bulk of his most characteristic expression preceded it,"[170] for much of *Drum-Taps* had already been completed when Walt went to Virginia to look for George. But in Whitman's letters to his mother and to Peter Doyle De Selincourt thinks that we observe for the first time "his actual personality by the side of the assumed personality of the hero of LEAVES OF GRASS, and find to our astonishment that the man is greater than the book, and different from it; in fact, that he is its complement."[171]

Bucke and Whitman himself would have approved this interpretation of the poet's spontaneous unconventionality:

His own wild music, ravishing, unseizable, like the song of a bird, came to him, as by his own principles it should have come, when he was not searching for it. And his greatness as a poet, when we regard his poetry on its formal side, is that conventional echoes damaged him so little, that in spite of unavoidable elements of wilfulness and reaction in his poetry, he was able to achieve so real an independence.[172]

Perhaps only a European critic could have declared finally that Walt Whitman "epitomised his people so perfectly that he could make no impression upon them."[173]

Four years later, in 1918, a French critic, Valéry Larbaud, voiced a revolt from the Bazalgette interpretation

[169] *Ibid.,* 31.
[170] *Ibid.,* 42-43.
[171] *Ibid.,* 45.
[172] *Ibid.,* 73.
[173] *Ibid.,* 241.

which was to be heard in ever-increasing volume in the next two decades. He rejected three Whitman legends, those of the prophet, the laborer, and the philosopher, and we might add a fourth, that of the American:

> Oui, il est Américan; mais c'est parce que nous flairons dans la partie vivante de son oeuvre une certaine odeur (indéfinissable) que nous trouvons aussi dans Hawthorne, Thoreau, roman de H. K. Viélé et trois nouvelles de G. W. Cable. Mais il n'est pas Américain parce qu'il s'est proclamé le poète de l'Amérique. Encore le démenti immédiat: il a été aussi méconnu aux États-Unis que Stendhal à Grenoble ou Cézanne à Aix. Sa doctrine est allemande, et ses maîtres sont anglais; par toute sa vie purement intellectuelle il fut un Européen habitant L'Amérique. Mais, surtout la plupart de 'happy few' vivent en Europe. C'est donc en Europe seulement qu'il pouvait être reconnu, et qu'il l'a été.[174]

In his chapter on Whitman in *Studies in Classic American Literature* (1918) D. H. Lawrence attacked savagely a mystical doctrine and a personal characteristic of the poet in a manner wholly new in biography and criticism of him. When Whitman looks at the slave, says Lawrence, he *merges* with him, vicariously shares his wounds —"is it not myself who am also bleeding with wounds?" But, "This was not *sympathy*. It was merging and self-sacrifice."[175] The merging theme is morbid and disintegrating. Whitman starts out boldly on the open road— explorer, adventurer, pioneer—but then he wants to merge with everything, all people, nature, the womb, finally

---

[174] *Walt Whitman: Oeuvres Choisis,* op. cit., 50.
[175] D. H. Lawrence, "Whitman," *Studies in Classic American Literature,* (New York: Albert Boni, 1923), 260.

with Death. He confounds sympathy (which would help the slave to free himself or the prostitute to secure medical and economic aid) with sentimental Christianity.

But the prophet and carpenter legend died hard. As late as 1921 Will Hayes, one of the last fundamentalists, published in London a book called *Walt Whitman: the Prophet of the New Era,* with chapters on "The Christ of Our Age," "The Carpenter of Brooklyn," and "A Sermon on the Mount." The book is too trivial to mention except as an example that the old faith still lingered on.

The extent to which Rossetti's attitudes toward Whitman had survived in Great Britain is evidenced in Gerald Bullett's *Walt Whitman: A Study and a Selection,* 1924. "If we regard a poet as an infallible seer," says Bullett, "we are at once saved the trouble of reading his work intelligently, with critical faculty alert," and this, he thinks, is exactly what some of Whitman's countrymen have done, they "who regard every word that he wrote, every comma that he omitted, as so infinitely precious that they reprint even his juvenile metrical verse, his temperance novel, and his newspaper reports."[176]

"Apart from the defect in taste that blemished his literary expression, he possessed personal idiosyncrasies that were due largely to an excess of qualities admirable in themselves. His occasional mawkishness, the endearments and kisses bestowed on the men who were his dearest friends . . . this, I feel, was but the odious superflux of a

---

[176] Gerald Bullett, *Walt Whitman: A Study and a Selection,* (London: Grant Richards Ltd., 1924), 27. Bullett has in mind Cleveland Rodgers and John Black's *The Gathering of the Forces* [From *Brooklyn Daily Eagle*], (New York: G. P. Putnam's Sons, 1920), 2 vols.; and Emory Holloway's *Uncollected Poetry and Prose of Walt Whitman,* (New York: Doubleday, 1921), 2 vols.

generous affection."[177] Like most of the British critics, Bullett censures Whitman for blabbing about intimate details of life that should be kept secret and accuses him of utter lack of artistic sense and taste. "Why make bones about it that Whitman at thirty-five was a satyr, and some of the first LEAVES OF GRASS the natural expression of a satyr?"[178] He knew nothing of selection. But he was not lacking in poetic power. He was best when he was cosmic. And when by "sheer strength of thought or depth of passion" his work escapes from graphic journalism it rises to the realm of great literature.[179]

John Bailey's *Walt Whitman* (1926) stands in about the same relation to the English biographies as G. R. Carpenter's book to the American biographies. It is reliable, complete, and always reasonable and conservative in interpretations, without adding anything new or especially significant. Bailey has great respect for those men fortunate enough to have known the poet personally and yet is always suspicious of their unrestrained enthusiasm. "In a man's lifetime lucky or unlucky personal characteristics often lead to his receiving more praise, or less, than his achievement deserved. But the function of later criticism is to take the book, or other work, and judge it as it is, apart from all prejudices of personal liking or disliking."[180] These words adequately summarize the state of Whitman biography and criticism in 1924. The influence of the "hot little prophets" had almost faded out completely and sober criticism both of the man's life and

---

[177] *Ibid.*, 30.
[178] *Ibid.*, 3.
[179] *Ibid.*, 45.
[180] John Bailey, *Walt Whitman*, (New York: The Macmillan Co., 1926), 197.

his work were becoming well established. As the living personality of Walt Whitman faded from the memory of men, the scholar and the critic began to turn a concentrated light upon the poetry itself and to read it with increasing depth of understanding and appreciation. After all, the man and the book were not exactly one and the same, even in a mystical sense, for the man had passed on but the book remained.

RESEARCH AND TEXTUAL STUDY:
HOLLOWAY, CATEL, SCHYBERG

Emory Holloway laid the foundation for a new era in Whitman studies when he published in 1921 the *Uncollected Poetry and Prose of Walt Whitman,* containing the poet's private notebooks, early journalistic writings, and other juvenilia in poetry and prose.[181] Since then Holloway and his assistants have continued to salvage and edit practically every journalistic scrap that can be assigned to Whitman, along with some that can be credited to him only hypothetically. Consequently, when Holloway got ready to publish his biography, *Whitman, An Interpretation in Narrative* (1926), he was undoubtedly familiar with more of the poet's total life output of writings than anyone else. His greatest achievement, therefore, was the first full account of Walt Whitman's life as journalist and editor. And on the natural assumption that the child is father to the man, he attempted to explain the mature poet in terms of his early life and intellectual development.

Holloway's book begins, therefore, not with the poet's ancestors—about which, after all, little can ever be known

---

[181] See note 176 above.

except names, dates, places of residence, and occupations
—but with the journalistic years in Brooklyn, a subject on
which the author had already become a recognized authority. Perhaps, as Holloway remarks, Whitman could hardly
have become the poet of Democracy without his training
and experience in the newspaper office. But the astonishing thing is that the more we learn of the mediocre mind
and expression of Walt Whitman the journalist, the
greater seems the miracle of his becoming, in the short
space of four or five years, a genuine poet. Some of the
relaxed, undisciplined habits of thought and expression
were carried over into LEAVES OF GRASS, but in his more
inspired moments he does seem literally a new man.

No one has ever been more aware of this miracle than
Professor Holloway himself. In fact, so conscious is he
of it, and so inadequately do the journalistic writings
provide any satisfactory clues, that once more the biographer must fall back upon two of the earlier hypotheses,
viz., Dr. Bucke's mysticism and Binns's New Orleans romance. Practically all the biographers are unanimous on
Whitman's mystical experiences, but Holloway's acceptance of the New Orleans conjecture shows the ironical
dilemma he is in, for he himself had convincingly de-
molished the whole "romance"-school in an earlier article.[182] One of the supposed bits of evidence nearly always cited to support the New Orleans theory is the
poem, *Once I Pass'd through a Populous City,* but Professor Holloway discovered that in the manuscript the
poem was addressed to a man rather than a woman and

---

[182] Emory Holloway, "Walt Whitman's Love Affairs," *The Dial,*
LXIX, 473-483 (November, 1920). In this interesting article Holloway
also discusses the evidence for an affair with a married woman in Washington.

belonged, therefore, to the *Calamus* group. Perhaps one poem does not prove or disprove the theory, but so great is Holloway's dilemma that he now cites the same poem once more to substantiate the love-affair which he had once rejected on the basis of this poem. "I am convinced," he explains, by many years of study and investigation that the gossip which linked the young journalist with the peculiar *demi monde* of New Orleans was substantially true."[183] No new and conclusive evidence, however, is brought forth.

The reader has the feeling that the biographer knows more than he dares to tell. Commenting on the first edition of LEAVES OF GRASS, Holloway says, "Indeed, had [Whitman] known as much about psychology as we do today, he might not have had the temerity to publish such a book."[184] In discussing the *Calamus* poems Holloway says of Whitman, "he did not carefully distinguish between . . . the sort of affection which most men have for particular women and that which they experience toward members of their own sex,"[185] and he adds that these poems were born of "an unhealthy mood."[186]

Perhaps the basis for these paradoxes is the fact that, as Holloway accurately points out, LEAVES OF GRASS contains several kinds of sex poems: (1) the "sentimental lyrics born of an ideal romance" (*i.e.,* normal sexual love), (2) celebrations of procreation (philosophical), (3) "emotions which accompany the initial act of paternity," (physiological); and to these the biographer at least im-

---

[183] Emory Holloway, *Whitman: An Interpretation in Narrative,* (New York: Alfred A. Knopf, 1926), 66.

[184] *Ibid.,* 123.

[185] *Ibid.,* 169.

[186] *Ibid.,* 173 ff.

plies a fourth type, the poems celebrating what the poet called "manly attachment."[187] Which of these types represents Whitman's real nature? Or is it possible for one man to experience all of these different sexual emotions? These questions are not answered, though perhaps Holloway inclines to a belief in the poet's emotional versatility, for he regards as pathetic and almost tragic the craving for manly affection in the third edition. "The emotion venting itself was so great as to carry with it, for a time, Walt's every ambition. The book was published when his craving for affection was at its height."[188] Later he succeeded in spiritualizing the passion. On the strength of Mrs. O'Connor's testimony Holloway accepts the story of Whitman's being in love with a married woman in Washington, apparently believing that soon after the third edition he recovered from his "unhealthy mood."

Perhaps in line with this interpretation, Holloway finds a great change in Whitman after 1870. He now "makes rendezvous, not with the Great Companions, but with the Comrade perfect."[189] He who declared in 1856, "Divine am I inside and out," now has ideals for his gods. "He sings, not the 'average man', but the 'Ideal Man'. . ." The meaning of the poems written in former periods now takes on a new significance for the poet himself. Concerning the *Children of Adam* poems, for example, "It was characteristic of his type of mind that he should himself have read into these poems, not merely the youthful impulses out of which they were born, but the religious aspirations which succeeded."[190]

In making these illuminating interpretations Holloway

---

[187] *Ibid.*, 169-170.
[188] *Ibid.*, 172.

[189] *Ibid.*, 245.
[190] *Ibid.*, 260.

went considerably beyond any previous biographer and opened the way for further searches for the poet's psyche in his unconscious betrayals in LEAVES OF GRASS.

And Whitman biography did not have long to wait. In Jean Catel's *Walt Whitman: La Naissance du Poète* the soul of the poet was exhumed for a psycho-analytical autopsy. With clinical thoroughness this critic searches, like Holloway, through every fragment of juvenilia, through diaries, letters, and finally LEAVES OF GRASS, for the key to Whitman's genius, and there in the first edition he believes he finds the answer.

In LEAVES OF GRASS we discover what escapes us in his real life and emotion. And of LEAVES OF GRASS, it is the first edition which retains in its music the secret that Whitman consecrated his life to disguise. If it is not there, it is nowhere. It is not in his public life, nor his journalistic articles, nor in his relations with a group of friends as ardent as they were blind. It is not in the biographical notes which he wrote himself, nor in those which he asked Horace Traubel to transmit to posterity. So much concern on his part lest he be misunderstood must arouse our suspicion.

Thus for what he hid Whitman substituted the soul of a poet ready to receive the habiliments of glory. To his real self he preferred a legend. He forgot only one thing—for one can not remember everything—: that first edition, all aquiver in a revolt which maturity and old age were to repudiate. After that edition is pruned, recast, and diluted into the later editions of LEAVES OF GRASS it lacks the air of reality of that first long, revealing cry."[191]

---

[191] Jean Catel, *Walt Whitman: La Naissance du Poète,* (Paris: Les Editions Rieder, 1929), 11. (Translation by present author.)

Once more biography has returned to the identification of the poet and his work, but a vast gulf of psychology separates Catel from Bucke. Dr. Bucke believed that the poet was able to tap the sources of intellectual power of a "cosmic consciousness" but he scarcely thought of searching in the subconscious for the hidden motives of daily action.

The first illusion which Catel attempts to dispel is Walt Whitman's sound ancestry. He finds it impossible "to agree with the optimism of Mr. Bazalgette . . . [that] 'The union of the two races [English and Dutch] was the extraordinary promise of a completer human type, one profiting by all the power of a new soil.' On the contrary, everything tended to create a type of mediocre humanity, harassed by anxiety."[192] In short, the marriage of the discontented and austere Walter Whitman with the loving, sunny Louisa Van Velsor was an unfortunate union. "Some would say that it was a fortunate mis-mating, since it produced a poet. Undoubtedly true, but this poet was not the product of a perfect equilibrium of physical and moral forces, as he and his devoted friends thought and said."[193]

Believing from the study of other writers, such as Dickens and Chateaubriand, that the adolescent impressions registered on the memory are the ones that reappear in the images and imaginative scenes of the creative mind of an author, Catel searches Whitman's writings for clues to his youth. What he discovers is a boy who felt himself from all sides "pushed out of doors, for at the time when the home is the most solid reality to the average child, it did not exist for him. At fifteen he felt himself to have

---

[192] *Ibid.*, 22, note 2 .   [193] *Ibid.*, 22.

no part in the house which his father had built and was living in temporarily." Therefore, "young Whitman, having only the loosest home ties, roamed the streets of Brooklyn and they received him with affection; they were like a home to him."[194] Thus does Catel account for the vividness with which the mature poet describes moving crowds, trips on the ferry, and the pleasure of merging his own ego with the mass of humanity.

Catel's thorough examination of Whitman's journalistic writings before he began LEAVES OF GRASS reveals a maladjusted young man, unsuccessful in the economic world, unsure of himself, unable to make social adjustments. In New Orleans, far from having "found himself" as some biographers believed, he was faced by the same necessities as in Brooklyn and New York, and once again failed miserably to meet them, having to return home after a row with his employer. But by this time one of the chief causes of his difficulties becomes apparent. There is some peculiarity in his sexual nature. Catel finds strong indications that Whitman had had experiences with "professional love" in New York or Brooklyn[195] but this sauntering, dreaming, introspective young man did not find satisfaction in these relationships, for he was naturally "auto-erotic."[196] And it is this peculiarity which accounts for his maladjustment to life.

After returning to Brooklyn, and unsuccessfully trying journalism again, he abandoned so far as possible the

---

[194] *Ibid.*, 38, 39.

[195] Il est certain, d'un côté, que Walt n'entretenait pas avec les jeunes filles de ces relations sentimentales (à la Byron) dont il s'est moqué et que, d'un autre côté, Walt fréquentant les heux de plaisir, il ne pouvait étranger aux joies sexuelles . . . Il est probable que le jeune Walt connut le plaisir des sens et que, sans doute, New-York lui offrit les facilités de l'amour professionnel . . ." *Ibid.*, 254.

[196] *Ibid.*, 435.

physical struggle for adjustment to the world of reality and began to create a compensating inner world of fantasy and imagination, which found expression through his poems. Thus does Catel explain Whitman's almost miraculous acquisition of literary power without recourse either to mysticism or a sexual awakening in the romantic city of the South. Furthermore, the explanation gives a revealing significance to the style, the egoism, and the motifs of LEAVES OF GRASS.

> The myself that Whitman 'celebrates' on each page . . . is the projection of the unconscious. If in reading Whitman's work, the reader will replace mentally the *I* or the *myself* by 'my unconscious', while giving to this word the dynamic sense which we have indicated, then he will understand better: first, the origin, the profound reason for the first edition of LEAVES OF GRASS; second, the end, what certain critics have called the messianic in Whitman.[197]

Being in his conscious mind agitated by a sense of failure, frustration, and loneliness, his poetic imagination returns to an idealized childhood of peace, innocence, and purity, and it is then that he feels in his soul that he is the equal of God.

Books became a powerful force in Whitman's attempt to find happiness through artistic creation. The subjective philosophy of the post-Kantians in America, and of Emerson especially, provided both a framework and a rationalization for the psychological adjustments which his inner nature compelled him to make. Perhaps he was only dimly aware of his great debt to Emerson, but Tran-

---

[197] *Ibid.*, 400-401.

scendentalism, like a religion, opened up a new life to Walt Whitman. Like many a man who has experienced a religious conversion, from this time forth Whitman's whole life, outer as well as inner, became harmonized and tranquilized. He had found a pattern and a purpose.

As the years passed and the adjustment became more settled and habitual, perhaps the poet himself forgot, or may never fully have understood, the emotions which he first conquered in LEAVES OF GRASS. Certainly he was inclined more and more to interpret those first naïve confessions with a disingenuousness that has baffled many a biographer. A study of the successive editions reveals the life-long effort which he gave to revising, deleting, and disguising those first outpourings of his subconscious in his attempt to spiritualize and sublimate the record of his inner life. But there in the 1855 edition is the secret of the whole life and the completed book—the key to Whitman's poetic stimulus, his literary expression, his symbolism, and his unceasing efforts to perpetuate an "official portrait" of himself.

The prodigious researches of Holloway and the Freudian interpretations of Catel culminated in 1933 in the most extensive study of the editions and of Walt Whitman's place in world literature so far accomplished, Frederik Schyberg's *Walt Whitman*—still, unfortunately available only in Danish. Although Schyberg's language predetermined a small audience for his book, his nationality and geographical location gave him advantages not possessed by American or English biographers. Like most Danish scholars, possessing a knowledge of several languages, including English, and being thoroughly familiar with the history of European literature, Schyberg was able to interpret and judge Whitman in terms of the international currents of thought and poetic theory to which he was unconsciously indebted.

Schyberg's first chapter, an attempt to orient Whitman with respect to the national history and the culture of the poet's land, is superficial and has little value for the American student. His second chapter, a strictly biographical sketch, is of interest mainly because it indicates the author's sources and attitudes. Here we see that Schyberg is fully aware of his debt to Catel, though he does not accept Catel's whole thesis and eventually goes far beyond him. He calls the publication of the journalistic writings "negative research";[198] they "contributed to destroy the myths, but offered nothing to fill the gap." We can see Schyberg's indebtedness to Catel in the statement that, "The myths which [Whitman] invented to conceal the uneventful periods in his life (and not a great deal did happen to Whitman . . .),—or to shield some innate weakness of character—, he thought concerned himself and himself alone."[199] Thus, the Danish biographer believes with Catel that there were truths and secrets which the poet concealed, either consciously or unconsciously, but he makes less use of Freud than the French biographer did. He is equally sure, however, that the New Orleans romance never existed except in the brain of Bazalgette and his followers, but he disagrees with Catel on the auto-eroticism;[200] he thinks that Whitman was simply abnormally slow in his biological development, and that he always retained some feminine char-

---

[198] Frederik Schyberg, *Walt Whitman*, (København: Gyldendalske Boghandel, 1933), 9.
[199] *Ibid.*, 10.
[200] *Ibid.*, 63.

acteristics (as even John Burroughs had observed.)[201]
On one fundamental point Schyberg agrees with Bertz:
"At one time Whitman's disciples wanted to make him
more than a poet. They wanted to make him a philosopher
and a prophet as well. Both rôles were impossible . . .
Whitman was a lyricist, not a logician; he was a mystic,
not a philosopher."[202] Schyberg acknowledges that he was
a religious prophet in the same sense and degree that
Nietzsche and Carlyle were, but no more. In his lyric
forms and his treatment of sex Walt Whitman created a
new epoch and became a major figure in world literature,
and these were superlative achievements, but Schyberg
sweeps aside all other claims for the American poet.

Although the earliest biographers often quoted the
poet's idealization of himself, his ancestry, and his conception of his own mission in LEAVES OF GRASS, no one
before Schyberg had examined all the editions to discover
Whitman's biography in the *changes* and *growth* of the
editions.

Schyberg's long and intricate analysis of the first edition
belongs rather to the subject of textual criticism[203] than
biographical interpretation, but significant here is the fact
that he also finds "the joy, confidence, and arrogance" of
the first volume a literary rather than a biographical
reality.[204] And in the comparison of the wording and the
feeling of Whitman's cosmic visions and pantheistic sentiments with the works of many European romanticists we
see that they were not unique and that they need not,

---

[201] *Ibid.*, 63 and 89. See Barrus, *op. cit.*, 339.
[202] *Ibid.*, 12.
[203] See Chap. II.
[204] *Ibid.*, 56 and 101.

therefore, have been the product of distinctly abnormal psychology.

The second edition of LEAVES OF GRASS, coming only one year after the first, was similar to the '55 version. It was the third edition, in Schyberg's opinion, not the first, that recorded the poet's psychological crisis. If Whitman did experience a tragic romance, it must have been between 1855 and '60, for in this 1860 edition traces of some sort of defeat are plainly visible. Since most of the private notebooks for this period are missing (possibly destroyed by the poet himself), Schyberg wonders whether he might not have led a "disgraceful and dissolute saloon life"[205] until the war broke out in 1861, when he recorded his dedication of himself to inaugurating a new regime which would give him "a purged, cleansed, spiritualized, invigorated body."[206] Soon he walked out of Pfaff's restaurant and turned his back on the New York Bohemians. But whatever the secret of this period may be, Whitman guarded it well—except for the emotional tone of that third edition. The key poems express personal grief and discouragement.

"The unspoken word, 'the word' which Whitman sought so zealously and so arrogantly at the conclusion of 'Song of Myself', and of which he said at that time:

It is not chaos or death—it is form, union, plan—
it is eternal life—it is Happiness[207]

that word Whitman found in the years between 1856-1860, and it was both chaos and death—but primarily

---

[205] *Ibid.*, 164.

[206] *Ibid.*, 163-164. Notebook entry for April 16, 1861, first quoted by Binns, *op. cit.*, 181.

[207] *Song of Myself*, Sec. 50.

death."[208] What loved one had died we do not know, but the real theme of *Out of the Cradle* is "Two together", and the fact that in later revisions the poet generalized and partly disguised the extremely personal tone of the first version lends credence to the suspicion that the original poem gave expression to some deep and genuine experience between the second and third editions. Schyberg notes also a sense of frustration and despair in *As I Ebb'd with the Ocean of Life*.[209] The "ship-wreck motif" is prominent in this edition. And it is highly significant that LEAVES OF GRASS has become "a few dead leaves." Certainly, "The arrogant pantheism of the earlier editions had become a despairing pantheism."[210]

The only clue to the morbidity of the 1860 LEAVES is probably the *Calamus* poems of that edition. In future revisions the poet gradually blurred the original impulses, even eliminating some poems altogether (despite his refusal to expurgate a single line for Thayer and Eldridge). On the basis of the later versions, Binns and Bazalgette tried to interpret these poems as a social program, but Schyberg thinks they are just as unmistakably love poems as Sappho's are, and the only love poems that Whitman ever wrote[211]—for the *Children of Adam* group is philosophical rather than personal. *In Paths Untrodden*, which gives the "program" of this group, suggests that there is something different and rather daring in this love. And it is significant that two of the most revealing poems were later deleted: *Long I Thought that Knowledge Alone Would Suffice* expresses the poet's willingness to give up his songs because his Lover is jealous, and in *Hours Con-*

---

[208] Schyberg, *op. cit.*, 167.
[209] *Ibid.*, 169.
[210] *Ibid.*, 170.
[211] *Ibid.*, 181.

tinuing Long, Sore and Heavy-Hearted we find him in utter dejection because he has lost his Lover: "Hours sleepless . . . discouraged, distracted . . . Hours when I am forgotten . . ."

> Sullen and suffering hours! (I am ashamed—but it is useless—I am what I am;)
> Hours of my torment—I wonder if other men ever have the like, out of the like feelings?

Schyberg thinks that the latter poem, and the experience it reveals, rather than a tragic New Orleans romance, gives the real origin of *Out of the Cradle Endlessly Rocking.* However, he adds that, "Probably Whitman wrote these poems quite innocently and published them without realizing how they betrayed himself, and they were tragic because they sprang out of an unrequited love."[212] Both D. H. Lawrence and Whitman "released their erotic impulses in their work, not in their lives."[213] Furthermore "the puberal and effeminate character of Whitman's erotic mentality"[214] is paralleled in the writings of other mystics, such as the medieval Heinrich Suso and the Persian Rumi. It is not an isolated phenomenon in LEAVES OF GRASS but is common in the history of religious and poetic mystics. Furthermore, after the first impulse of the poems had passed, *Calamus* became for Whitman a "city of friends,"[215] and in *Democratic Vistas* (1871) he was able to give it a genuine social interpretation.

The 1860 edition contains not only the record of the great spiritual crisis of Whitman's life—in which he seems to have contemplated suicide—, but it also reveals the

---

[212] *Ibid.*
[213] *Ibid.,* 182, note 2.
[214] *Ibid.,* 183.
[215] *Ibid.,* 190.

means by which he saved himself. This is a discovery of vast importance both to Whitman biography and the critical interpretation of LEAVES OF GRASS. Though "torn and wracked by conflicts within,"[216] he was struggling for both a personal and a literary unity (the *Poem of Many in One*—later *By Blue Ontario's Shore*—is characteristic). "Conflicts within himself would be conquered because they were found collected in one body as the many poems were collected in one book."[217] And by a kind of unconscious ironical symbolism, the nation was becoming divided as Walt Whitman had been. Thus, "He proclaimed the union when the states were on the verge of a break. He hailed adhesiveness, though he had not found it."[218] In *To a President, To the States,* and other poems we find "spontaneous admissions of the real state of affairs."[219] Thus it was not entirely accidental that "Whitman came to consider the democratic fiasco as corresponding to the fateful character of his love in 'Calamus' and thus corroborated the duality in the book's message."[220] But presently he turned his attention to America's future greatness, and thus regained his faith and confidence. *On the Beach at Night* in the 1871 edition answers the despairing question of *As I Ebb'd with the Ocean of Life* in the 1860 edition. By this time Whitman's spiritual crisis was completely over.

What saved him, above all else, was the unifying effect of the Civil War—not only through his own patriotic and devoted services in the army hospitals, but also because the war gave Whitman and the nation Abraham Lincoln.

---

[216] *Ibid.,* 175.
[217] *Ibid.*
[218] *Ibid.,* 200.

[219] *Ibid.,* 194.
[220] *Ibid.*

Lincoln and Whitman complemented each other. Lincoln saved the union and he probably saved Whitman spiritually and practically, and it is also interesting that he appreciated LEAVES OF GRASS. ". . . in Lincoln Whitman found his great Camerado, and the funeral hymn speaks of him as 'my departing comrade'. At any rate, at that time a revolution took place in Whitman's inner life, a recovery from the 1860 psychosis."[221] Because the "Wound-Dresser" became "a man who personally did what he had celebrated as an ideal," Schyberg finds *Drum-Taps* (1865) "a great and remarkable advance in Whitman's art."[222] The poet's sex emotions have become completely sublimated in his hospital work and in his poetry. "Washington was a climax in Whitman's life, a great strain, but also a great release and a great freedom."[223] After *Drum-Taps* Whitman's works really became a unity, though gradually, step by step.

Discouragements returned to the poet after the Washington period, as in his *Prayer of Columbus* (written 1874), in which the mood of the "batter'd, wreck'd old man" is that of the paralyzed and dependent poet himself;[224] but the progress toward personal and literary unity continued until in "A Backward Glance" (*November Boughs,* 1888) he could relax the struggle and look back upon his work as an evolution, a growth. The links in the stages of development, however, had been obscured by the earlier efforts for unity, and the 1892 edition remained a record of the life Whitman wanted remembered, not entirely the one he had actually lived.

In his final chapter Schyberg says:

---

[221] *Ibid.,* 203.
[222] *Ibid.,* 204.
[223] *Ibid.,* 210.
[224] *Ibid.,* 256-257.

An evaluation of Whitman in world literature is an evaluation of those he resembles and those who resemble him. To limit the discussion to his followers and pupils in contemporary literature would deprive it of the major portion of interest. In the history of literary relationships, the influence of author on author is merely half the story and often the least interesting part, whereas the real problem and real interest centers on the question of types and common patterns of thought among authors who probably never knew each other.[225]

Since Whitman's place in world literature is the subject of the final chapter in this *Handbook* it is sufficient for the present to point out that Schyberg's study has an important bearing on Whitman biography, for it reveals the American poet as less of a unique phenomenon and an anomaly than his friends and most of the biographers have thought. His temperament, conduct, and characteristic expression link him with the lives and writings of the great mystics of all ages and all lands. And in his typical thought and poetic form he was preceded and followed by similar poets in the current of European romanticism. This interpretation not only makes Walt Whitman personally less abnormal but it also helps to explain his astounding world-fame and influence.

PRESENT STATE OF WHITMAN BIOGRAPHY: MASTERS AND SHEPHARD TO FURNESS AND CANBY

Edgar Lee Masters' poorly-organized *Whitman* (1937), the first full-length life in the United States after Catel

---

[225] *Ibid.,* 275.

and Schyberg's books in France and Denmark, made no significant contribution to Walt Whitman scholarship or biography, but it did plainly indicate changing attitudes toward the life of the American poet. Here we find a frank discussion of Whitman as one of those "sports" in nature which sex pathologists call "Uranians." Masters applies to Whitman de Joux's definition: "They are enthusiastic for poetry and music, are often eminently skilful in the fine arts, and are overcome with emotion and sympathy at the least sad occurrence. Their sensitiveness, their endless tenderness for children, their love of flowers, their great pity for beggars and crippled folk are truly womanly."[226] The same authority on the conduct of this type of man: "As nature and social law are so cruel as to impose a severe celibacy on him his whole being is consequently of astonishing freshness and superb purity, and his manners of life as modest as those of a saint."[227] Thus on the basis of modern psychology Whitman's character is now defended with a new tolerance and veneration.

The poet of Spoon River thinks Whitman's "poems of nakedness" not a "survival of youthful exhibitionism," but the result of "his free and barbaric innocent days in the country, by the sea . . . and of his own wonderful health and vitality."[228] And of *Calamus:* "Whitman took America for his love and his wife, in somewhat the same way as Vachel Lindsay did later."[229] Masters admits that

---

[226] Edgar Lee Masters, *Whitman,* (New York: Charles Scribner's Sons, 1937), 142. The authorities used by Masters are: Edward Carpenter, *The Intermediate Sex;* De Joux, *Die Enterbten des Liebes glückes;* and Havelock Ellis, *Psychology of Sex.*

[227] Masters, 142-143.

[228] *Ibid.,* 44.

[229] *Ibid.,* 45.

there was unusual warmth in the poet's affection for Doyle but does not think there was anything shameful about it. "Foreigners have remarked that men in America are not really friends, and that love is not so passionate, so tender, among Americans as among the Latin races, or the Germans."[230]

In the opinion of Masters, Whitman's greatest achievements were his literary pioneering and his breaking the bonds of narrow conventionalism. "He was a great influence in inaugurating this better respect for the body which we know today. He stood for sanity in matters of sex and for the outspoken championship of sexual delight as one of the blessings of human life."[231] As poet "he felled to some extent the encumbering forest and let later eyes see in part what the lay of the land was . . ."[232]

In the following year (1938) the bitterest attack on Whitman since Bertz's *Yankee-Heiland* was published in the United States by Esther Shephard as *Walt Whitman's Pose*. Mrs. Shephard would deny that it was an attack, but so disillusioned was she by her "discoveries" that she branded Whitman's whole literary career as a "pose" and a calculated attempt to deceive the public. She found such striking parallels between LEAVES OF GRASS and the epilogue of George Sand's *Countess of Rudolstadt* that she concluded the American poet got the first conception of his literary rôle from George Sand's "vagabond poet, dressed in laborer's garb, who goes into a trance and composes what is described as 'the most magnificent poem

---

[230] *Ibid.*, 132.
[231] *Ibid.*, 323.
[232] *Ibid.*, 327.

that can be conceived'."[233] Likewise Sand's *Journeyman Joiner,* which Whitman reviewed in 1847, gave him ideas for this pose:

> It is a story of a beautiful, Christ-like young carpenter, a proletary philosopher, who dresses in a mechanic's costume but is scrupulously clean and neat. He works at carpentering with his father but patiently takes time off whenever he wants to in order to read, or give advice on art, or share a friend's affection. In short, he is very much the kind of carpenter that Walt Whitman became in the time of the long foreground . . .[234]

There can be no doubt that Whitman read George Sand before writing the first edition of LEAVES OF GRASS, and he was also certainly influenced by the French novelist. Mrs. Shephard admits that, "If LEAVES OF GRASS is a great book, it does not matter that Walt Whitman was a sly person and a poseur,"[235] but in her whole discussion she makes him sound like a fraud and seems to cast suspicion not only on his honesty but also on the value of his literary creation.[236] Undoubtedly her discovery will have some influence on future Whitman biography, for she has at least proven that books had a great deal more im-

---

[233] Esther Shephard, *Walt Whitman's Pose,* (New York: Harcourt, Brace and Co., 1938), 141. Mrs. Shephard, however, was not the first to exploit the "pose" theory. That doubtful honor goes to Harvey O'Higgins, for his bitter attack on the poet in "Alias Walt Whitman," *Harper's Magazine,* CLVIII, 698-707 (May, 1929), later published (same title) in New York: W. M. Stone, 1929, 49 pp., limited edition, 1930. For a sensible critique of both O'Higgins and Shephard see F. I. Carpenter, "Walt Whitman's 'Eidólon'," *College English,* III, 534-545, (March, 1942).

[234] *Ibid.,* 201.

[235] *Ibid.,* 237.

[236] Whitman "never possessed a great poet's imagination" nor "mastery over his materials," and "he revised and rejected not as an artist but rather as the poseur that he was, fame-greedy and fearful lest his secret be betrayed," *Ibid.,* 242.

portance in his life than most of the biographers have yet realized. But there were other writers aside from George Sand whom he could—and certainly did draw upon too.[237] Nearly every critic who reviewed Mrs. Shephard's book agreed that she had exaggerated the importance of this one source. And anyway, like the "Happy Hypocrite" of Max Beerbohm's delightful little allegory, Whitman wore his mask with such sincere intention that underneath he too became, no less than Beerbohm's reformed rake, an exact and genuine facsimile of the former disguise. At the beginning of his career as the poet of LEAVES OF GRASS, Walt Whitman may have assumed a pose in his life and his book, but all eye-witnesses of his conduct and personality confirm the belief of most biographers that to a remarkable degree he actually became the person and poet he wished to be.

By a lucky coincidence, Haniel Long's *Walt Whitman and the Springs of Courage* (1938) answered the skepticism of Mrs. Shephard's "pose theory", though unfortunately the book was published by an obscure press[238] and is not yet well known. "Wars and pestilence and pestilential literary fashions come and go," says Long, "but literature remains the picture of man adapting himself to the new-old necessities of intimacy with the universe and himself."[239] This book is not, properly speaking, a biography but it is a critical interpretation which reveals Whitman's biography in a new light. As the author says, "To examine Whitman's life with an eye

---

[237] Cf. Gay W. Allen, "Walt Whitman and Jules Michelet," *Études Anglaises*, I, 230-237 (May, 1937).

[238] Haniel Long, *Walt Whitman and the Springs of Courage*, (Santa Fe, New Mexico: Writers' Editions Inc., 1938).

[239] *Ibid.*, 142-143.

to observing what his springs of courage were, is simply
to respond to our need of outwitting and defying those
forces in society today which would rob us of the last shred
of self-confidence."[240] Or to put it a little differently:

> Now I will begin writing what I can discern of the
> things that gave Whitman trouble, and the things that
> gave him no trouble; and how, in spite of troubles
> which were his fault, or the fault of others, or merely
> the result in any age of being born, he was able to grow
> into a tremendous oak, root himself well in the soil,
> and extend wide branches for any who for centuries to
> come might be needing shade.[241]

Since this book is not, as stated above, a conventional
biography, Whitman's faults and troubles are not treated
specifically, but anyone familiar with the story of his life
knows in general what they were. Starting then, with a
recognition that Walt Whitman's life was haunted by
doubts, uncertainties, and human fraility, what was the
secret of the healing courage which he attained and all
men desire? "First of all is the diverting fact that Whitman, like Rilke's Fraulein Brahe, lived in wonderland—
though his sojourn there was brief."[242] This wonderland
was phrenology. Every student of Whitman's life knows
that at one time he took stock in this pseudo-science and
cherished for years the flattering interpretation that had
been made of his own cranial bumps. One scholar, Edward Hungerford, even reached the conclusion that the
phrenologist's extremely favorable reading of Whitman's
"chart of bumps" first gave him the serious ambition of

---

[240] *Ibid.*, 3.   [242] *Ibid.*, 9.
[241] *Ibid.*, 7.

trying to be a poet[243]—a theory perhaps as overly-simplified as Mrs. Shephard's. Long does not know whether "phrenology told Whitman correctly where he was strong and where he was weak", but, "We need to be praised, we need to be alarmed, about ourselves,"[244] and phrenology temporarily served this purpose.

That pseudo-science furnished Whitman a picture of a balanced and harmonious life, from which if one were sensible nothing human need be excluded: which makes it an important factor in his growth. Its terminology has not stuck, its names seem fantastic. Yet it achieved an enviable simplification, and above all it heartened one with its moral blessings and warnings. American life was neither balanced nor harmonious, nor was Whitman's own life. By including all aspects of his being, and by indicating certain aspects of himself he might well guard against, phrenology left him with a vigorous hope for himself, and for his native land. It was part and parcel of the gospel of the 'healthy-mindedness', and Whitman became its poet.[245]

Thus phrenology met the pragmatic test for Walt Whitman, as religion and all sorts of rag-tags of philosophy do for other men.

The second spring of courage for Whitman was Emerson.[246] First of all his essays, his poems, and his transcendentalism; and second, that generous, impulsive greeting of the 1855 LEAVES OF GRASS. The letter went to Whitman's head for a while and made him do some

---

[243] Edward Hungerford, "Walt Whitman and His Chart of Bumps," *American Literature*, II, 350-384 (January, 1931).

[244] Long, *op. cit.*, 14.

[245] *Ibid.*, 15.

[246] *Ibid.*, 16 ff.

silly things, but it gave him courage at a time when he most needed it and ultimately strengthened his self-reliance until he had less need for Emerson. The arrogant tone of the first two editions is misleading; actually, "Whitman exceeded the rest of the brotherhood of writers in his anxiety to make sure of bouquets."[247] He needed more, not less, than most men to find "springs of courage."

This need was intensified by the hostile opposition which he encountered on almost every side: prudish conventionalism, the Bostonians' belief that American culture should "stay close to the mother culture of England,"[248] and ignorant blindness of readers unconditioned to a new poetic art. Much of Long's book is taken up with the courage the poet derived from his contact with common people, personal friends, Mrs. Gilchrist, Peter Doyle, and from the philosophy and religion which he painfully worked out for himself. This book might be called *an intellectual biography.* It attempts to lay bare the organic pattern of ideas and faiths, and the expression of them which integrated one man's life and gave it the strength of an oak tree with shade for future generations of men.

Newton Arvin's *Whitman* is even less biography than Long's book, for it is mainly a study of Whitman's social thinking, but it deserves to be mentioned among the memorable publications of 1938 which future biographers must take into consideration in their re-evaluations of LEAVES OF GRASS and its author. Arvin finds two powerful and opposing intellectual currents in the life and thought of Whitman. "He was so powerfully worked upon by the romantic mood of his generation that it has largely been forgotten or ignored how much he had been

---

[247] *Ibid.,* 26.   [248] *Ibid.,* 40.

affected, in boyhood and earliest youth, by an older and tougher way of thought . . . he was the grandchild of the Age of Reason."[249] Arvin makes out Whitman's father to have been a sort of intellectual rebel himself, a subscriber to the "free-thought" journal edited by Frances Wright and Robert Dale Owen, a follower of the unorthodox Hicksite Quakers, and a democrat of the Jefferson and Paine tradition. No other critic or biographer has given Walter Whitman credit for so much intellectual curiosity and vitality.

Although he raises in the mind of the reader the possibility of an intellectual antithesis in the Whitman home, the father leaning toward eighteenth-century rationalism and the mother toward romantic mysticism, Arvin is careful to point out that this contradiction was actually characteristic of the age in which the poet grew up. Even the leading scientists, "almost to a man . . . succeeded in 'reconciling' their inherited Calvinism or Arminianism with their Newtonian or their Darwinian knowledge."[250]

Nevertheless, the Quaker influence which Whitman derived in part at least through his family was unfortunate because the "inner light" doctrine encouraged him "in a flaccid irrationalism,"[251] and "for the poet whose book was allegedly to be pervaded by the conclusions of the great scientists, this was hardly the wisest habit to form." Arvin thinks that Whitman's anti-intellectualism and obscuritanism grew with age. In the first edition he found the earth sufficient, but as he became older he found it

---

[249] Newton Arvin, *Whitman*, (New York: The Macmillan Co., 1938), 161.
[250] *Ibid.*, 170-171.
[251] *Ibid.*, 174.

less and less sufficient and he sought assurance in "world-weary and compensatory mysticisms."[252]

On the vexing question of Whitman's sex "anomaly", Arvin is unequivocal. "There was a core of abnormality in Whitman's emotional life," but it was not the whole of his nature; "he remained to the end, in almost every real and visible sense, a sweet and sane human being . . . who had proved himself capable of easy and genial friendship with hundreds of ordinary people."[253] Arvin expresses the opinion that "it would not be incredible if even the most personal poems in 'Calamus' should come to be cherished, as Shakespeare's sonnets have been, by thousands of normal men and women,"[254] and adds the information that André Malraux and Thomas Mann have accepted Whitman's "virile fraternity" and "a patriotism of humanity" as social and political slogans.[255]

The duality which Arvin finds in Whitman's age and in the poet's own life and conduct gives this critic himself a divided attitude toward his subject. Though he bitterly denounces Whitman's refusal to take an active part in the Abolitionist[256] movement—believing to the last that the Civil War was only a struggle to preserve the Union—and deplores his indifference to socialism and trade unionism, Arvin nevertheless concluded that LEAVES OF GRASS is a full and brave "anticipatory statement of a democratic and fraternal humanism."[257]

Whether or not Long and Arvin's books will occupy a

---

[252] *Ibid.*, 229.
[253] *Ibid.*, 277.
[254] *Ibid.*, 278.
[255] *Ibid.*, 282.
[256] "We shall find no other dose so acrid or so hard to swallow . . . [as] his rather inglorious record in the days of the Abolitionists," *Ibid.*, 33.
[257] *Ibid.*, 290.

permanent place in Whitman scholarship, they did at least contribute intelligent discussions of fundamental critical and biographical problems. But the old schools were not dead. In 1941 Frances Winwar published *American Giant: Walt Whitman and His Times,* an inaccurate, sentimental and journalistic rehash of the worst features of nearly all the previous biographies, though it was audaciously advertised as a "definitive life." Here we find the dust brushed from the hoary New Orleans romance, even the Washington romance revived from Holloway, and the most dogmatic denial of any taint of homosexual psychology in the *Calamus* poems. Despite her fanciful idealization of her hero, she perpetuates the inaccurate story of the "thousands of dollars" which the supposedly indigent poet spent in the building of his tomb. The whole Whitman family is sentimentalized, but especially is this true of "Mother Whitman", who is made into an ideal mother and housekeeper and a sort of moral saint.

Clifton Furness, the editor of the *Workshop,*[258] who has for years been at work on a scholarly biography which may well prove to be the definitive life, corrected the worst of Winwar's errors in a long review in *American Literature.*[259] From unpublished manuscripts he quotes passages to show the real emotions back of one of the poems which she used to support her belief in a normal love-affair in New Orleans, and he quotes from Mother Whitman's illiterate letters to show the confusion, squalor, bickering, and complaining in her household.

---

[258] Clifton J. Furness, *Walt Whitman's Workship;* a Collection of Unpublished Manuscripts, (Cambridge, Mass.: Harvard University, 1928). Contains some of the most illuminating critical notes on the poet which have been published.

[259] *American Literature,* XIII, 423-432 (January, 1942).

Meanwhile, Mrs. Katharine Molinoff had already published a monograph, *Some Notes on Whitman's Family* (1941),[260] which reveal sufficient reason for Mother Whitman's dejection and her whining letters. Her daughter Mary was capricious and headstrong.[261] Her youngest son, Edward, was a life-long cripple and imbecile, a constant care and worry to Walt and his mother. The oldest son, Jesse, died in the lunatic asylum. Andrew, an habitual drunkard, married a disreputable woman, who after her husband's death of tuberculosis of the throat, "became a social outcast and set her children to beg on the streets." Hannah married a mean, improvident artist who starved and beat her—not without "ample cause"—until she became psychopathic.

The whole picture is almost incredibly sordid, and yet there are only the vaguest hints in the biographies of these conditions. Furness and Mrs. Molinoff, in these brief and pathetic glimpses into Walt Whitman's family relationships, give us a better understanding of "that baffling reluctance to mention any member of his family which is so puzzling to biographers."[262] Furthermore, Walt's letters to his mother, his constant financial help for her and Eddie, and his worrying and planning for them, reveal his devotion, unselfishness, and gentleness as no biographer has done. In these relationships he is truly and incontrovertably heroic. When the full story is finally told, we may learn a great deal more about the processes of poetic sublimation.

---

[260] Privately printed by the author.

[261] The description of the "capricious and headstrong—but tender and very affectionate"—sister Mary in Whitman's juvenile short story, "The Half Breed" is evidently his own sister. See Molinoff, p. 4 ff.

[262] *Ibid.*, 5.

Until Furness publishes his biography we are not likely to get the whole truth of Walt Whitman's life, for no one else has attempted to assemble all the facts; but meanwhile the books continue to roll from the presses. In 1942 Hugh I'Anson Fausset published a new study, *Walt Whitman: Poet of Democracy*.[263] The title is somewhat misleading, for Fausset is less concerned with the poet's democratic ideas than Arvin was. Whitman is presented as the poet of democracy in somewhat the same way that Rossetti and Dowden had done, and more or less Symonds and Bailey, *i.e.*, as the true representative of a raw, undeveloped, undiscriminating American culture.

The thesis of Fausset's book is that Whitman was a split personality who was never able to achieve poise, serenity, and unity in either art or life. This thesis leads Fausset into a dilemma which has now become familiar to the reader of Whitman biography. The man he reveals is mentally indolent, uncritical, almost sloven; as a personality he is by turns affectionate and secretive, egotistical and shrinking; as a poet, undisciplined, unsure of his technique, a "true poet" only on rare and lucky occasions. Yet Fausset wrote the book because he was convinced of the importance of Walt Whitman as a poet, a man whose heart was in the right place but head always undependable. The biographer, in short, finds himself unable to explain the literary power and world-wide fame of the man he attempts to analyze.

It is a happy coincidence that this survey of Whitman biography can be terminated by an examination of Henry Seidel Canby's *Walt Whitman: An American* (1943),[264]

---

[263] Published by the Yale University Press.
[264] Published by Houghton Mifflin Co., Boston.

for Canby's book epitomizes the best of recent Whitman scholarship, resolves many of the biographical cruxes with plausible and sensible conclusions, and leaves the reader with the conviction that Walt Whitman, both as man and poet, deserves the reputation and influence which he has attained throughout the modern world.

Canby has not presumed to write a "final book on Whitman", or to assemble, "for the benefit of scholars, . . . all known information about his friends, his family, and his daily doings"—information "much needed, and . . . soon to be made readily accessible in a book by my friend, Mr. Furness"[265]; his book is, frankly an interpretation, an attempt to "make intelligible Whitman himself and his 'Leaves'."[266] Canby's success is due in part to his basic assumption that, "Walt Whitman's America was not a real America, though the real America was his background and a source of his inspiration. It was a symbolic America, existing in his own mind, and always pointed toward a future of which he was prophetic."[267] He agrees with Catel and confirms Schyberg (whom he has not read) that "a satisfactory biography of Whitman must be essentially a biography of an inner life and of the mysterious creative processes of poetry."[268] But he does not psychoanalyze or draw sensational contrasts between fiction and reality:

This biographer and that, using hints or boastings, or the dubious evidence of poems, has endeavored to spice this daily life with hypothetical journeys, unverified quadroon lovers, illegitimate children, and dark suggestions of vice and degeneracy. Yet even if all the

---

[265] Canby, iv and v.   [267] Ibid., v.
[266] Ibid., vi.   [268] Ibid., 2.

stories about Whitman's hidden activities were true, they would not account for a passionate fervor that has deeper and more burning sources.[269]

For despite the fact that he was "a poseur sometimes, and often a careless carpenter of words", Whitman "made articulate and gave an enduring life in the imagination to the American dream of a continent where the people should escape from the injustices of the past and establish a new and better life in which everyone would share."[270]

Most biographers have attempted to explain the mystery of this ordinary youth who suddenly revealed himself as a poetic genius. Some have thought he was aroused by a "dark lady", others by psychological frustration, but most have been inclined to believe that mystical experience "made him a prophet and a poet." Canby finds no mystery at all—except in so far as poetic genius is always something of a miracle. During Whitman's childhood in Brooklyn and his youthful contact with the country and village people of Long Island, he was storing up experiences and impressions which enabled him to become a "representative" poet of nineteenth-century America. Small towns, printing offices, country schools, political newspapers, all these were important during the formative years when the future poet's "imagination was like a battery charging."[271] Canby thus makes little of Whitman's boasted heredity, much of his environment.

This approach enables Canby to avoid some of the pitfalls of other biographers, for he is content to describe Whitman's social and intellectual milieu instead of at-

---

[269] *Ibid.*, 3.
[270] *Ibid.*

[271] *Ibid.*, 29.

tempting to create or reconstruct his inner life before he became articulate. "He was a happy familiar of streets and market-places, and a spokesman for society [through his editorials], before he began to be egoist, rebel, and prophet."[272] After 1847, when Whitman began to record in his notebooks his poetic ambitions and his intimate thoughts, subjective biography is possible, and with these as the primary source this critic-biographer begins the "inner life" of his subject.

When the young journalist turns poet and mystic, the biographer meets his first real test. To Whitman's contemporaries, and even to many later critics, "This self-assumed apostleship, this mantle of a prophet put on at the age of twenty-eight, seems a little strong."[273] But Canby shows that, "This new Walt Whitman proposes to inspire because he is inspired. Greatness is growth, he says, and his soul has become great because in mystical, imaginative experiences it has grown until it identifies itself with the power of the universe."[274] He was misunderstood because his "I" was neither his own ego nor the editorial "We", "but 'my soul', by which he meant an identification of himself with the power for greatness which he felt intuitively to be entering his own spirit." The poet thus began the long career of dramatizing this "soul", presenting "a 'Walt Whitman' who was symbolic, yet in his knowledge of men and cities and scenes and emotions of the common man was also representative of the merely human Walt who had been absorbing the life of America so passionately for many years."[275] No previ-

---

[272] *Ibid.*, 72.

[273] *Ibid.*, 92.

[274] *Ibid.*

[275] *Ibid.*, 93.

ous biographer has so subtly reconciled the "symbolic" Whitman with the objective Whitman.

This reconciliation, however, does not eliminate the "problems" which have harassed the biographers for half a century; nor does it necessarily "solve" them, but what it does do above all else is to undermine their former importance. No doubt in some cases, too, it is too facile—too subtle. For example, Canby, like Schyberg, recognizes in the 1860 edition the evidences of spiritual "crisis", and he readily admits that during the later 1850's the poet was troubled by "deep perturbations of sexual passion,"[276] but Canby's thesis leads him to attribute Whitman's crisis to national rather than personal causes—"this was a decade of rising hate", and hate was the antithesis of the poet's dream of an "ideal democracy."

Canby does not, however, attempt to deny or disguise the sex problem in Whitman's life and writing; he refuses to conjecture or theorize where there is no evidence. "There may of course have been, as his later biographers think, other journeys, other residences in the South before 1860—perhaps lovers, perhaps a mother of his alleged children. We do not know, and there is no real evidence."[277] Discussing the *Children of Adam,* Canby says, "This man's greatness is in some respects a function of his excessive sexuality. Whole sections of the 'Leaves' are either rhetorical fantasy or the articulation and sublimation of experience." But, he adds, "Of that experience we know actually very little . . ."[278] Unfortunately, much has to be omitted because we simply have no facts and in all probability never will have."[279]

[276] *Ibid.,* 162-163.
[277] *Ibid.,* 168.
[278] *Ibid.,* 186.
[279] *Ibid.,* 187.

Like Catel, Schyberg, and Masters, Canby recognizes in Whitman a kind of extraordinary sexual versatility which is at least in part responsible for his universal love and cosmic imagination. Canby calls this characteristic "auto-eroticism", but thinks it was psychological rather than physical:

> He could feel like a woman. He could feel like a man. He could love a woman—though one suspects that it was difficult for him to love women physically, unless they were simple and primitive types. He could love a man with a kind of father-mother love, mingled, as such love often is, with obscure sexuality. Because all reference was back to his own body, he seemed to himself to be a microcosm of humanity. There are, I think, no truly objective love poems in the 'Leaves of Grass.'[280]

Schyberg thought that Whitman's "turmoils" were calmed by his active participation in the war through his hospital work, and Canby adds more weight to the argument, extending the influence from the personal to the intellectual realm. The poet "becomes less interested in himself as a religion incarnate, less rhetorical about democracy, more certain of his confidence that democracy has firm ground in human nature."[281] Fully aware of the "corruption, degeneracy, pettiness, both physical and spiritual,"[282] in his post-war America, Whitman attempted to counteract these evils by preaching respect for the individual personality and the dangers of selfishness. No other biographer or critic has succeeded so well in combatting the superficial belief that Whitman's democratic teachings

---

[280] *Ibid.*, 204-205. Cf. *supra,* p. 67 for Schyberg's contrasting opinion— see also Chap. II, p. 152.
[281] *Ibid.*, 230.
[282] *Ibid.*, 263.

and public misunderstanding and indifference to the first three editions of LEAVES OF GRASS. Partly to bolster the defence, but more especially because of the poet's remarkable personal fascination and the literary theory by which he himself interpreted his own character, these friends attempted to found a cult to worship at the shrine of their modern Messiah. Some of these disciples were more infatuated and deceived than others by the conscious deification of their subject, but all of them, from O'Connor to Kennedy, resented objective criticism, and they made it difficult for scholarly biography to begin. They glorified the poet's ancestry, his youth, his education by contact with reality instead of books and culture, and thought that in his magnificent physique and his "cosmic mind" nature had produced a new and unique type of human being.

Though Whitman's intimate friends liked to reproach America for failing to recognize and appreciate her own genius long after he was accepted and admired in Great Britain, the first steps in the destruction of the legends built up by O'Connor, Bucke, and Burroughs were taken by two British friends and biographers, Symonds and Edward Carpenter. Both found it difficult to forgive Whitman's self-advertizing and his tendency to conceal or distort the actual facts of his private life. They were the first to express suspicions about the psychology of the *Calamus* poems, and it was through them that the story of the illigitimate children was brought to light. It was also an English biographer, Binns, who first concocted the theory of the New Orleans love affair with a Creole mistress, the starting point for a new mythology.

When Bliss Perry finally published a genuinely critical life of Whitman in 1906, the attitude of the public toward

LEAVES OF GRASS still made an unbiased interpretation of the poet's life difficult. The cult still existed,[287] and—a greater obstacle—so did widespread antagonism toward both the thought and the forms of the poems, even to some extent still against the character of the unconventional poet. In the next decade the progress of naturalism and realism in literature made Whitman's frankness and shirtsleeves manners seem less crude and objectionable; and expressionism in music and painting, as well as the effects of the recent French symbolist movement, removed much of the former unintelligibility from the style and form of LEAVES OF GRASS. Perry helped greatly to bring about a more intelligent attitude toward both the man and his work. His greatest achievement, however, was his sympathetic unmasking of the legendary Whitman and his revelation of a real man, subject to human frailities though nonetheless a literary genius and one of America's greatest poets.

After Bliss Perry's book in America, Whitman scholarship passed back to Europe for a time. This was probably due in part to the translation of LEAVES OF GRASS into German, French, Italian, and Russian, but perhaps more to the direction in which European literature had developed. Readers familiar with Nietzsche, Novalis, George Sand, Verhaeren, André Gide, Tolstoi, Wergeland, Almquist—to mention only a few—were better prepared to understand Whitman than Americans were until

[287] Harrison S. Morris's *Walt Whitman: A Brief Biography with Reminiscences* (Cambridge: Harvard University Press, 1929) might be regarded as the last word from the cult, for his attitude and expression are quite similar to the rhapsodies of the "hot little prophets." And like theirs, Morris's reminiscences are of some value to the modern student and biographer.

much later. At any rate, it is significant that the two most important books on Whitman between Perry and Holloway were by Bazalgette in France and De Selincourt in England. Both shared with the earliest American biographers a sympathy and *rapport* with their subject which made them impressionistic rather than judicial critics, but in their attempt to uncover the mystery concealed by the foliage of the poems they prepared the way for later psychological biographers. European critics have always been more curious and more outspoken about Whitman's sex-pathology than American biographers, and Bazalgette and De Selincourt were no exceptions, though they insisted that the poet was normal and healthy.

In the 1920's Whitman biography returned to its native land. This was the period of research in the journalistic writings of the poet and the reprinting of the juvenilia. In these activities Emory Holloway led the way, and his biography in 1926 was the first after Perry's to be based on a great amount of new material. Although Holloway through his editions and biography inaugurated a new era in Whitman scholarship, on which he has had a really profound influence, he did not start a new school in Whitman biography, for his interpretations were not radically different from those of Binns, Perry and De Selincourt.

Then once more the Europeans took the lead. Catel, stimulated by the problems raised by Binns and Bazalgette and profiting from Holloway's researches, thought he had found the key to all the mysteries in the unconsciously autobiographical confessions of the 1855 edition. His intensive reading of the poems and subtle search for their origins in the poet's inner life was a *tour de force* comparable to John Lowes's *Road to Xanadu.*[288] Jean Catel's achievement was the use of a new critical technique to discover the biography unconsciously recorded in the fossil remains of the poet's works.

But Catel had merely laid bare one layer of this rich field for biographical and critical exploration. He was followed in a few years by Schyberg in Denmark, who dug through the whole ten layers and found internal evidence that illuminated many of the problems which the biographers had never satisfactorily solved. Confirming and supplementing Catel, he interpreted the Great Companions, the Spiritual Democracy, and the Poet-Prophet rôles as sublimations of Whitman's creative imagination. This psychological method of explaining the poet's life can be given either a positive or a negative interpretation. It may lead a Shephard to the blind abyss of skepticism—making the poet's whole life a "pose" and a deception—or a Long to lay bare the springs of human courage. The method is the same either way, but the evaluation is diametrically opposed.

However, the biographers who point out Whitman's little-known intellectual sources, or who, like Arvin, call attention to the duality of his action and thought, serve a useful purpose in forcing the student to a critical evaluation and understanding of all phases of the man and his work.

---

[288] It is unlikely, however, that *The Road to Xanadu* had any influence on Catel, for it was not published until 1927. A more likely influence is Charles Baudouin, *Etudes de psychanalyze* (Paris, 1922), a psychoanalytical study of the imagery of Émile Verhaeren, the Whitmanesque Belgian poet. This book is a good introduction to this type of literary criticism and indirectly throws a good deal of light on Whitman. There is an English translation by Eden and Cedar Paul, *Studies in Psychoanalysis* (London: George Allen and Unwin, 1922; New York: Dodd, Mead and Company, 1924).

Furness and Mrs. Molinoff, through their researches into the family background of Whitman, are now revealing a life so much more realistic and painful than any biographer has so far presented that they could bring about a crisis in the biography and reputation of the poet. But that this is not to be the next development seems abundantly clear from the recent life by the well-known critic, Henry Seidel Canby; for in this latest biography we find a reaffirmation of Whitman's fundamental achievements in poetry and democratic theory, with a consequent de-emphasizing of his personal eccentricities. In the attempt to solve psychological mysteries, to understand the poet's sex pathology, to expose his sublimated search for companions, to establish literary sources, and the dozens of other curiosities of Whitman scholarship and biography—all too often these searchers have neglected the importance of Whitman's message and his indisputable world-wide influence. Many of these modern biographies have failed to reveal a mind and personality capable of writing one of the greatest books in modern literature. The latest of these split-personality biographies is Mr. Fausset's, but within one year it was followed by Mr. Canby's reintegration of Walt Whitman.

We can never again blindly accept the poet's own interpretation as naïvely as Burroughs and Bucke did—Symonds, De Selincourt, Holloway, Catel, Schyberg, and many others, have at least done that much for us—; but so dynamic was the poet's message, and so challenging to each generation since his death, that it seems quite unlikely that the biography of Whitman and the interpretation of his work has yet reached full maturity. Like LEAVES OF GRASS itself, the life of our great poet is becoming an imperishable fable in which each generation attempts to find its own expression and the answers to its moral and spiritual problems.

SELECTED BIBLIOGRAPHY

BIBLIOGRAPHY[289]

ALLEN, GAY W. *Twenty-Five Years of Walt Whitman Bibliography: 1918-1942.* Boston: The F. W. Faxon Co., 1943. 57 pp.
[Supplements Holloway and Saunders—see below.]

HOLLOWAY, EMORY, and SAUNDERS, HENRY S. "[Bibliography of Walt] Whitman." *Cambridge History of American Literature.* New York: G. P. Putnam's Sons. 1918. Vol. II, pp. 551-581.
[Best up to 1918.]

SHAY, FRANK. *The Bibliography of Walt Whitman.* New York: Friedmans'. 1920. 46 pp.
[Editions.]

TRIGGS, OSCAR LOVELL. "Bibliography of Walt Whitman." *Complete Writings of Walt Whitman.* New York and London: G. P. Putnam's Sons. 1902. Vol. X, pp. 139-233.
[Useful description of editions with extended list of biographical and critical material before 1902.]

WELLS, CAROLYN and GOLDSMITH, ALFRED F. *A Concise Bibliography of the Works of Walt Whitman.* Boston: Houghton Mifflin and Co. 1922. 107 pp.
[A descriptive checklist of editions with a selected list of fifty books about Whitman.]

---

[289] Clifton Joseph Furness and Henry S. Saunders—with the assistance of Emory Holloway, David Goodale, and Florence M. Chace—have compiled an exhaustive, complete bibliography which is now awaiting publication.

BIOGRAPHY[290]

ARVIN, NEWTON. *Whitman.* New York: The Macmillan Co.
1938. 320 pp.
[Whitman as social thinker.]

BAILEY, JOHN. *Walt Whitman.* London and New York: The
Macmillan Co. 1926. 220 pp.
[Reliable but unoriginal life in the English Men of Letters
Series.]

BARRUS, CLARA. *Whitman and Burroughs: Comrades.* Boston:
Houghton Mifflin and Co. 1931. 392 pp.
[Contains valuable correspondence of Burroughs, Whitman
and their friends—also reliable criticism.]

BAZALGETTE, LÉON. *Walt Whitman, L'Homme et son oeuvre.*
Paris: Mercure de France. 1908. 513 pp.
[A romantic biography.]

————. *Walt Whitman, the Man and His Work.* Translated
by Ellen Fitzgerald. Garden City: Doubleday. 1920. xviii,
355 pp.
[The translation is expurgated and slightly edited.]

BERTZ, EDUARD. *Der Yankee-Heiland.* Dresden: Carl Reissner.
1906. 253 pp.
[An attack on Whitman's claim as a prophet and thinker;
analysis of sex pathology.]

BINNS, HENRY BRYAN. *A Life of Walt Whitman.* London:
Methuen and Co. 1905. 369 pp.
[First exhaustive life—very sympathetic. Binns started the
theory of the New Orleans romance.]

BLODGETT, HAROLD. *Walt Whitman in England.* Ithaca, N. Y.:
Cornell University Press, 1934. 244 pp.
[Not a biography but discusses the English biographies.]

BORN, HELENA. *Whitman's Ideal Democracy.* Boston: Everett
Press. 1902. 88 pp.

---

[290] This list includes all biographies of any significance.

[Impassioned defense of Whitman by a devoted socialist friend.]

BUCKE, RICHARD MAURICE, M.D. *Walt Whitman*. Philadelphia: David McKay. 1883. 236 pp.

[An "official portrait," edited and partly written by Whitman himself. Contains also: "Appendix: *The Good Gray Poet* reprinted from the pamphlet of 1866, with an Introductory Letter (1883), written for this volume by William D. O'Connor."]

BUCKE, RICHARD MAURICE; HARNED, THOMAS B.; and TRAUBEL, HORACE L. "Introduction" [biographical] to *The Complete Writings of Walt Whitman*. New York: G. P. Putnam's Sons. 1902. Vol. I, pp. xiii-xcvi.

[Last official biography by Whitman's literary executors.]

BULLETT, GERALD. *Walt Whitman, a Study and a Selection*. London: Grant Richards. 1924. Philadelphia: J. B. Lippincott. 1925. 166 pp.

[Discriminating biographical essay, pp. 3-24.]

BURROUGHS, JOHN. *Notes on Walt Whitman as Poet and Person*. New York: American News Co. 1867. 108 pp. Sec. Ed., New York: J. S. Redfield. 1871.

[Whitman wrote a large part of this first book on his life.]

―――. "The Flight of the Eagle." *Birds and Poets*. Boston: Houghton Mifflin and Co. 1877, 1895. Pp. 185-235.

―――. *Whitman, A Study*. Boston: Houghton Mifflin and Co. 1896. 268 pp.

[Mainly critical rather than biographical.]

CANBY, HENRY SEIDEL. *Walt Whitman, An American*. Boston: Houghton Mifflin and Co. 1943. 381 pp.

[Reassertion of Whitman's importance as national poet and critic of democracy. A valuable contribution to Whitman interpretation rather than of biographical fact.]

CARPENTER, EDWARD. *Days with Walt Whitman: with Some Notes on His Life and Works.* London: George Allen; New York: The Macmillan Co. 1906. 187 pp.

[Friendly but critical—first publication of Whitman's letter to Symonds claiming the paternity of six children. An important book in the growth of Whitman biography.]

CATEL, JEAN. *Walt Whitman: la Naissance du Poète.* Paris: Les Éditions Rieder. 1929. 483 pp.

[Psychological study of the origin of *Leaves of Grass.* Oversimplifies the problem, but illuminating.]

CLARKE, WILLIAM. *Walt Whitman.* London: Swan Sonnenschein and Co.; New York: Macmillan and Co. 1892. 132 pp.

[Of little value to modern student; good at time of publication.]

DE SELINCOURT, BASIL. *Walt Whitman: A Critical Study.* London: Martin Secker. 1914. 250 pp.

[Another romantic life like Bazalgette's, though more critical. New Orleans romance still flourishes.]

DEUTSCH, BABETTE. *Walt Whitman, Builder for America.* New York: Messner. 1941. 278 pp.

[A competent biography for juveniles.]

DONALDSON, THOMAS. *Walt Whitman, the Man.* New York: Francis P. Harper. 1896. 278 pp.

[By an intimate friend of the Camden period; adds little to Bucke and Burroughs, but somewhat more critical.]

DOWDEN, EDWARD. "The Poetry of Democracy: Walt Whitman." *Studies in Literature: 1789-1877.* London: C. Kegan Paul and Co. 1878. Pp. 468-523.

[Interprets Whitman as product and representative of American invironment, life, and unstabilized culture.]

ELLIOT, CHARLES N. *Walt Whitman, as Man, Poet and Friend.* Boston: Badger. 1915. 257 pp.

[Autograph tributes of friends and admirers; a curiosity, but of little biographical value.]

FAUSSETT, HUGH I'ANSON. *Walt Whitman: Poet of Democracy.* New Haven: Yale University Press. 1942. 320 pp.
[Presents Whitman as a divided personality.]

GLICKSBERG, CHARLES I. *Walt Whitman and the Civil War: A Collection of Original Articles and Manuscripts.* Philadelphia: University of Pennsylvania Press. 1933. 201 pp.
[New source of material for the Civil War period.]

HAYES, WILL. *Walt Whitman: the Prophet of the New Era.* London: C. W. Daniel. n.d. [1921]. 194 pp.
[Continuation of the literal interpretation of Whitman's prophetic rôle.]

HOLLOWAY, EMORY. *Whitman: an Interpretation in Narrative.* New York: Knopf. 1926. 345 pp.
[Still one of the major biographies.]

KENNEDY, WILLIAM SLOANE. *Reminiscences of Walt Whitman,* with extracts from his letters and remarks on his writings. London: Alexander Gardner. 1896. 190 pp.
[First-hand account by a friend of the Camden period—very sympathetic. Excellent discussion of the poet's "organic" theory of style.]

LAWRENCE, D. H. "Whitman." *Studies in Classic American Literature.* New York: Albert Boni. 1923. Pp. 241-264.
[A condemnation of Whitman's sentimental Christianity.]

LONG, HANIEL. *Walt Whitman and the Springs of Courage.* Sante Fe: Writers' Editions, Inc. 1938. 144 pp.
[On the origins of the poet's self-confidence and intellectual history.]

MASTERS, EDGAR LEE. *Whitman.* New York: Charles Scribner's Sons. 1937. 342 pp.
[A mediocre biography but frank treatment of the "Calamus" problem.]

MOLINOFF, KATHERINE. *Some Notes on Whitman's Family: Mary Elizabeth Whitman, Edward Whitman, Andrew and Jesse Whitman, Hannah Louisa Whitman.* Introduction by Oscar Cargill. Brooklyn: privately printed by the author. 1941. 43 pp.
[New and important information.]

MORRIS, HARRISON S. *Walt Whitman, a Brief Biography with Reminiscences.* Cambridge, Mass.: Harvard University Press. 1929. 122 pp.
[Interesting for the reminiscences; otherwise of slight value.]

O'CONNOR, WILLIAM DOUGLAS. *The Good Gray Poet, A Vindication.* New York: Bunce and Huntington. 1866. Pamphlet.
[Reprinted in Bucke's *Walt Whitman,* 1883, q.v.]
[A defense of Whitman's life and character after his dismissal by Harlan. The first biography and the beginning of the "Modern Christ" legend.]

PERRY, BLISS. *Walt Whitman, His Life and Work.* London: Archibald Constable and Co.; New York: Houghton Mifflin and Co. 1906. 318 pp.
[The first scholarly biography; still one of the best.]

RIVERS, W. C. *Walt Whitman's Anomaly.* London: George Allen. 1913.
[Study in sex pathology—circulation limited to the medical profession.]

ROGERS, CAMERON. *The Magnificent Idler: The Story of Walt Whitman.* Garden City: Doubleday, Page and Co. 1926. 312 pp.
[Fictionized and romanticized, but faintly anticipates Catel and Schyberg.]

SCHYBERG, FREDERIK. *Walt Whitman.* København: Gyldendalske Boghandel. 1933. 349 pp.
[Continues the interpretation of Catel by searching through all the editions of *Leaves of Grass* for autobiographical reve-

lations; also orients the poet in the currents of world literature to which he was unconsciously indebted.]

SHEPHARD, ESTHER. *Walt Whitman's Pose.* New York: Harcourt, Brace and Co. 1938.
[A source study affecting biographical interpretation.]

SMITH, LOGAN P. "Walt Whitman." *Unforgotten Years.* Boston: Little, Brown and Co. 1939. Pp. 79-108.
[Charming reminiscences of the poet's visits in the Smith home.]

SYMONDS, JOHN ADDINGTON. *Walt Whitman, A Study.* London: George Routledge; New York: E. P. Dutton. 1893. 160 pp.
[Critical study by a friend and admirer—still valuable.]

THOMSON, JAMES. *Walt Whitman, the Man and the Poet.* With an introduction by Bertram Dobell. London: Bertram Dobell. 1910. 106 pp.
[Biographical details mainly from Burroughs and Bucke, but some critical comments by a great poet give the work value.]

TRAUBEL, HORACE. *With Walt Whitman in Camden, March 28-July 14, 1888.* Boston: Small Maynard and Co. 1906. 473 pp. Second Volume, *July 16-October 31, 1888.* New York: D. Appleton and Co. 1908. Third Volume, *March 28-July 14, 1888; November 1,* 1888-*January* 20, 1889. New York: Mitchell Kennerly, 1914.
[This record of daily conversations with Whitman, though often tedious and trivial, is nevertheless a source-book for the poet's later years.]

TRAUBEL, HORACE; BUCKE, RICHARD MAURICE; and HARNED, THOMAS B. *In Re Walt Whitman.* Edited by his Literary Executors. Philadelphia: David McKay, 1893. 452 pp.
[Along with much worthless praise by the "disciples," some valuable new testimony from Doyle, George Whitman, etc., and translations of critical essays from French, German, and Danish.]

TRIMBLE, W. H. *Walt Whitman and Leaves of Grass, an Introduction.* London: Watts and Co. 1905. 100 pp.

[Of slight biographical importance but interesting because compiled from lectures given in Dunedin, New Zealand, 1904.]

TROWBRIDGE, JOHN TOWNSEND. *My Own Story: with Recollections of Noted Persons.* Boston: Houghton Mifflin and Co., 1903. Pp. 360-401.

[Valuable for poet's own testimony to Trowbridge of Emerson's influence.]

WINWAR, FRANCES. *American Giant: Walt Whitman and His Times.* New York: Harper and Brothers. 1941. 341 pp.

[Journalistic and sentimental narrative—unreliable.]

ARTICLES OF BIOGRAPHICAL VALUE

BRADLEY, SCULLEY. "Walt Whitman on Timber Creek." *American Literature,* V, 235-246 (November, 1933).

[Based on visits to the place.]

CARPENTER, F. I. "Walt Whitman's Eidólon." *College English,* III, 534-545 (March, 1942).

[Refutation of O'Higgins and Shephard; Whitman achieved his ideal in his poetry if not in his own life—anticipation of Canby's "Symbolical Whitman."]

FURNESS, CLIFTON JOSEPH. Review of Winwar's *American Giant: Walt Whitman and His Times. American Literature,* XIII, 423-432 (January, 1942).

[Although ostensibly a book review, this essay contains new and startling information about Whitman's family and the motives of some of his poems.]

HOLLOWAY, EMORY. "Walt Whitman's Love Affairs." *The Dial,* CXIX, 473-483 (November, 1920).

[The discovery that in the original manuscript of *Once I Pass'd Through a Populous City* was a "Calamus" poem led Holloway to reject the New Orleans romance.]

O'HIGGINS, HARVEY. "Alias Walt Whitman." *Harper's Magazine*, CLVIII, 698-707 (May, 1929).
[Anticipates Esther Shephard's interpretation of Whitman's "pose"; a relentless attempt to expose the poet as a fraud.]

CHAPTER II

THE GROWTH OF *LEAVES OF GRASS*
AND THE *PROSE WORKS*

I myself make the only growth by which I can be
appreciated,
I reject none, accept all, then reproduce all in
my own forms.[1]

THE "ORGANIC GROWTH"

Every reader acquainted with LEAVES OF GRASS and the circumstances under which it was written knows that it is not a single work, a book, like the *Faerie Queene* or one of Shakespeare's plays, but the whole *corpus* of Walt Whitman's verse published between 1855 and 1892. During these years not one but nine books[2] bore the title LEAVES OF GRASS, seven of these quite different in organization and even content, though each edition after the first contained most of the poems of its predecessor in revised form, and often under new titles.

If the final edition were simply an unabridged accumulation of the poems of all former publications, the earlier editions would be of interest only to scholars or readers curious about the genesis of the poet's style or his artistic growth, and a scholarly edition of LEAVES OF GRASS similar to the *Variorum Spenser* would be sufficient for these purposes. But the 1892 LEAVES is more than an accumula-

---

[1] *By Blue Ontario's Shore,* sec. 2.
[2] Not counting reprints of the main editions—see Bibliography on p. 227. The tenth edition (1897) contained a section of posthumous poems called *Old Age Echoes.*

tion. The metaphor "growth" has often been applied to the work,[3] and is perhaps the best descriptive term to use, but even assuming that many branches have died, atrophied, been pruned away, and new ones grafted on, the metaphor is still not entirely accurate—unless we think of a magical tree that bears different fruit in different seasons, now oranges, now lemons, occasionally a fragrant pomegranate. Not only by indefatigable revising, deleting, expanding, but also by constant re-sorting and re-arranging the poems through seven editions did Whitman indicate his shifting poetic intentions. Thus each of the first seven or eight editions has its own distinctive form, aroma, import, though nourished by the same sap.

Why does the critic fall so easily into these biological metaphors in discussing the "growth" of the editions of LEAVES OF GRASS? The nature of the work, the manner of its publication, and the theory by which the poet composed and interpreted his poems indicate the answer. In the first place, the seminal conception of the first edition was a new sort of allegory—we might even say an attempt, extending over nearly half a century, to make a life into a poetic allegory. In a novel and daringly literal application of the "organic"[4] theory of literary composition, Walt Whitman began his first edition with the attempt to "in-

---

[3] For example: "[LEAVES OF GRASS must be] considered as a growth and as related to the author's own life process. . . . Succeeding editions have the character of expansive growths, like the rings of a tree . . .," Oscar Triggs, "The Growth of 'Leaves of Grass'," *The Complete Writings of Walt Whitman* (New York and London: G. P. Putnam's Sons, 1902), X, 102. But Frederik Schyberg declares that: Bogen er nok et levende Hele, men dens Historie fremgaar ikke af Ringene i den som de nu er lagt" ["The book is a living unit but in its present state its history is not shown by annual rings of growth"], *Walt Whitman* (København: Gyldendalske Boghandel, 1933), 17.

[4] The "organic principle" is discussed in Chap. III as one of Whitman's "fundamental ideas"—see p. 292 ff.

carnate"[5] in his own person the whole range of life, geography, and national consciousness of Nineteenth-Century America.

Simultaneously the poet of LEAVES OF GRASS tries to express: (1) his own ego, (2) the spirit of his age and country,[6] (3) the mystical unity of all human experience, (4) and all of these in a pantheistic[7] justification of the ways of God to man. Thus he can call the United States themselves "essentially the greatest poem" and without inconsistency attempt to span his country from coast to coast, while "On him rise solid growths that offset [*i.e.,* tally or symbolize] the growths of pine and hemlock and liveoak," etc. Also he can transcend time and space, for "The prescient poet projects himself centuries ahead and judges performer or performance after the changes of time."

The very mystical nature of these poetic ambitions explains why Walt Whitman did not plan, write, and finish one book but continued for the remainder of his life to labor away at the same book. He was writing not an autobiography in the ordinary sense, nor a creative history of an age like Dos Passos's *U. S. A.*—tasks which can be definitely completed—but was attempting to express the inexpressible. Like all mystics, he could give only "hints," "indirections," symbols.[8] Hence, so long as the afflatus moved him, he could not finish his life-work or feel satisfied with the tangible words, pages, bound volumes. On his birthday in 1861, and again in 1870, Whitman declared of his book, "The paths to the house are made—but where **is** the house? . . . I have not done the work and cannot

---

[5] 1855 Preface.   [7] Cf. p. 259.
[6] *Ibid.*   [8] Cf. p. 430.

do it. But you [the reader] must do the work and make what is within the following song [*i.e.*, LEAVES OF GRASS]."[9] And not long before the end of his life he could still refer to his decades of effort as, "Those toils and struggles of baffled impeded articulation."[10] None of these statements, however, were published. Although Whitman always insisted that the real poem was what the reader made out of the printed words themselves, he nevertheless found it expedient in his prefaces and public utterances about LEAVES OF GRASS to make the most of what unity he could find in the work.

Furthermore, the "organic" theory helped not only to explain the poet's fundamental intentions but also rationalized the form at any given stage. After the fifth edition he believed with Burroughs that the whole volume was best understood when viewed "as 'a series of growths, or strata, rising or starting out from a settled foundation or centre and expanding in successive accumulations',"[11] and a similar statement is found in Dr. Bucke's biography, which Whitman co-authored.[12] Of the 1882-83 edition, Bucke declared: "Now it appears before us, perfected, like some grand cathedral that through many years or intervals has grown and grown until the original conception and full design of the architect stand forth."[13] The influence of this partly self-inspired explanation is inter-

---

[9] From a manuscript draft of an unpublished preface, dated first May 31, 1861, then redated May 31, 1870—printed in Clifton J. Furness, *Walt Whitman's Workshop*, (Harvard University Press, 1928), 135-137. (The first sentence was used in *Thou Mother with Thy Equal Brood*).

[10] Found in a rejected passage for "A Backward Glance," printed in "Notes and Fragments" by Dr. R. M. Bucke, *Complete Writings of Walt Whitman*, (New York: G. P. Putnam's Sons, 1902), IX, 17.

[11] Furness, *op. cit.*, 9-10.

[12] R. M. Bucke, *Walt Whitman*, (Philadelphia: David McKay, 1883), 147.

[13] *Ibid.*, 155.

estingly echoed by the poet's friend, E. C. Stedman, in a letter to Burroughs, in which he declared after Whitman's death: "Before he died . . . he rose to synthesis, and his final arrangement of his life-book is as beauteously logical and interrelated as a cathedral."[14] This authorized interpretation was officially repeated and emphasized by Dr. Oscar L. Triggs in 1902 in the essay, "The Growth of 'Leaves of Grass'," published in the *Complete Writings*.[15] Though ostensibly the first critical study of the editions, this essay is of value mainly for its bibliographical information, with some comments on textual changes. The initial assumption on which it was based prevented genuine critical analysis:

> LEAVES OF GRASS has a marked tectonic quality. The author, like an architect, drew his plans, and the poem, like a cathedral long in building, slowly advanced to fulfillment. Each poem was designed and written with reference to its place in an ideal edifice.[16]

Of considerably more value is Dr. Triggs's "Variorum Readings" compiled for the *Complete Writings*.[17] No critical evaluation of the editions is possible without detailed textual comparisons, and this work will always be a landmark in the study of Whitman's texts, but Dr. Triggs's interpretations made little advance over those of Bucke, Burroughs, and Whitman himself.

The accuracy and truth of this "organic" defence of the unity of LEAVES OF GRASS cannot be decided until we have examined all the editions, but the important point

---

[14] Quoted by Clara Barrus, *Whitman and Burroughs, Comrades,* (Boston: Houghton Mifflin Co., 1931), 318; letter dated Feb. 12, 1896.
[15] See note 3, above.
[16] *Ibid.*, 101.
[17] *Ibid.*, III, 83-318 (including "Rejected Poems").

here is that the biological and architectural metaphors
have to a great extent prevented most readers and critics
from going back of the final, "authorized," edition of
LEAVES OF GRASS. Both the rejected passages of the
manuscript of "A Backward Glance"[18] and the published
preface (1888) show plainly that the poet was still
conscious of the imperfect realization of his original intentions, but having in 1881 achieved the most satisfying
unity so far accomplished, and being conscious of his
waning physical strength and poetic energy, Whitman
began to say with increasing conviction that he had accomplished his purpose. He continued to add poems until
the year of his death, but attempted no major revision or
rearrangement after 1881.

Finally convinced that he had done his best to express
and "put on record" his life and his age, he authorized
his literary executors to publish only the 1892 edition
(with the inclusion of the posthumous *Old Age Echoes*)
and practically anathematized anyone who might dare to
disturb the bones of the earlier versions of his work.[19] So
sympathetically has this wish been obeyed that to this day
no other complete edition of LEAVES OF GRASS has ever
been published.[20] In fact, not until De Selincourt, did any
biographer or scholarly critic question the full truth of the
claim that the final LEAVES OF GRASS is a perfect organism
or logical structure. Concerning the organization of the
book, De Selincourt declared in 1914: ". . . being a poor
critic of his own writings, [Whitman] finally arranged

---

[18] See note 10, above.

[19] See "An Executor's Diary Note, 1891," in Emory Holloway's Inclusive Edition of *Leaves of Grass* (New York: Doubleday, Doran, 1931),
539.

[20] Stuart P. Sherman's chronological edition of *Leaves of Grass* (New
York: Scribner's, 1922), contains none of the poems published after 1881.

them without regard for their poetic value, considering merely in what order the thought of each would be most effective in its contribution to the thought of all."[21] And of the additions after 1881: "The whole of the latter part of LEAVES OF GRASS . . . exists only as a sketch."[22]

This admirable beginning, however, was not immediately followed by other investigations of the editions. The next contribution was William Sloane Kennedy's chapter, "The Growth of 'Leaves of Grass' as a Work of Art (Excisions, Additions, Verbal Changes)," in *The Fight of a Book for the World;* but this, like Dr. Triggs's essay, is superficial, being concerned mainly with a few verbal improvements in the text. The first biographer to become skeptical of the cathedral analogy was Jean Catel, who found the 1855 edition interesting for its unconscious psychological revelations,[23] and he deserves credit for stimulating research on the growth of the final text.

A few years after the publication of Catel's biography Floyd Stovall made a study of Whitman's emotional and intellectual growth as revealed in the key-poems of the various editions, which he called "Main Drifts in Whitman's Poetry."[24] This was the first really significant critical contribution to the subject. It was followed two years later by Killis Campbell's "The Evolution of Whitman as Artist,"[25] based on a more extensive examination of verbal changes than Kennedy's study, but agreeing

---

[21] Basil De Selincourt, *Walt Whitman: A Study,* (London: Martin Secker, 1914), 164.

[22] *Ibid.,* 180.

[23] Jean Catel, *Walt Whitman: La Naissance du Poète,* (Paris: Editions Rieder, 1929), discussed in this HANDBOOK on p. 59.

[24] Floyd Stovall, "Main Drifts in Whitman's Poetry," *American Literature,* IV, 3-21 (March 1932).

[25] Killis Campbell, "The Evolution of Whitman as Artist," *American Literature,* VI, 254-263 (November, 1934).

in the main with the conclusions of Triggs and Kennedy that Whitman's revisions improved the style and thought of his poems.

Meanwhile Frederik Schyberg in Denmark had made the most extensive of all attempts "to unravel the difficult pattern, to present LEAVES OF GRASS in its gradual evolution through the eight editions from 1855 to the final edition in 1889,"[26] but his book is still known to few Whitman scholars in America and has had almost no influence—so little, in fact, that in 1941 Irving C. Story could declare, "no detailed comparative study that considers the several editions as units, and as successive stages in an evolution toward a final product has yet been made."[27] Story was the first scholar in the United States to attempt "a complete picture of the relations of the successive editions"[28] and to point out the necessity of a variorum edition of LEAVES OF GRASS for a complete understanding of Whitman's message and artistic achievement.

The need for a variorum edition was further emphasized in 1941 by Sculley Bradley in a paper read at the English Institute,[29] in which he discussed the problems that must be solved in preparing such an edition. He concluded that the text must be based on the last edition, because Whitman's purposes are apparent only in his final grouping of the poems. Here, as in Schyberg's study, we see that one

---

[26] Schyberg, *op. cit.*, 17.

[27] Irving C. Story, "The Growth of *Leaves of Grass:* A proposal for a variorum edition," *Pacific University Bulletin*, XXXVII, 1-11 (February, 1941).

[28] *Ibid.*, 4.

[29] "The Problem of a Variorum Edition of Whitman's *Leaves of Grass*," *English Institute Annual, 1941*, (New York: Columbia University Press, 1942), 128-157.

of the major problems for the critic is understanding the poet's intentions as indicated by his continued experiments in grouping his poems. The following year, 1942, Story in a second study, "The Structural Pattern of LEAVES OF GRASS,"[30] further corroborated this conclusion. It is significant that three scholars, widely separated and working independently, reached virtually the same judgment. Among them, they have probably indicated most of the problems to be encountered in a study of the editions and have even suggested procedures to follow.

The following discussion of the growth of LEAVES OF GRASS is not intended to be a definitive exposition of the subject (probably an impossibility until a complete and scholarly variorum edition is available) but to indicate the general trends in the development of the editions, including the main prose works, and thus to prepare the way for more exhaustive studies. Above all else, the author hopes it may stimulate others to read the earlier editions.

FIRST EDITION, 1855

Although Walt Whitman published a number of poems in various journals during the 1840's and early '50's, his poetic début took place with the publication of the 1855 LEAVES OF GRASS, printed for him by the Rome Brothers in Brooklyn. It was a thin quarto of ninety-five pages bound in green cloth stamped with an elaborate rococo design of flowers and foliage. The title, printed in gold, sprouted roots, leaves and branches from all sides, perhaps intended to symbolize the "organic" theory on which the poems were written. Especially symbolical is the por-

---

[30] *Pacific University Bulletin*, XXXVIII, No. 3, 1-12 (January, 1942).

trait inside facing the title page and taking the place of
the author's name, which is found only in the copyright
notice and on page 29 of the poem later called *Song of
Myself*, "Walt Whitman, an American, one of the roughs,
a kosmos . . ." The portrait shows the poet in the characteristic rôle of this poem, in shirt sleeves, the top of his
colored undershirt showing, standing in a slouch posture,
wearing a large black hat and a scraggly beard—"one of
the roughs."

The book contains a prefatory essay in prose (though
parts were later arranged as verse in *By Blue Ontario's
Shore*) and twelve poems, none of which have separate
titles. Though the Preface is well known, the importance
of the first edition cannot be accurately indicated without
a summary. Whitman's first avowed purpose is to give expression to his own national life and age. America, he
realizes, is still in the formative state—"the slough still
sticks to opinions and manners and literature while the
life which served its requirements has passed into the new
life of the new forms." This national self-reliance leads
to the theory that the poet must "incarnate" his country,
since "The United States themselves are essentially the
greatest poem." And the expression must be "transcendent
and new."

Accepting Emerson's doctrine that "the poet is representative" and "stands among partial men for the complete man,"[31] Whitman defines his poet as a "seer" and
an individual who "is complete in himself . . . the others
are as good as he, only he sees it, and they do not." He
is a "kosmos," a leader and an encourager of other poets.

[31] Cf. "The Poet," second paragraph.

He will show men and women "the path between reality and their souls."

Whitman anticipates "Pragmatism" and much of the realistic literary theory of the twentieth century in his belief that the poet shall be enamored of *facts* and *things;* that with "perfect candor" and sound health he shall represent nature, the human form, and life accurately—empirically. Hence he will strive for art without artificial ornamentation. But this must not be at the expense of spirituality. "The largeness of nature or the nation were monstrous without a corresponding largeness and generosity of the spirit of the citizen." He "does not moralize or make application of morals; . . . he knows the soul."

In a similar duality, the poet shall flood himself "with the immediate age as with vast oceanic tides" and at the same time he shall be universal: to him shall be "opened the eternity which gives similitude to all periods and processes and animate and inanimate forms." Like Shelley and Emerson, Whitman thinks "There will soon be no more priests; a new breed of poet-prophets shall take their place, and every man shall be his own priest."

But the final "proof of the poet is that his country absorbs him as affectionately as he has absorbed it."

Nearly half of the volume is taken up with the first poem, here untitled, later called *Walt Whitman,* and finally in 1881 *Song of Myself.* It is undoubtedly, as the title indicates, his most personal poem, and it appropriately dominates the first edition, which is certainly the most personal of all the editions, the most naïve and rudimentary. Without a guiding title, without section numbers, and covering forty-three quarto pages—no wonder the first readers could make little sense out of it. In fact, Carl F.

Strauch was the first critic ever to print a defence of its logic.[32] His outline of the structure deserves to be quoted:

1. Paragraphs 1-18, the Self; mystical interpenetration of the Self with all life and experience

2. Paragraphs 19-25, definition of the Self; identification with the degraded, and transfiguration of it; final merit of Self withheld; silence; end of the first half

3. Paragraphs 26-38, life flowing in upon Self, then evolutionary interpenetration of life

4. Paragraphs 39-41, the Superman

5. Paragraphs 42-52, larger questions of life—religion, faith, God, death; immortality and happiness mystically affirmed.[33]

Since Strauch analyzed the final version, he may have found more logic in the poem than one can discover in the first printing. The variorum readings are over half as long as the finished poem; only two sections (9 and 27) were unrevised. However, a close examination reveals that the fundamental ideas were not changed, though the revisions improved the rhythm,[34] diction, and coherence.

In this poem we find not only an epitome of Whitman's poetic thought in 1855 but an introduction to the main ideas of all editions of LEAVES OF GRASS. In succeeding editions he made considerable advance in the use of these ideas, and the culmination of his poetic growth certainly came much later; but just as the 1855 Preface announced the central esthetic doctrine of Whitman's life-work, so

---

[32] Carl F. Strauch, "The Structure of Walt Whitman's Song of Myself," *English Journal* (College Ed.), XXVII, 597-607 (Sept., 1938).

[33] *Ibid.*, 599.

[34] *E.g.*, the first line read, "I celebrate myself," and was not balanced until 1881 by "and sing myself."

does this poem serve as a program (not conscious, deliberate, and logical, but sub-conscious and intuitive) for the life-poems. Perhaps, therefore, a more elaborate summary will be useful.

In sections 1 through 4 the poet is intoxicated by the joy of physical sensations—with breathing, the beating of his heart, the smell of vegetation, and the feeling of health—, "But they are not the Me myself." In sec. 5 a mystical experience between "Me" and the "Soul"[35] gives the poet his mystical convictions:[36]

> And I know that the spirit of God is the eldest brother of my own,[37]
> And that all men ever born are also my brothers . . . .[38]
> and the women my sisters and lovers,
> And that a kelson of the creation is love . . .

This introduces (sec. 6) the symbol of the pantheistic grass, "itself a child . . . the produced babe of the vegetation,"—and "The smallest sprout shows there is really no death." Sections 7-8 develop the thesis that it is just as lucky to die as to be born. Here, potentially, are all the sentiments and philosophy of Death to be found in later poems; the only difference is variation in the intensity of the emotion expressed.

---

[35] Note that Catel, *op. cit.*, would make the Soul the "unconscious," p. 400. See p. 62, *ante*.

[36] Cf. William James, *Varieties of Religious Experience* (New York: Modern Library, n.d. [Longmans, Green, 1902]), Lectures XVI-XVII.

[37] After 1855 Whitman eliminated the effective word "eldest" from this line.

[38] In the first edition Whitman used freely four dots to punctuate a pause or separate loosely connected clauses. In these quotations four dots indicate Whitman's original punctuation, three editorial omission, as at the end of this quotation.

This philosophy of Death and the poet's rôle as "caresser of life" rests on a pantheistic belief in the transmigration of souls,[39] the "souls moving along." Thus vicariously he joins in the haying (9), lives in the wilderness with the hunters and trappers (10), or protects the runaway slave. He is the erotic young woman who watches the bathers from the window (11), a curious revelation of an abnormally acute sensitivity to touch—[40] perhaps a key to the sex poems of the next edition, and an anticipation of sections 27-30 in *Song of Myself.*

The structure of the poem is not primarily logical (though Professor Strauch's defence of the logic is helpful because it demonstrates that the poem has a structure); neither thought nor emotion advances in orderly sequence. The best analogy for the structure is the symphony—an analogy of which the poet himself was not unaware.[41] A theme (*i.e.,* an idea or a sentiment) is advanced briefly in one section and later developed in more detail in other sections, so that the movement is often more spiral, or even circular, than forward. Thus one cannot say that a given theme or "movement" (in the symphonic sense) begins precisely at a given point and extends over exactly so many lines or sections. For example, in sections 12-13 the poet vicariously visits and observes with a sculptor's delight the butcher-boy, blacksmith, and negro at work. Then as he continues his mythical ramble his tread "scares the wood-drake and wood-duck," and this motif develops

---

[39] See Chap. III, p. 267.

[40] Cf. Carl Van Doren, "Walt Whitman, Stranger," *American Mercury,* XXXV, 277-285 (July, 1935).

[41] Cf. Furness, *op. cit.,* 201-262. Also Furness's lecture on "Walt Whitman and Music," given before the Boston chapter of the Special Libraries Association, and printed in the (S. L. A.) *News Bulletin,* November, 1937. See also Chap. V, p. 421.

in section 14 as an exemplification of the poet's "incarnating" the fauna of his country. The pantheistic doctrine is emphasized again when he sees in the animals and himself "the same old law," *i.e.,* pantheistic evolution, reincarnation and transmigration.[42]

These sympathetic observations of the brother animals lead to a catalog tour of occupations (15), resulting in a universal, Christ-like, sympathy; he speaks for all people in all places (16). His thoughts "are the thoughts of all men in all ages and lands, they are not original with me" (17). This sympathy leads him to play marches not for victors only but for the conquered and slain also (18), and to eat with the "wicked just the same as the righteous" (19). Even the arrogant worship of his own body (20), which Catel finds auto-erotic,[43] is symbolic, for "In all people I see myself." As the poet of body and the soul he chants "a new chant of dilation or pride" in human existence (21), and through combined sea and sex imagery accepts good and evil alike (22).

Section 23 is a brief interlude announcing a program of modernity—"And mine a word of the modern . . . . a word en masse"— and a "Hurrah for positive science!" Perhaps this sketchy section is unconsciously prophetic, for Whitman was never to have a definite social program and sympathy rather than accurate knowledge was the basis for his claim to being the poet of science also.[44]

In section 24 the poem returns to the theme of the body as a temple, a central motif in the song, which is developed

---

[42] See C. J. Furness, "Walt Whitman and Reincarnation," *The Forerunner,* III, 9-20 (Autumn, 1942); also Chap. III, p. 267.

[43] See *ante,* p. 61. Cf. H. S. Canby *Walt Whitman* (Boston: Houghton Mifflin Co., 1943), 199-206.

[44] Newton Arvin gives the best discussion of this point. See *ante,* p. 79.

with sections on human sensations: sounds (26), touch (27-30), and procreation and fecundity[45] are supported by the pantheistic philosophy: "I believe a leaf of grass is no less than the journey work of the stars"(31), and he thinks he finds in the animals "tokens" of himself which his soul must have dropt as it moved "forward then and now and forever" (32).

This thought leads to a mystic transcending of time and space in which the poet, afoot with his vision, "merges" with the hounded slave, the wounded person, the bruised fireman. After brief interruptions to narrate some historical incidents—the Alamo (34) and an "old fashioned frigate" fight (35)—the vicarious suffering theme, the Christ-motif, runs through several sections, culminating in the announcement of a "new Messiah," who incorporates "the old religions" and supplants them: "Accepting the rough deific sketches to fill out better in myself . . . bestowing them freely on each man and woman I see."

Beginning with section 42 this new Messiah preaches a sermon, like Christ addressing the multitude, his voice resounding in the open air.

A call in the midst of the crowd,
    My own voice, orotund sweeping and final.
Come my children,
Come my boys and girls, and my women and household
    and intimates,[46]
Now the performer launches his nerve . . . . he has
    passed his prelude on the reeds within.

---

[45] Fecundity is a necessary consequence of Whitman's pantheism. (See Chap. III, p. 284.)

[46] Present reading: "Come my boys and girls, my women, household and intimates, . . ."

Easily written loosefingered chords! I feel the thrum of
their climax and close.[47]

He looks over the crowd: "Music rolls, but not from the
organ" (noise of the crowd?): they are strangers, absorbed in their own selfish lives, but he accepts them all,

The weakest and shallowest is deathless with me,
What I do and say the same waits for them,
Every thought that flounders in me the same flounders
in them.

What he preaches is a "faith" that encloses "all worship
ancient and modern" (43). The sermon continues: "What
is known I strip away. . . . I launch all men and women
forward with me into the unknown." The theology is
pantheistic evolution: "That which fills its period or place
is equal to any . . . Before I was born out of my mother
generations guided me . . ." (44) He invites the audience
to accompany him on the "perpetual journey" (46) as
traveling companions (47). The lesson is self-reliance.
(47). He repeats his central message (48):

I have said that the soul is not more than the body,
And I have said that the body is not more than the soul,
And nothing, not God, is greater to one than one's-
self is . . .

He sees God in the faces of men and women and finds
"letters from God dropped in the street" (48). And what
is Death? Life is "the leavings of many deaths"; the suns

---

[47] The organ metaphors, though rather ambiguous, intensify the religious connotations. Perhaps one could find in this passage a suggestion
of a church service, the organ music followed by the oral discourse; but
it is more likely that the "reeds within" are the vocal chords and the
"loose-fingered chords" are the music of spontaneous oratory.

and the grass of graves are "perpetual transfers and promotions." (49) Thus the prophet can declare finally (52):

I bequeath myself to the dirt to grow from the grass
     I love,
If you want me again look for me under your bootsoles.

         .   .   .

Failing to fetch me at first keep encouraged,
Missing me one place search another,
I stop some where waiting for you.

The second poem in the first edition, [*A Song for Occupations*], is a further development of the occupations-
theme in *Song of Myself*. It is like a sermon continued
from the first poem on the "drift" of the message—the
impulse to preach dominated Whitman in 1855. The poem
has poor unity and coherence, even in the final version.
The extremely intimate appeal to his readers in the first
seven lines—"Come closer to me, / Push closer my lovers
and take the best I possess"—was dropped in later
editions, drastically changing the motivation. Here it is a
forerunner of the search for companions and anticipates
the *Calamus* group—though after it was revised and
shifted to a position in the midst of the later "Songs," the
reader could scarcely guess its origin.

The third poem, [*To Think of Time*], is also a further
treatment of a major theme in *Song of Myself,* a pantheistic interpretation of Death. There is no death. Everything
has a soul: in cosmic processes are "promotion" and
"transformation" but no death: "there is nothing but immortality! . . . all preparation is for it . .[48] and identity is
for it . . and life and death are for it."

---

[48] Here Whitman used two instead of four dots.

The fourth poem, [*The Sleepers*], is the most successfully motivated, and the most interesting psychologically,
of any in the first edition. Though again taking his theme
from the universal sympathy motif of *Song of Myself,*
Whitman achieves both poetic and mystic unity by pro-
jecting himself like a spirit among the sleepers of all
lands, visiting, healing, and soothing each in turn. Dr.
Bucke made one of his most acute observations when he
called this poem "a representation of the mind during
sleep," made of "connected, half-connected, and discon-
nected thoughts and feelings as they occur in dreams, some
commonplace, some weird, some voluptuous, and all given
with the true and strange emotional accompaniments that
belong to them."[49] To what extent the imagery may have
been chosen deliberately or subconsciously (as may easily
happen in "stream-of-consciousness" composition) we do
not know, but the boldness of the sex imagery leads one
to suspect that the poem may have special psychological
significance. The invocation to "darkness" to "receive me
and my lover too . . . . he will not let me go without him"
sounds like a line from *Calamus.* But more revealing is
an eleven-line passage which was dropped in 1881. It
gives a description of adolescent awakenings to the sensations of sex: the poet is "curious to know where my feet
stand . . . .and the hunger crosses the bridge between."[50]
Walt Whitman was thirty-six years old when he published
this poem. No other composition is so revealing of the
methods by which he sublimated his life into the universal
symbols of poetry, and this first version is a great deal

---

[49] Bucke, *op. cit.,* 171.

[50] Schyberg, *op. cit.,* 138, says this passage "is absolutely invaluable
for the insight it gives into the peculiar erotic emotion of the first
edition . . ."

more revealing than the pruned version of the later editions. Shifting the poem to a position in LEAVES OF GRASS after *Autumn Rivulets* and *Passage to India* still further blurred its original significance.

The next poem, [*I Sing the Body Electric*], also gains in meaning when read after *The Sleepers*. In the *Children of Adam* group it seems generic rather than personal. Here, minus the somewhat mechanical descriptions of the parts of the body added in 1856,[51] the doctrine that the body and the soul are inseparable seems to have intimate connotations for the poet.

The sixth poem, [*Faces*], gives vivid expression to the doctrine of transmigration first encountered in *Song of Myself*. As the poet looks at faces, especially those of the wicked, the deformed, the diseased, he is consoled by the belief that this is but a temporary abode for the soul: he will "look again in a score or two of ages" and will "meet the real landlord perfect and unharmed."

> Off the word I have spoken I except not one . . . . red
>   white or black, all are deific,
> In each house is the ovum . . . . it comes forth after a
>   thousand years.
> Spots or cracks at the windows do not disturb me,
>
>   .   .   .   .
>
> I read the promise and patiently wait.

Since the biographical revelations of Mrs. Molinoff and Professor Furness,[52] this doctrine has acquired a new pathos and yields greater insight into the poetic mind of Walt Whitman. The poem underwent few changes

---

[51] Retained as Sec. 9.   [52] See p. 81, *ante*.

but was finally placed near the end of the LEAVES in a group called *From Noon to Starry Night*.

The remaining poems in the first edition have no great importance. The seventh, [*Song of the Answerer*], was extensively revised and shifted around in later editions. To the question, how shall you know the poet when he comes?, the reply is that he is the answerer and the common denominator of humanity. He is at ease and an equal among all men, all accept him as friend and brother. It is a restatement of one of the doctrines of the Preface.

One poem, No. 8 [*Europe*], had been published before, as *Resurgemus* in the New York *Daily Tribune*, June 21, 1850, the only poem in the volume not appearing for the first time. The thought is undistinguished, *viz.* that the spirits of men murdered by tyrants will live on to fight for Liberty, but Schyberg has found the poem important for a psychological reason:

> It describes a defeat, but its tone is optimistic and confident. Thus it shows the basic impulse of all Whitman's lyrics. As his love lyrics grew out of the disparity between his dreams and achievements, so his political lyrics were the result of the incongruity between the America he saw and the America he wished for. That is the background for Whitman's entire paradoxical political attitudes throughout all the editions of LEAVES OF GRASS . . . Optimism in sheer defiance— that is the foundation of Whitman's lyricism.[53]

The ninth poem, [*A Boston Ballad*], was probably written in 1854, for the subject is a slave delivery which took

---

[53] Schyberg, *op. cit.*, 72. Without contradicting Schyberg, it might be added that the poem was obviously inspired by the failure of the cause of democracy in the 1848 Revolution in France, which Whitman probably read about in American newspapers.

place in Boston that year. It is, therefore, chronologically close to the other poems in the '55 edition, but in manner it is unlike anything else in LEAVES OF GRASS, for it is a satire and Whitman did not later find this sarcastic tone congenial.[54] In a jig tune the poet declares that King George's coffin should be exhumed and the king shipped to Boston. Since it was Whitman's intention to use no explanatory notes in LEAVES OF GRASS, he later intended to delete this poem, but Trowbridge persuaded him to let it stand.[55]

The tenth poem, [*There was a Child Went Forth*], was much edited in later editions. The subject is the influence of natural objects on the life of a child—no doubt the poet himself—, "And the first object he looked upon . . . that object he became . . ." The loving portrait of the mother and the description of the father as "mean, angered, unjust" give further evidence of the personal nature of this first edition, for nearly all biographers accept the poem as autobiographical despite Whitman's denials. Of minor interest is the fact that the months are conventionally named, not yet called "Fourth-month" and "Fifth-month" after the Quaker custom.[56]

The last two poems, [*Who Learns my Lesson Complete*] and [*Great are the Myths*], are probably the weakest in the volume. The former merely asserts again that immortality is wonderful but that existence and the physical universe are just as wonderful and miraculous. It was probably written hastily and carelessly. The ideas were to be much better expressed later in *Salut au Monde!*,

---

[54] Quite different, but also satirical, is the 1856 *Poem of the Propositions of Nakedness*—see p. 131.

[55] W. S. Kennedy, *The Fight of A Book for the World* (West Yarmouth, Mass.: Stonecroft Press, 1926), 153 and 175.

[56] See Trowbridge, *op. cit.*, 396-397.

Song of the Rolling Earth, and elsewhere. The final poem, eventually rejected, exclaims, even less effectively, that everything is great. Perhaps it does serve as a general summary of the themes in the edition, though in no systematic manner, but it contains no helpful interpretations or application. Furthermore, its position is anti-climactic.

Catel thinks that Walt Whitman unconsciously revealed himself in the 1855 edition as in no other,[57] but this interpretation is based on the theory that the *secret* of LEAVES OF GRASS is that the poet created his poems as an intellectual compensation for his own physical failures, frustrations, and shabby origins. Undoubtedly we do see in the first edition the processes of sublimation at work, and we get many hints of the poet's psychology. But historically it is important because it shows the materials and methods which were to go into the creation of the final LEAVES OF GRASS. Here in 1855 Whitman has a poetic theory fairly complete, he has a mass of unorganized ideas, and the foundations of his philosophy are well established. In his first poem he tries to include all of these, with the result that it lacks the unity and power even of *The Sleepers,* but it remains a good summary of his ideas and philosophy, and the structure illustrates the symphonic organization of his materials. Furthermore, here, before he had been screeched and howled at by scandalized critics, he expressed himself with a freedom and abandon unequalled again except possibly in the expanded edition of the next year. His fervor was at its height, but his poems were yet in a formative stage and he still had much to learn about editing and organizing his work.

---

[57] See p. 59.

SECOND EDITION, 1856

Soon after the abortive publication of the first edition, Whitman must have begun preparation of his second edition of LEAVES OF GRASS, for he published it the following year, with Fowler and Wells acting as agents. This phrenological firm withheld its name from the title page and soon renounced all responsibility for the book, fearing that the bad reputation it was getting would injure their thriving business.

The new book was a small volume, 16 mo, of 384 pages, with a green cloth binding stamped with floral designs not quite so ornate as those of the first edition. On the backstrip, in gold letters, appeared "I Greet You at the/ Beginning of A/ Great Career/ R. W. Emerson," which Whitman had quoted from Emerson's spontaneous letter without bothering to ask permission. So great was the influence of this letter upon the second edition of LEAVES OF GRASS, and probably upon Whitman's whole subsequent career as a poet, that it deserves to be quoted in full. In thanks for his complimentary copy of the first edition Emerson wrote:

Concord, Massachusetts, 21 July, 1855
Dear Sir—I am not blind to the worth of the wonderful gift of "Leaves of Grass." I find it the most extraordinary piece of wit and wisdom that America has yet contributed. I am very happy in reading it, as great power makes us happy. It meets the demand I am always making of what seemed the sterile and stingy nature, as if too much handiwork, or too much lymph in the temperament, were making our western wits fat and mean.

I give you joy of your free and brave thought. I have great joy in it. I find incomparable things said incomparably well, as they must be. I find the courage of treatment which so delights us, and which large perception only can inspire.

I greet you at the beginning of a great career, which yet must have had a long foreground somewhere, for such a start. I rubbed my eyes a little, to see if this sunbeam were no illusion; but the solid sense of the book is a sober certainty. It has the best merits, namely, of fortifying and encouraging.

I did not know until I last night saw the book advertized in a newspaper that I could trust the name as real and available for a post-office. I wish to see my benefactor, and have felt much like striking my tasks and visiting New York to pay you my respects.

R. W. EMERSON[58]

The controversy stirred up by the publication of this letter has scarcely died down even yet; but whether or not Whitman was justified in using it as he did, its importance in the preparation of the second edition of his poems can scarcely be overestimated. Whitman's friends report that he was tremendously "set up" by it, and during the summer of 1855 he carried the letter around with him in his pocket. It may even have encouraged him to go on writing and printing his poems despite his recent fiasco. Certainly the exuberant confidence of the second edition is remarkable.

Not content with printing the letter in an appendix to the new volume, Whitman wrote a boastful and garrulous reply in which he addressed Emerson as "Master." The reply begins, "Here are thirty-two Poems, which I send

---

[58] *Leaves of Grass* (Brooklyn, 1856), 345-346.

you, dear Friend and Master, not having found how I
could satisfy myself with sending any usual acknowledgment of your letter."[59] Then without regard to the true
circumstances, he claims that the thousand-copy edition
of the first volume readily sold and that he is printing several thousand copies of the second. He expects in a few
years a sale of ten or twenty thousand copies. Then he
launches into a theoretical discussion which is especially
revealing and shows plainly that Whitman himself was
not unaware of the paradox mentioned by Schyberg, the
incongruity between his dream and reality. In the spirit
of the literary nationalism of his day, he complains that
the genius of America is still unexpressed in art. His
evaluation of American life and character is almost as
heroic as Paul Bunyan folklore, but the magnificence is
latent, not actual. "Up to the present . . . the people, like
a lot of large boys, have no determined tastes, are quite
unaware of the grandeur of themselves, and of their destiny, and of their immense strides . . ."[60] At present
America is only "a divine true sketch."

In addition to helping complete the "sketch," Whitman
recognizes another responsibility in the development and
recording of American culture: it is the honest, truthful
expression of sex:

the body of a man or woman . . . is so far quite unexpressed in poems . . . Of bards for These States, if it
come to a question, it is whether they shall celebrate in
poems the eternal decency of the amativeness of Nature, the motherhood of all, or whether they shall be
the bards of the fashionable delusion of the inherent

---

[59] *Ibid.,* 346.   [60] *Ibid.,* 352.

nastiness of sex, and of the feeble and querulous modesty of deprivation.[61]

Plenty of sex imagery is to be found in the first edition, especially in *Song of Myself* and *The Sleepers,* but beginning with the second edition it is now to be a program, a "cause," a campaign against both asceticism and puritanism.

In the twenty new poems which Whitman added in the second edition to the twelve of the former collection, his faith in himself, his sanguinary hopes, and the crystallization of his "program" are clearly discernible. The poems now have titles and their arrangement is the poet's first experiment in working out a dramatic-allegorical sequence. Omitting the '55 Preface, which was gradually being transferred to new compositions in verse,[62] he begins the volume with the poem which in all editions will continue to be a good theme-catalog, here called *Poem of Walt Whitman, an American* (finally *Song of Myself*), and progresses through the gamut of personal identity, sex, friendship, evolution, cosmic sympathy, to eternity and immortality. Neither here nor later do the poems treat the perpetual journey of the soul from the germ to the grave in a narrative or logical manner, but already they are falling into a kind of abstract allegory resembling Carlyle's "out of eternity, into eternity."[63]

In 1856 Whitman's "sex program" was still so intimately a part of his whole inspiration that the new sex poems are scattered throughout the whole book. Following *Song of Myself* comes *Poem of Women* (later *Un-*

---

[61] *Ibid.,* 356.

[62] Mainly *Poem of Many in One* (1856), later called *By Blue Ontario's Shore* (1881).

[63] "Aus der Ewigkeit, zu der Ewigkeit hin," in *Sartor Resartus.*

folded out of the Folds). The theme is both maternity and self-reliance: "First the man is shaped in the woman, he can then be shaped in himself." The treatment is abstract, ethical, and ideal; only physically and morally strong women can produce a strong race. It is one aspect of Whitman's dream of the future glory of America.

The next sex poem is No. 7, now called *Poem of the Body* (*I Sing the Body Electric*), taken over from the first edition but considerably revised. Number 13, *Poem of Procreation* (*A Woman Waits for Me*), further extends the theme that "sex contains all." Number 28, *Bunch Poem* (*Spontaneous Me*), is the least abstract and most bizarre of the group. The "bunch" is a seminal figure, like "herbage" in *Scented Herbage of My Breast* (1860), which, however, is a *Calamus* poem, and hence not procreative. *Bunch Poem* is definitely auto-erotic, for the poet is conscious of his own body rather than the body of his lover. It celebrates the life impulse latent in him, but it is not in imagery, feeling, or thought a love poem, and may be indicative of ambiguous emotions in Whitman himself at this period.

The *Poem of the Propositions of Nakedness* is not, as the title might indicate, a sex poem, except indirectly. It is composed of a long list of satirical paradoxes for those who distrust nakedness, sex, truth, democracy, love, nature, themselves—note the relation of sex to the whole "program." After his ironical mood had passed (Cf. *Boston Ballad* in the first edition), Whitman apparently did not know exactly what to do with this poem. It was included in *Democratic Chants* (1860) as poem No. 5, later called *Respondez* and finally in 1881 rejected except for the six lines of *Reversals* and three of *Transpositions.*

Though the second edition contained no poem equal in power to the lilac elegy of 1865, it did include four or five of his most successful compositions. The first of these (No. 3) is *Poem of Salutation* (*Salut au Monde!*), in which the national "incarnation" ambition of the '55 Preface has expanded into a lyric embrace of the whole world:

> My spirit has passed in compassion and determination around the whole earth,
> I have looked for brothers, sisters, lovers, and found them ready for me in all lands.

This poem contradicts the theory of many critics that after failing to gain acceptance in his own country, Whitman developed an international sentiment as a compensation. And as within him "latitude widens, longitude lengthens," Walt Whitman gains tremendously in poetic power. World sentiment invigorated and stimulated his lyric growth and came in the flush of his inspiration, not afterwards.

Broad-Axe Poem (*Song of the Broad-Axe*) contains a good deal of Whitman's earlier nationalism, perhaps imperialism, but this is due in part to the spirit of "arrogant, masculine, naïve, rowdyish" perfect health in which the broad-axe symbolizes the human activity of all lands. "Muscle and pluck forever! What invigorates life, invigorates death." The prophecy of one hundred Free States, "begetting another hundred north and south," is less imperialistic in its context than out of it, for the vision of "the shapes of fullsized men" and of vigorous women to be their equals[64] includes all lands and peoples, "Shapes

---

[64] The ideal of vigorous women in this poem is reminiscent of the tradition which Whitman liked to tell about his mannish grandmother— see *Specimen Days*.

bracing the whole earth, and braced with the whole earth."

In *Sun-Down Poem* (*Crossing Brooklyn Ferry*), Thoreau's favorite and one of Whitman's most sustained lyric achievements, we can feel the rhythmical and emotional strength, no less than tranquil mystical assurance, which the poet's expanding ego has attained.

> It avails not, neither time nor place—distance avails not,
> I am with you, you men and women of a generation,
> or ever so many generations hence,
>
> . . . . . .
>
> You furnish your parts toward eternity.

Whitman had already handled the idea in several poems, but here in the unifying ship motif, carrying humanity toward eternity, he becomes a truly inspired poet.

Even in the carefree, light-hearted *Poem of the Road* (*Song of the Open Road*), the poetic vision expands over the whole world—and finally the universe: "Afoot and lighthearted I take to the open road! Healthy, free, the world before me! . . . The earth expanding . . . I will scatter myself among men and women as I go." The themes of travel, physical joy, and companionship are happily blended. Phrenological "adhesiveness,"[65] which was building for the poet a "city of friends"[66] where "manly affection" would reign, is defined by the question: "Do you know what it is as you pass to be loved by strangers?" The poet travels always toward the "great companions." His poem is a new *Pilgrim's Progress:*

---

[65] For a complete explanation of Whitman's phrenological vocabulary see Edward Hungerford, "Walt Whitman and His Chart of Bumps," *American Literature,* II, 350-384 (Jan., 1931). See also Chap. I, p. 76, *ante.*

[66] Cf. Long, discussed on p. 75.

> To know the universe itself as a road—as many roads—
> as roads for traveling souls! . . .
> All parts away for the progress of souls,
> All religion, all solid things, arts, governments—all
> that was or is apparent upon this globe or any globe,
> falls into niches and corners before the processions of
> souls along the grand roads of the universe, . . .

He probably knew little about Hegelianism at this time,[67] but he could declare,

> Now understand me well—it is provided in the essence
> of things, that from any fruition of success, no mat-
> ter what, shall come forth something to make a
> greater struggle necessary.
>
> . . . . .
>
> My call is the call to battle—I nourish active rebellion,

thus preparing the way for his justification of evil in *Chanting the Square Deific* a decade later.

Even the religious concept of individualism, first form-ulated in the '55 Preface, takes on new depth and breadth when whole passages of the Preface are transferred to *Poem of Many in One* (later *By Blue Ontario's Shores*) and are motivated with cosmic significance. In addition to singing a new nation, which is to build on the past and henceforth lead the world, the poet has taken on a philo-sophical search for the meaning of the universe.

> I match my spirit against yours, you orbs, growths,
> mountains, brutes,
> I will learn why the earth is gross, tantalizing, wicked,
> I take you to be mine, you beautiful, terrible, rude
> forms.

---

[67] See Chap. VI, p. 455.

This search for the meaning of life and existence also has considerable bearing on the poet's theory of language. In the Preface he had declared that "The English language befriends the grand American expression. . . . it is brawny enough and limber and full enough," and concluded that, "It is the medium that shall well nigh express the inexpressible." The more mystic his poems become, the more Whitman strives to "express the inexpressible," and this leads to a fuller development of his theory of words.[68] As a consequence of the Neo-platonic doctrine in the Preface that "All beauty comes from beautiful blood and a beautiful brain," Whitman explains in *Poem of Many in One* that to use the language the poet must "prepare himself, body and mind." Linguistic expression is thus the product of character. In *Poem of the Sayers of the Words of the Earth* (*Song of the Rolling Earth*), Whitman gives this idea an Emersonian interpretation; in fact, he is probably indebted to the Transcendentalist belief that "Words are signs of natural facts."[69] *Words* are not sounds or marks on paper, says Whitman, but reality; the words of the poem are "the words of the eloquent dumb great mother."[70]

> I swear I begin to see little or nothing in audible words!
> I swear I think all merges toward the presentation of the unspoken meanings of the earth!
> Toward him who sings the songs of the body, and of the truths of the earth,

[68] See Chap. V, pp. 428-437.

[69] "Language," in *Nature,* 1836. See Emerson Grant Sutcliffe, "Emerson's Theories of Literary Expression," *Studies in Language and Literature* (University of Illinois, 1923), VIII, 17. Cf. Jean Gorley, "Emerson's Theory of Poetry," *Poetry Review* (August, 1931), 263-273.

[70] Cf. F. O. Matthiessen, *American Renaissance* (New York: Oxford University Press, 1941), 518 ff. See also Chap. V of this HANDBOOK, pp. 428-437.

Toward him who makes the dictionaries of the words
that print cannot touch.

Hence the need for symbols, for "indirections"—"This
is a poem for the sayers of the earth—these are hints
of meanings," which echo the tones and phrases of souls.
Perhaps the greatest importance of the second edition
is the testimony it bears to the courage and fortitude of
Walt Whitman in the face of literary failure. Nearly
every new poem in the book radiates his faith in himself,
in his ideas, and in his newly-invented technique. And
despite the brashness and bad taste of the open-letter to
Emerson, this edition shows unmistakable growth in lyric
power, especially when the cosmic emotion or universal
sympathy carries his Muse on a vicarious journey into
all lands and ages, as in *Salut au Monde!, Crossing Brooklyn Ferry,* or *Song of the Rolling Earth.* Even in his most
personal sex lyrics, which seem to reflect some inner
struggle or irrespressible urge, he is already striving to
sublimate the emotion. He has, in short, not yet attained
the poise and tranquility which grew upon him after his
service in the army hospitals; but as the first edition reveals the main stream of his essential ideas, so does the
second map out the lyric and psychological paths which
he is to follow through succeeding editions of LEAVES
OF GRASS.

THIRD EDITION, 1860

In 1860 a reputable publisher in Boston, Thayer and
Eldridge, brought out the third edition of LEAVES OF
GRASS; however, this firm went into bankruptcy in 1861
and later the plates were obtained by a dishonest printer

who distributed many pirated copies. The new edition was a fat book, 8vo, bound in cloth, with 456 pages. The frontispiece was a steel engraving of the poet at the age of forty, from a painting by Charles Hine. Whitman's love of symbolical bindings and decorations extended this time to the inside of the volume, three emblematical tail-pieces, probably designed by the author himself, being used several times throughout the book. The first of these, a hand with a butterfly poised on the forefinger, was also stamped on the backstrip of the binding; the second, a globe in space revealing the western hemisphere, was used both on the front cover and inside; and the third was a sunrise at sea. These were probably intended to signify Whitman's global and cosmic inspiration and his con-viction that all creatures were his intimate friends.

The new edition contains 124 new poems, extensive re-visions of the old ones, many new titles (some of them final) ; and the experimental grouping of the poems shows clearly for the first time the allegorical-dramatic order that Whitman was beginning to attempt. The book opens with *Proto-Leaf* (*Starting from Paumanok*), which gives more specific autobiography and poetic intentions than even *Song of Myself,* and ends with the farewell-prophetic *So Long!,* which was to terminate all subsequent editions (with the exception of annexes). Most of the new poems are found in the groups called *Chants Democratic* (fifteen out of the twenty-two being new), *Enfans d'Adam* (*Chil-dren of Adam*—twelve of the fifteen being new), *Cal-amus* (all forty-five poems new), *Messenger Leaves* (thirteen new to two old), and the miscellaneous frag-mentary group, *Thoughts* (composed of six new poems and one old poem, later rejected). *Children of Adam* and

Calamus were to be retained, with a few alterations in contents, in all future editions, and have no doubt become the most famous groups of the 1860 edition—though all four of these major sections deserve to be discussed in detail.

Proto-Leaf (or *Starting from Paumanok*),[71] which was to precede *Song of Myself* in all future editions, is a self-characterization and summary of Whitman's poetic program. Here, even more than in the '55 Preface or the '56 *By Blue Ontario's Shore*, genuine autobiography and Whitman's poet-prophet rôle become inseparably blended.

> Free, fresh, savage,
> Fluent, luxuriant, self-content, fond of persons and
>   places,
>
> Fond of fish-shape Paumanok, where I was born, . . .

But the "Boy of Mannahatta" is soon breathing the air of California, Texas, and Cuba, which he had visited only in fancy, and living "rude in my home in Kanuck woods." Furthermore, the poet, "Solitary, singing in the west," striking "up for a new world," is celebrating less his contemporary United States of 1860 than life which "has come to the surface after so many throes and convulsions," *i.e.,* the evolution of the human race. With clairvoyant vision he sees the whole globe revolving in time and space, with "the ancestor-continents" and the "present and future continents."

---

[71] The main revisions were made for the 1867 edition, though further alterations are found in the 1881 version. The long passages dropped were from sections (as finally numbered): 1 (sixteen lines), 3 (two stanzas transferred to sec. 1 of *Song of Myself* in 1881), and 14.

See, vast, trackless spaces,
As in a dream, they change, they swiftly fill,
Countless masses debouch upon them,
They are now covered with the foremost people, arts,
    institutions known.

As in the 1856 *Sun-Down Poem* (*Crossing Brooklyn Ferry*) the poet dips into the future and sees for himself "an audience interminable." And as in the '55 Preface, he sings modernity with reverence for the Past:

In the name of These States, shall I scorn the antique?
Why These are the children of the antique, to justify it.

The key-word is *justify*. Like Milton justifying the Puritan theology, Whitman justifies cosmic evolution—and something comparable to Bergson's *élan vital*.[72]

Although ostensibly nationalistic, and writing "from an American point of view," he "will trail the whole geography of the globe, and salute courteously every city large and small."[73] So much has been said about Whitman's arrogant patriotism during these early years that his cosmic imagination and universal sympathy have often been overlooked. But it is of fundamental importance to observe that he feels his inspiration to be a timeless current which flows through himself and his age:

O strain, musical, flowing through ages—
    now reaching hither,
I take to your reckless and composite chords—
    I add to them, and cheerfully pass them forward.[74]

This cosmic inspiration, which finds expression in the

[72] Cf. p. 271.
[73] *Starting from Paumanok*, sec. 6.
[74] Sec. 37.

most lyrical strophes of the poem, is tied to a more personal theme, which may indeed have been the psychological *drive* motivating the mystical inspiration. This theme is "the song of companionship" or the "ideal of manly love." The following lines give a clue to the origin of these emotions, and possibly Whitman's inmost necessity for poetic expression:

> I will therefore let flame from me the burning fires
>   that were threatening to consume me,
> I will lift what has too long kept down those smouldering fires,
> I will give them complete abandonment,
> I will write the evangel-poem of comrades and of
>   love, ...[75]

Along with the cosmic motif and the evangel of "manly love," Whitman also announces that he will inaugurate a new religion which shall include evil as well as good. The ending of this poem leaves little doubt that the "pensive aching to be together" with his comrade is the basic experience underlying the poet's need for lyric utterance. It is perhaps also significant that in contrast to *Proto-Leaf,* the succeeding poem *Walt Whitman* (or *Song of Myself*), is abstract and philosophical, though in the first edition it too had seemed highly personal.

Although *Proto-Leaf* hints that the most urgent theme in the 1860 edition is that of comradeship or "Calamus," the *Calamus* section is preceded by *Chants Democratic,* followed by a group of twenty-four numbered but untitled poems called simply *Leaves of Grass,* and then *Enfans d'Adam* (later called *Children of Adam*). This ar-

---

[75] Sec. 22.

rangement would seem to be a deliberate attempt to so-
cialize and transmute Whitman's personal experience.
Since Emerson had failed to argue the sex-poems out of
the book, they must be included in the program, but they
were not permitted to dominate, even to the extent that
they had in 1856.

Chants Democratic—subtitled "And Native American"
—is a collection of sixteen new poems[76] and six old ones
apparently intended to celebrate the nationalistic purposes
which had been promised in the 1855 Preface. It is introduced by the exclamatory poem, *Apostroph,* which enumerates, often in phrases later repeated in this group of
poems, the various themes and intentions of the *Chants.*
This poem was rejected in all subsequent editions, probably not only because of its hysterical style but also
because when this group was broken up and the poems
redistributed, its purpose vanished. It is interesting here
only because it shows Whitman's growing tendency to
use prologue-poems to introduce his groups.

The first numbered poem in the *Chants Democratic*
group is the 1856 version of the '55 Preface, called *Poem
of Many in One* in '56 and in 1881 given the final title of
By Blue Ontario's Shore. It proclaims Whitman's theory
of the "nation announcing itself," and appropriately precedes the '56 *Song of the Broad-Axe* and the '55 *Song for
Occupations.* As Schyberg has remarked, it is ironical that

---

[76] The new poems are: *Apostroph* (later rejected); *Our Old Feuillage;
With Antecedents; Song at Sunset; Thoughts,* sec. 1; *To a Historian;
Thoughts,* sec. 2; *Vocalism,* sec. 1; *Laws for Creation; Poets to Come;
Mediums; On Journeys through the States; Me Imperturbe; I Was
Looking a Long While; I Hear America Singing; As I Walk these Broad
Majestic Days.* The old ones are: *Poem of Many in One (By Blue On-
tario's Shore); Song of the Broad-Axe; Song for Occupations; Re-
spondez!; Poem of Remembrance for a Girl or Boy of These States;* and
Poem of the Heart of the Son of Manhattan Island (Excelsior, 1867).

just before the outbreak of the Civil War Whitman should sing the unity of The States, which he declares in poem No. 4 (*Our Old Feuillage*) to be as united in "one identity" as the parts of his own body. But it is a theoretical identity, transcending political borders, uniting the poet and his countrymen with the "antecedents" of all lands (Cf. No. 7, later called *With Antecedents*), and prophetic of "the ideal man, the American of the future" (No. 10, *To a Historian*). These *Chants* are less a celebration of national achievement than a search for the foundations of an ethical Democracy, which the poet finds at last (No. 19) not in history, nor in fables or legends, but in a culmination of all existence in the average life of today, in things, inventions, customs, people. Therefore he proclaims as the most solid of all realities, Liberty, Freedom, and the "divine average" (No. 21),

> And our visions, the visions of poets . . .
> Democracy rests finally upon us . . .
> And our visions sweep through eternity.

Before discussing the second group of poems in the third edition, called ambiguously *Leaves of Grass,* we need to examine *A Word Out of the Sea* (in 1871 renamed *Out of the Cradle Endlessly Rocking*), which was first published in 1859. The poems of this group form a rather indefinite unit, the first one being later the second of *Sea-Drift,* in which *Out of the Cradle* stands first. The order of these two poems in *Sea-Drift* suggests a biographical as well as a chronological association. The "reminiscence" of the little boy who watched and listened to the mocking bird from Alabama grieving for his mate and heard the ocean whispering the answer in the sooth-

ing word "death," is so musically and poignantly told that
most critics have taken it as a symbolical account of the
poet's own bereavement, probably of his lover. Holloway
is unable to identify the lover, but he says that, "Surely
some lover had died, and he could find solace only in
song."[77] Since no conclusive evidence of any kind has ever
been found for interpreting the grief of the poem as either
actual or vicarious, this chapter is hardly the place for
further conjecture. But in order to understand the mood,
tone, and distinguishing characteristics of the third edition,
it is important to observe that the poet who declares that
the bereaved mocking bird "poured forth the meanings
which I, of all men know," and who records the "reckless despairing carols" of lonesome love and death, is not
the same as the irrepressible optimist of *Song of Myself*
or the sanguinary author who addressed Emerson as
"Master." As Schyberg puts it,

> The unspoken word, "the word" which Whitman
> sought so zealously and so arrogantly at the conclusion
> of "Song of Myself" and of which he said at that time
> > It is not chaos or death—it is form, union, plan—it is
> > eternal life—it is happiness[78]
> that word Whitman found in the years between 1856-60
> and it was both chaos and death—but primarily death.[79]

Schyberg also thinks[80] it significant that one line in
the original conclusion, which read,

---

[77] Emory Holloway, *Whitman: An Interpretation in Narrative* (New
York: Knopf, 1926), 162.

[78] Sec. 50.

[79] Schyberg, *op. cit.*, 167. Schyberg is alluding especially to a parenthesis later deleted from the last section of *Out of the Cradle:*
> O a word! O what is my destination? (I fear it is
> henceforth chaos;)...

[80] *Ibid.*, 168.

But fuse the song of two together,

was generalized in later editions to read,

But fuse the song of my dusky demon and brother . . .

The present motif of "two together" does without a doubt seem more personal in the 1859 and '60 versions. But whatever the interpretation of this debatable question, all readers must agree that in the intensity of the pathos and the reconciliation to Death, this poem marks a new depth in Whitman's verse. Undoubtedly it is the masterpiece of the third edition and one of the three or four most moving poems that he ever wrote.

In the other great sea-poem of this edition, *As I Ebb'd with the Ocean of Life,* "the fierce old mother" no longer rocks her cradle but "endlessly cries for the castaways." Now the poet is "baffled, balked" and perceives he has "not understood anything—not a single object—and that no man ever can." His poems have become "a few dead leaves"; the attempt to express himself, begun so confidently in *Song of Myself,* has been frustrated. Nature, "here, in sight of the sea," darts upon him and stings him because he had dared to open his mouth to sing at all; hence his conclusion that he too is but "a trail of drift and debris." He throws himself upon the land— "your breast, my father"—and asks the Old Mother, moaning her endless cry for her castaways, not to deny him. Nowhere else in LEAVES OF GRASS does the poet abandon himself to such fatalistic pessimism as in the ending of this poem:

> We, capricious, brought hither, we know not whence, we
>   spread out before You, up there, walking or sitting,
> Whoever you are—we too lie in drifts at your feet.

Both *Out of the Cradle Endlessly Rocking* and *As I Ebb'd with the Ocean of Life* were foreshadowed in 1856 in the posing of the riddle of existence in *On the Beach at Night Alone,* but the ship-wreck motif, with the father-land and mother-ocean symbols, characterize the 1860 edition. The same theme, with a vague, optimistic answer, was treated again in 1871 in *On the Beach at Night.*

A study of the mood of these poems and the *Calamus* group led Schyberg to conclude that the third edition records a spiritual crisis through which Walt Whitman passed about 1859-60. The cause of this crisis, if such it was, must be left for the biographers to settle, but no reader of the original versions of these poems can doubt the tragic grief of *Out of the Cradle* or the negation of *As I Ebb'd with the Ocean of Life.* By 1871 the mood had passed, to judge by *On the Beach at Night,* but so had the power-giving inspiration, for this is a feeble poem in comparison with the 1860 sea-shore lyrics.

Although Whitman's vicarious suffering of the sins and afflictions of all men was present in the first edition, especially in *The Sleepers,* this theme becomes more personal, a more intimate conviction (at times almost like a confessional) in the third edition. Three poems in the *Leaves of Grass* group may be cited as examples. In No. 13 (*You Felons on Trial in Courts*) the poet declares,

> I feel I am of them—I belong to those convicts and prostitutes myself,
> And henceforth I will not deny them—for how can I deny myself?

In No. 17 (*I Sit and Look Out*) he is subdued and resigned,

> I sit and look out upon all the sorrows of the world, . . .
> See, hear, and am silent.

Though not inconsistent with his earlier pantheism, No. 18 (*All is Truth*) sounds like a personal solution to "the sorrows of the world."

> I feel in myself that I represent falsehoods equally with
>   the rest,
> And that the universe does . . .
> And henceforth I will go celebrate anything I see or
>   am,
> And sing and laugh, and deny nothing.

What experience (or experiences) accounts for the mental depression and tragic brooding of the 1860 edition and Whitman's defiant celebration of the evil in himself and others, the biographers have not yet settled. Schyberg conjectures that Whitman may have led a dissolute life between 1856 and '60,[81] but practically the only evidence he can find is the subjective testimony of the poems in this period. The failure of the first and second editions to win recognition had so discouraged the poet that in *So Far and So Far* (No. 20 in the *Leaves of Grass* section), which was never again published in his lifetime, he confessed his wavering poetic ambition: "whether I continue beyond this book, to maturity . . . (the sun . . . has not yet fully risen) . . . [depends upon] you, contemporary America." In view of this confession, No. 24 (*Now Lift Me Close*)—also rejected in later editions—is pathetic in its attempt to establish a personal intimacy with the reader. The 1860 LEAVES OF GRASS "is in reality no book, nor part of a book, It is a man, flushed and full-blooded . . ."

---

[81] *Ibid.*, 163.

The parting kiss which he gives the reader is a significant
gesture, repeated again at the end of the book in *So Long!*

The tone of *Poem of Joys* (later *Song of Joys*) is more
like the 1856 *Song of the Open Road* than most of the
poems of the 1860 edition, though the exclamatory style
resembles *Longings for Home*. The desire to express "the
voices of animals . . . the dropping of rain-drops . . . the
sunshine and motion of waves" is a new lyrical statement
of the "organic" theory[82] of the '55 Preface, and many
of the "joys" are as reminiscent of boyhood scenes and
experiences as *Song of Myself* or *By Blue Ontario's Shore*.
But as the poem advances it takes up the themes and
moods characteristic of the third edition. The poet calls
for,

> O something pernicious and dread!
> Something far away from a puny and pious life!
> Something unproved! Something in a trance!
> Something escaped from the anchorage, and driving
> free.[83]

Ironically, he longed in 1860 for "the joys of the soldier!"

> To go to battle! To hear the bugles play, and the drums
> beat!
>
> . . . . .
>
> To see men fall and die and not complain!
> To taste the savage taste of blood! to be so devilish!
> To gloat so over the wounds and deaths of the enemy.[84]

How far these romantic longings for action and danger
were from reality, Whitman was soon to learn in military
camp and hospital. These artificial joys are followed in

---

[82] For definition and discussion see Chap. III, p. 292.
[83] Sec. 21.
[84] Sec. 23.

these poems by a somewhat detailed description of "the whaleman's joys"[85]—a passage likely inspired by the reading of *Moby Dick*.[86]

But especially significant is the "joy" of Death:
O the beautiful touch of Death, soothing and benumbing a few moments, for reasons . . .

The poet seems exhilarated by the thought of "discharging my excrementitious body" and "returning to the purifications, further offices, eternal uses of the earth."[87] Characteristically, this idea is quickly followed by imagery of the shore and bathing in the ocean. The section on "the joy of suffering,"[88] however, is not morbid but merely a Faust-like desire of the poet to bare his breast to every experience,

To struggle against great odds! to meet enemies undaunted!

The *Poem of Joy* ends with the brash confidence and egoistic ambitions of the earlier poems:

To lead America—to quell America with a great tongue.

. . . . .

To confront with your personality all the other personalities of the earth.

. . . .

O to have my life henceforth my poem of joys!

After the *Leaves of Grass* section in the third edition, and the miscellaneous poems which have already been

---

[85] Sec. 24.
[86] Schyberg, *op. cit.*, 196, seems to have been the first to point out this possible source.
[87] Sec. 30.
[88] Sec. 36.

discussed, we find the notorious *Enfans d'Adam* (called *Children of Adam* in 1867 and thereafter). Although twelve of these fifteen poems are new, the theme had been announced in sec. 40 of *Song of Myself:*

> On women fit for conception I start bigger and nimbler babes,
> (This day I am jetting the stuff of far more arrogant republics.)

Indeed, these poems may have been a conscious attempt to develop this earlier theme. Thoreau believed that in the group Whitman "does not celebrate love at all. It is as if the beasts spoke."[89] D. H. Lawrence's comment was: ". . . what is Woman to Walt Whitman? Not much. She is a great function—no more."[90] The *Calamus* poems sound like genuine love poems; but the expression of *Children of Adam* is theoretical and philosophical. In No. 1 (*To the Garden the World*) *love* is presented as the means of pantheistic transmigration: ". . . here behold my resurrection, after slumber,/ The revolving cycles, in their wide sweep, having brought me again. . ." Even in the second poem, which later had such a suggestive title as *From Pent-up Aching Rivers,* the poet sings "something yet unfound, though I have diligently sought it, ten thousand years." He later changed this line to "sought it many a year," thus eliminating the connotation of transmigration. It is interesting that he attempted to make these poems more rather than less personal, as in his usual revisions, such as we have noticed in *Out of the Cradle.*

---

[89] In letter to Harrison Blake, *Thoreau's Familiar Letters* (Boston: Houghton Mifflin & Co., 1894), 345.

[90] "Appreciation of Walt Whitman," *The Nation* (London), XXIX, 617 (July 23, 1921).

But it is perhaps still more remarkable that in this poem on the theme of birth and procreation he also sings "the song of prostitutes." This sexual attraction he declares to be "the true song of the Soul."

No. 3 in this group is less polemical and more lyrical, showing an artist's delight in the contours of the human form, especially of the body in motion. But in No. 4 we find one of the first crude attempts to give this sex program a social meaning: "I shall demand perfect men and women out of my love-spendings. . ." No. 5 (*Spontaneous Me*) was first published in the second edition. Despite the careful descriptions of both male and female erotic sensations, it is vividly personal in the sense of touch, but it is auto-erotic, as we have already observed.[91] It contains the fantastic figure "bunch" for seminal seed, which suggests the botanical imagery characteristic of the *Calamus* poems.

The central procreative theme is by no means uniformly or consistently maintained in the *Children of Adam* group. In No. 6 (*One Hour to Madness and Joy*) the emotion is promiscuous, "O to be yielded to you, whoever you are," and the free love doctrine blends into the literary program of reckless abandon to impulse. In No. 7 (*We Two How Long We Were Fool'd*) the "two" were apparently fooled by abstinence, by artificial repression; and there is a suggestion again of pantheistic transmigration in, "We have circled and circled till we have arrived home again—we two have. . ." No. 8 (*Native Moments*) is a paen of "libidinous joys only."

> I am for those who believe in loose delights—I share the midnight orgies of young men, . . .

---

[91] See p. 131.

and No. 9 (*Once I Pass'd through a Populous City*) was originally, as Holloway discovered,[92] a *Calamus* poem. No. 10 (*Facing West from California's Shores*) is connected with the procreation theme only in a vague pantheistic manner, being an anticipation of the *Passage to India* motif: "I, a child, very old, over waves, toward the house of maternity, the land of migrations, look afar . . ." No. 15 (*As Adam Early in the Morning*) serves as an epilogue for the group and returns to the Garden of Eden allegory, closing the section with lyric praise of the human body, especially the sense of touch. Thus the *Children of Adam* poems contain several mingled themes and motifs carried over from the first two editions and overlap the purposes of several other poems in the third edition. The central thought is a pantheistic interpretation of procreation, but some of the poems are personal in the revolt against conventional attitudes toward sex and in the author's abnormally acute sensitivity to touch. They are in no sense love poems. The ones which are not abstract and philosophical are auto-erotic or hedonistic. The poet reveals a love only for his own sensibility, and accepts indiscriminately all stimuli. Although his reverence for the origins of humanity is almost religious, he gives scarcely a hint of any social control of the sexual emotions.

Calamus is the most unified group in the third edition. All forty-five poems are new, and though the "great companions" motif had appeared in *Proto-Leaf* and was a part of Whitman's earliest poetic program, the tender feeling and shy expression in *Calamus* was entirely absent in *Children of Adam* and was never again duplicated in LEAVES OF GRASS. In short, *Calamus* contains Whitman's

---

[92] See p. 56.

love poems. As Schyberg puts it: "Whitman first celebrated the emotion of love in all its nuances in 'Calamus'. In 'Children of Adam' he was self-confident and supercilious, in 'Calamus', shy, hesitant, wistfully stuttering."[93]

The kind of love which these poems reveal will perhaps always be debated among Anglo-Saxon critics, who cannot enjoy the lyrics of Sappho without first assessing her morality. It is like the controversy over the *Book of Canticles,* whether it is erotic or a veiled allegory of church history. Let those who wish interpret *Calamus* as an allegory of democratic brotherhood. The fact remains that the expression is the poetry of love, and sometimes almost as tender and beautiful as the expression of affection and friendship in Shakespeare's sonnets, which these poems parallel in a number of ways.[94]

The first poem in the group gives the setting: a secluded spot beside a pond "in paths untrodden." The theme is "manly attachment"; the mood is shy, secretive, utterly unlike the boastful, erotic display in *Children of Adam.* In this damp retreat, the "Scented Herbage of my Breast" imagery in the second poem becomes morbidly symbolical:

> Scented herbage of my breast,
> Leaves from you I yield, I write, to be perused best afterwards,
> Tomb-leaves, body-leaves, growing up above me, above death.

In *Song of Myself* and *This Compost* "leaves" grow out of death and corruption but symbolize resurrection and the eternal cycles of life. Here they seem to be a private

---

[93] Schyberg, *op. cit.,* 180.
[94] In length and structure they might be called free verse sonnets.

confession of some hidden secret, and remembering the "bunch" metaphor of *Spontaneous Me,* we guess that the leaves also have a sexual symbolism. But they and the fragrant calamus root likewise suggest Death:

> Yet you are very beautiful to me, you faint-tinged
>   roots—you make me think of Death,
> Death is beautiful from you—(what indeed is beautiful
>   except Death and Love?)

What is the connection between this association of Death and Love and the tragic tone of *Out of the Cradle* and *As I Ebb'd with the Ocean of Life?* The biographers have not told us, but this association is the outstanding characteristic of the third edition of LEAVES OF GRASS. The poet who doted on himself in 1855 and declared "The scent of these arm-pits [is] aroma finer than prayer,"[95] now writes like this:

> Do not fold yourselves so in your pink-tinged roots,
>   timid leaves!
> Do not remain down there so ashamed, herbage of my
>   breast!
> Come, I am determined to unbare this broad breast of
>   mine—I have long enough stifled and choked...

Something of the psychological origin of these poems is indicated in No. 3 (addressed to *Whoever You Are*): the author writes to solicit love, and like a lover he is jealous and all-demanding; furthermore, he gives "fair warning" that he is "not what you supposed ... The way is suspicious" (Cf. also No. 12). In No. 4 (*These I Singing in Spring*) he gives tokens to all, but the calamus root "only to them that love, as I myself am capable of

---

[95] *Song of Myself,* sec. 24.

loving." These select lovers are obviously a minority; they seem to be in some way different from the mass. However, in No. 5 (*For you O Democracy*) the poet makes an attempt to evolve from these calamus roots and leaves[96] a general democratic symbolism. His kind of "new friendship" shall compact the States.

> Affection shall solve every one of the problems of freedom,
> Those who love each other shall be invincible ...

As in Shakespeare's sonnets, however, it is difficult to trace a consecutive story of an experience in these poems. They are not arranged either in the chronology of the experience or in the order of a psychological drama. The social application of the love emotion in No. 5 may be the culmination of the "Calamus" experience, but in the group it is followed by several poems which reveal a crisis that must surely have preceded the solution and the catharsis. No. 7, for example, presents *The Terrible Doubt of Appearances*. For a while all existence seems a dream and a delusion, but then all doubts "are curiously answered by my lovers, my dear friends." Whether these were real friends or vicarious lovers created by poetic fancy, the poem does not reveal.

More revealing is No. 8 (*Long I Thought that Knowledge Alone would Suffice*), and one wonders why it was never again printed. Had the sentiment passed or was it too personal? Whitman must have known himself that

---

[96] To judge by a note preserved by Dr. Bucke in *Notes and Fragments, op. cit., p.* 169, Whitman planned at one time to call these poems "Live Oak Leaves." The note reads: "A string of poems (short etc.) embodying the amative love of woman—the same as Live Oak Leaves do the passion of friendship for man." Evidently *Children of Adam* was written more or less to balance *Calamus*.

it was a good poem, and several admirers protested its rejection. John Addington Symonds confessed it was this poem which first aroused his interest in LEAVES OF GRASS and was one of the great experiences of his life.[97] The story that the poem tells is the following: the poet believed at one time that knowledge alone would suffice, and he aspired to be the orator of his country; then, "to enclose all, it came to me to strike up the songs of the New World," but now the lands must find another singer:

> For I can be your singer of songs no longer—One who
>   loves me is jealous of me, and withdraws me from all
>   but love,
> With the rest I dispense—I sever from what I thought
>   would suffice me, for it does not—it is now empty
>   and tasteless to me,
> I heed knowledge, and the grandeur of The States, and
>   the example of heroes, no more,
> I am indifferent to my own songs—I will go with him
>   I love,
> It is to be enough for us that we are together—We
>   never separate again.

The very next poem, No. 9 (*Hours Continuing Long, Sore and Heavy-Hearted*) was also published only once. It is the most painful of the group, and one of the most deeply moving in LEAVES OF GRASS. The poet feels himself to be so tormented and lonely that he wonders if he is not an anomaly.

> Hours sleepless . . . discouraged, distracted . . . when
>   I am forgotten . . .
> Hours of my torment—I wonder if other men ever have
>   the like, out of the like feelings?

---

[97] John Addington Symonds, *Walt Whitman: A Study* (London: George Routledge & Sons, 1893), 158.

Is there even one other like me—distracted—his friend,
his lover, lost to him?

No. 16 (*Who is Now Reading This*) was likewise rejected in 1867, possibly because it was also too personal,
too revealing. The poet confesses that he is puzzled at
himself:

As if I were not puzzled at myself!
Or as if I never deride myself! (O conscience-struck!
O self-convicted!)
Or as if I do not secretly love strangers!
(O tenderly, a long time, and never avow it;)
Or as if I did not see, perfectly well, interior in myself,
the stuff of wrong-doing,
Or as if it could cease transpiring from me until it must
cease.

The mood of loneliness and discouragement returns
again (or perhaps was the same occasion as in No. 9) in
No. 20, *I Saw in Louisiana a Live-Oak Growing.*

... I wondered how it could utter joyous leaves, standing alone there, without its friend, its lover near—
for I knew I could not . . .

Here we have also another, though similar, clue to the
"leaves" symbolism. The word "utter" especially suggests that Whitman's *leaves* were his poems, and between
the jealousy of the lover who will permit no rival dis-
traction and the dejection of the poet when he feels his
love to be unreturned, the LEAVES OF GRASS experiment
seems near an end.

Paradoxically, however, both of these frustrations drive
the poet to a vicarious release in verse. In fact, he now
has a new poetic ambition (No. 10); he wants to be

known not so much for his poems as for the "measureless oceans of love within him,"

> Nor speak of me that I prophesied of The States, and led them the way of their glories; . . . [but]
> Publish my name and hang up my picture as that of the tenderest lover . . .

This poem is followed by the most ecstatic in the group (No. 11), and perhaps the most beautiful. It would be difficult to find in the whole literature of love a more tender and convincing description of the joyous day when the lover returns. Also tender, but a great deal more obscure, is No. 17, the poet's dream of his lover's death. Curiously the dream seems to reconcile the poet to death, which he henceforth finds everywhere. This experience is obviously connected in some way with the theme of *Out of the Cradle* and Whitman's philosophy of death, but just how we do not know.

Poem No. 23 shows that the "Calamus" emotions underlie Whitman's universal sympathy and his international sentiments. The poet's yearning for love leads him to think of men of other lands who might also be yearning and he decides that they could all "be brethren and lovers" together. In the next poem he would establish "The institution of the dear love of comrades." In No. 26, however, he returns to the theme of "two together." This poem, like *Song of the Open Road,* probably describes an ideal rather than an actuality. Two boys roam the lands, enjoying all activities, "One the other never leaving." But the general application of the "Calamus" emotion revives again in No. 34, which describes how the poet "dreamed in a dream" of a "new City of Friends," and in No. 35 he believes that the germ of exalted friendship is "latent in all men."

In the brief, four-line poem numbered 39, the steps of the process of sublimation are clearly indicated:

> Sometimes with one I love, I fill myself with rage, for fear I effuse unreturned love;
> But now I think there is no unreturned love—the pay is certain, one way or another,
> Doubtless I could not have perceived the universe, or written one of my poems, if I had not freely given myself to comrades, to love.

And this explanation is amplified in poems No. 41 and 42, in which we can plainly see Whitman's rôle as prophet and teacher, seeking followers and pupils, originating in the emotions of *Calamus*.

This interpretation is still further strengthened by No. 44, which repeats and emphasizes the confessional introductory poems. "Here", says the poet, are "the frailest leaves of me, and yet my strongest lasting." In these "leaves" he hides his thoughts, and "yet they expose me more than all my other poems." Could anything say more plainly that the *secret* of Walt Whitman's poetic inspiration is recorded in the *Calamus* poems? Because his emotions of love for other men were abnormally strong, so strong that the poet himself felt lonely and different from other men, many critics have twisted the meaning of these poems into fantastic allegories, like some of the interpretations of the passionate *Songs of Solomon*. But since out of these emotions grew Whitman's Christ-like love for humanity, his St. Francis-like sympathy for all living things, and the psychic turmoil for which he could find ex-

pression and release only in his life-book, we do the
memory of our great poet a disservice by distorting or
concealing the meaning of the *Calamus* group. In fact,
in these poems we can sympathetically understand Walt
Whitman better than in any other section of LEAVES OF
GRASS. Their relationship to the whole book is appropriately indicated by Whitman himself in the final
poem of this group, No. 45, in which he speaks to his
readers of a century or more hence, and invites the reader
of the future to be his lover. In the 1860 edition this poem
provided a transition to *Crossing Brooklyn Ferry,* which
immediately followed the *Calamus* group. This sequence
is so fortunate and meaningful that it is difficult to understand why Whitman used it only in this one edition—
though it is not the only example that the 1860 edition
LEAVES OF GRASS is the most revealing of all editions.

A poem in the third edition which some biographers
have used to support their theories of a New Orleans
romance[98] is *Longing for Home* (later *O Magnet South*).
Such lines as

O Magnet-South! O glistening, perfumed South!
  My South!
O quick mettle, rich blood, impulse, and love!
  Good and evil! O all dear to me!

lend themselves to these romantic speculations, but as a
whole the diction is trite and sentimental, in the "Carry
me back to Old Virginny" tradition. The poet sings of
the "trees where I was born" and the rivers in Florida,
Georgia, and Carolina—which he never saw, so far as
we know—and ends like a popular song-writer with, "O

[98] Holloway, *op. cit.,* 81.

I will go back to old Tennessee, and never wander more!"
Even as an example of Whitman's desire to include the
South in his "incarnating" program, this florid compo-
sition is of little importance.

The remainder of the third edition is fragmentary,
though it contains one more large group, *Messenger
Leaves,* and several smaller and even less developed
groups, such as *Thoughts* and *Says.* *Messenger Leaves*
has no well-defined theme, though the Messiah-rôle is
prominent in several poems, such as *To Him That was
Crucified, To One Shortly to Die, To a Common Prostitute,* and *To Rich Givers.*

Although neither in the sequence of themes nor in the
biological experiences of the poems does the 1860 edition
of LEAVES OF GRASS convey the impression of a life-allegory, the final poems in the book show that Whitman
was working toward such an arrangement. Near the end
we find *To Think of Time* (1855), now renamed *Burial,*
and this is followed by *To My Soul* (in the 1871 edition
renamed *As the Time Draws Nigh* and used to introduce
a new section called *Songs of Parting*). In this poem a
premonition of death seems to be tremendously strong,
thus emphasizing the themes of both the sea-side and
Calamus poems of 1860. The final poem, *So Long!,* which
was hereafter to remain the valedictory of all editions
through the final arrangement in 1881, has a double farewell meaning, serving both as an *au revoir* and an *adieu.*
The poet concludes his message, anticipates the end of
his life, and prophesies his influence on the "plentiful
athletic bards" and the "superb persons" which LEAVES
OF GRASS is intended to generate. With a parting kiss
and a "so long!" he writes his final lines:

Remember my words—I love you—I depart from
    materials,
I am as one disembodied, triumphant, dead.

Of all editions of LEAVES OF GRASS before the final
arrangement of the poems in 1881, the third gives us the
clearest insight into Walt Whitman's growth as a poet.
In the first place, the very bulk of the new poems shows
that this volume is the product of his most creative period,
and *Out of the Cradle Endlessly Rocking* is probably next
to the best poem he ever wrote. The two main themes,
love and death, were prominent in the first two editions,
but in the third they take on such overwhelmingly tragic
significance that we perceive Walt Whitman, in his tormented struggle to reconcile them, becoming a major poet.
Here the sensitive reader will feel closer to Whitman
than in any of the later editions. Here he comes nearest
laying bare his heart. At times he seems almost ready to
give up the struggle and renounce his bold ambition to
be the poet of his age and country, and even in his final
invocation in *So Long!* he seems to have a premonition
either that death is near or that this may be his last appearance in his poetic-drama. This mood of tragic fore-
boding gives to the 1860 edition, however, an intensity, a
sincerity, and a tenderness almost entirely lacking in 1855
and '56. Yet despite this evidence that Whitman was
growing in creative imagination and lyric skill, this might
have been the last publication of his poems had not the
national crisis in 1861 rescued him from his morbid
obsession with his own inner problems. He was destined,
like Faust in Goethe's fable, to find happiness in service
to his country—in extroverted activity.

DRUM-TAPS, 1865

In "A Backward Glance O'er Travel'd Roads," the preface to *November Boughs* (1888), Walt Whitman estimated the influence of the Civil War on his life and works:

> I went down to the war fields in Virginia (end of 1862), lived thenceforward in camp—saw great battles and the days and nights afterward—partook of all the fluctuations, gloom, despair, hopes again arous'd, courage evoked—death readily risk'd—*the cause,* too—along and filling those agonistic and lurid following years, 1863-'64-'65—the real parturition years (more than 1776-'83) of this henceforth homogeneous Union. Without those three or four years and the experiences they gave, "Leaves of Grass" would not now be existing.

Precisely what Whitman meant by the last sentence it is difficult to say, though if he referred to LEAVES OF GRASS in the 1881 or '88 editions, he was no doubt speaking accurately. As we have already noticed, he closed the 1860 edition as if he expected it to be his last, and the tone of the poems of that period support this conclusion. Furthermore, all biographers agree that Whitman's war experiences were of great importance. Charles I. Glicksberg states that, "The influence of the Civil War on his work can . . . hardly be exaggerated. It was for Whitman a national crisis, a living epic, a creative force."[99] Schyberg adds that the poet who declared in 1855,

> Behold I do not give lectures or a little charity,
> When I give I give out of myself.

[99] Charles I. Glicksberg, *Walt Whitman and the Civil War* (Philadelphia: University of Pennsylvania Press, 1933), 8.

was through his wound-dressing services successful in actually realizing his ideal.[100]

After the war finally ended, and the Union had been preserved, Whitman published in New York in 1865 a seventy-two page pamphlet of a collection of poems entitled *Drum-Taps,* to which he presently added a "Sequel," *When Lilacs Last in the Door-Yard Bloom'd,* Washington, 1865-6, of twenty-four more pages. These two publications, usually known as *Drum-Taps* and *Sequel to Drum-Taps,* were added to the 1867 edition of LEAVES OF GRASS as annexes, but in 1870-1 were incorporated into the main body of the LEAVES.

Drum-Taps contains 53 poems, all new.[101] The emotions generated by the out-break of the war, the horrifying shock of the Confederate victory at Bull Run, and later Whitman's first-hand observations at the front in Virginia and in the war hospitals of Washington—all these experiences found expression in these poems, and gave them a greater unity and coherence than is to be found in his works of any other period. Not all of *Drum-Taps,* however, was written in the same place or near the same time. A large number seem to have been composed in Brooklyn between the attack on Fort Sumter in April 1861 and Whitman's leaving home in December 1862 to search for his wounded brother in Virginia. Walt left the manuscript with his mother and he mentions it in his letters to her, cautioning her to take good care of it.[102]

We have no way of knowing precisely which were the

---

[100] Schyberg, *op. cit.,* 204.

[101] The *Drum-Taps* of the final edition contains only about half of the original collection. Twenty-three poems were shifted to other sections and thirteen were added to the group after 1865.

[102] Letter dated March 31, 1863, in *The Wound Dresser,* reprinted in *Complete Works,* VII, 142.

poems in this manuscript, but a number of the poems obviously reflect the "shock electric" felt in the metropolis at the first war news and the surge of patriotic fervor which followed. In the initial poem, untitled but beginning "First, O songs, for a prelude!" we feel this nervous enthusiasm: "It's O for a manly life in the camp!" *Beat! Beat! Drums!* and *City of Ships* catch the excitement of parades and marching feet. The poem called *1861* states that the poet for the "arm'd year . . . of struggle" must be "a strong man, erect, clothed in blue clothes, advancing, carrying a rifle on your shoulder." Perhaps Whitman is thinking of enlisting. At any rate, the war is still adventurous—and remote.

Then there are other poems which, whether or not they were written after Whitman's visit to the front, at least show a sympathetic understanding of the life of camp and battle field. Among these are *By the Bivouac's Fitful Flame*—solemn, thoughtful, a little homesick—, *Vigil Strange I Kept on the Field One Night, A Sight in Camp in the Day-Break Dim and Grey,* and *A March in the Ranks Hard-Prest, and the Road Unknown.* They sound authentic. They do not glorify war or the cause. In fact, they are forerunners of realism and give us the impression that the poet is not writing from theory or standing aloof from the conflict.

Not all poems in *Drum-Taps* are directly about the war, though even when Whitman treats other themes we can see the impact of the national crisis upon his thinking and feeling. For example, *Shut Not Your Doors to Me Proud Libraries* is an obvious war poem in *Drum-Taps* but later Whitman revised and transferred it to *Inscriptions,* where it is a general plea for acceptance of LEAVES OF GRASS;

but in the 1867 version of this poem the poet thinks he has a patriotic service to render through his songs. In *From Paumanok Starting I Fly Like a Bird* we have an interesting example of the patriotic application of an idea from the "program-poem" *Proto-Leaf* (*Starting From Paumanok*); the preservation of the union fits easily into Whitman's whole poetic program since 1855.

Apparently this grave period left its imprint upon every subject that Whitman attempted to handle during this time. In 1861 he was engaged in writing a series of antiquarian articles about Brooklyn. But as he wrote about the past, he kept finding reminders of the present emergency. For example, Washington Park in Brooklyn inspires *The Centenarian's Story*. And his pleasant rambles on Long Island must be given up for "the duration." In *Give Me the Splendid Silent Sun* he renounces the sun, the woods, and Nature for people who are aroused by the passions of war. Similarly, in *Rise O Days from Your Fathomless Deeps* he has "lived to behold man burst forth, and warlike America rise;"

> Hence I will seek no more the food of the northern solitary wilds,
> No more on the mountains roam, or sail the stormy sea.

In subject-matter and imagery *Pioneers! O Pioneers!* seems remote enough from the fratricidal war of the '60's. The theme is somewhat patriotic, since it celebrates "pioneers," and of course the word suggests the great American migration; but Whitman uses it especially for the marching army of civilization— a theme that always facinated him. What specifically distinguishes this composition as originally a *Drum-Taps* poem (it was later shifted to *Birds of Passage*) is the trochaic meter and almost conventional stanza pattern. It is a marching poem. Under the strong emotional stress of a country engaged in deadly combat, Whitman's rhythms become more regular. That is true of nearly all the poems in this collection. The fact that they are less philosophical and introspective, more concerned with some definite experience or exact spot, and with the simple emotions of courage, loyalty, or pity may account to some extent for their being briefer, more unified, and nearer conventional patterns. Perhaps they were written more hastily, "on the spot," than the earlier poems. Some critics have thought them artistically inferior to the earlier work, and no doubt the greater regularity of form is inconsistent with Whitman's literary theory; but it is also interesting to find him so absorbed in external events, and so dedicating himself to a worthy cause that for the time-being he can forget himself and his theory.

One of the most puzzling poems in the original *Drum-Taps* is *Out of the Rolling Ocean, the Crowd,* which seems to be a perfect description of Whitman's meeting his English adorer, Mrs. Gilchrist—but the poem was published several years before he even knew of her existence, and long before her visit to America. At any rate, except for the date of composition the poem does not belong in *Drum-Taps* (unless some unknown love affair in the poet's life took place during the war, and there is no other evidence in *Drum-Taps*) ;[103] in the next edition it was shifted

---

[103] However, Clara Barrus, in *The Life and Letters of John Burroughs* (Boston: Houghton Mifflin Co., 1925) says that Miss Juliette H. Beach was "The friend to whom Whitman wrote 'Out of the rolling ocean.' She wrote many beautiful letters to Walt which J. B. tried in vain to get her consent to publish. She died many years ago," I, 120, note.

to *Children of Adam*—though the sentiment and imagery are nearer *Calamus*.

Death is no less prominent in *Drum-Taps* than in the third edition of LEAVES OF GRASS, but the treatment is neither morbid nor romantic, as in the Novalis-like blend in *Out of the Cradle*. *Come Up from the Fields, Father* cannot be strictly autobiographical, but it accurately conveys the meaning of a soldier's death to his family back home. And toward the end of the collection we get a close-up view of death, as Whitman himself finally observed it, in *Camps of Green* (later shifted to *Songs of Parting*), *As Toilsome I Wander'd Virginia's Woods, Hymn of Dead Soldiers,* and others.

Though no poet could be more deeply moved by the sight of a fallen comrade or the grave of an unknown soldier than Walt Whitman, these experiences did not embitter or disillusion him but aroused his great motherly compassion, which embraced the stricken of both armies and found a prophetic reconciliation in his poems. His *Calamus* love found an outlet in his activities as a "wound-dresser" (Cf. *The Dresser,* later renamed *The Wound-Dresser*).

> The hurt and the wounded I pacify with soothing hand,
> I sit by the restless all the dark night—some are so young;
> Some suffer so much—I recall the experience sweet and sad;
> (Many a soldier's loving arms about this neck have cross'd and rested,
> Many a soldier's kiss dwells on these bearded lips.)

In 1881 Whitman added three lines to this poem which significantly interpret the *Drum-Taps* collection:

(Arous'd and angry, I'd thought to beat the alarm, and
urge relentless war,
But soon my fingers fail'd me, my face droop'd and I
resign'd myself,
To sit by the wounded and soothe them, or silently
watch the dead;) ...

This all embracing-sympathy enabled Whitman to affirm in *Over the Carnage Rose Prophetic a Voice* that
"Affection shall solve the problems of Freedom yet."
This is a new and sublimated *Calamus* poem. In *Years
of the Unperform'd* (*Years of the Modern*) he envisions,
in the spirit of his earliest poems, "the solidarity of races,"
and in *Weave in, Weave in, My Hardy Life* (later shifted
to *From Noon to Starry Night*) he uses the imagery of
war to describe "the campaigns of peace." But the complete catharsis for the war-tragedy is the pantheistic dirge,
Pensive on Her Dead Gazing, I Heard the Mother of All:

Pensive, on her dead gazing, I heard the Mother of all,
Desperate, on the torn bodies, on the forms covering the
battle-fields gazing;
As she call'd to her earth with mournful voice while she
stalk'd;
Absorb them well, O my earth, she cried—I charge you,
lose not my sons! lose not an atom;

. . . . . .

Exhale me them centuries hence—breathe me their
breath—let not an atom be lost;
O years and graves! O air and soil! O my dead, an
aroma sweet!
Exhale them perennial, sweet death, years, centuries
hence.

The poet has now covered the whole gamut of his own

and his country's war emotions, from beating the drums
for the first volunteers to burying the dead, and he ends
with an epilogue in which he states his final claim for
these poems:

> I have nourish'd the wounded, and sooth'd many a
>   dying soldier;
> And at intervals I have strung together a few songs,
> Fit for war, and the life of the camp.

Although *Drum-Taps* was issued as a separate publication, containing eighteen new poems, the *Sequel* may be
thought of as part of the same work. In the first place, it
was soon combined in a second issue of *Drum-Taps*. Wells
and Goldsmith state in their *Concise Bibliography of Walt
Whitman* that, "A few copies were issued containing
'Drum Taps' only. On the death of Lincoln, Whitman
held up the edition and added 'When Lilacs Last in the
Dooryard Bloom'd,' with separate title-page and pagination."[104] Moreover, the *Sequel* is a continuation of Drum-
Taps in other and more intrinsic ways. For one thing,
many poems were shifted from the *Sequel* to the final
text of *Drum-Taps,* such as *Spirit Whose Work is Done,
As I Lay with my Head in Your Lap, Camerado, Dirge
for Two Veterans, Lo! Victress on the Peaks!,* and *Reconciliation.* The first of these is an invocation to the spirit
of war to inspire the poet's martial songs; the second is a
remotivated "Calamus" sentiment, though not a love
poem; and the last continues the theme of reconciliation
begun in *Drum-Taps*—". . . my enemy is dead, a man
divine as myself is dead."

---

[104] Carolyn Wells and Alfred F. Goldsmith, *A Concise Bibliography
of the Works of Walt Whitman* (Boston and New York: Houghton
Mifflin Co., 1922), 11.

If *Chanting the Square Deific* has any special significance in this collection, it is difficult to perceive. As an
epitome of Whitman's eclectic religion, clearly announced
in *Song of Myself* and *Proto-Leaf* and alluded to elsewhere, it is a poem of great importance; but in tone it
has much of the arrogance of the second edition, and as
Sixbey has shown,[105] the ideas had been crystalizing for
ten years. Possibly, as Sixbey has also mentioned, Whitman's deification of the spirit of rebelliousness may have
been influenced by the rebellion against the Union.[106] At
any rate, Whitman's earlier indignation had now given
way to conciliating sympathy and forgiveness. Possibly
also this spirit may have influenced the expression of the
side of the "Consolator most mild," especially the following one line deleted in 1881:

(Conqueror yet—for before me all the armies and
    soldiers of the earth shall yet bow—and all the
    weapons of war become impotent:) ...

But the main poems in the *Sequel,* for which Whitman
stopped the press, were the Lincoln elegies, later grouped
as *Memories of President Lincoln.* The first of these,
When Lilacs Last in the Dooryard Bloom'd, is universally
admitted to be his masterpiece. In structure it resembles
the other great poem on death, *Out of the Cradle Endlessly Rocking,* especially in the use of the bird song. But
his use of symbols, the "Lilac blooming perennial and the
drooping star in the west," and the song of the thrush, are
handled with a skill found nowhere else in LEAVES OF
GRASS. The lilac with the "heart-shaped leaves" of love,

---

[105] G. L. Sixbey "Chanting the Square Deific—A study in Whitman's
Religion," *American Literature,* IX, 174 (May, 1937).
[106] *Ibid.,* 172.

the hermit thrush singing his "song of the bleeding heart,"
the resurrection of the "yellow-spear'd wheat" in the
spring, the coffin journeying night and day through the
Union that Lincoln had preserved—these are interwoven
in a mighty symphony of imagery and sound, each theme
briefly advanced, then developed in turn, finally summarized in a climax[107] and then repeated gently once more
as the "sweetest, wisest soul of all my days and lands"
comes to rest,

> There in the fragrant pines, and the cedars dusk and
>   dim.

Not since the third edition, in which love and death
were so inseparably intertwined, had Whitman used sea
imagery in any striking manner. Perhaps this may have
been because he had, as he said, renounced his pleasant
contacts with nature for the duration of the war, or it
may have been because in Washington he had little time
for the sea-shore. A better explanation, however, is that
Drum-Taps is less subjective and introspective than
Calamus or *Out of the Cradle* and *As I Ebb'd with the
Ocean of Life.* Whatever spiritual and emotional crisis
Whitman had passed through, the wound-dressing preoccupations had completely cured him. Now once more,
when he is stirred to the depths of his being by the tragic
death of Lincoln, sea imagery comes back to him, and
the word that the ocean whispers is the same: "lovely and
soothing Death" undulating "round the world." But the
"Dark Mother, always gliding near, with soft feet," brings
redemption and delivery, not chaos and despair.

[107] First part of sec. 16.

> Approach, encompassing death—strong Deliveress!
> When it is so—when thou hast taken them, I joyously
>   sing the dead,
> Lost in the loving, floating ocean of thee,
> Laved in the flood of thy bliss, O Death.[108]

In this great elegy Walt Whitman attained a spiritual poise and emotional tranquility that was never again wholly to leave him—except possibly for one brief period (see *Prayer of Columbus*).

After the lilac poem, the other verses in the *Sequel to Drum-Taps* are an anti-climax. *O Captain! My Captain!*, in almost conventional iambic metre and regular stanzaic pattern, is similar to the beating of the drums in *Drum-Taps*. The music is more like Poe than Whitman, and Whitman himself later became sick of it. True, it has its merits, but it is almost impossible to appreciate the poem soon after reading the lilac symphony.

The original *Sequel* ends with a prophecy, in *To the Leaven'd Soil They Trod*, which remained largely unfilled,

> The Northern ice and rain, that began me, nourish me
>   to the end;
> But the hot sun of the South is to ripen my songs.

The poet felt deeply this wish to reconcile the North and the South through his songs, and it is an appropriate application of his earliest poetic program, but except in a remote symbolical sense the wish was never realized. Walt Whitman was, however, soon to become a more truly *National* poet.

---

[108] Sec. 14.

Fourth Edition, 1867

The 1867 LEAVES OF GRASS might be called "The Workshop Edition," for the revisions indicate great creative activity, although in organization it is the most chaotic of all the editions. Exclusive of the annexes (two of which have been discussed above), this edition contains only eight new poems,[109] all short and of minor significance. What makes it important is Whitman's great exertion to rework the book by deletion, emendation, and rearrangement of the poems. The confused state of the published work, therefore, bears testimony to the poet's literary and spiritual growth during the War.

The manner of publication is no less confused than the contents. The book was printed for Whitman (whose name appears only in the copyright date, 1866),[110] by a New York printer, William E. Chapin, and was bound and distributed during the year in at least four different forms: (1) LEAVES OF GRASS, 338 pp.; (2) LEAVES OF GRASS with *Drum-Taps* (72 pp.) and *Sequel to Drum-Taps* (24 pp.); (3) LEAVES OF GRASS with *Drum-Taps, Sequel to Drum-Taps,* and *Songs Before Parting* (36 pp.). Wells and Goldsmith say: "This edition was crude and poorly put together. [The copies] were probably bound up in small lots as sold. This may account for the many variations."[111]

The first poem in this edition, one of the new compositions, is *Inscription (One's-Self I Sing)*, which was henceforth to stand as the opening poem in all subsequent

---

[109] They are: *Inscription (One's-Self I Sing), The Runner, Tears! Tears! Tears!, Aboard at a Ship's Helm, When I Read the Book, The City Dead-House, Leaflets (What General), Not the Pilot.*

[110] This is also the first edition to omit a portrait of the author.

[111] Wells and Goldsmith, *op. cit.,* 114.

editions. *Inscription* outlines the main subjects of the collection of the LEAVES and gives a suggestion of their order.
These subjects are: (1) "one's-self," or individualism; (2)
"Man's physiology complete, from top to toe"; (3) "the
word of the modern ... En-Masse";[112] (4) "My days I
sing, and the Lands—with interstice I knew of hapless
war"; (5) finally a personal appeal to the reader to journey with the poet. These subjects correspond roughly to
(1) the personal poems, *Starting from Paumanok* and
Walt Whitman (*Song of Myself*); (2) the physiological
Children of Adam poems, which now follow *Walt Whitman;* (3) the consciousness of social-solidarity and world-
citizenship of all humanity found both in *Calamus* and
the succeeding major poems, such as *Salut au Monde!* and
Song of the Broad-Axe; (4) the war-experiences in the
annex *Drum-Taps;* and (5) the final appeal to the reader
in *So Long!*, which now stands at the end of the last annex,
Songs before Parting, where it would remain. So well did
Whitman like the scheme outlined in this prologue that
he finally expanded it to twenty-four *Inscriptions*—though
few of the poems were written specifically for this purpose, most of them having been used first in various other
groups. But in the 1867 *Inscription* we have a skeleton
plan of the final LEAVES OF GRASS, a revelation of the
emerging purposes and the congealing form.

The extent to which Whitman revised his work for the
fourth edition is obvious in the first poem after the *Inscription,* which is now called *Starting from Paumanok*—
originally *Proto-Leaf* in the third edition, where it also
served as an introduction. Nearly every section contains

---

[112] In his final revision (1871) of this poem Whitman reversed the
order of "1" and "2" as summarized here.

some revisions, but the first illustrates the nature, general purpose, and extent of the changes. *Proto-Leaf* began:

> Free, fresh, savage,
> Fluent, luxuriant, self-content, fond of persons and places,
> Fond of fish-shape Paumanok, where I was born,
> Fond of the sea—lusty—begotten and various,
> Boy of the Mannahatta, the city of ships, my city,
> Or raised inland, or of the south savannas,
> Or full-breath'd on Californian air, or Texan or Cuban air,
> Tallying, vocalizing all — resounding Niagara — resounding Missouri,
> Or rude in my home in Kanuck woods,
> Or wandering and hunting, my drink water, my diet meat,
>
> .   .   .   .
>
> Aware of the mocking-bird of the wilds at daybreak,
> Solitary, singing in the west, I strike up for a new world.

This becomes:

> Starting from fish-shape Paumanok, where I was born,
> Well-begotten, and rais'd by a perfect mother;
> After roaming many lands—lover of populous pavements;
> Dweller in Mannahatta, city of ships, my city—or on southern savannas;
> Or a soldier camp'd or carrying my knapsack and gun— or a miner in California;
> Or rude in my home in Dakotah's woods, my diet meat, my drink from the spring;
>
> .   .   .   .

Having studied the mocking-bird's tones, and the moun-
tain hawk's,
And heard at dusk the unrival'd one, the hermit thrush
from the swamp-cedars,
Solitary, singing in the West, I strike up for a New
World.

Aside from the improvements in diction and rhythm,
and the beginning of the mannerism of writing past participles with *'d,* in the new version the poet attempts to
give the impression that he has now experienced what he
expressed as poetic theory in 1860. The "Boy of Mannahatta . . . raised inland, or of the south savannas . . .,
Tallying, vocalizing all" on the basis of the '55 program,
now extends his rôle to "roaming many lands . . . Or a
soldier camp'd . . . Or rude in my home in Dakotah's
woods . . ." It is not a new rôle, rather the application
of the "incarnating" doctrine of the first Preface, incorporating the poet's *Drum-Taps* experiences, his contact
with frontiersmen (*i.e.,* soldiers from Dakota and other
remote places), and his wider knowledge of America.
The 1867 edition is thus an attempt to bring the poetic
record up to date.

In this interim of revision Whitman tears apart most of
the groups which he had started in 1860 but he has not
yet had sufficient time to construct new groups. He de-
molishes *Chants Democratic,* one of the major groups in
the third edition, and redistributes the poems. The group
previously called *Leaves of Grass,* with twenty-four numbered poems, disappears as a unit, although five miscellaneous groups (including one in the annex, *Songs Before
Parting*) are given this ambiguous title. The only two sec-

tions to remain more or less intact are *Children of Adam*
(formerly called *Enfans d'Adam*) and *Calamus*. Of
these two, the former has been changed least, though it
is shifted from the center of the book toward the front—
in accordance with the plan of the *Inscription*.

Calamus, however, needed considerable revision to bring
it into line with Whitman's newest intentions. Perhaps
the most disturbing reminder which he found of his
1860 mood was the three poems[113] which he felt compelled to delete entirely, *Long I Thought that Knowledge
Alone Would Suffice* (No. 8), *Hours Continuing Long,
Sore, and Heavy-Hearted* (No. 9), and *Who is Now
Reading This?* (No. 16). In 1867, having watched and
even participated in the tragedies of the national struggle
and found healing catharsis in the *Drum-Taps* experiences,
Whitman blotted from the record these morbid confessions of the third edition.

Calamus poem No. 5 of 1860 provides another interesting example of the effect of Whitman's war experiences
on his original "Calamus" program. In 1860 he had already socialized this program:

> States!
> Were you looking to be held together by the lawyers?
> By an agreement on a paper? Or by arms?
> Away!
> I arrive, bringing these, beyond all the forces of courts
> and arms,
> These! to hold you together as firmly as the earth itself
> is held together.

But he brashly wished to make his "manly affection" an
evangelism associated with his own name:

---

[113] See pp. 154-156.

There shall from me be a new friendship—It shall be
  called after my name,

. . . . .

Affection shall solve every one of the problems of freedom,
Those who love each other shall be invincible,
They shall finally make America completely victorious,
  in my name.

Whitman never ceased believing that affection could solve
all problems, but his personal desire for recognition became sublimated in his enlarged patriotism. In the 1867
edition a large part of this poem is rejected and the remainder is divided into two compositions, the first being
one of the most musical of the new *Calamus* group, called
A Song, (For You O Democracy), with a stanzaic pattern and a repetend, and the second being a *Drum-Taps*
poem, *Over the Carnage Rose Prophetic A Voice.* Thus
without renouncing his earlier doctrines of comradeship,
Whitman now blends them with his new nationalism.

It would be a mistake, however, to conclude that the
revised *Calamus* group is depersonalized. No. 10, called
in '67 *Recorders Ages Hence,* is a good illustration. In
1860 it began:

You bards of ages hence! when you refer to me, mind
  not so much my poems,
Nor speak of me that I prophesied of The States, and
  led them the way of their glories;
But come, I will take you down underneath this im-
  passive exterior—I will tell you what to say of me:
Publish my name and hang up my picture as that of the
  tenderest lover, . . .

This becomes:

> Recorders ages hence!
> Come, I will take you down underneath this impassive
>   exterior—I will tell you what to say of me;
> Publish my name and hang up my picture as that of the
>   tenderest lover, . . .

The poet believes in his Calamus-program as strongly as ever, but he is acutely aware that his prophecies of The States have not "led them the way of their glories."

Some of the revised *Calamus* poems are considerably more personal than the earlier versions, like No. 39, *Sometimes with One I Love,* which originally ended:

> Doubtless I could not have perceived the universe, or
>   written one of my poems, if I had not freely given
>   myself to comrades, to love.

This becomes:

> (I loved a certain person ardently, and my love was
>   not return'd;
> Yet out of that, I have written these songs.)

The chief difference, therefore, between these two versions of *Calamus* is not a change in motive or conviction, but in tone and emphasis. The poet has carefully erased most of the record of morbidity and discouragement of 1860, along with the temporary whim to abandon his poet-prophet rôle for the rôle of tender lover.

Perhaps the only safe conclusion to draw from the five groups (counting the third annex) called *Leaves of Grass* in the fourth edition is that Whitman had evidently not decided yet what to do with these poems. If these group-

ings have special significance it is not obvious to the
present observer. Most of the poems appeared in the
1855, '56, and '60 editions and have merely been re-
shuffled. They are drawn from several previous groups and
were later placed in various other groups. It is of some
importance, however, that No. 20 (*So Far and So Far,
and on Toward the End*) of the third edition was dropped
permanently in '67. In 1860 Whitman confessed in this
poem that his poetic powers had "not yet fully risen," and
that

> Whether I shall attain my own height, to justify these
>   [songs], yet unfinished,
> Whether I shall make THE POEM OF THE NEW WORLD,
>   transcending all others—depends, rich persons, upon
>   you,
> .   .   .   .
>
> And you, contemporary America.

In 1867 Whitman was almost as unrecognized by "contemporary America" as in the depth of his discouragement
seven years previous; but the poet of *Drum-Taps* and the
Sequel had inner resources of courage and strength which
he had not had before the War.

Some of the revised *Leaves* also reveal the poet's
growth, both in art and mental poise. One of these is
On the Beach at Night Alone (*Clef Poem* in 1856; *Leaves
of Grass,* No. 12, in 1860). The fifteen verses of the '67
version have a far greater unity than the thirty-four of
1856-60, and this is sufficient justification for the revision.
But in the original version the emphasis is on the poet's
personal and physical satisfaction with this life:

This night I am happy; . . .
What can the future bring me more than I have?[114]

whereas in the '67 text the central theme is the mystic
intuition which comes to the poet "On the beach at night
alone," that "A vast similitude interlocks all." The "similitude" section was also in the original composition, but it
was preceded by seven stanzas of personal conviction that
nothing in eternity can improve upon the goodness and
completeness of the poet's present existence. This is not a
doctrine which Whitman ever rejected, but in various
periods he expressed it with different emphasis.

Since we have already discussed two of the annexes to
this volume, *Drum-Taps* and the *Sequel,* which were attached to the fourth edition without revision, they need
not be mentioned further here. But the third annex, *Songs
Before Parting,* is a major attempt in reorientation and is,
therefore, one of the most important sections of the book.

In this annex we have the beginning of a new and permanent group, *Songs of Parting.* But none of the poems
were new in 1867, two of them being from '56, *As I Sat
Alone by Blue Ontario's Shore* and *Assurances,* and eleven
from 1860, of which five were from *Leaves of Grass* (Nos.
18, 19, 21, 22, and 23). In the fifth edition this group
became the final section of LEAVES OF GRASS, where it
remained (exclusive of annexes) throughout all future
editions. But in 1871 the number of poems was pared to
eight, of which only three were retained from '67, and in
the final version the number was increased to seventeen,
including only four of the original group. Thus about all

---

[114] Although Whitman let these lines stand in 1860, they obviously
express his sanguinary mood of '56.

that finally remained of *Songs Before Parting* was the allegorical intention of the name and the use of *So Long!* as a half-personal, half-prophetic benediction.

The introductory and concluding poems in *Songs Before Parting* were extensively revised for this annex, and these changes probably reveal not only Walt Whitman's intentions in 1867 for the group but his broader purposes also. *As I Sat Alone by Blue Ontario's Shore* appeared first in the '56 edition as *Poem of Many in One,* in '60 as No. 1 of *Chants Democratic* (the longest and perhaps the most ambitious group of the third edition), and was finally called *By Blue Ontario's Shore* in the last arrangement of the LEAVES, where it is still one of the major poems.

The 1856-60 version of this poem is merely a poetic arrangement of the 1855 Preface, even retaining many of the same phrases and clauses. It begins with the motif of "A nation announcing itself," but the central theme is that of "the bard [who] walks in advance, the leader of leaders," teaching "the idea of perfect and free individuals, the idea of These States." In the 1867 version the whole composition has been greatly improved both in coherence and dramatic effect by the addition of an introduction, with the present shore motif, and a conclusion, changing the "Many in One" motif to the more impressive mystic vision of "the free Soul of poets," and of the "Bards" capable of singing "the great Idea" of Democracy, "the wondrous inventions . . . the marching armies," the times, the land, and the life of The States.

In 1867 Whitman developed one of the subordinated ideas of the 1856-60 poem,

Others take finish, but the Republic is ever constructive,
    and ever keeps vista,[115]

as the major theme—the throes of Democracy—now symbolized by the apostrophes to the "Mother" figure. To
show how Whitman has amplified the call for "Bards"
in *Poem of Many in One* into the new theme of Democracy in travail, the whole first section (all new) needs to
be quoted:

As I sat alone, by blue Ontario's shore,
As I mused of these mighty days, and of peace return'd,
    and the dead that return no more,
A Phantom, gigantic, superb, with stern visage, accost'd
    me;
Chant me a poem, it said, *of the range of the high Soul
    of Poets,*
*And chant of the welcome bards that breathe but my
    native air—invoke those bards—;*
*And chant me, before you go, the Song of the throes of
    Democracy.*
(Democracy—the destined conqueror—yet treacherous
    lip-smiles everywhere,
And Death and infidelity at every step.)[116]

These parenthetical interpolations run like a contrapuntal
theme throughout the poem, exposing the danger to
Mother-Democracy and the Sister-States—as later in
Democratic Vistas—, but also indicating the hope and
the means of political salvation:

(O mother! O sisters dear!
If we are lost, no victor else has destroy'd us;

---

[115] Sec. 8.   [116] See also sec. 7.

It is by ourselves we go down to eternal night.)[117]

.   .   .   .   .

(Soul of love, and tongue of fire!
Eye to pierce the deepest deeps, and sweep the world!
—Ah, mother! prolific and full in all besides—yet how
    long barren, barren?)[118]

.   .   .   .

(Mother! with subtle sense—with the naked sword in
    your hand,
I saw you at last refuse to treat but directly with indi-
    viduals.)[119]

.   .   .   .

(Mother! bend down, bend close to me your face!
I know not what these plots and deferments are for;
I know not fruition's success—but I know that through
    war and peace your work goes on, and must yet
    go on.)[120]

The tragic war has been fought and the honor of the
national flag preserved ("Angry cloth I saw there leap-
ing!"),[121] but it is not to celebrate the past that the poet
invokes the Muse:

O my rapt song, my charm—mock me not!
Not for the bards of the past—not to invoke them have
    I launch'd you forth, . . .
But, O strong soul of Poets,
Bards for my own land, ere I go, I invoke.[122]

One of the unconscious ironies of this poem is that
Whitman's new call for native bards leads him into an
excessive nationalism—which he dropped when he re-

[117] Sec. 2.
[118] Sec. 9.
[119] Sec. 15.
[120] Sec. 20 (sec. 18 in final version).
[121] Sec. 11.
[122] Sec. 22.

vised the composition again for the 1881 edition. For
example, the characteristic robust-health motif of 1856,

> How dare a sick man, or an obedient man, write poems?
> Which is the theory or book that is not diseased?[123]

became in '67:

> America isolated I sing;
> I say that works made here in the spirit of other lands,
>   are so much poison in These States.
> How dare these insects assume to write poems for
>   America?[124]
> For our armies, and the offspring following the
>   armies [?]

If the "great Idea" was still largely unachieved in These
States, why would "works made . . . in the spirit of other
lands" be worse poison than the sinister forces already
working here against Democracy? Furthermore, these
"isolationist" sentiments are oddly at variance with the
universal sympathy and cosmic themes of the poet's earlier
works, as he himself no doubt later realized. Possibly this
inconsistency arose from the fact that in *As I Sat Alone
by Blue Ontario's Shore* Whitman was still groping his
way toward the theory of *Democratic Vistas*.

In the final poem of *Songs Before Parting,* the revised
So Long! of the third edition, we find eliminated the tentative, discouraged tone of 1860, when the poet evidently
despaired of accomplishing his ambitious program of
1855. For example, in 1860 strophe 2 read:

> I remember I said to myself at the winter-close, before
>   my leaves sprang at all, that I would become a candid
>   and unloosed summer-poet.

---

[123] Lines 20 and 21.   [124] Sec. 4.

I said I would raise my voice jocund and strong, with
reference to consummations.

In 1867 this reads:

I remember I said, before my leaves sprang at all,
I would raise my voice jocund and strong, with reference
to consummations.

A number of lines have been dropped in which Whitman had claimed to be not the Messiah but a John the
Baptist preparing the way:

Yet not me, after all—let none be content with me,
I myself seek a man better than I am, or a woman better
than I am,
I invite defiance, and to make myself superseded,
All I have done, I would cheerfully give to be trod
under foot, if it might only be the soil of superior
poems.
I have established nothing for good,
I have but established these things, till things farther
onward shall be prepared to be established,
And I am myself the preparer of things farther onward.

In 1867 Walt Whitman no longer regards his poems
either as failures or as tentative experiments for which
he must apologize. Through the *Drum-Taps* years he had
gained tremendously in poise and self-confidence (real
confidence instead of the bravado of '55-'56), and he now
begins in earnest to prepare his book for posterity.

DEMOCRATIC VISTAS, 1871

Although in his youthful and journalistic days Walt
Whitman published a great deal more prose than poetry,
it was not until 1871, with the publication of *Democratic*

Vistas, that he made a serious contribution to prose literature. Financially the book was no more successful than
the editions of LEAVES OF GRASS had been, and even to
the present day Whitman has gained only a few admirers
for his prose, which always remained extremely loose,
mannered, and improvised; but nothing else he ever wrote
so clarifies and rounds out both his literary and democratic
theory as this essay.

Many of the ideas in *Democratic Vistas* were first expressed in the 1855 Preface, and touched upon in many
poems, such as *Song of Myself, Salut au Monde!, Song
for Occupations,* and *Starting from Paumanok*—as indicated in the discussion of the fourth edition of LEAVES OF
GRASS—; but the immediate starting point of the essay
seems to have been some short papers which Whitman
published in *The Galaxy* in 1867 and '68. The first of
these, entitled "Democracy," was an attempt to answer
Carlyle's attack on democracy in *Shooting Niagara.* But
the more Whitman studied the problem, the more he
came to agree with Carlyle's charges, though not with his
whole condemnation. The second forerunner of *Democratic Vistas* was an essay on "Personalism," the central
doctrine in the book, and a philosophical term which the
American poet seems to have introduced into America.[125]
In writing these papers Whitman's thinking for the past
fifteen or twenty years apparently came to a head and he
felt the necessity of publishing a more complete treatment.
It is interesting also that in doing so he was returning to
a purpose which he had once dreamed of achieving
through oratory, *i.e.,* leading his country through the
eloquence of words.

[125] See Chap. III, p. 302.

This purpose is partly indicated by the word *Vistas:* "Far, far, indeed, stretch, in distance, our Vistas!"[126] He is writing more of the future of democracy than of its achievements to date, and makes a powerful homiletic appeal to his countrymen to turn their professed democratic ideals into reality.

> Sole among nationalities, these States have assumed the task to put in forms of lasting power and practicality, on areas of amplitude rivaling the operations of the physical kosmos, the moral political speculations of ages, long, long deferr'd, the democratic republican principle, and the theory of development and perfection by voluntary standards, and self-reliance.[127]

But no one is more aware than Walt Whitman that these "moral [and] political speculations of ages" have not yet been honestly tried in America:

> . . . society in these States, is canker'd, crude, superstitious, and rotten . . . Never was there, perhaps, more hollowness at heart than at present . . . here in the United States . . . The depravity of the business classes of our country is not less than has been supposed, but infinitely greater . . . Our New World democracy . . . [despite]—materialistic development . . . is, so far, an almost complete failure in its social aspects . . .[128]

What kind of people make up the American nation? Looking around him, Whitman observes almost everywhere low morals, poor health, and bad manners. Here his dilemma is most acute, but he attempts to solve it by an analysis of the mass *vs.* the individual. He agrees that

---

[126] *Prose Works* (Philadelphia: David McKay, n.d. [1892]), 226.
[127] *Ibid.*, 203.
[128] *Ibid.*, 210-211.

"man, viewed in the lump, displeases, and is a constant puzzle and affront" to what he calls "the merely educated classes."[129] Despite the fact, however, that the masses lack taste, intelligence, and culture, the "cosmical, artist-mind" sees their "measureless wealth of latent power." The war justified Whitman's faith in the common man, for the "unnamed, unknown rank and file" were responsible for the heroic courage, sacrifice, and "labor of death," and these were "to all essential purposes, volunteer'd," even in the face of "hopelessness, mismanagement, [and] defeat."[130]

Whitman thinks that the function of government in a democracy is often misunderstood. It is not merely "to repress disorder, &c. but to develop, to open up to cultivation."[131] Democracy is not so much a political system as a "grand experiment"[132] in the development of individuals. He is not concerned either with the romantic theory of the innate goodness of the masses or with the political theory of the sovereignty of the people, but with Democracy as a moral and ethical ideal—in fact, a religion: "For I say at the core of democracy, finally, is the religious element. All the religions, old and new, are there."[133] He admits that he has had his doubts, especially "before the war" (around 1860?), and that "I have everywhere found, primarily thieves and scallawags arranging the nominations to offices, and sometimes filling the offices themselves"; yet he still believes that, "Political democracy, as it exists and practically works in America, with all its threatening evils, supplies a training school for making first class men."[134]

---

[129] *Ibid.*, 215.
[130] *Ibid.*, 215-216.
[131] *Ibid.*, 218.
[132] *Ibid.*, 219.
[133] *Ibid.*, 220.
[134] *Ibid.*, 223.

At this point Whitman reiterates, in a more specific context and as the corner-stone of his democratic idealism, the literary theory which he had advanced in the 1855 Preface, and continued to reword in the versions of *By Blue Ontario's Shore*. Although the American people have, he still believes, a great potential capacity for democracy, their genius (or potentiality) is still unexpressed.[135] There is as yet no Democratic Literature to guide them; hence America's greatest need is a new school of artists and writers. This call for native authors is subject to misunderstanding, and at times Whitman's own enthusiasm misleads him into an excessive patriotism; but in the larger implications, it is clear that his nationalism is a consequence and not the original motive of his plea for indigenous art. The function of literature is to unite the people with common social and ethical ideals and to establish a moral pattern for its citizens. Thus Whitman's nationalistic poets would combat the greatest enemy of These States, their own moral and, therefore, political corruption. Current literature and "culture" are rejected because they do not provide sufficient moral guidance for a democratic people.

Personalism[136] is the term which Whitman uses to cover his whole program, an all-round development of the self and the individual, including health, eugenics, education, cultivation of moral and social conscience, etc. He rejects institutionalized religion, but a genuine, personal

---

[135] This belief, in view of Whitman's own efforts at such expression for over fifteen years, is interesting. Does it show that he is, in such a moment of sincerity and frankness, more modest than is commonly thought? Or does he regard his own efforts as failures? Either way, we see him in a new light.

[136] For definition and discussion of the personalism as an "idea," see Chap. III, p. 302.

religious life is of paramount importance. Personalism fuses all these developments, including participation in politics and removing the inequality of women. Since the future American democracy depends upon the development of great persons (or personalities) such as the world has never known before, literature and art must not be imitative or derivative of other times or nations, for none of them possessed or attempted to achieve the great American dream of a transcendent democracy.

Here Whitman's Calamus sentiments become completely socialized and emotionally reinforce his democratic idealism:

> Many will say it is a dream, and will not follow my inferences: but I confidently expect a time when there will be seen, running like a half-hid warp through all the myriad audible and visible worldly interests of America, threads of manly friendship, fond and loving, pure and sweet, strong and life-long, carried to degrees hitherto unknown—not only giving tone to individual character, and making it unprecedentedly emotional, muscular, heroic, and refined, but having the deepest relations to general politics.[137]

This new democratic literature needs also the help of empiricism and modern science, even necessitating a "new Metaphysics."[138] True, science and materialism have further endangered American democracy by intensifying the greed for things and by "turning out . . . generations of humanity like uniform iron castings."[139] But by believing, like all romanticists, in the goodness and friendliness of Nature to man, Whitman thinks that further knowledge

[137] *Prose Works*, 247 note. [139] *Ibid.*, 256.
[138] *Ibid.*, 249.

of the processes of cosmic melioration will aid mankind in conceiving and establishing a society of perfect equality and human development. Thus Whitman's democracy is finally pantheistic and cosmic,[140] and he believes that his social and literary ideals are predestined by the laws of the universe to triumph eventually.

FIFTH EDITION, 1871-72

As with the fourth edition of LEAVES OF GRASS, the fifth is difficult to define satisfactorily. The first issue appeared in 1871, and contained 384 pages, but a second issue included *Passage to India* and 71 other poems, a few of them new, adding 120 extra pages, numbered separately. In 1872 this edition was reissued, from Washington, D. C., dated 1872 on the title page but copyrighted 1870. All the latter copies contain *Passage to India,* still with separate pagination, and a later issue includes another supplement, *After All Not to Create Only,* with 14 extra pages. One of the '72 issues may have been an English pirated edition.[141]

In the following discussion the fifth edition will be regarded as the 1871-72 LEAVES OF GRASS (practically identical in all issues), plus the annex, *Passage to India.*

At first glance this does not appear to be an especially important edition, for aside from the annexes it contains only thirteen new poems, all fairly short and individually of no great distinction. But this hasty impression is entirely misleading, for in the revisions and the new poems (including the *Passage to India* supplement) LEAVES OF GRASS comes to a great climax, and probably what Walt

---

[140] See Chap. III.
[141] See Wells and Goldsmith, *op. cit.,* 118.

Whitman intended to be the end of this book and the beginning of a new one, as the prefaces of '72 and '76 plainly indicate.

To begin at the first of the fifth edition, we notice that the *Inscription* of the fourth edition has now been increased to a whole section containing nine poems, though only two of them are new. Whitman is still trying to clarify the purposes and themes of the book by these prologue poems. *One's-Self I Sing* has become the permanent summary of the themes of LEAVES OF GRASS, but the other inscriptions also indicate the nature of the 1871 version.

In 1867 the themes were the great national tragic conflict and the ensuing reconciliation. The war scenes and experiences were naturally still the poet's most vivid memories, though he had come through the tragedy spiritually purged and ennobled. Now the war years have retreated into the background, and both the poet and the nation are busy with reconstruction. In *As I Ponder'd in Silence* a phantom arises and tells the poet that all bards who have achieved a lasting reputation have sung of war. He replies that he too sings of war, the greatest of all, the eternal struggle of life and death. And as we shall see, in his new poems Whitman channels his war emotions and energies into new outlets.

The third *Inscription* (second new poem), *In Cabin'd Ships at Sea,* is prophetic not only of the thought of the fifth edition but is also a radical departure from Whitman's former sea imagery. Heretofore, and especially in the great emotional poems of 1860, his imagination always returned to the sea-shore, where the fierce old mother incessantly moaned, whenever he was deeply moved by an experience or a memory. *Sea-Shore Memories* is an accurate title for the group of poems in the *Passage to India* supplement, which contains *Out of the Cradle* and *Elemental Drifts* (*As I Ebb'd,* &c.) In 1871, however, we find the poet venturing beyond the shore, even embarking on ships and vicariously sailing the oceans. Why Walt Whitman was no longer shore-bound we can best decide after further examination of this edition.

But first let us complete the tour of the '71 LEAVES. The order of the main part of the book has now become settled, almost as in the final arrangement. After *Inscriptions* come the unclassified *Starting from Paumanok* and *Walt Whitman* (soon to become *Song of Myself*). These are followed by *Children of Adam* and *Calamus.* The addition to the latter group of *The Base of All Metaphysics* makes further progress toward the sublimation and reinterpretation of the original personal confessions.

> Yet underneath Socrates clearly see—and underneath
> Christ the divine I see,
> The dear love of man for his comrade—the attraction
> of friend to friend, . . .

The *Calamus* sentiment is now so generalized that it is to be the foundation, as in *Democratic Vistas,* of a New World "metaphysics."

Drum-Taps, now in LEAVES OF GRASS for the first time, has been considerably revised and many of the poems redistributed in sections called *Marches Now the War is Over* and *Bathed in War's Perfume.* The title of *Songs of Insurrection* may possibly have been suggested by the war, but the contents are such early poems as *To a Foil'd European Revolutionaire* and *France, the 18th Year of These*

States. The new grouping is merely an attempt to give these poems a context in the aftermath of the national struggle.[142]

The fact that in this edition Whitman feels the necessity of giving his poems a topical connotation is of considerable importance, for it offers further testimony that the war enabled him to enter more fully into the life of the nation and think less about himself than he did while writing and editing the 1860 edition. In fact, he is even becoming an "occasional" poet. For example, *Brother of All with Generous Hand* is a memorial to George Peabody, the philanthropist. *The Singer in Prison* records the concert of Parepa Rosa in Sing Sing Prison. Most of the remaining war poems are occasional in a general sense, like *A Carol of Harvest, for 1867 (Return of the Heroes),* which is a memorial to the Civil War dead on the occasion of a harvest of peace and returning prosperity. (The most *occasional* of all, *Song of the Exposition* and *Passage to India,* we will consider later.)

The 1871 LEAVES OF GRASS, exclusive of annexes, ends with the section called *Songs of Parting.* On the surface there is nothing remarkable in this fact, for the poems are not new, and since 1860 Whitman has been ending his book with *So Long!* However, it rounds out LEAVES OF GRASS in such a manner that we wonder if the poet is not planning to make this the last of all the editions. That this is his intention becomes clear during the next six years.

The best of all indications that Whitman is planning a major change in strategy is that nearly a third of his col-

---

[142] The prefatory poem (no separate title) was later removed from *Drum-Taps* and incorporated into *The Wound Dresser,* sec. 1.

lected poems, including much of his best work, has been removed from LEAVES OF GRASS proper and rearranged in *Passage to India*. It is significant that in planning a new collection Whitman did not start out with writing a new book, but began by writing an introductory poem and pulling out of his completed and published work enough pieces to fill out a 120-page pamphlet, which he would presently tack onto the LEAVES as a supplement. This is characteristic of his method through the remainder of his life.

The title poem in the supplement, *Passage to India*, was occasioned by three events of the greatest international importance: the completion of the Suez Canal, connecting Europe and Asia by water; the finishing of the Northern Pacific Railroad, spanning the North American continent; and the laying of the cable across the Pacific Ocean, thus joining by canal, rail, and cable Europe, North America, and Asia. In celebrating these great scientific and material achievements, Whitman was at last fulfilling one of the announced intentions of his 1855 program: he was now giving expression to the times in which he lived. Thus *Passage to India* is the most important occasional poem in the 1871 edition.

But *Passage to India* is a great deal more than a poetic celebration of nineteenth-century engineering feats, though no other poet of the age seems to have so fully appreciated these materialistic achievements. Having always been fascinated by the history of the human race and its long upward journey through the cycles of evolution, Whitman now sees these events as symbols and spiritual prophecies.

Lo, soul! seest thou not God's purpose from the first?
The earth to be spann'd, connected by net-work,
The people to become brothers and sisters,
The races, neighbors, to marry and be given in marriage,
The ocean to be cross'd, the distant brought near,
The lands to be welded together.[143]

Once more, as in *Salut au Monde!,* the poet's cosmic
vision returns to him:

O, vast Rondure, swimming in space!
Cover'd all over with visible power and beauty!

And with the lyric inspiration of his pre-war poems he
sketches the history of the race,[144] saluting the restless soul
of man, which has explored the continents and founded
the civilizations. Returning to his old poetic conviction,
Whitman announces once more that after the engineers,
inventors, and scientists

Finally shall come the Poet, worthy that name;
The true Son of God shall come, singing his songs.[145]

All this is repetition in a new context of the poet's great
dream of 1855-56, but here both the expression and the
application of the theory take on the imagery and meaning
of the fifth edition.

We too take ship, O soul!
Joyous, we too launch out on trackless seas![146]

No longer does the poet search for the meaning of life
and death in the sibilant waves that wash the shore of
Paumanok. Fearlessly he and his soul set out on a voyage,

---

[143] Sec. 3.   [145] Sec. 6.
[144] Sec. 6.   [146] Sec. 8.

singing their songs of God. Both the theme and mood
have changed, for instead of questioning, now the poet
affirms. And instead of addressing himself vaguely to
"whoever you are up there,"[147] he now prays,

Bathe me, O God, in thee—mounting to thee,
I and my soul to range in range of thee.

. . . . .

O Thou transcendant!
Nameless—the fibre and the breath!
Light of the light—shedding forth universes—
    thou centre of them![148]

Then comes the final development and culmination of
the *Calamus* motif: "Waitest not haply for us, somewhere
there, Comrade perfect?"[149] First the love poems of 1860
developed into a search for lovers among the readers,
then came the creation of an ideal "city of friends," which
gradually became a social and patriotic program. Now the
poet in his old age looks to God for perfect comradeship.

This is not to say, however, that in *Passage to India*
Whitman's religion has become orthodox. Though his
language and imagery have profoundly altered, his conception of death and immortality is as pantheistic as in
1855.

Swiftly I shrivel at the thought of God,
At Nature and its wonders, Time and Space and Death,
But that I, turning, call to thee O soul, thou actual Me,
And lo! thou gently masterest the orbs,
Thou matest Time, smilest content at Death,
And fillest, swellest full, the vastness of Space.[150]

---

[147] See p. 144.   [149] Sec. 8.
[148] Sec. 11.   [150] *Ibid.*

His "soul" is "greater than stars or suns." He and his soul take "passage to more than India"; sounding "below the Sanscrit and the Vedas," they voyage to the shores of the "aged fierce enigmas," plunge to the "secret of the earth and sky," through "seas of God." In 1855-56 Death was a philosophical problem, in 1860 it was chaos and frustration, but now the concept and expectation have become joyous, personal liberation—though still pantheistic in intellectual context.

Whispers of Heavenly Death, the title poem of a new group by this name, comes nearest to returning to the older imagery,

> Labial gossip of night—sibilant chorals, . . .
> Ripples of unseen rivers—tides of a current, flowing,
>   forever flowing; . . .

but even this poem ends with calling death a "parturition" and an "immortal birth,"

> Some Soul is passing over.

"Some Soul is passing over"—soaring, sailing, bidding the shore good-bye (Cf. *Now Finale to the Shore*), such are the emotions of the *Passage to India* collection, which ends with *Joy, Shipmate, Joy!* The old poems here grouped as *Sea-Shore Memories* merely emphasize the contrast.

In the other great poem in this collection, *Proud Music of the Storm,* we also find the same spiritual exaltation and emotional catharsis. It is not one of Whitman's most famous works, but nowhere else did he use his characteristic symphonic structure with greater unity of effect or with richer symbolism. It is his only poem which is literally a symphony of sound, like Lanier's deliberate musical experiments.

The orchestration of the storm ranges through the elemental sounds of all creation and the music of humanity,

> Blending, with Nature's rhythmus, all the tongues of
> nations, . . .[151]

raising allegories with every blast, which it would be unprofitable to attempt to analyze here. It is a private performance, anyway, for the poet's own "Soul":

> Come forward, O my Soul, and let the rest retire;
> Listen—lose not—it is toward thee they tend;
> Parting the midnight, entering my slumber-chamber,
> For thee they sing and dance, O Soul.[152]

First comes a "festival song" of marriage, followed by the beating of war drums and the "shouts of a conquering army," but this gives way to "airs antique and medieval," and then by contrast "the great organ sounds,"

> Bathing, supporting, merging all the rest—
> maternity of all the rest;
> And with it every instrument in multitudes,
> And players playing—all the world's musicians, . . .[153]

It is a symphony in which man, who has strayed from Nature like Adam from Paradise, returns,

> The journey done, the Journeyman come home,
> And Man and Art with Nature fused again.[154]

Section 7 revives the theme of the 1855 *There was a Child Went Forth:*

> Ah, from a little child,
> Thou knowest, Soul, how to me all sounds become
> music; . . .

---

[151] Sec. 1.
[152] Sec. 2.
[153] Sec. 5.
[154] *Ibid.*

But equally sweet to the poet are "All songs of current lands," and the vocalists whom he heard as a young man, best of all the "lustrous orb—Venus contralto," Alboni herself. In section 9 he lists his favorite operas, then passes on (10) to "the dance-music of all nations," Egypt, China, Hindu (11), and (12) Europe.

Finally the poet wakes from his trance, and tells his Soul that he has found the clue he sought so long. What the Soul has heard was not the music of nature or of other lands and times, but

> . . . a new rhythmus fitted for thee,
> Poems, bridging the way from Life to Death, vaguely
>   wafted in night air, uncaught, unwritten,
> Which, let us go forth in the bold day, and write.[155]

There we have the significance of the supplement to the 1871 LEAVES OF GRASS. At this time Walt Whitman plans to close his first life-book, his poems of "physiology from top to toe" and his songs of "Modern Man," described in the first *Inscription,* and begin a new collection of "Poems bridging the way from Life to Death." *Proud Music of the Storm* announces the new intention and *Passage to India* was evidently planned to launch this new poetic voyage.

THE 1872 PREFACE

The poems in Whitman's two pamphlet publications of 1871 and '72, *After All, Not to Create Only (Song of the Exposition)* and *As a Strong Bird on Pinions Free (Thou Mother with Thy Equal Brood),* are of distinctly minor importance. The fact that they were both written

---

[155] Sec. 15.

by invitation, the one for the 40th Annual Exhibition in New York City and the other to be read at the Dartmouth College commencement in 1872—and may therefore have been composed under forced inspiration—might explain their perfunctory tone. Both are poetic restatement of the nationalistic ideas in *Democratic Vistas.*

However, the Preface[156] which Whitman wrote for the latter pamphlet, *As a Strong Bird on Pinions Free,* is highly important in the history and growth of LEAVES OF GRASS because in it the poet states unequivocally that he has brought the LEAVES to an end and is starting a new book. He says, in words that need to be italicized, that his *"New World songs, and an epic of Democracy, having already had their published expression, as well as I can expect to give it, in LEAVES OF GRASS, the present and any future pieces from me are really but the surplusage forming after that Volume, or the wake eddying behind it."*[157] The suspicion that the *Passage to India* supplement was intended to start a new book is here confirmed. In the same paragraph Whitman makes a further confession, no less revealing. He is not sure of his new literary intentions, and he is at least vaguely aware (perhaps subconsciously, we might say) that he has written himself out. Now in retrospect he feels sure that in LEAVES OF GRASS he "fulfilled ... an imperious conviction, and the commands of my nature as total and irresistible as those which make the sea flow, or the globe revolve."[158] To what extent the "organic" metaphor may have influenced the exaggerated finality of this pronouncement, we can-

---

[156] *Prose Works,* op. cit., 275-280.
[157] *Ibid.,* 275-276.
[158] *Ibid.,* 276.

not say; but never before had Whitman spoken with such finality of LEAVES OF GRASS. As for the new project:

> But of this Supplementary Volume, I confess I am not so certain. Having from early manhood abandoned the business pursuits and applications usual in my time and country, and obediently yielded myself up ever since to the impetus mentioned, and to the work of expressing those ideas, it may be that mere habit has got dominion of me, when there is no real need of saying anything further . . .[159]

No doubt Whitman intended this comment to apply to the supposedly finished book, but the seven poems of this pamphlet, like the 1871 *Song of the Exposition,* lack the fervor and conviction of the 1860's. They are the work of a poet who is tired, written out, and on the brink of physical collapse, for it was only a few months before he would be stricken down by paralysis, never entirely to recover.

Even the remainder of this Preface is simply a repetition of the nationalistic ideal which he had already expressed in *Democratic Vistas:*

> Our America to-day I consider in many respects as but indeed a vast seething mass of *materials,* ampler, better, (worse also,) than previously known—eligible to be used to carry toward its crowning stage, and build for good the great Ideal Nationality of the future, the Nation of the Body and the Soul . . .[160]

The finished book and the projected book are to be differentiated in this way:

---

[159] *Ibid.*   [160] *Ibid.,* 277.

LEAVES OF GRASS, already published, [*note!*] is, in its intentions, the song of a great composite *Democratic Individual,* male or female. And following on and amplifying the same purpose, I suppose I have in my mind to run through the chants of this Volume, (if ever completed,) the thread-voice, more or less audible, of an aggregated, inseparable, unprecedented, vast, composite, electric *Democratic nationality.*[161]

Notice the uncertainty: "I *suppose* I have in my mind"— and "if ever completed."

Only two of the seven new poems in the 1872 pamphlet are of sufficient importance to be mentioned, and of these two, *As a Strong Bird on Pinions Free (Thou Mother with Thy Equal Brood)* merely repeats earlier ideas and moods. Once again the poet declares his function to be the initiator of democratic nationalism.

> The paths to the house I seek to make,
> But leave to those to come the house itself.

The motif of the "strong bird on pinions free" is also reminiscent of Shelley's *Skylark,* even though Whitman asserts that "The conceits of the poets of other lands I'd bring thee not." But more important: the poem is merely a restatement of the nationalistic literary program of the '55 Preface, *By Blue Ontario's Shore,* and other early works.

More significant is *The Mystic Trumpeter,* but it is also a summing up rather than a new achievement in thought or lyric expression. Professor Werner has advanced the interesting theory that the poem is an autobiographical record of

---

[161] *Ibid.,* 279-280.

moods parallel to Whitman's own life: his early fond-
ness for Scott's feudalism; his celebration of love in
the early *Leaves;* the Civil War; his post-war despair
at the evils of humanity; and his final optimism and
ecstasy. Thus interpreted, the poem seems no longer
utterly formless, nor an assembly of the chief poetic
themes, but a chronological summary of Whitman's
poetic life.[162]

SIXTH EDITION, 1876

Despite his grave illness, Whitman was able to commemorate 1876 with a two-volume Centennial Edition of
LEAVES OF GRASS and *Two Rivulets,* the former being a
reprint of the fifth edition and the latter composed of
prose, eighteen new poems, and the *Passage to India*
annex of the fifth edition. This is the first of the two-
volume editions of poetry and prose. The *Two Rivulets*
has a Preface which, according to Whitman's statement
in a footnote, "is not only for the present collection, but,
in a sort for all my writings, both Volumes."[163]

In this Preface we learn that *Passage to India,* which
is referred to as "chants of Death and Immortality," had
been intended "to stamp the coloring-finish of all, present
and past. For terminus and temperer to all, they were
originally written; and that shall be their office to the
last." Having had to give up the plan of making *Passage
to India* the nucleus of a new collection of songs, he now
plans to regard it as a sort of epilogue of all his poems,
but by reprinting it in *Two Rivulets* he postponed the
time when it would become a part of LEAVES OF GRASS.

---

[162] W. L. Werner, "Whitman's The Mystic Trumpeter as Autobiography," *American Literature,* VII, 458 (Jan., 1936).

[163] *Two Rivulets* (Camden, 1876), 5, footnote.

It is thus still unassimilated, though regarded as an epitome of the LEAVES. In a long footnote Whitman says that "*Passage to India,* and its cluster, are but freer vent and fuller expression to what, from the first, and so on throughout, more or less lurks in my writings, underneath every page, every line, everywhere." This is a good example of the way the poet would continue to improvise and compromise in his plans during the remaining editions of LEAVES OF GRASS.

In this same footnote he confesses that he has had to relinquish his plan to write a second collection of poems:

> It was originally my intention, after chanting in LEAVES OF GRASS the songs of the Body and Existence, to then compose a further, equally needed Volume, based on those convictions of perpetuity and conservation which, enveloping all precedents, make the unseen Soul govern absolutely at last. . . . But the full construction of such a work (even if I lay the foundation, or give impetus to it) is beyond my powers, and must remain for some bard in the future.[164]

Characteristically, however, he does not entirely give up his earlier scheme: "Meanwhile, not entirely to give the go-by to my original plan, and far more to avoid a mark'd hiatus in it, than to entirely fulfill it, I end my books with thoughts, or radiations from thoughts, on Death, Immortality, and a free entrance into the Spiritual world."[165] This intention can be plainly seen in the constant resorting and rearranging of the poems up until the year of Whitman's death.

---

[164] *Two Rivulets,* 6, footnote: *Holloway,* Inclusive Edition, *op. cit.,* 513.

[165] *Two Rivulets,* 6; Holloway, 514.

A note in this Preface, dated May 31, 1875, reveals the second spiritual crisis in Whitman's life (the first being visible in the third edition): "O how different the moral atmosphere amid which I now revise this Volume, from the jocund influences surrounding the growth and advent of LEAVES OF GRASS."[166] As he indicates presently, the "moral atmosphere" to which he refers is his extreme mental depression following his mother's death, a shock from which he seems never to have recovered, and his "tedious attack of paralysis." This depression is also partly responsible for Whitman's interpretation of the first volume (i.e., LEAVES OF GRASS) as radiating "Physiology alone," whereas "the present One, though of the like origin in the main, more palpably doubtless shows the Pathology which was pretty sure to come in time from the others." Although the later poems do lack the "vehemence of pride and audacity" to be found in the earlier editions—"composed in the flush of my health and strength—,"[167] it is not strictly true that the first six editions of LEAVES OF GRASS dealt exclusively with "Birth and Life,"[168] For Death and Immortality are prominent themes in every edition, including the first, though the treatment does vary somewhat from period to period. But in his sickness and old age Whitman was inclined to idealize the physiological vigor and joy of his healthier and happier days.

In another reminiscence, however, he makes one of his most revealing confessions about the psychological origins of much of the earlier LEAVES:

[166] *Two Rivulets,* 7, footnote; Holloway, 514.
[167] *Two Rivulets,* 8; Holloway, 515.
[168] *In Former Songs* (1876—*Two Rivulets,* p. 31) stresses this division in Whitman's poems, but it was dropped after '76, no doubt because the poet had given up the intention of dividing his songs into two books.

Something more may be added—for, while I am about
it, I would make a full confession. I also sent out
LEAVES OF GRASS to arouse and set flowing in men's
and women's hearts, young and old, (my present and
future readers,) endless streams of living, pulsating
love and friendship, directly from them to myself, now
and ever. To this terrible, irrepressible yearning, (surely
more or less down underneath in most human souls,)—
this never-satisfied appetite for sympathy, and this
boundless offering of sympathy—this universal democratic comradeship—this old, eternal, yet ever-new inter-
change of adhesiveness, so fitly emblematic of America
—I have given in that book, undisguisedly, declaredly,
the openest expression.[169]

Aside from the phrenological term "adhesiveness," which
Whitman uses to indicate the "Calamus" emotion, no
clearer statement can be found of the fact that the impulse
of Whitman's songs came not from the desire to express
love experiences but to compensate for the absence of
experience. In 1876 Whitman still needs sympathy, but
the "terrible, irrepressible yearning" came to a climax in
the third edition, was appeased through the activities of
the "wound-dresser," and is now almost entirely sublimated in the democratic idealism of such poetry and
prose as *Democratic Vistas, Thoughts for the Centennial,*
the centennial songs, and other pieces in *Two Rivulets,*
including the Preface, which summarizes Whitman's social
and literary theory.

The dominant mood of Whitman during the first years
of his invalidism is poignantly mirrored in the chief poems
of *Two Rivulets,* the *Prayer of Columbus* and the *Song*

---

[169] *Two Rivulets,* 11, footnote; Holloway, 518, note.

of the Red-Wood Tree. The poet was obviously thinking of himself when he described Columbus in his late
years as, "A batter'd, wreck'd old man." Almost with the
grief of Job, Columbus reminds God that not once has he
"lost nor faith nor ecstasy in Thee." He is resigned to
"The end I know not, it is all in Thee." In a climax of
pathos he feels mocked and perplexed, but then

> As if some miracle, some hand divine unseal'd my eyes,
> Shadowy vast shapes smile through the air and sky,
> And on the distant waves sail countless ships,
> And anthems in new tongues I hear saluting me.

No doubt a similar dream of future reward and recognition in "new tongues" sustained Walt Whitman in the
hour of his deepest suffering and discouragement.

We might say that in *Prayer of Columbus* the poet's
solution is some variety of religious faith, whereas in *Song
of the Red-Wood Tree* it is a philosophical consolation,
perhaps derived indirectly from Hegel. The subject of this
poem is the death-chant of a "mighty dying tree." It
too has "consciousness, identity," as "all the rocks and
mountains have, and all the earth." In typical Whitmanesque fashion the spirit of the tree is projected into
the future—the poet's *"Vistas"*—, "Then to a loftier
strain" the chant turns to the "occult deep volitions" which
are shaping the "hidden national will,"

> Clearing the ground for broad humanity, the true
>   America, heir of the past so grand,
> To build a grander future.[170]

The philosophical thought and the imagery of this
poem are perhaps more clearly explained in *Eidólons,*

---

[170] Sec. 3.

which in 1881 was shifted to the *Inscriptions* group, thus
indicating that Whitman regarded it as one of the keys
to LEAVES OF GRASS. It is an abstract treatment of Whitman's subjective and idealistic philosophy. Each object,
as well as rivers, worlds, and universes, has a spirit, soul,
or "eidólon", and the seer tells the poet to celebrate these
instead of physical things. This "eidólon" is the poet's
"real I myself," and his soul is a part of the great Nature-
soul of all creation, so that the only genuine and ultimate
reality is eidólons.[171]

The *Song of the Universal* is another Hegelian expression of the *Democratic Vistas* faith in the ultimate triumph
of the poet's ideals:

> In this broad earth of ours,
> Amid the measureless grossness and the slag,
> Enclosed and safe within its central heart,
> Nestles the seed perfection.[172]

"Nature's amelioration" is constantly evolving the universal "good" out of the "bad majority."[173]

In *Song of Myself* this doctrine was a pantheistic[174] belief in cosmic evolution, and was then expressed with a
"plenitude"[175] in harmony with the poet's exuberant vigor
and audacious ambitions. It is still essentially the same
doctrine, but it has now been modified by Whitman's discovery of Hegel and by the calming influence of sickness
and old age. In 1855 Whitman gave lyric utterance to
philosophical ideas; in 1876 the lyric power has largely
evaporated and even the language has become abstract.

---

[171] See discussion of Whitman's "panpsychism," p. 256.
[172] Sec. 1.
[173] Cf. p. 290.
[174] See p. 255.
[175] See p. 278.

This is the great change that had taken place over the years. In the 1876 edition of LEAVES OF GRASS and *Two Rivulets,* Walt Whitman's poetic fire has notably cooled; but as his inspiration slackens and his vigor ebbs away, he turns more resolutely than ever to critical commentary and editorial revision of his life's work.

SEVENTH EDITION, 1881-82

Whitman's bad luck with Boston publishers held until the end, for soon after James R. Osgood and Company brought out the 1881-82 edition of LEAVES OF GRASS the District Attorney of Boston threatened prosecution if the book were not withdrawn from the mails or expurgated. When Whitman refused permission to delete any lines whatever, Osgood abandoned publication and turned the plates over to the author, who soon secured a new publisher in Rees Welsh and Company, Philadelphia, and the book was reissued in 1882. Later the same year David McKay took over this edition and remained Whitman's loyal friend and publisher for the rest of his life. McKay imprints of the seventh edition are also dated 1883, 1884, and 1888, but they are from the same plates—though some copies are on larger paper, and in 1888 a small batch was printed with *Sands at Seventy* as an annex.[176]

Whether in 1881-82 Whitman intended this to be the last version of LEAVES OF GRASS, we do not know; nevertheless, in this edition the poems received their final revisions of text, their last titles, and their permanent positions. Whitman continued to write poems almost up to his death in 1892, but two installments of these he at-

---

[176] This edition contains 404 instead of 382 pages. See Wells and Goldsmith, *op. cit.,* 27.

tached in 1888-89 and 1892 as annexes and he left in-
structions that his posthumous verse be placed in a third
annex, thus leaving the 1881 LEAVES intact and unaltered.
The 1881 edition, therefore, is essentially the final,
definitive LEAVES OF GRASS, though all modern "Inclusive" editions contain also the three annexes.

The seventh edition contains twenty new poems, placed
in various groups. All of these new compositions, however, are comparatively short and none is of major importance. Several reflect the old-age activities of the poet,
such as his reading Hegel (*Roaming in Thought*), his
trip to the West (*The Prairie States, From Far Dakota's
Canons, Spirit that Form'd this Scene*), and his anticipa-
tions of the end of his life (*As at thy Portals also Death*).
A short poem called *My Picture Gallery* is highly indicative
of Whitman's old-age editorial methods. It is actually, as
Professor Holloway discovered,[177] a fragment of a very
early poem, one of the ur-LEAVES, parts of the original
manuscript having been used in various places. The printing of this unused fragment in 1881 as a new poem indicates that Whitman was salvaging, re-sorting, and editing
his old manuscripts—perhaps scraping the bottom of the
barrel. The two new bird poems in this edition are also
significant. *To the Man-of-War-Bird* is actually a translation from Michelet,[178] and John Burroughs has testified
that *The Dalliance of the Eagles* was written from an account which he gave Whitman.[179] As he grew older,

---

[177] See Emory Holloway, "Whitman's Embryonic Verse," *Southwest Review*, X, 28-40 (July, 1925); also Introduction to *Pictures: An Un-published Poem by Walt Whitman* (London: Faber and Gwyer, 1928).

[178] See Adeline Knapp, "Walt Whitman and Jules Michelet, Identical Passages," *Critic*, XLIV, 467-468 (1907); also Gay W. Allen, "Walt Whitman and Jules Michelet," *Études Anglaises*, I, 230-237 (May, 1937).

[179] See Barrus, *op. cit.*, xxiv.

Whitman made greater use of borrowed observations, journalistic articles, and events in the day's news.

In 1860 Whitman began groping toward the organization of LEAVES OF GRASS which he finally adopted and made permanent in 1881. The nine *Inscriptions* of 1871 have now been increased to 24, though only one, a final two-line dedication to *Thou Reader,* is new. Half of these, however, were first published in 1860, before Whitman had started this group, and the final section is thus an improvised prologue rather than a carefully planned unit. At first glance it seems to be a poetic index, or "program", for the contents of LEAVES OF GRASS, but on close examination the program-symbolism is vague, unsystematic, incomplete, though some of the intentions and motifs are suggested. The first *Inscription* announces the theme of "One's Self", the third the ship motif (like Shelley's West Wind, the ship carries Whitman's poems to all lands), in *Poets to Come* the "main things" are expected from future bards, and the group ends with a solicitation of friendship and personal intimacy from the reader. Considering the fact that nearly all these poems were first published in other groups, such as *Chants Democratic, Drum-Taps, Calamus, Two Rivulets,* etc., and were transferred to this group over a period of ten years, it is surprising that they serve as well as they do to introduce LEAVES OF GRASS. And it is characteristic of Whitman that instead of deliberately planning and writing an introductory poem, or series, he selected, like an anthologist, poems already completed under various circumstances and impulses.

The *Inscriptions* also characterize the arrangement of the whole book in a manner that is not obvious to the reader who has not studied the poems chronologically.

Since Whitman's avowed purpose was to put on record his own life, which he regarded as typical and representative, we would expect the poems of his life-record to be arranged either in chronology of their composition (which is to say, the chronology of his poetic and emotional development) or classified so that their subject-matter at least suggests a natural biographical sequence. Although the prologue poems are followed by the most ostensibly autobiographical works in the book, *Starting from Paumanok* and *Song of Myself* (new title in 1881), and the collection ends with groups symbolizing old age and approaching death, the life-allegory arrangement is still quite general and unsystematic, and there is little visible attempt at chronology inside the groups.

This observation will become clarified and illustrated as we survey the remaining groups in this final arrangement. The two especially autobiographical and doctrinaire poems are followed by *Children of Adam* and *Calamus,* groups which do, of course, typify Whitman's psychology and sentiments from about 1855 to '60, but both groups have since then been considerably revised and edited— and *Calamus,* as we have seen, has even been remotivated.

Then come the great songs in an unnamed group. The earliest of these are *Song of the Answerer* and *A Song for Occupations* (1855) and the latest is *Song of the Redwood-Tree* (1874). The group begins with *Salut au Monde!* and contains *A Song of the Rolling Earth,* both cosmic in theme and imagery, and they help give unity to these poems in which the poet's universal sympathy and his cosmic lyric inspiration were at white-heat intensity (about 1856, the date of five of these poems). Thus chronologically these poems should precede *Children of*

Adam and *Calamus,* but they were probably placed after these groups in order that the physiological and sex motifs might precede the cosmic ones—a logical arrangement in terms of Whitman's general philosophy.

The first of the new groups is *Birds of Passage,* a title which seems to compare life to the migrations of the bird kingdom. The poems come from various periods, but the general theme of the collection is the evolution and migration of the human race through Time and Space, as in *Song of the Universal, Pioneers! O Pioneers!,* and *With Antecedents.* The group has very little personal significance or relation to the life-allegory motif of the whole book. There is, however, a certain appropriateness in placing the "pioneer" motif after the great cosmic songs.

The next group has been renamed *Sea-Drift* (called *Sea-Shore Memories* in 1871). It contains the two major sea poems, *Out of the Cradle Endlessly Rocking* (1859) and *As I Ebb'd with the Ocean of Life* (1860), but also represents different moods from various periods, as in *Tears* (1867), *On the Beach at Night Alone* (1856) and *On the Beach at Night* (1871). In chronological sequence Whitman's sea-shore poems reveal the major crises of his poetic career and form a psychological drama, but this grouping suggests only that the sea provided much of the poet's inspiration. The group is unified by a common subject and locale, and is not without its own logic, but the student must search through other groups to complete the experiences vaguely hinted here.

Another new group is *By the Roadside,* a miscellaneous collection of short poems on many topics and extending from *Europe* (1850) and *Boston Ballad* (1854) to *Roam-*

ing in Thought (1881). They are merely samples of experiences and poetic inspirations along Whitman's highway of life.

Drum-Taps has been considerably revised and enlarged since 1865, and the introductory poem of 1871-76 has been discarded. *Virginia—The West* is a good example of the way Whitman shifted poems around. It first appeared in *As a Strong Bird on Pinions Free* (1872), then in *Two Rivulets* ('76), and now comes to rest in *Drum-Taps*. Also the poem which introduced this group in '71 and '76 is now a part of section 1 of *The Wound-Dresser* —"Arous'd and angry, I'd thought to beat the alarum," etc. Several poems first published in *Sequel to Drum-Taps* have finally been placed in this group, thus making it a record not only of the war but of the aftermath too, except for the memorial poems for President Lincoln, which are now called *Memories of President Lincoln*.

The latter group is followed by perhaps the most revised composition in LEAVES OF GRASS, now called for the first time, after the sixth change in title, *By Blue Ontario's Shore*. In 1856 Whitman incorporated parts of his '55 Preface in this poem, and with each succeeding edition until 1881 made extensive revisions. Perhaps his difficulty in making up his mind what to do with the composition was due in part to his having meanwhile expressed and exemplified his poetic theory in many ways. At any rate, in subject-matter this poem is akin to *Starting from Paumanok* and *Song of Myself,* but it now appears after the war and Lincoln poems because in 1867 Whitman had remotivated it as a "Chant ... from the soul of America," singing the "throes of Democracy" and victory (a transition from *Drum-Taps* to *Democratic Vistas*).

Autumn Rivulets, another new group-title, does not signify poems associated with the autumn of the poet's life,
although in the introductory *As Consequent,* etc. he compares these songs to "wayward rivulets" flowing after the
"store of summer rains." He also thinks of his life and
the experiences which he has recorded in his poems as
"waifs from the deep, cast high and dry" onto the shore.
Instead of Emerson's Over-Soul metaphor, Whitman uses
"the sea of Time," from whence his own identity has come
and toward which it is ever flowing, there to blend finally
with "the old streams of death." Thus in the imagery of
his group-title Whitman re-expresses his philosophy of
life and death through this new poem.

But this symbolism is found only in the lead poem. In
the other poems of the group, from the 1855 *There was
a Child Went Forth* to the 1881 *Italian Music in Dakota*
neither these images nor "Autumn Rivulets" motifs reappear. Furthermore, the majority of the poems date back
to 1856 and '60 and reflect the moods and sentiments of
those periods: *This Compost* ('56), *To a Common Prostitute* ('60), *O Star of France* ('71), etc. *My Picture-
Gallery* was evidently rescued from the barrel of old
manuscripts.

Throughout the remainder of LEAVES OF GRASS the
poems are in general arranged to emphasize the "spiritual"
purposes which Whitman professedly began with *Passage
to India.* Even here, however, he often places an earlier
poem, like *The Sleepers* ('55) or *To Think of Time* ('55),
both of which come between *Passage to India* and the 1871
group—still retained—, *Whispers of Heavenly Death.*
Then, after a brief interval, comes the new section called
From Noon to Starry Night, a title which happily permits

the poet to follow his usual procedure of selecting typical poems from various periods of his career. The group is introduced by a new poem, *Thou Orb Aloft Full-Dazzling,* a prayer to the sun, with which the poet feels a special affinity and a reminder of his own prime:

> As for thy throes, thy perturbations, sudden breaks and
>   shafts of flame gigantic,
> I understand them, I know those flames, those perturba-
> tions well.

He adores the sun also because it "impartially infoldest all" and liberally gives of itself. He invokes the sun to prepare his "starry nights." The section ends patly with a short epilogue-poem, *A Clear Midnight,* on the images of "Night, sleep, death and the stars."

The final group, also with a new title, is the inevitable *Songs of Parting,* which of course ends with the 1860 *So Long!* The theme is death in its many connotations: personal anticipation, memory of the poet's mother, the death of soldiers in the war, the assassination of President Garfield, and the triumphant journey of the soul into the realms of eternity. But the anticipated end of the poet's life did not come for eleven years and he was spared to write many more postscripts and epitaphs.

As editor of his own work, Whitman is ingenious. His final group titles are appropriate for this anthology of his life-work, and there is a certain kind of poetic logic in his arrangement of the poems inside the various groups. But the student who has closely examined the growth of the editions will also find serious objections to Whitman's belief that the 1881 LEAVES OF GRASS is as unified as a cathedral or as inevitable in structure as an organism in nature. In chronological order his poems do tell the inner story of the poet's long struggle to put on record his own life and the literary ambitions which he was trying to achieve, but in this final arrangement the story is inconsecutive and often obscured by the deletions and emendations which Whitman had made throughout the years as his concept of his own poetic rôle fluctuated. Perhaps he had deliberately obscured it. His arrangement of the poems by subject-matter seems to indicate that this is true. An inconsistency, however, remains. Such group titles as *Autumn Rivulets, From Noon to Starry Night,* and *Songs of Parting* suggest a chronology of life-experiences, but the contents of these groups reveal ideational rather than biological sequences. Furthermore, often the symbolism of these titles scarcely carries beyond the introductory poem and possibly an epilogue.

Perhaps critics will never agree upon the poet's success in this final arrangement, for everything depends upon what one wants in an edition of LEAVES OF GRASS. The very fact that this was so indisputably Walt Whitman's final choice, and that he was still satisfied with it a decade later, leaves no doubt that this edition does show his intentions—especially his intention to suggest (*indirectly,* as he might have said) that this "is no book" but a man's life, though he reserved the right to erase and emend any parts of the record that violated his later ideals, and to arrange the parts so that they would not suggest the realism of biography. After all, this is a *poetic record,* not objective history or prosaic autobiography. Thus the reader of Whitman will no doubt always cherish the poet's own final edition. But for the student who is interested in the growth of Whitman's thought or the

development of his prosodic techniques and artistry, or
the solution of psychological mysteries, a chronological
text is well-nigh indispensable.

SPECIMEN DAYS, 1882

About one-third of the material in *Specimen Days* was
published in 1875 in pamphlet form as *War Memoranda,*
but in 1882 Whitman collected this and other prose pieces,
including *Democratic Vistas,* into what was historically
the second edition of the *Complete Works* in two volumes
(volume one being a reprint of the 1881 LEAVES) but
what was now essentially the *Complete Prose.*

Whitman himself called *Specimen Days* a "way-ward
book," and it is certainly improvised, much of it having
been copied from note-books, diaries, and scraps of manuscript, evidently with little revision—though these notes
are perhaps more authentic "specimens" for not having
been rewritten.[180] The book covers three main subjects,
the first being a brief autobiography which Whitman says
he wrote for a friend in 1882;[181] the second being war
memoranda, taken from "verbatim copies of those lurid
and blood-smutch'd little note-books" written in Washington and Virginia from the end of 1862 through
'65; and the third being diary and nature-notes for
1876-81 and miscellaneous short essays and articles.

The autobiography throws some light on the growth
of Whitman as a poet because we can see in the glorification of his ancestry and the importance he attaches to his
environment some of the processes by which he trans-
muted the commonplace into the idealism of his verse.

---

[180] See *Prose Works, op. cit.,* 7, note.
[181] See "Answer to an Insisting Friend."

In the war memoranda, however, we get a side of Whitman which is almost entirely lacking in his poems and which therefore supplements the poetry. In his graphic descriptions of the camp of the wounded, with the amputated arms and legs lying under the trees, he anticipates later American realism. And the exact account of many individual cases of the wounded documents the record. Atrocities are told with great anguish of spirit but without partisanship. Without preaching Whitman reveals the bestiality of war. He concludes that, "the real war will never get in the books," and adds that it was so horrible that perhaps it should not. But he comes nearer telling it than anyone else in America was to do for nearly a century to come, and he tells it all without the sentimentality or propaganda for pacifism which followed World War I.

The third part of *Specimen Days* reveals still another side of Whitman's life. Before the war he had been a great nature lover, and nature plays a prominent part in all his poems, but the record of his Timber Creek experiences reads almost like a summer idyl. More amateurish than Thoreau in his botanical and ornithological observations, even priding himself on deficiency in exact information, Whitman's enjoyment of nature is as intimate and personal as one can find in romantic prose. But it is probably not accidental that he now expresses himself in loose, informal language, for he seems to have been living in the most satisfying repose of his life. The great sea-shore poems were not written in such a mood of quiet resignation. Even in the accounts of his travels of 1889, which he seems to have enjoyed as thoroughly as his youthful trip across the Alleghanies on his way to St.

Louis, we find this same repose, this Indian summer atmosphere, which *Specimen Days* more clearly reflects than any of the old-age poems.

November Boughs, 1888

Specimen Days marks the transition to Whitman's final attitude toward life and his art in *November Boughs*, which contains sixty-two new poems and a Preface, *A Backward Glance O'er Travel'd Roads*. Here in prose and verse we find the resumé. His critical theory now approaches Wordsworth's doctrine of "emotion recollected in tranquility." These old-age poems are mainly the product of reflection, November reminiscences. And after completing his poems, he is "curious to review them in the light of their own (at the time unconscious, or mostly unconscious) intentions, with certain unfoldings of the thirty years they seek to embody."[182]

Gone are the ambitious boastings, the grandiose claims to fame. With tranquil confidence and utmost frankness Whitman now admits, "I have not gain'd the acceptance of my own time, but have fallen back on fond dreams of the future." Yet despite the fact that Leaves of Grass has always been a financial failure, "I have had my say entirely in my own way, and put it unerringly on record—the value thereof to be decided by time."[183] The work was always an experiment, "as, in the deepest sense, I consider our American Republic itself to be, with its theory." He is content that he has "positively gain'd a hearing."[184]

---

[182] Holloway, "Inclusive Edition" of Leaves of Grass, *op. cit.*, 522.
[183] *Ibid.*, 523.
[184] *Ibid.*

Once more Whitman reiterates his original purpose: "to exploit [his own] Personality, identified with place and date, in a far more candid and comprehensive sense than any hitherto poem or book."[185] With this part of his original program he is still satisfied, but he is not so sure about another intention:

> Modern science and democracy seem'd to be throwing out their challenge to poetry to put them in its statements in contradistinction to the songs and myths of the past. As I see it now (perhaps too late,) I have unwittingly taken up that challenge and made an attempt at such statements—which I certainly would not assume to do now, knowing more clearly what it means.[186]

We would certainly like to have this last statement amplified, but Whitman says no more. Exactly why he now doubts this part of his program we shall probably never know, but there can be little doubt that he succeeded better in expressing his own personality than in giving voice to modern science. Moreover, his mysticism was always stronger than his rationalism, and he can still say that, "It almost seems as if poetry with cosmic and dynamic features of magnitude and limitlessness suitable to the human soul, were never possible before."[187]

It is interesting and a little pathetic that Whitman's failure to gain wide acceptance in his own time and country has now convinced even him that "in verbal melody and all the conventional technique of poetry, not only the divine works that to-day stand ahead in the world's reading, but dozens more, transcend (some of them im-

---

[185] *Ibid.*, 524.   [187] *Ibid.*, 526.
[186] *Ibid.*

measurably transcend) all I have done, or could do," though he still believes that "there must imperatively come a readjustment of the whole theory and nature of Poetry . . ."[188] Today, after such a readjustment has taken place, it is difficult for us to understand the nineteenth-century intolerance in poetic technique.

For the most part, the remainder of this Preface merely re-affirms Whitman's familiar doctrines: that the function of a poem is to fill a person "with vigorous and clean manliness,"[189] that American democratic individuality is yet unformed, and that the great poet will express the goodness of all creation.

The poems in this book scarcely need much discussion. They seem to be mainly fragments from unpublished manuscripts or stray thoughts and echoes from earlier compositions. Some are epigrammatic or short, senten-tious reflections. Some are reminiscences, "thoughts," long after the passing of the emotions and experiences which first gave rise to lyric utterance. Whitman him-self is fully conscious of his true condition. In *Memories* he refers to the "sweet . . . silent backward tracings," and in *As I Sit Writing Here* he fears that the old-age vexations of the flesh "May filter in my daily songs." With conscious effort he is trying to make his last days hap-piest of all, "The brooding and blissful halcyon days" (*Halcyon Days*).

In his last years the poet also feels close to the sea once more, and at times both the sight of the ocean and his recollections almost fan to life the old lyric sparks, as in his *Fancies at Navesink* or the "sudden memory-flash . . . back" in *The Pilot in the Mist*. The ocean revives the

---

[188] *Ibid.*, 527.　　　　　[189] *Ibid.*, 532.

emotional symbolism of his greatest poems. *With Husky-Haughty Lips, O Sea:*

The tale of cosmic elemental passion,
Thou tellest to a kindred soul.

But these are merely echoes too, like *Old Salt Kossabone,* the family tradition about the sailor on his mother's side which he had already used in section 35 of *Song of Myself.* And *Going Somewhere* revives the theme of two 1867 poems, *Small the Theme of my Chant* and the first *Inscription.* As in *After Supper and Talk,* the old poet is "loth to depart" and "garrulous to the very last."

NINTH EDITION, 1892

These poems in *November Boughs* became, without revision, *Sands at Seventy,* the "First Annex," in the 1892 edition, which also reprinted *A Backward Glance.* In a Preface Note to the Second Annex, *Good-Bye My Fancy,* Whitman wonders if he had "better [not] withold (in this old age and paralysis of me) such little tags and fringe-dots (maybe specks, stains) as follow a long dusty journey," but he had always followed the principle of putting everything on record, not "afraid of careless touches, . . . nor of parrot-like repetitions—nor platitudes and commonplaces;"[190] so once more he submits another accumulated batch of poems, or post-scripts, as it were, to print. Since he has already accurately assessed their value, little more need be said about this Second Annex. Not only does he say farewell to his Fancy but he reiterates once more the faiths by which he has lived and sung. He is especially emphatic about his belief in the soul and in

---

[190] Holloway, Inclusive Edition, *op. cit.,* 537.

the "Unseen Buds,"[191] the germs of life awaiting, "Like babes in wombs, latent, folded, compact, sleeping." Once more he has returned to the imagery of pantheistic trans-migration[192]—returned, or merely echoed again?

The final, posthumous, annex, *Old Age Echoes,* is similar in content and quality to the other annexes. Whitman himself chose the title to apply "not so much to things as to echoes of things, reverberant, aftermath."[193] In a few the rhythm is excellent, like *To Soar in Freedom and in Fullness of Power.* But for the most part they are indeed echoes of the old themes and motifs: the journey of the human race, evolution (Cf. *A Thought of Colum-bus*), and even "Calamus" (*Of Many a Smutch'd Deed Reminiscent*). *To be at All* is another version of stanza 27 of *Song of Myself.* In accordance with Whitman's wish, these poems were attached to the collection in 1897-98, and have since been reprinted in every "Inclusive" edition.

In "An Executor's Diary Note, 1891" Whitman indi-cated his final wish:

> . . . I place upon you the injunction that whatever may be added to the LEAVES shall be supplementary, avowed as such, leaving the book complete as I left it, con-secutive to the point I left off, marking always an un-mistakable, deep down, unobliteratable division line. In the long run the world will do as it pleases with the book. I am determined to have the world know what I was pleased to do.[194]

---

[191] *Unseen Buds.*
[192] See Chap. III, p. 267.
[193] Holloway, Inclusive Edition, *op. cit.,* 539.
[194] *Ibid.*

The wish has been fulfilled, and this wayward, inconsistent, often puzzling, but still living and inspiring book has been kept as Walt Whitman left it.

SELECTED BIBLIOGRAPHY

THE MAIN EDITIONS OF WHITMAN'S WRITINGS
(Listed Chronologically)

Leaves of Grass. [First edition.] Brooklyn, New York. 1855. 95 pp. quarto.
[No name on title-page but copyrighted by Walter Whitman. Frontispiece, steel engraving of the poet in shirt sleeves. Poems preceded by a twelve-page Preface. Volume contains twelve poems without titles.]

————. Facsimile of 1855 edition. Portland, Maine: Thomas Bird Mosher and William Francis Gable. 1919. [Introduction by Mosher.]

————. Facsimile of 1855 edition. With an introduction by Clifton Joseph Furness. Facsimile Text Society, Publication No. 47. Columbia University Press. 1939.

Leaves of Grass. [Second edition.] Brooklyn, New York. 1856. 385 pp. 16mo.
[Frontispiece same as first edition. Stamped in gold on backstrip: "I Greet You at the/ Beginning of a Great Career/ R. W. Emerson." An appendix called "Leaves Droppings" contains Emerson's "Greeting" letter, dated July 21, 1855, and Whitman's open-letter reply to the "Master." This section also contains reviews of the first edition. The poems are numbered and titled, Nos. 14 to 33 being new. The 1855 Preface is omitted.]

Leaves of Grass. [Third edition.] Boston: Thayer and Eldridge. 1860-61. 456 pp. 12mo.

[Frontispiece, steel engraving from painting by Charles Hine, 1859. Poems added since second edition: 124. Many pirated copies were later printed from the plates of this edition.]

Walt Whitman's Drum-Taps. New York. 1865. 72 pp. 12mo.
[Reissued same year with *Sequel to Drum-Taps,* and included in 1871 *Leaves of Grass* as annex.]

Leaves of Grass. [Fourth edition.] New York. 1867. 470 pp. 8vo.
[No portrait. Annexes: *Drum-Taps* (1865), *Sequel to Drum-Taps* (1865-66), and *Songs Before Parting.* Eight new poems aside from the annexes, which contain 71.]

Democratic Vistas. Memoranda. Washington, D. C. 1871.
[Copyrighted by author, 1870.] 84 pp. narrow 12mo.
[Text same as in *Prose Works* except for first paragraph and a few foot-notes.]

Leaves of Grass. [Fifth edition.] Washington, D. C. 1871.
384 pp. 8vo.
[A reprint in 1872 contains *Passage to India* with 120 added pages. Thirteen new poems exclusive of the annexes in the later printings. In the fifth edition the groupings and revisions approach the final arrangement.]

Leaves of Grass. [Sixth edition.] Camden, New Jersey. 1876.
384 pp. 8vo.
[Called *Author's Edition,* with autograph and two portraits. Printed from 1871-72 plates and issued as vol. I of the first edition of the *Complete Works*—see *Two Rivulets* below.]

Two Rivulets. Including *Democratic Vistas, Centennial Songs,* and *Passage to India,* Camden, New Jersey. 1876. 384 pp. 8vo.
[Vol. II of *Author's Edition* of the *Complete Works.* Eighteen new poems. Title from poem, "Two Rivulets Side by Side," rejected in later editions.]

Leaves of Grass. [Seventh edition.] Boston: James R. Osgood and Co. 1881. 382 pp. 12mo.

[Reprinted in Philadelphia by Rees Welsh and Co. in 1882 and David McKay in 1888. The poems received their final arrangement in this edition, later poems being added without disturbing this grouping. After the book was banned in Boston, it was reissued in Philadelphia, as indicated above.]

Specimen Days and Collect. Philadelphia: Rees Welsh and Co. 1882-83. 374 pp. 8vo.

[This was regarded as vol. II of the *Complete Works,* to accompany the 1881 *Leaves* reprinted by Rees Welsh.]

November Boughs. Philadelphia: David McKay. 1888. 140 pp. 8vo.

[Frontispiece, portrait of Whitman in 70th year. The prose includes "A Backward Glance O'er Travel'd Roads," and miscellaneous notes printed in the 1892 *Prose Works,* pp. 375-476. The poems are *Sands at Seventy,* the First Annex in the 1892 *Leaves of Grass.*]

Complete Poems and Prose of Walt Whitman, 1855-1888. [Eighth edition of the poems; third of *Complete Works.*] Philadelphia: published by the author. 1888. 900 pp. large quarto.

["Portrait from Life—Autograph . . . also profile portrait." Portraits facing p. 29 and frontispiece from *November Boughs,* from which new poems are taken.]

Leaves of Grass, with *Sands at Seventy* and *A Backward Glance O'er Travel'd Roads.* [Eighth separate edition of poems.] Philadelphia. 1889. 422 pp. 12mo.

[Special autograph edition, with portraits, celebrating the poet's seventieth birthday.]

Leaves of Grass. [Ninth edition.] Philadelphia: David McKay. 1892. 438 pp. 8vo.

[Also sold as vol. I of the fourth edition of *Complete Works* (see *Complete Prose Works,* below). This edition, super-

vised and approved by Whitman himself, is the final "authorized" text of all later editions. To p. 381 it is a reprint of
the 1881 edition, new poems being those of the annex
pp. 381-411).]

Leaves of Grass. [Tenth edition.] Boston: Small, Maynard and
Co. 1897. 455 pp. crown octavo.

[In addition to the 1892 text, this edition contains "posthumous additions" in *Old Age Echoes.*]

Complete Prose Works. Philadelphia: David McKay. 1892. 522
pp. large 8vo.

[Sold as vol. II of *Complete Works,* later redated 1894 and
1897. Still later issued as *Prose Works,* undated. Contains:
Specimen Days and *Collect* (1882), prose of *November
Boughs* (1888), and *Good Bye My Fancy* (1891). *Complete
Prose Works* also published by Small, Maynard, Boston,
1898.]

The Complete Writings of Walt Whitman. Issued under the
editorial supervision of the Literary Executors, Richard Maurice Bucke, Thomas B. Harned, and Horace L. Traubel, with
additional bibliographical and critical material by Oscar
Lovell Triggs, Ph.D. New York and London: Putnam's
Sons. The Knickerbocker Press, New York. 1902. 10 vols.,
small quarto.

[Published in several limited editions, with different paper
and various bindings. In addition to Whitman's collected
poetry and prose, this work also contains a biographical
essay by the literary executors, letters of the poet to his
mother, *Notes and Fragments* previously edited by Dr. Bucke,
and other miscellanies.]

Leaves of Grass. Inclusive edition. Garden City, New York:
Doubleday, Doran and Co. 1929. 728 pp. 8vo.

[Contains "authorized" text, with prefaces and Variorum
Readings compiled by Triggs.]

Complete Poetry, and selected prose and letters. Edited by Emory Holloway. New York: Random House. 1938. xxxix, 1116 pp.

["Authorized" text of 1892; a handy modern edition.]

UNCOLLECTED WRITINGS
(In Order of Publication)

Calamus. A Series of Letters Written during the Years 1868-1880. By Walt Whitman to a Young Friend (Peter Doyle). Edited with an introduction by Richard Maurice Bucke, M.D. Boston: Laurens Maynard. 1897. viii, 172 pp.

The Wound Dresser. A Series of Letters Written from the Hospitals in Washington during the War of Rebellion By Walt Whitman. Edited by Richard Maurice Bucke, M.D. Boston: Small, Maynard and Co. 1898. viii, 201 pp.

Notes and Fragments. Edited by Dr. Richard Maurice Bucke. (Printed for Private Distribution Only.) London, Ontario, Canada. 1899. 211 pp.

[Manuscript fragments of both poetry and prose, including some early notebooks and a list of magazine and newspaper clippings kept by the poet. A valuable source book for the study of the development of Whitman's thought and form— though most of the fragments are undated or unreliably dated. This collection was republished in *The Complete Writings of Walt Whitman,* vol. IX.]

Letters Written by Walt Whitman to His Mother From 1866 to 1872. Together with Certain Papers Prepared from Material now First Utilized. Edited by Thomas B. Harned. New York and London: G. P. Putnam's Sons. 1902.

[Excerpt from *Complete Writings,* Vol. VIII, reprinted by Alfred F. Goldsmith, with an Introductory Note by Rollo G. Silver. New York. 1936. 71 pp.]

Walt Whitman's Diary in Canada. With Extracts from other of his Diaries and Literary Note-Books. Edited by William Sloane Kennedy. Boston: Small, Maynard and Co. 1904. 73 pp.

An American Primer. With Facsimiles of the Original Manuscript. Edited by Horace Traubel. Boston: Small, Maynard Co. 1904. 35 pp.

The Letters of Anne Gilchrist and Walt Whitman. Edited by Thomas B. Harned. New York: Doubleday, Doran and Co. 1918. 241 pp.

The Gathering of the Forces. Editorials, Essays, Literary and Dramatic Reviews and other material Written by Walt Whitman as Editor of the Brooklyn Daily *Eagle* in 1846 and 1847. Edited by Cleveland Rodgers and John Black. With a foreword and a sketch of Whitman's Life and Work During Two Unknown Years. New York and London: G. P. Putnam's Sons. 1920. 2 vols.

The Uncollected Poetry and Prose of Walt Whitman. Much of Which Has Been But Recently Discovered with Various Early Manuscripts Now First Published. Collected and Edited by Emory Holloway. New York: Doubleday, Doran and Co. 1921. 2 vols. Reprinted by Peter Smith. New York. 1932. [The most useful of all the "uncollected" publications; indispensable for Whitman research.]

Pictures. An Unpublished Poem by Walt Whitman. With an Introduction and Notes by Emory Holloway. New York: The June House, 1927. London: Faber and Gwyer. 1928. 37 pp.

[One of the ur-*Leaves;* important in the genesis of Whitman's art. Professor Holloway first published the manuscript in "Whitman's Embryonic Verse," *Southwest Review,* X, 28-400 (July, 1925).]

The Half-Breed and Other Stories. Edited by Thomas Ollive Mabbott. New York: Columbia University Press. 1927. 129 pp.

[Juvenile writings published in popular magazines.]

Walt Whitman's Workshop. Edited by Clifton Joseph Furness. Cambridge: Harvard University Press. 1928. 278 pp.

[Contains speeches and unpublished prefaces. Also a valuable Introduction and many Notes by the editor. Indispensable for research or serious study of Whitman.]

The Eighteenth Presidency! Voice of Walt Whitman to each Young Man in the Nation, North, South, East and West. With note by Jean Catel. Montpellier, France: Causse, Graille and Castelnau. 1928. 31 pp.

[Also in *Walt Whitman's Workshop.*]

A Child's Reminiscence. Collected by Thomas O. Mabbott and Rollo G. Silver, with Introduction and Notes. (University of Washington Quartos, No. 1.) University of Washington Book Store. 1930. 44 pp.

[Interesting for light on growth of the poem.]

I Sit and Look Out. Editorials from the Brooklyn *Daily Times.* Selected and Edited by Emory Holloway and Vernolian Schwartz. New York: Columbia University Press. 1932. xii, 248 pp.

[Less valuable than *The Uncollected Poetry and Prose*—the gleanings are running thin.]

Walt Whitman and the Civil War. A Collection of Original Articles and Manuscripts. Edited by Charles I. Glicksberg. University of Pennsylvania Press. 1933. xii, 201 pp.

New York Dissected. A Sheaf of Recently Discovered Newspaper Articles by the author of *Leaves of Grass.* Introduction and Notes by Emory Holloway and Ralph Adimari. New York: Rufus Rockwell Wilson. 1936. 257 pp.

[Some of doubtful authenticity.]

Textual Studies

(Arranged Alphabetically)

Bradley, Sculley. "The Problem of a Variorum Edition of Whitman's *Leaves of Grass." English Institute Annual, 1941.* New York: Columbia University Press. 1942. Pp. 129-157.

[Argues that a satisfactory Variorum Edition must be based on the 1881 text.]

Campbell, Killis. "The Evolution of Whitman as Artist." *American Literature,* VI, 254-263 (November, 1934).

[Traces the poet's growth by means of his textual improvements—main source: Triggs's *Variorum Readings.*]

Catel, Jean. *Walt Whitman: La naissance du poète.* Paris: Les Éditions Rieder. 1929. 504 pp.

[Regards the first edition as the most revealing. Interpretation highly subjective.]

De Selincourt, Basil. *Walt Whitman: A Study.* New York: Mitchell Kennerley. 1914. London: Martin Secker. 1914.

[Chap. VI, "Plan," traces the "skeleton design" of Leaves of Grass.]

Kennedy, William Sloane. "The Growth of 'Leaves of Grass' as a Work of Art (Excisions, Additions, Verbal Changes)." *The Fight of a Book for the World.* West Yarmouth, Mass.: Stonecroft Press. 1926. 304 pp.

[Some interesting examples but the essay is a feeble attempt to trace the "growth" of the work.]

Schyberg, Frederik. "Leaves of Grass 1855-1889 (En Bogs Vækst Og En Digters)." *Walt Whitman.* København: Gyldendalske Boghandel. 1933. Pp. 95-272.

[The first extensive critical examination of all the editions. Unfortunately not available in translation.]

STORY, IRVING C. "The Growth of Leaves of Grass: a Proposal for a Variorum Edition." *Pacific University Bulletin,* XXXVII, 1-11 (February, 1941).

————. "The Structural Pattern of Leaves of Grass." *Pacific University Bulletin,* XXXVIII, 1-12 (January, 1942).
[Both of these essays are valuable contributions.]

STOVALL, FLOYD. "Main Drifts in Whitman's Poetry." *American Literature,* IV, 3-21 (March, 1932).
[Traces certain major developments chronologically but does not characterize the separate editions. Not a systematic textual study, though of value as literary criticism.]

STRAUCH, CARL F. "The Structure of Walt Whitman's Song of of Myself." *English Journal* (College Edition), XXVII, 597-607 (September, 1938).

TRIGGS, OSCAR LOVELL. "The Growth of 'Leaves of Grass'." *Complete Writings of Walt Whitman.* New York: Putnam's Sons. 1902. Vol. X, pp. 99-134.
[Written by a man who knew all the editions—having compiled the *Variorum Readings*—but superficial in critical interpretation.]

CHAPTER III

WHITMAN'S FUNDAMENTAL IDEAS

*These are really the thoughts of all men in all ages
and lands, they are not original with me . . .*[1]

WHITMAN AS PHILOSOPHER

To what extent Walt Whitman took himself seriously
as a "philosopher" it is difficult to say. Certainly he
relished the title of "prophet"—playing the rôle with
such devotion that some critics have thought him a poseur[2]
—; and he conceived the poet's function to be that of
leader and teacher of mankind.[3] But a teacher can not
teach without subject-matter or a prophet prophesy without a message. Whether or not Bertz was correct in his
belief that Whitman wanted to be "the founder of a
tenable scientific religion with a definitely philosophic
world outlook,"[4] there can be little doubt that he wished
above all else to affect profoundly the thinking of his own
and succeeding generations.

Moreover, in his poems he raises and attempts to answer
many philosophical questions of fundamental importance.
Thus on metaphysics:

---

[1] *Song of Myself*, sec. 17.

[2] Cf. p. 40.

[3] Cf. 1855 Preface. Shelley, in his "Defense of Poetry," expresses a
similar theory of the poet's function.

[4] Eduard Bertz, *Der Yankee-Heiland* (Dresden: Reissner, 1906), 100:
"Aber zu seinem Unglück, wollte er vor allem Prophet sein, und zwar,
wie wir sahen, der Verkünder einer wissenschaftlich haltbaren Religion,
also einer einheitlichen philosophischen Weltanschauung, und unter
diesem Gesichtspunkte versagt seine Geistesart . . ."

What is a man anyhow? what am I? what are you?[5]
Or ontology:

To be in any form what is that?[6]

And the central theme of LEAVES OF GRASS as summarized
in the first *Inscription* is the attempt to answer the question of the self, "identity"; what is a person and what is
his relation to society?

One's-self I sing, a simple separate person,
Yet utter the word Democratic, the word En-Masse.[7]

In the 1855 Preface Whitman declared: "The poets of the
kosmos [*i.e.,* the kind of poet he was trying to be] advance
through all interpositions and coverings and turmoils and
stratagems to first principles."[8] And in *Passage to India*
he prophesied that:

Nature and Man shall be disjoin'd and diffused no more,
The true son of God [the Poet] shall absolutely fuse
    them.[9]

All of these purposes and intentions are ethical and
philosophical, but the fact that Whitman propounds such
questions and then attempts to answer them in his
prophetic-poetic utterance does not make him a formal
metaphysician or ontologist. Nor did he intend to be.
In one of his early notebooks he confided:

I will not be a great philosopher, and found any school,
    and build it with iron pillars, and gather the young men

[5] *Song of Myself,* sec. 20.
[6] *Ibid.,* sec. 27.
[7] *One's-Self I Sing.*

[8] 1855 Preface, paragraph 20.
[9] *Passage to India,* sec. 5.

around me, and make them my disciples, that new
superior churches and politics shall come.[10]

In 1860 he repeated this injunction and indicated why he
did not wish to be the founder of a theory or school:

I charge that there be no theory or school founded
out of me,
I charge you to leave all free, as I have left all free.[11]

The poet was not, in fact, either in temperament or ambition, a systematic or aggressive student of philosophy.
He has, himself, accurately characterized his limitations:

Beginning my studies the first step pleas'd me so much,
The mere fact consciousness, these forms, the power of
motion,
The least insect or animal, the senses, eyesight, love,
The first step I say awed me and pleas'd me so much,
I have hardly gone and hardly wish'd to go any farther,
But stop and loiter all the time and sing it in ecstatic
songs.[12]

In view of such a confession, the truth of which is borne
out in the whole bulk of his poems, we cannot accept
literally the poet's claim to

Having studied the new and antique, the Greek and
Germanic systems,
Kant having studied and stated, Fichte and Schelling
and Hegel,[13]
Stated the lore of Plato, and Socrates greater than Plato,

[10] Manuscript Notebook for 1847, in Emory Holloway, *Uncollected Poetry and Prose of Walt Whitman* (New York: Peter Smith, 1932), II, 66. (This collection is hereafter referred to as *Uncollected Poetry and Prose.*)
[11] *Myself and Mine* (1860).
[12] *Beginning My Studies* (1867).
[13] See p. 455.

And greater than Socrates sought and stated, Christ
divine having studied long, . . .

This passage is found in a poem with the pretentious
title, *The Base of All Metaphysics,* but the "base and
finalè too for all metaphysics" turns out to be Whitman's
favorite doctrine of

The dear love of man for his comrade, the attraction
of friend to friend,
Of the well-married husband and wife, of children and
parents,
Of city for city and land for land.

This is, however, no burlesque of philosophy, for Whitman held no doctrine more sincerely than this one, and
he probably called it "metaphysical" in order to show
his profound seriousness. But the "philosophy" of this
poem is plainly ethical, religious, and mystical rather than
speculative or dialectical.

Because Whitman often used names and terms famous
in the history of philosophy, critics have been frequently
puzzled and irritated by what they thought to be his
philosophical pretentions. For example, Robert Louis
Stevenson:

[Whitman's philosophy] is the language of transcendental common sense, such as Thoreau held and sometimes uttered. But Whitman, who has a somewhat
vulgar inclination for technical talk and the jargon of
philosophy is not content with a few pregnant hints;
he must put the dots upon his i's; he must corroborate

the songs of Apollo by some of the darkest talk or human metaphysics.[14]

A more sympathetic critic, John Addington Symonds, declared that, "It is useless to extract a coherent scheme of thought from [Whitman's] voluminous writings ... But though he may not be reducible to system, we can trace an order in his ideas."[15] This opinion has been corroborated by a recent critic, Matthiessen:

> No arrangement or rearrangement of Whitman's thoughts ... can resolve the paradoxes or discover in them a fully coherent pattern. He was incapable of sustained logic, but that should not blind the reader into impatient rejection of the ebb and flow of his antitheses. They possess a loose dialectic of their own ...[16]

And the most recent critic to date, Miss Parsons, says that Whitman was "poet first and philosopher afterward, if precisely speaking, he can be called a philosopher at all (except, of course, as a mystic). He at no time worked out a systematized body of philosophical principles."[17]

If these critical opinions are well-founded—and they are at least typical of modern writers on the subject—, then we would be wasting our time to search in Whitman's writings for a systematic or professional philosophical theory; but he obviously adapted, applied, and per-

---

[14] *Familiar Studies of Men and Books* (New York: Scribner's Sons, 1896), 101.

[15] John Addington Symonds, *Walt Whitman: A Study* (London: George Routledge, 1893), 42.

[16] F. O. Matthiessen, *American Renaissance* (New York: Oxford University Press, 1941), 526.

[17] Olive W. Parsons, "Whitman the Non-Hegelian," *Publications of Modern Language Association*, LVIII, 1077 (December, 1943).

haps even developed philosophical *ideas* in his poetry and prose, whether systematically or not.

We shall, therefore, speak from now on not of Walt Whitman's "philosophy" but of his "thought" and "ideas". And we may discover that in their own context—which is to say, in relation to sources (whether personal or literary) and poetic use or linguistic environment—they are less chaotic, contradictory, and incoherent than they appear to the casual or uninformed reader.

Furthermore, one seldom goes to a poet for philosophy, but to philosophers themselves. Poets hardly ever originate philosophical ideas, but they often adapt them to their own purposes, and Whitman was one of the world's most prolific adapters. Some knowledge of the theories and concepts which he was trying to express in his own lyric way is indispensable for an understanding and appreciation of his message and his technique of expressing it. Without such knowledge, much of his poetic vocabulary remains esoteric, and his technique as confusing as most of his contemporaries found it to be.

MYSTICISM: THE BACKGROUND OF WHITMAN'S THOUGHT

Nearly all critics agree that Whitman was a mystic, and biographers have sought in a "mystical experience" or similar psychic phenomenon for the clue to his almost miraculous acquisition of creative power in the 1850's.[18] The term *mystic,* however, is ambiguous and lends itself to confusion even in scholarly and critical discussions. Thus one critic will call Blake and Wordsworth mystics and others will deny that they were. Emerson has often

---

[18] See pp. 14, 56.

been called a mystic, but he himself contrasted unfavorably the mystic and the poet.[19]

Mystics themselves desire above all else to come somehow into direct contact with the supernatural, and they are usually labeled on the basis of the strength of their convictions or the vividness with which they describe their experiences. But how do we know that they have established relations with unseen forces, or that they speak truthfully? Obviously neither proof nor accurate standards are possible. The very nature of the experience indicates the unavoidable ambiguity of analysis and criticism. The greatest variable, however, is the interpretation. One of the most widely-accepted authorities on this subject, Dr. Rufus Jones, says:

> . . . the fundamental fact of first-hand mystical experience, the direct encounter with the living revealing God in the depths of the soul, is pretty much of the same type in all ages, in all lands, and in all religions. What varies is the interpretation of the experience through the attempt to communicate it and to make others see the significance of the inward event. Here in this business of interpretation and communication come into play the whole background stock of ideas and the prevailing philosophy or theology of any given period.[20]

Viewing mysticism as a psychological phenomenon, we can, with William James, observe and enumerate the external characteristics. He discovered, after studying many

---

[19] In "The Poet": "Here is the difference betwixt the poet and the mystic, that the last nails a symbol to one sense, which was a true sense for a moment, but soon becomes old and false." Poets use universal symbols. This citicism implies the superiority of the poet over the mystic.

[20] Rufus M. Jones in a review of *Jewish Mysticism*, by G. Scholen, *Harvard Theological Review*, XXXVI, 156 (April, 1943).

cases, that the person who has had a "mystical experience" usually reports four characteristics, which James calls: (1) *ineffability,* (2) *noetic quality,* (3) *transiency,* and (4) *passivity.*[21] To translate: the first means that the experience defies expression; it cannot be imparted to others. The second means that despite the ineffability, the subject feels a great desire to communicate the experience, *feeling* that he has some great wisdom to impart; hence the familiar mystical recourse to symbols and "indirections" (Whitman's favorite word). The third term means that the "mystical state" passes quickly: "Except in rare instances, half an hour, or at most an hour or two, seems to be the limit beyond which they fade into the light of common day."[22] The fourth characteristic needs little explanation; the subject feels himself to be completely *passive,* his own will in abeyance, and sometimes he has a conviction of having been grasped, held, sustained, etc. by some superior will or power.

Notice, however, that this is a psychological description. It is a description of someone who has a conviction that he has *experienced* something supernatural. Failure to notice this fact is the source of much of the confusion in discussions of mystics. James describes such an experience as Paul of Tarsus had on the road to Damascus, or Swedenborg in his visions of Paradise—or as Blake claims to have had, though they may have come from his poetic imagination, so that it is perhaps impossible to say whether they are literally truthful or symbolically truthful.

Most of the authorities on mysticism fail to take into account derivative, literary, or borrowed mysticism. A

[21] William James, *Varieties of Religious Experience* (New York: Longmans, Green, 1925), 380-382.
[22] *Ibid.,* 381.

person who has never experienced a "mystical state" may have been influenced in his personal contact with someone who has had such an experience, or he may pick up ideas, attitudes, and vicarious experience in his reading. Perhaps we might distinguish these as primary and secondary mysticism, but the distinction cannot be more than theoretical, for the one sort of mystic can easily become the other kind.

This distinction, however, will be useful in studying Whitman's mysticism. It is difficult to prove that he was a "primary" mystic, though Dr. R. M. Bucke, an intimate friend during the poet's old age, claims that he was. In fact, it seems to have been from his acquaintance with Whitman that this Canadian psychiatrist got his idea that in the course of evolution some rare, fortunate human beings develop a third[23] and superior kind of consciousness, or "Cosmic Consciousness,"[24] a term which Dr. Bucke explained in this way:

> Whitman, who has an immense deal to say about [Cosmic Consciousness], speaks of it in one place as "ineffable light—light rare, untellable, lighting the very light—beyond all signs, descriptions, languages." This consciousness shows the cosmos to consist not of dead matter governed by unconscious, rigid, and unintending law; it shows it on the contrary as entirely immaterial, entirely spiritual and entirely alive; it shows that death is an absurdity, that everyone and everything has eternal life; it shows that the universe is God and that God is the universe, and that no evil ever did or ever will enter

---

[23] The other two are of course the conscious and the subconscious or unconscious.

[24] Richard Maurice Bucke, *Cosmic Consciousness* (New York: E. P. Dutton, 1923—other editions in 1901, 1905, 1912, and 1922).

into it; a great deal of this is, of course, from the point of view of self consciousness, absurd; it is nevertheless undoubtedly true. Now all this does not mean that when a man has cosmic consciousness he knows everything about the universe.[25]

We notice in this description of cosmic consciousness, or more commonly known as mysticism, not only definite attitudes toward life, God, and man's relationship to the unseen world, but also philosophical ideas: matter is alive and spiritual, God and the universe are the same, evil is an illusion, etc. Mysticism is not itself a philosophy, but a mystic cherishes certain typical ideas.

Since we are interested primarily in Whitman's *ideas,* it does not matter exactly where he got them, whether from "cosmic consciousness," from reading and memory, or from cognition. The point is that certain of Whitman's fundamental ideas are commonly found in the literature of mystics and mysticism, and this is why we need some knowledge of the subject to understand and appreciate his ideas.

One of the most useful summaries of the ideas of mysticism is contained in Bertrand Russell's lecture on *Mysticism and Logic.* Mysticism and logic are commonly thought to be mutually contradictory and incompatible, but if metaphysics be defined, as Mr. Russell defines it, as "the attempt to conceive the world as a whole by means of thought,"[26] then we see that there may be even a kind of mystical metaphysics—even a mystical logic. Bergson has remarked that there are "two profoundly different

---

[25] *Ibid.,* 17-18.

[26] Bertrand Russell, *Mysticism and Logic and Other Essays* (London: Longmans, Green, 1921), 1.

ways of knowing a thing. The first implies that we move round the object; the second that we enter into it."[27] The mystic tries to obtain knowledge by the second means.

Russell summarizes the central ideas in practically all mysticisms:

1. Insight—knowledge is obtained by intuition.
2. Unity—plurality and division are illusory.
3. Unreality of Time and Space.
4. Evil is mere appearance.

"Mysticism does not maintain that such things as cruelty, for example, are good but it denies that they are real: they belong to that lower world of phantoms from which we are to be liberated by the insight of the vision."[28] In other words, this idea is an aspect of the belief in Unity, one of the oldest doctrines in religion and philosophy, known in the former as pantheism and in the latter as monism, though the logic of this indivisible Whole began with Parmenides and culminated in Hegel.[29]

Although Russell's essay is a defence of the scientific rather than the mystic method of acquiring knowledge, he admits that, "Even the cautious and patient investigation of truth by science, which seems the very antithesis of the mystic's swift certainty, may be fostered and nourished by that very spirit of reverence in which mysticism lives and moves."[30]

Before proceeding to examples of Whitman's mysticism, one more distinction must be made. It is often assumed that mystics of all lands and ages are surprisingly alike,

---

[27] Quoted, *Ibid.*, 14, from *Introduction to Metaphysics*, p. 1.
[28] *Ibid.*, 10-11.
[29] *Ibid.*, 18.
[30] *Ibid.*, 12.

especially that East and West (Orient and Occident) meet in mysticism. The similarities are so astonishing that the dissimilarities are often overlooked. In a comparative study of this relationship, Rudolf Otto says, "In spite of much formal agreement, mystical experience is capable of great diversity. Its content can be curiously varied. The moods and feelings which it arouses can differ from one another even to the extent of being diametrically opposed."[31]

Taking Śankara, one of the greatest of all Hindu mystics—the classical example—as typical of the East, and the Medieval German mystic, "Meister" Eckhart, as representative of the West, Otto discovers a fundamental contrast, which he calls "static" and "dynamic":

> The goal for Śankara is the stilling of all Karmāni, all works, all activity of will: it is quietism, tyāga, a surrender of the will and of doing, an abandonment of good as of evil works, for both bind man to the world of wandering.[32]

But for Eckhart:

> God is, in Himself, tremendous life movement. Out of undifferentiated unity He enters into the multiplicity of personal life and persons, in whom the world and therewith the multiplicity of the world is contained.[33]

As Eckhart himself would say: God "loves and creates without ceasing. Work is His nature, His being, His life, His happiness."[34] Or in Otto's summary:

---

[31] Rudolf Otto, *Mysticism East and West* (New York: Macmillan, 1932), 39.
[32] *Ibid.*, 173.
[33] *Ibid.*, 170.
[34] *Ibid.*, 173.

Only in the being of the creature does God Himself come to His own goal and purpose. That is to say, only as the eternal and ceaselessly creating God, is He God. For only thus is He a 'living' God. This is the Christian God, who is not like the God of the ancient world sufficient unto Himself, blessed in Himself.[35]

Thus the eastern mystic may speak of cycles and transmigrations, but he does not believe in progress, evolution, amelioration. The greatest misfortune to the "soul" is to have to enter into other forms of life, to continue the journey. The highest objective is obliteration of individuality by coming to rest—to negation—in the Eternal, the Over-Soul, or *nirvana*. The western mind may be attracted by quietism, and in certain moods may long for it, but the Faust-soul is typically occidental. The spiritual goal must be attained through turmoil, struggle, and suffering. It is no accident that Schopenhauer's theory of the world as will, Fichte's philosophy of the *ego*, or Nietzsche's "will to power" developed in the West. Eastern mysticism may have curbed the aggressiveness of Thoreau and Emerson, but every critic and biographer admits that they remained Yankee for all that.[36] Though Whitman's poetic utterance sounds familiar to the Hindus themselves,[37] we shall understand his mysticism more readily if we look for its dynamic rather than static characteristics.

---

[35] *Ibid.*, 175.

[36] Cf. Arthur Christy, *The Orient in American Transcendentalism* (New York: Columbia University Press, 1932), 223.

[37] "Vedantic views are at times [in *Leaves of Grass*] expressed with such originality and energy as to have brought a smile of delight to the serene immobile countenance of a Hindu friend, to whom I read them," William A. Guthrie, *Walt Whitman the Camden Sage* (Cincinnati: Robert Clark Co., 1897), 25. See also Edward Carpenter, *Days with Walt Whitman* (London: George Allen, 1906), 250.

Both in LEAVES OF GRASS and in his prose Whitman has given a number of descriptions of experiences almost exactly parallel to examples in books on mysticism.[38] Perhaps the most famous is section 5 of *Song of Myself:*

I believe in you my soul, the other I am must not abase
    itself to you,
And you must not be abased to the other.

Loafe with me on the grass, loose the stop from your
    throat,
Not words, not music or rhyme I want, not custom or
    lecture, not even the best,
Only the lull I like, the hum of your valvèd voice.

I mind how once we lay such a transparent summer
    morning,
How you settled your head athwart my hips and gently
    turn'd over upon me,
And parted the shirt from my bosom-bone, and plunged
    your tongue to my bare-stript heart,
And reach'd till you felt my beard, and reach'd till you
    held my feet.

Swiftly arose and spread around me the peace and
    knowledge that pass all the argument of the earth,
And I know that the hand of God is the promise of
    my own,
And I know that the spirit of God is the brother of
    my own,
And that all the men ever born are also my brothers,
    and the women my sisters and lovers,
And that a kelson of the creation is love,

---

[38] James, *op. cit.*, quotes in Lecture XVI the core of Section 5 of *Song of Myself.*

And limitless are leaves stiff or drooping in the fields,
And brown ants in the little wells beneath them,
And mossy scabs of the worm fence, heap'd stones,
elder mullein, and poke-weed.

Whether this is the account of a psychological experience—something like a "vision"—or an imaginative creation to convey a literary intention, we have no way of knowing, and even if we had more data the distinction might be irrelevant. The passage, however, is an astonishingly complete description of almost all phases of a mystical experience, from the communication with the Soul[39] and the sensation of being penetrated and permeated by the supernatural, to the belief that the experience has brought with it clairvoyant knowledge and spiritual wisdom. Typical of the mystic are the resultant convictions of equality with God, brotherhood with all people, and love as the foundation of the whole universal creation. As a matter of fact, these over-beliefs resulting from the "vision" fairly accurately indicate the main "ideas" in the poem. And it is by such means as illustrated in this passage that the cosmic poet advances through coverings and turmoils to "first principles."[40] It is the clue which Whitman himself gives to the secret of his message.

Although we shall later analyze in detail Whitman's stylistic techniques, it is important at this point to notice his theory of inspiration. The first lines of the above quotation are clarified by a confession in a notebook, containing the germs of his first poems: "I cannot understand the mystery, but I am always conscious of myself

---

[39] It is characteristic of Whitman in his early period that he communicates with his own Soul instead of God.

[40] Cf. p. 237.

as two—as my soul and I: and I reckon it is the same with all men and women."[41] The "other I am," then, must be his ordinary consciousness, or possibly his physical self. In another place he records the thought that,

> A man only is interested [*i.e.*, is interested only] in anything when he identifies himself with it—he must himself be whirling and speeding through space like the planet Mercury—he must be driving like a cloud—he must shine like the sun—he must be orbic and balanced in the air, like this earth . . .[42]

And in a trial poetic flight, we get a glimpse of this "identification" in practice:

> Afar in the sky was a nest,
> And my soul flew thither and squat[ted], and looked out
> And saw the journeywork of suns and systems of suns,
> And that a leaf of grass is not less than they . . .[43]

In still another place he is so explicit that his self-instructions might be compared to yoga exercises—and perhaps they indicate the means by which he half-hypnotized himself into a sort of automatic composition:

> Abstract yourself from this book; realize where you are at present located, the point you stand that is now to you the centre of all. Look up overhead, think of space stretching out, think of all the unnumbered orbs wheeling safely there, invisible to us by day, some visible by night . . . Spend some minutes faithfully in this exercise. Then again realize yourself upon the earth, at the

[41] *Uncollected Poetry and Prose,* II, 66. Cf. C. J. Furness, *Walt Whitman's Workshop* (Harvard University Press, 1928,) 200, n. 36.
[42] *Uncollected Poetry and Prose,* II, 64.
[43] *Ibid.,* 70.

particular point you now occupy ... [Thinks of fou directions.] Seize these firmly in your mind, pass freely over immense distances. Turn your face a moment thither. Fix definitely the direction and the idea of the distances of separate sections of your own country, also of England, the Mediterranean Sea, Cape Horn, the North Pole, and such like distinct places.[44]

Thus by being conscious of his imaginative faculty as a distinct identity or personality, which he addresses as "my Soul," by "identifying" this poetic consciousness with whatever thing or place he chooses for treatment in verse, and by yoga-like limbering up and stretching of his mind, he succeeds now and then in composing like "one divinely possessed, blind to all subordinate affairs and given up entirely to the surgings and utterances of the mighty tempestous demon."[45]

I depart as air, I shake my white locks at the runaway
    sun,
I effuse my flesh in eddies, and drift it in lacy jags.[46]

But these intoxications during which the poet is "afoot with [his] vision," casting off material "ties and ballasts,"[47] are no mere mystical dypsomania. In 1871 Whitman explained the purpose of LEAVES OF GRASS in these lines:

---

[44] *Workshop, op. cit.,* 189.
[45] *Ibid.,* 37. The quotation is from a manuscript on Whitman's theory of oratory, but applies equally well to his conception of poetic inspiration. It is significant that in *Pioneers! O Pioneers!* the poet thinks of himself as a "trio,"
    I too with my soul and body,
    We, a curious trio . . .
[46] *Song of Myself,* sec. 52.
[47] *Ibid.,* sec. 33.

To put rapport the mountains and rocks and streams,
And the winds of the north, and the forests of oak and
    pine,
With you O soul.[48]

Like all mystics, Whitman regards his intuitive knowledge as incommunicable; words and logic[49] are paltry
and inadequate.

There is something that comes home to one now and
    perpetually,
It is not what is printed, preach'd, discussed, it eludes
    discussion and print,
It is not to be put in a book, it is not in this book, . . .[50]

In fact, he sees "little or nothing in audible words," but
he thinks that "All merges toward the presentation of the
unspoken meanings of the earth."[51] Knowledge of these
"meanings" consists mainly of a perception of analogies,
relations of parts (identities) to whole (unity, Absolute).

Here we come to the *emanations* doctrine. "The kernel
of every object that can be seen[,] felt or thought of,
has its relations to the soul, and is significant of something there."[52] Which is to say that "All truths wait in
all things . . ."[53]

Here is the test of wisdom, . . .
Something there is in the float of the sight of things
    that provokes it out of the soul.

[48] *As they Draw to a Close.*
[49] Cf.: Logic and sermons never convince,
    The damp of the night drives deeper into my soul.
[50] *A Song for Occupations,* sec. 2.
[51] *A Song of the Rolling Earth,* sec. 3.
[52] Quoted in *Workshop,* 236, note 138, from Emory Holloway, "A
Whitman Manuscript," *American Mercury,* III, 475 (Dec., 1924).
[53] *Song of Myself,* sec. 30.

. . . .

> The efflux of the soul comes from within, through em-
> bower'd gates, ever provoking questions, ...[54]

Or again,

> To me converging objects of the universe perpetually
> flow,
> All are written to me, and I must get what the writing
> means.[55]

Furness says that Whitman "eventually adopted the attitude of the older mystics toward perception, embracing
the view voiced by Nicholas of Cusa, and Valentine
Weigel, that 'all knowledge flows out from man into the
object,' but that 'the object has a reality in itself, which
awakens the knowledge in the spirit'."[56] But at least in
the earlier stages of his thought and poetic career he believed that these emanations of the soul flowed both ways,
from the object to him and from himself outward.[57]
Hence his desire to be in contact with things and people,
and also his belief that "The presence of the greatest poet
conquers" and that "If he breathes into anything that was
before thought small it dilates with the grandeur and life
of the universe."[58]

At this point, however, it is almost impossible to understand these doctrines of "dilation" and "emanation"
without studying the larger aspects of Whitman's "Idealism," or as it is commonly called, "Pantheism."

---

[54] *Song of the Open Road*, sec. 6-7.
[55] *Song of Myself*, sec. 20.
[56] *Workshop*, 236.
[57] Cf. *There Was a Child Went Forth* (1855) and *Crossing Brooklyn Ferry* (1856).
[58] The 1855 Preface.

PANTHEISM AND PANPSYCHISM:
DEFINITIONS

In 1888 the French critic, Gabriel Sarrazin, declared that, "The poetry of Walt Whitman proclaimed at the outset complete pantheism, with no extenuation, and with all its consequences (see 'Song of the Universal')."[59] Since then the term *pantheism* has been the word most frequently used to indicate the nature of Whitman's thought, though no one seems to have taken the trouble to define the term or to indicate which of the many possible definitions is most applicable to his ideas.[60]

Pantheism is almost as broad and ambiguous as *mysticism,* and the complexity of ideas which it embraces are perhaps as old in human thought and experience as mysticism. To use a dictionary definition, pantheism is "The doctrine that the universe, taken or conceived of as a whole, is God; the doctrine that there is no God but the combined forces and laws which are manifested in the existing universe..."[61] But this definition itself contains two almost diametrically opposed views: the first suggests a spiritual pantheism, the latter a materialistic pantheism—which some authorities deny being pantheism at all. The latter view, in fact, is often associated with atheism, and is also sometimes denounced by theologians

---

[59] "Walt Whitman," translated by Harrison S. Morris, in *In Re Walt Whitman* (Philadelphia: David McKay, 1893), 160.

[60] The chief authorities on pantheism are: C. E. Plumptre, *General Sketch of the History of Pantheism* (London: Samuel Deacon and Co., 1878), 2 vols. J. Allanson Picton, *Pantheism: Its Story and Significance* (London: Archibald Constable, 1905). Rev. John Hunt, *An Essay on Pantheism* (London: Longmans, Green, Reader, and Dyer, 1866).

[61] *Webster's Collegiate Dictionary,* fifth edition (1937). See also J. M. Baldwin, *Dictionary of Philosophy and Psychology* (New York: Peter Smith, 1940).

for its emphasis on the non-personality of God.[62]

In most views, however, pantheism is neither atheistic nor agnostic, but is rather a belief in spirit, God, and immortality to the extent of being mystical. Herein it is easily distinguished from *deism,* which conceives of creation as an act of imposing structure upon external material. The deist thinks of God as a maker or designer. The pantheist thinks of Him as *immanent* and creation as an *emanation.* Several varieties of pantheism may be mentioned as illustrations: *acosmism* is the belief that the universe is a creation of a divine mind (may or may not be pantheistic); *cosmotheism* is the belief that the physical universe is the only divinity (this may become materialistic pantheism); *Neoplatonism* teaches that there is a One above Reason and that men and things are not true beings but shadows, appearances, even illusions (as in Hindu mysticism). A pantheistic doctrine which strongly resembles Whitman's is that of Giordano Bruno, the Renaissance mystic, who taught that God is a world or cosmic personality. Akin to this doctrine is *panpsychism,* "the form of noumenal idealism which holds that the universe is a vast communion of spirits, souls of men, of animals, of plants, of earth and other planets, of the sun, all embraced as different members of the soul of the world."[63] In fact, panpsychism might be a more satisfactory term for Whitman's thought than pantheism, though at times pantheism seems more applicable to his

---

[62] An interesting example in America is Ebenezer Halley, *The Pantheism of Germany: A Sermon Delivered before the Synod of Albany, at Saratoga Springs, Oct. 9, 1850* (Albany: Gray and Sprague, 1850).

[63] *Encyclopedia Britannica* (metaphysics of Fechner and Paulsen), 10th ed., XXX, 659.

thought than this less familiar term,[64] and is therefore more convenient.

Plotinus and so-called Neo-platonists are in general pantheistic, but Spinoza is usually regarded as the father of modern pantheism. He taught that proof of God is the existence of nature, and that the created and creator are one; hence that it is not necessary to go outside the realm of nature to find God. Since God is indivisible, nature is interlocked by an all-pervading unity. If evil exists at all, it must exist in nature, and nature being indivisible, there is no evil; or what we call evil is only what displeases us. When the mind by intuitive insight catches a glimpse of God in nature, it perceives the immortal, which is to say, outside Time and Space (which have no more reality than evil). Thus immortality may be achieved here and now by the mind's identifying itself with God-in-nature. These doctrines, though greatly modified by Leibniz, Kant, Fichte, Schelling, Hegel, etc., form the background of German "Idealism." Thus Leibniz's doctrine that since monads, the ultimate reality, are indestructible, there is really no birth or death and rational souls pass on to other stages of existence. Central in Fichte's theory of the Ego is the belief that nature is physical in appearances but spiritual in reality and that thought—Idea—is the only Reality. In Schelling's philosophy the outer world is symbolic of the real or ideal (thought) world; in nature we see the *identity* of the ideal. Or as Whitman himself summarized this doctrine: *"the essential identity of the sub-*

---

[64] It is perhaps logically contradictory for Whitman's thought to be both pantheistic and panpsychic, for the former is usually thought of as universal spirit (or God) in nature whereas the latter teaches that each atom, particle, etc. has a distinct soul; since, however, there is an all-embracing kinship or unity among these souls, the distinction is subtle—certainly too subtle to have bothered the mind of Walt Whitman.

jective and objective worlds, or . . . what exists as mentality, intelligence, consciousness in man, exists in equal strength and absoluteness in concrete forms, shows [*i.e.,* appearances] and practical laws in material nature."[65] Schleiermacher, influenced by both Spinoza and Schelling, introduced pantheism into German theology.[66] He replaced the personal God of the Moravians with an impersonal Divinity of philosophy. For him nature was a continuous action of Divinity.[67]

To summarize the essense of pantheism: the universe is a Divine Unity, in which separation of parts and the existence of Time and Space, good and evil, birth and death have no ultimate reality but exist only artificially in temporarily finite minds (temporary because finite minds will soon return to the infinite Unity of all mind). Some pantheists tend to deny reality of any kind to the physical world, regarding it as illusory and evanescent, while others regard it as Divine Reality itself; but both are likely to treat natural objects as symbolical either of God or a higher and invisible Unity. Here pantheism and mysticism are inseparable, as in Fichte's statement that:

> We see Him (through the eye of conception) as stone, plant, animal; we see Him when we pass beyond these, as the law of nature, as the moral law. Yet all this is still not He. Always the form hides the Being from us. Always our seeing itself covers up the object of our seeing, and our own eye stands in the way of our sight.[68]

---

[65] Unpublished notes for projected lectures on German philosophy, *Notes and Fragments,* edited by Dr. Richard Maurice Bucke (London, Canada: privately printed, 1899), 138; reprinted in *The Complete Writings of Walt Whitman* (New York: Putnam, 1902), IX, 180.

[66] In this country Schleiermacher's *Discourses* influenced Theodore Parker to write and publish (1842) *A Discourse of Matters Pertaining to Religion.*

[67] Cf. Otto, *op. cit.,* 241.

[68] Quoted by Otto, *op. cit.,* 225.

WHITMAN'S PANTHEISM

It was Goethe who said, "We know the soul only through the medium of the body, and God only through Nature."[69] Goethe is not accused of being a materialist because he sang the beauties of physical life, for his pantheism is well known. But probably no other of Whitman's ideas has been so misunderstood and misrepresented as his doctrine that the body is the soul. As late as 1932 Floyd Stovall referred to "the inherent sensuality of Whitman's nature,"[70] and attempted to trace the poet's shift from a physiological to a spiritual philosophy and poetic expression. No doubt Whitman did shift his lyric emphasis as he grew older, feebler, and more conservative, but his pantheism was at no time stronger or more genuine than in his first edition. In fact, some of the clearest statements are found in the unpublished manuscripts, notes, and fragments which he wrote in preparation for the first poems. In his 1847 *Notebook* he wrote:

> The effusion or corporation of the soul is always under the beautiful laws of physiology—I guess the soul itself can never be anything but great and pure and immortal; but it makes itself visible only through matter—a perfect head, and bowels and bones to match is the easy gate through which it comes from its embowered garden, and pleasantly appears to the sight of the world.[71]

---

[69] Quoted by George H. Lewes, *The Life of Goethe* (London: Smith, Elder and Co., 1875 [third ed.]), 72. Goethe added: "Hence the absurdity, as it appears to me, of accusing those of absurdity who philosophically have united God with the world. For everything which exists, necessarily pertains to the essence of God, because God is the one Being whose existence includes all things." *Ibid.*

[70] Floyd Stovall, "Main Drifts in Whitman's Poetry," *American Literature*, IV, 5 (March, 1932).

[71] *Uncollected Poetry and Prose*, II, 65. See also p. 64.

Since *the soul makes itself visible only through matter,* this doctrine is easily misunderstood, especially because it led Whitman to sing of "reality" with a boldness that might be taken for "naive realism." Although his pantheism is essentially mystical, it is unlike either the Oriental or Carlylean mystical pantheism,[72] both of which regard the objective world as un-real and chimerical. In his attempt to combat this sort of "Idealism" Whitman wrote in his *Notebook* this experimental poem:

> I am the poet of reality
> I say the earth is not an echo.
> Nor man an apparition;
> But that all the things seen are real,
> The witness and albic dawn of things equally real
> I have split the earth and the hard coal and rocks and
>   the solid bed of the sea
> And went down to reconnoitre there a long time,
> And bring back a report,
> And I understand that those are positive and dense
>   every one
> And that what they seem to the child they are...[73]

This sounds like Dr. Johnson's naïve refutation of Berkeley's idealism by kicking a brick, and perhaps it is just that. But in other manuscript fragments we find a different interpretation of this apparent "materialism." For example:

> Why what do you suppose is the Body?
> Do you suppose this that has always existed—
>   this meat, bread, fruit that is eaten, is the body?

---

[72] Cf. Charles Frederick Harrold, *Carlyle and German Thought, 1819-1834* (New Haven: Yale University Press, 1934), 80-81.

[73] *Uncollected Poetry and Prose,* II, 69-70.

No, those are visible parts of the body, materials that
  have existed in some way for billions of years not
  entering into the form of the body,
But there is the real body too, not visible.

    .   .   .   .   .

Divine is the body—it is all—it is the soul also.
How can there be immortality except through mortality?
How can the ultimate reality of visible things be
  visible?
How can the real body ever die?[74]

This doctrine may have been influenced by the scientific
principle of the conservation of energy (the second law
of thermodynamics), but the poet's emphasis is mystical
rather than scientific. In *Song of Myself* he also sings what
might be taken as a materialistic pantheism:

And as to you Corpse I think you are good manure,
  but that does not offend me,
I smell the white roses sweet-scented and growing,
I reach to the leafy lips, I reach to the polish'd breasts
  of melons.[75]

and again:

I bequeath myself to the dirt to grow from the grass I
  love,
If you want me again look for me under your bootsoles.[76]

But in this same poem he declares that he hears and
beholds God in every object.[77] The doctrine of "signa-

---

[74] *Notes and Fragments,* 37-38. Whitman was not satisfied with this
passage in his manuscript, for he wrote, "Make this more rhythmic."
[75] *Song of Myself,* sec. 49.
[76] *Ibid.,* sec. 52.
[77] *Ibid.,* sec. 48.

tures"[78] is familiar in the literature both of mysticism and
pantheism:

> I see something of God each hour of the twenty-four,
>   and each moment then,
> In the faces of men and women I see God, and in my
>   own face in the glass,
> I find letters from God dropt in the street, and every
>   one is sign'd by God's name,
> And I leave them where they are, for I know that where-
>   soe'er I go,
> Others will punctually come for ever and ever.[79]

That this is really pantheism (or possibly panpsychism)
is abundantly borne out in many other poems:

> Strange and hard that paradox true I give,
> Objects gross and the unseen soul are one.[80]
> We realize the soul only by you, you faithful solids and
>   fluids,[81]

In *Starting from Paumanok* Whitman declares that all objects and particles of the universe have "reference to the
Soul,"[82] and that "the body includes ... and is the Soul."[83]
In *To Think of Time* he calls suspicion of death the worst
of all heresies because it denies "soul" for every particle
of the universe:

> I swear I see now that every thing has an eternal soul!

---

[78] The Hebraic teaching that man was made in the image of God is
paralleled by the pantheistic idea that every object in nature bears the
imprint or sign of God. Cf. Emerson's theory of symbols in *Nature* or
Goethe and Carlyle's image of the world as the "Garment of God" (*Faust*
and *Sartor Resartus*).
[79] *Song of Myself*, sec. 48.
[80] *A Song for Occupations*, sec. 5.
[81] *Sun-Down Poem (Crossing Brooklyn Ferry)*, 1856 edition, p. 221.
[82] *Proto-Leaf (Starting from Paumanok)*, 1860 edition, [sec. 46], p. 17.
[83] *Ibid.*, [sec. 51], p. 17.

The trees have, rooted in the ground . . . . the weeds of
  the sea have . . . . the animals.
I swear I think there is nothing but immortality!
That the exquisite scheme is for it, and the nebulous
  float is for it, and the cohering is for it,
And all preparation is for it . . . . and identity is for it
  . . . . and life and death are for it.[84]

This is a poem of 1855, but *Eidólons,* 1876, is a restatement of the same theme, and most of Whitman's later
treatments of death and immortality rest upon this doctrine as a background.

Now that we are sufficiently familiar with the extent to
which Whitman used this idea, it is time to examine applications or broader implications of pantheism. One of
the poet's key-words is *identity.* Notice in the above quotation that it is associated with "nebulous float," "cohering," and "preparation," all words suggesting cosmic
evolution. In *Crossing Brooklyn Ferry* we find the term
in a context in which the meaning is unmistakable:

I too had been struck from the float forever held in
  solution,
I too had receiv'd identity by my body, . . .[85]

And in *To Think of Time:*

It is not to diffuse you that you were born of your mother
  and father, it is to identify you, . . .
Something long preparing and formless is arrived and
  form'd in you,
You are henceforth secure, whatever comes or goes.[86]

---

[84] 1855 version; final version slightly different—see sec. 9.
[85] Sec. 5.
[86] Sec. 7.

Whitman's "float" corresponds to Emerson's Over-Soul, though the imagery comes more from science than Emerson's term, which is a translation of the Hindu *Atman*. It is of course not Darwinian, for Whitman was using it several years before the *Origin of Species* was published (1859), but it parallels the cosmic evolution of Leibniz, Schelling, Goethe, etc.

This then is life,
Here is what has come to the surface after so many
throes and convulsions, . . .[87]

At "birth" each object in nature becomes individualized momentarily, (*i.e.*, receives its "identity" through form or "body") and represents some portion of the soul-stuff which pervades the universe.[88] At times Whitman seems to think of this soul as a germ lying fallow, awaiting the "arousing touch" to start it on its life-journey[89]—he is fascinated by the symbolism of traveling,[90] because he believes in a universe in a state of constant development and amelioration: "All parts away for the progress of souls."[91] In this procession all forms of life and people have their places and "The law of promotion and transformation cannot be eluded."[92]

In various places in his writings Whitman treats one aspect of his evolution thought in a manner that suggests

---

[87] *Starting from Paumanok*, sec. 2.

[88] Cf. Emerson's *Over-Soul*: "Within man is the Soul of the whole . . . to which every part and particle is equally related; the eternal ONE."

[89] *Notes and Fragments*, 45.

[90] The significance of the "journey" motif in Whitman's thought is discussed by Gay Wilson Allen in "Walt Whitman's 'Long Journey' Motif," *Journal of English and Germanic Philology*, XXXVIII, 76-95 (January, 1939).

[91] *Song of the Open Road*, sec. 13.

[92] *To Think of Time*, sec. 7.

the Neo-platonic doctrine of the correspondence between external or physical beauty and internal or spiritual beauty, though his expression of the idea seems peculiarly his own. We first encounter this idea in the 1847 (or '48)[93] *Notebook:* "A twisted skull, and blood watery or rotten by ancestry or gluttony, or rum or bad disorders,—they are the darkness toward which the plant will not grow, although its seed lies waiting for ages."[94] Already we can see why in his theory of the poet in the 1855 Preface, in his early poems, and later in his self-inspired biography, Whitman will emphasize so fanatically his robust health, his physical beauty, and his biologically perfect ancestry. One wonders, also, what influence, if any, Walt's idiot brother may have had on this idea,[95] or why it appealed so strongly to the poet's imagination; but all that we can say with certainty is that the idea occupies a most important niche in the metaphysics of Whitman's poetry, as in *The Sleepers:*

The Soul is always beautiful,
The universe is duly in order, everything is in its place,
What has arrived is in its place, and what waits shall
    be in its place,
The twisted skull waits, the watery or rotten blood waits,
The child of the glutton or venerealee waits long, and
    the child of the drunkard waits long, and the
    drunkard himself waits long,
The sleepers that lived and died wait, the far advanced
    are to go on in their turns, and the far behind are
    to come on in their turns,

---

[93] See *Uncollected Poetry and Prose,* p. 63 note. Cf. also note 71, above.
[94] *Ibid.,* 65.
[95] See p. 82.

The diverse shall be no less diverse, but they shall flow
and unite—they unite now.[96]

In *Faces* this doctrine becomes clearer:

Do you suppose I could be content with all [*i.e.,* faces,
appearances, life as it is observed] if I thought them
their own finalè?

.   .   .

Off [*sic*] the word I have spoken, I except not one—
red, white, black, are all deific,
In each house is the ovum, it comes forth after a
thousand years.

Spots or cracks at the windows do not disturb me,
Tall and sufficient stand behind and make signs to me,
I read the promise, and patiently wait.[97]

This potential divinity in all men and all things considerably modifies Whitman's worship of the spirit in the
flesh—we might say the spirit or soul made manifest in
the flesh. All being and all life are incomplete and imperfect at any given moment in their transitory existence
but will in due course of cosmic evolution come nearer to
perfection.

Like Pythagoras, Bruno, and other pantheists, Whitman
does not fear death but welcomes it as part of the cosmic
scheme of change. Souls are indestructible, and unceasingly journey from body to body and abode to abode, always carrying out some divine scheme; therefore death
is "The word of the sweetest song, and all songs."[98]

I do not think Life provides for all and for Time and

---

[96] Sec. 7.
[97] *Faces,* sec. 2 and 4.
[98] *Out of the Cradle Endlessly Rocking.*

Space, but I believe Heavenly Death provides for all.[99]

I have sung . . . the songs of Life and of Birth—and shown that there are many births.[100]

To what extent Whitman believed literally in transmigration is debatable, but there can be no doubt that it is a basic idea in his cosmic evolution, though it is not entirely analogous to Hindu transmigration. To understand and appreciate his use of this idea is to understand and appreciate the apparently extreme individualism, egotism, and messianic rôle of the poet in LEAVES OF GRASS.

Most critics have long been aware that Whitman's "I" is generic and cosmic rather than personal, but the student will also discover an almost limitless range and potentiality of his "I" as a representative migrating "soul":

I exist as I am, that is enough,
If no other in the world be aware I sit content,
And if each and all be aware I sit content.

One world is aware and by far the largest to me, and that is myself,
And whether I come to my own to-day or in ten thousand or ten million years,
I can cheerfully take it now, or with equal cheerfulness I can wait.
My foothold is tenon'd and mortis'd in granite,
I laugh at what you call dissolution,
And I know the amplitude of time.[101]

---

[99] *Assurances.*
[100] *So Long!* (1871 version).
[101] *Song of Myself,* sec. 20.

> And as to you Life I reckon you are the leavings of
>   many deaths,
> (No doubt I have died myself ten thousand times be-
>   fore.)

> I hear you whispering there O stars of heaven,
> O suns—O grass of graves—O perpetual transfers and
>   promotions, . . .[102]

Whitman says nothing of retrogressions of the soul, as
in Brahmanism; it is "transfers" and "promotions." But
this pantheistic transmigration explains his feeling of kinship with all parts of creation, and his doctrine that each is
equally perfect and equally divine with all others—no less
than a complete and uncompromising cosmic democracy!

> I find I incorporate gneiss, coal, long-threaded moss,
>   fruits, grains, esculent roots,
> And am stucco'd with quadrupeds and birds all over,
> And have distanced what is behind me for good reasons,
> And call any thing back again when I desire it.[103]

Of course the "call anything back again, when I desire it"
is mystical and poetic rather than volitional, but his sympathy with the animals is more than an imaginative identification of his ego with theirs:

> I wonder where they get those tokens,
> Did I pass that way huge times ago and negligently
>   drop them?

> Myself moving forward then and now and forever,
> Gathering and showing more always and with velocity,
> Infinite and omnigenous, . . .[104]

---

[102] *Ibid.,* sec. 49.   [104] *Ibid.,* sec. 32.
[103] *Ibid.,* sec. 31.

It is in this sense also that the poet feels himself to be "an acme of things accomplish'd" and "an encloser of things to be."[105] And it is in this sense that he worships his own body and glorifies his heredity:

Before I was born out of my mother generations guided
    me,
My embryo has never been torpid, nothing could over-
    lay it.[106]

Therefore he can say that "nothing, not God, is greater to one than one's self is."[107] What he is deifying is not himself in the ordinary sense but *the self,* the cosmic "soul."

This doctrine likewise accounts for Whitman's worship of sex, for it is by means of sex that the soul receives its identity and perpetually fulfills the cosmic plan:

Ages and ages returning at intervals,
Undestroy'd, wandering immortal,
Lusty, phallic, with the potent original loins, . . .[108]

Practically the whole of *Children of Adam* is an exemplification of this thought and is, as we observed in Chapter II, philosophical rather than personal. Of course Whitman exploited this idea as a means of combatting asceticism and prudery, but he regarded asceticism as philosophically wrong. Of course his own temperament may have colored the conviction, or at least made it possible for the idea to take such a strong hold of him. Is this not true of every man's ideas?

Much of Whitman's lyric inspiration as well as his warm humanitarianism springs from the strong appeal

---

[105] *Ibid.,* sec. 44.
[106] *Ibid.*
[107] *Ibid.,* sec. 48.
[108] *Ages and Ages Returning at Intervals.*

which this idea of the wandering soul made to his impressionable fancy. In fact, it may have been the origin of the poems, for one of Whitman's early literary themes was the origin and progress of the human race. Asia interested him particularly as the birthplace of mankind, as seen in his personification of himself as the human race:

I, a child, very old, over waves, towards the house of
    maternity, the land of migrations, look afar, . . .
Long having wander'd since, round the earth having
    wander'd,
Now I face home again, very pleas'd and joyous,
(But where is what I started for so long ago?
And why is it yet unfound?)[109]

This pantheistic transmigration provides the chief motif in Whitman's "new" religion. Out of the "great pride of man in himself," he conceives God in his own image because God is incarnate in the body: "I only am he who places over you no master, owner, better, God, beyond what waits intrinsically in Yourself."[110] Believing in the migrations of the soul through all forms of life, he can even declare: "I am myself waiting my time to be a God."[111]

Without entering into that useless argument as to the allegorical interpretations of *Chanting the Square Deific,* which seems to be a perennial pastime with Whitman critics,[112] we may notice that the pantheistic-transmigration

---

[109] *Facing West from California's Shores.* Cf. note 90.

[110] *To You* (1856).

[111] *Notes and Fragments,* p. 47, sec. 160.

[112] See Mrs. Alice Lovelace Cooke "Whitman's Indebtedness to the Scientific Thought of his Day," *Studies in English (The University of Texas Bulletin),* July 8, 1934, p. 113 ff; and G. L. Sixbey's "Chanting the Square Deific—A Study in Whitman's Religion," *American Literature,* IX, 171-195 (May 1937).

doctrine makes even this poem fairly intelligible. Out of the "one" [The Absolute or "the square entirely divine"] advance the various religions of the past, the poet eagerly and vicariously identifying himself with each in turn, including the pagan, the Christian, the anti-Christian [Satan — evil, revolt], but culminating with "Santa Spirita, breather, life, . . ." This life-spirit, which includes all beings and is the "life of the real identities," is nothing but a kind of pantheistic Over-Soul.[113] This soul is personified, as in many other poems, by the "I" of the poet:

Life of the great round world, the sun and stars,
    and of man, I, the general soul,
Here the square finishing, the solid, I the most solid,
Breathe my breath also through these songs.

In some of the old-age poems, such as *Passage to India,* Whitman's imagery of the soul in flight and his symbolism of immortality come much nearer orthodox Christian conceptions than in the bolder pantheism of his earlier works. He and his soul take ship for "unknown shores on waves of ecstasy to sail," and they flow through Time and Space and Death, mounting to God.

Swiftly I shrivel at the thought of God,
At Nature and its wonders, Time and Space and Death,
But that I, turning, call to thee, O soul, thou actual Me,
And lo, thou gently masterest the orbs,
Thou matest Time, smilest content at Death,
And fillest, swellest full the vastnesses of Space.[114]

Even here, however, the imagery of the soul filling space is more pantheistic than conventionally Christian—though

---

[113] Perhaps, however, Bergson's *élan vital* is a closer parallel than Emerson's "Over-Soul."
[114] Sec. 11.

there is nothing in the poem that need conflict with the spirit or intention of Christianity.

As Plumptre says, Evil is the great logical problem for pantheism.[115] If God pervades everything, how can anything be evil or the world contain any part of evil? However, this is almost as great a logical problem for monotheism, for if God is good how can any of his works be bad? In dealing with this problem many Christian theologians have rejected their monotheism and unconsciously embraced polytheism. Especially is this true of the Calvinists with their vivid conception of the great cosmic drama of the two gods, the eternal struggle between the Good God and the Bad God.

The Hindu mystic solves the problem by regarding evil as an illusion of limited human faculties. By devotion and religious exercises the mind can rise above the deceptive appearances. A simpler pantheistic solution is to regard evil as the result of transgressing the laws of nature. For the man who is completely in harmony with nature and her laws, there is no evil. Still another answer is Hegel's theory of the merging of opposites into unity; on the cosmic scale evil is always in the process of losing its identity in the Absolute, which is Good.

Whitman was no logician or dialectician, and his answer is not so clear-cut as any of these. But he does give one which is not inconsistent with the pantheism which we have so far traced. In many places he asserts that he includes evil as well as good and attempts to equalize good and evil, but one quotation will serve to indicate his typical expression:

Omnes! omnes! let others ignore what they may,

---

[115] Plumptre, *op. cit.*, 22.

I make the poem of evil also, I commemorate that part
  also,
I am myself just as much evil as good, and my nation
  is—and I say there is in fact no evil,
(Or if there is I say it is just as important to you, to the
  land or to me, as any thing else.)[116]

It is perhaps not so much statements as this, however,
as his expression of socially tabood subjects—his flaunting
his own worst characteristics ("The wolf, the snake, the
hog, not wanting in me"),[117] and his comradely greeting
of prostitutes and low characters—that has convinced most
readers that Whitman denied the existence of evil, or at
least refused to make moral distinctions. The key to Whitman's attitude is the above *omnes;* he is the poet of *all*—
all life, all existence, every object and particle in the universe equally necessary, perfect and therefore good. In
order to shock his readers into an awareness of the full
implication of this doctrine he mentions the unmention-
able, dwells on the ugly, the crude, the taboo, not because
they are more important than the beautiful or the socially
amenable but to force their inclusion in the whole of life,
nature and the cosmic scheme.

One of the most enlightening discussions on this point
is Maximilian Beck's "Whitman's Intuition of Reality."[118]
He says:

There is a fundamental philosophical thesis in all
Whitman's writings—that the value of anything that
exists does not lie in its specific quality, in what it is,
but purely in its own being . . . Many passages of his

---

[116] *Starting from Paumanok,* sec. 7.
[117] *Crossing Brooklyn Ferry,* sec. 6.
[118] Maximilian Beck, "Walt Whitman's Intuition of Reality," *Ethics,*
LIII, 14-24 (October, 1942).

poems seem merely shocking or tiresome unless understood as a means of emphasizing his infinite delight in pure real existence[119]. . . . He does not merely praise life; he praises the absolute worth of every particular and individual person. He stresses the worth of everything and everyone, thus fighting a supposed hierarchy of value. His most important thesis is that of the *absolute equality in worth of every real existing being.*[120]

Thus Whitman did not reject value; he found value not in distinct forms but "in reality itself." Far, then, from actually denying evil, he accepts it as part of reality. He denies only the ignoring of evil, and the categorizing of evil. Certainly no poet who, according to all testimony, was so charitable, so humane, so kind as Walt should be accused of championing evil. As Beck remarks,[121] he does not approve evil as Nietzsche did. What Whitman does is assert that all reality is good, for "Reality is not dead but is steadily being born anew. He saw it himself and forced others to see it also through the power of his personality and poetry."[122]

The place of evil in Whitman's thought is further clarified by his idea of "prudence," which is similar to the Hindu *karma,* a mystical law of cause and effect: no good deed is ever lost, at least in the eternal count. Whitman had developed this idea at least as early as 1856, for we find it hinted in *Poem of the Sayers of the Words of the Earth* in which "The song is to the singer and comes back most to him," etc., and each person is held responsible for his own development:

---

[119] *Ibid.,* 14.　　　[121] *Ibid.,* 20.
[120] *Ibid.,* 19.　　　[122] *Ibid.,* 23.

Each man to himself, and each woman to herself,
   is the word of the past and present, and
   the word of immortality,
Not one can acquire for another—not one!
Not one can grow for another—not one![123]

And in the same year the idea is explicitly stated and developed under the term "prudence," in the poem called *Poem of the Last Explanation of Prudence* (1856) and later (1881) *Song of Prudence*. As the poet ponders Time, Space, and Reality, he places "abreast with them Prudence," and then explains:

The soul is of itself,
All verges to it, all has reference to what ensues,
All that a person does, says, thinks, is of consequence,
Not a move can a man or woman make, that affects him
   or her in a day, month, any part of the direct lifetime, or the hour of death, but the same affects him
   or her onward afterward through the indirect lifetime.[124]

The "indirect life-time" is of course, as the remainder of the poem establishes beyond all doubt, the immortal existence of the soul, for "Not one word or deed . . . but has results beyond death, as really as before death." The reward motif is elaborated in the succeeding line: "Who has been wise receives interest," and every action "will forever affect, all of the past, and all of the present, and all of the future."

Whitman has often been accused of inconsistency and his famous lines on his own contradictions[125] have been

---

[123] *Leaves of Grass* (Brooklyn, 1856), 328.
[124] [Sec. 2], 1856 edition, 257.
[125] Do I contradict myself?
   Very well, then I contradict myself;
   (I am large—I contain multitudes.) *Song of Myself*, sec. 51.

quoted again and again to indicate his indifference to logic, but the truth is that in his basic pantheism he carries his consistency almost to absurdity (if indeed he does not often cross the line). Not only does he, as we have seen, insist on the absolute equality, divinity, and immortality of all being, but he now claims that every deed and every act is likewise of eternal consequence: "All suggestions of the divine mind of man, or the divinity of his mouth, or the shaping of his great hands;" and

> All that is henceforth to be thought or done by you,
>   whoever you are, or by any one,
> These inure, have inured, shall inure, to the identi-
>   ties from which they sprang, or shall spring.[126]

But this doctrine of pantheistic determinism must not be confused with the usual theological belief in the divine punishment of sin. As with *life, being, soul,* Whitman makes no divisions or distinctions.

> What is prudence, is indivisible,
> Declines to separate one part of life from every part,
> Divides not the righteous from the unrighteous, or the
>   living from the dead . . .[127]

What then is the test of right conduct? The only answer is a dark one: "Whatever satisfies souls is true . . ."[128] Here it is easy for both the poet and the reader to lose themselves in mysticism, but the implication of all Whitman's poems is that intuitive knowledge of the *soul* leads to bodily health, love of all creation, sympathy with all creatures, and the promotion of happiness in one's self

---

[126] *Poem of the Last Explanation of Prudence,* 260. *(Song of Prudence).*
[127] *Ibid.,* 260-261.
[128] *Ibid.,* 260.

and others. This poem on prudence also implies the goodness of courage and fortitude, for the prudent person "neither hurries nor avoids death," and "he who never peril'd his life, but retains it to old age in riches and ease, has probably achiev'd nothing for himself worth mentioning." Here we are reminded of the Christian paradox, "He who loses his life shall find it," but it is perhaps nearer the Hindu doctrine of *karma*[129] and transmigration.

> Of your real body and any man's or woman's real body,
>   [*i.e.,* spiritual or immortal as opposed to physical and temporal],
> Item for item it will elude the hands of the corpse-cleaners and pass to fitting spheres,
> Carrying what has accrued to it from the moment of birth to the moment of death.[130]

THE GREAT CHAIN OF BEING

Most of the ideas which have been discussed above under "pantheism" and "panpsychism" could be treated just as appropriately under the subject of "The Great Chain of Being," a concept which dominated European thought from Plato and Aristotle until well into the nineteenth century.[131] However, though an exhaustive comparative study needs to be made of the relations of Whitman's thought to the Chain of Being, for the present purpose a brief discussion will serve, first because we can

---

[129] "In Hinduism and Buddhism, the whole ethical consequence of one's acts considered as fixing one's lot in the future existence," *Webster's Collegiate Dictionary,* fifth edition.

[130] *Starting from Paumanok,* sec. 13.

[131] The authoritative, exhaustive study of the subject is by Arthur O. Lovejoy, *The Great Chain of Being: A study of the History of an Idea* (Cambridge, Mass.: Harvard University Press, 1936).

thereby reduce to a minimum the repetition of points already discussed, and, second, because Whitman himself did not specifically mention the Chain of Being or the technical terms which once accompanied this philosophical concept and may have been unaware of the resemblances between his assumptions and those once associated with the Chain metaphor. But the comparison cannot be overlooked entirely, for it will serve two useful purposes: (1) demonstrate the extent to which European thought got woven in the woof and warp of Whitman's thought and (2) at the same time illustrate that his ideas are so closely knit that when we pull out one thread we unravel the whole design.

The concept of the Chain of Being is first observable in the writings of Plato, who held two theories of God, which might be labeled *other worldly* and this *worldly*.[132] In the "other worldly" theory, God is the Idea of the Good; He is perfect, self-sufficient, and the highest "good" and happiness which a human being can attain consists in the contemplation of Him—a doctrine strongly resembling the "static" mysticism of the East, where it may have originated. But a "this worldly" theory of God is found in Plato's idea that God (or the Absolute), being perfect, cannot deny existence to any Idea or being. To envy the existence of any possible being would contradict the goodness and perfection of God; He must therefore express or realize His goodness by creating all possible beings. This is the principle of *plenitude*. Notice, however, that in this

---

[132] For this whole summary the author is, of course, greatly indebted to Professor's Lovejoy's book, but he has had the good fortune to direct a gifted student, Miss Margery Suhre, in writing a Master of Arts thesis on "The Chain of Being in *Leaves of Grass*." The thesis is on file in the University Library at Bowling Green, Ohio.

doctrine God is not self-sufficient but is perfect only to the extent that he expresses His goodness in creation, in "God's plenty." This God is dynamic, and the doctrine emphasizes the importance of this world, here and now, rather than a supernatural world.

Aristotle rejected plenitude but originated a second principle, *continuity,* which complements the Platonic doctrine of necessary "fullness." Aristotle, sometimes thought of as the father of science, observed that the qualities or characteristics of the various forms of *beings* overlap or resemble each other; hence the figure of the Chain of Being, with a continuity of links, each joined to the next. Aristotle also added what came to be known as the third principle, that of *gradation.* Nothing except God is perfect; therefore, everything in creation has in it undeveloped potentialities, so that all beings may be graded upward according to their degree of progress toward perfection or completeness of development or downward according to their mere potentiality. We now have the three principles of the Chain of Being concept: *plenitude* (creation of all possible forms), *continuity* (unbroken relationship, all species contiguous), and *gradation* (the scale extending from simplest to most complex, lowest to highest, etc.)

If the principle of plenitude is assumed to populate the universe at every moment with all possible beings, then the Chain is static. In the middle ages it was usually thought to be immutable, for speculators reasoned that the very possibility of additions of any kind to the fullness or variety of creation would mean that the Chain was imperfect and would thereby contradict the goodness and omnipotence of the Creator. One of the great ideas of the

Renaissance, however, was the assumption that other planets are inhabited, and since space was now thought to be infinite, the possibilities of existence, of being, of life, were also limitless. Thus without disputing the immutability of the Chain, it was given a wider range of applicability and thus actually became less static.

In the seventeenth century Spinoza was of course interested in the fullness of creation, but he did not have much to say about the Chain of Being. Leibniz, however, discussed the three principles, giving them first a static and then a dynamic interpretation. Though the latter was inconsistent with his monad theory,[133] it had great influence on the future of the idea. On the basis of the principle of continuity, for example, he predicted the biological discovery of "zoophytes," or "plant animals," to fill the gap between plants and animals.[134] He also expressed the theory that human souls were formerly animal souls; but once having taken abode in human beings they became reasonable and able henceforth to "advance and ripen continually, like the world itself, of which they are but images."[135] This doctrine of universal and perpetual progress led Leibniz to abandon pure optimism in favor of meliorism, i.e., this is not "the best of all possible worlds," and never will be; it is only in the process of becoming better.

The eighteenth century held two views of the Chain of Being, the one static and the other an extension of Leibniz's meliorism. The two most admired philosophical poems of the century, Pope's Essay on Man and Akenside's Pleasures of the Imagination, illustrate these views. Ac-

---

[133] See Lovejoy, op. cit., 259-61.   [135] Quoted, Ibid., 258.
[134] Ibid., 256 ff.

cording to Pope, the Chain is completely static and this
is the best of all possible worlds because it already contains all possible beings—*i.e.,* perfection. Even in the
realm of society and politics, no further progress is possible. Moreover man occupies the middle link of the
Chain, far alike from the lowest form of life or the
highest, which is God; and he can bring unhappiness upon
himself by striving to climb higher, thus upsetting the
divine scheme of things.

Akenside begins with the Platonic Idea or Absolute,
from whom all beings have acquired their form, but he
does not think that the "Sovereign Spirit of the world . . .
self-collected from eternal time" completed his work in
the beginning; rather that

> he at once,
> Down long series of eventful time,
> So fix'd the dates of being, so dispers'd
> To every living soul of every kind
> The field of motion and the hour of rest,
> That all conspir'd to his supreme design,
> To universal good . . .

By *fixing the date of being,* by allowing some forms to
exist in one period and others at another time, Akenside's
God permits "all things which have life [to] aspire to
God":

> in their stations all may persevere
> To climb the ascent of being, and approach
> For ever nearer to the life divine.

This is what Lovejoy calls "temporalizing" the Chain
of Being:[136] the principles of plenitude, continuity, and

<hr>

[136] *Ibid.,* Chap. **IX.**

gradation apply to a long range of time; God creates all possible forms but not simultaneously. All links of the Chain were possible from the beginning but God creates them when they are needed. This interpretation turns the Chain of Being into a ladder, up which all forms of life may climb, and holds out unlimited hope for man and all God's creatures.

Kant's theory of cosmic evolution was another contribution to the temporalizing of the principle of plenitude, in accordance with the astronomical knowledge of the age. Kant presupposes the existence of the particles of matter, but in the beginning these were diffused and unorganized. By mechanical means, which he does not altogether make clear, these particles were condensed and set into revolution (cf. the nebular hypothesis of astronomy), thereby forming planets and solar systems. These are infinite in number and will progress eternally through cycles extending from a maximum of diffusion to a maximum of condensation (as if universes were constantly winding and unwinding themselves); but the process does not take place uniformly in all places, so that at any given moment different stages of evolution may be going on in different universes. Partly on the basis of this theory Kant thought that souls could migrate from one cosmic system to another—and that they too were subject to evolutionary processes.[137]

Similar to Kant's transmigration of souls is Robinet's "germ" theory, which is cosmic evolution in different terms. Like Leibniz and others, he maintained that the germs of all things are immortal and that they are propelled by some inner force or principle through the "uni-

---

[137] See *Ibid.*, 265-268.

versal scale." Thus, "nature is always at work, always in travail, in the sense that she is always fashioning new developments, and generations."[138]

This temporalizing of the Chain of Being led to a romantic delight in change and diversity. God was thought to manifest himself through change and becoming. He too had become temporalized. Schelling asserted that God was potentially all-perfect from the beginning but that actually He evolves with the universe.

If evil is lack of goodness and perfection, then this evolutionary concept of God eliminates any absolute evil; as God becomes more perfect through his creation, evil is eliminated. And similar to this interpretation is denial of death, for life arises from death, not death from life. In this vein Hegel postulates an *a priori* Absolute or World-stuff and uses a dialectic to show how the Absolute develops by the merging or harmonizing of contradictions into Unity. Thus God delights in change, conflict, and strife by means of which he realizes His nature.

These interpretations led to profound changes in the theory of art. As Lovejoy says, in the theory of the German romantics it was thought that "the artist's task is to imitate, not simply Nature's works, but her way of working, to enter into the spirit of the universe by aiming, as it does, at fullness and variety without end."[139] The romantics thought with Frederich Schlegel, that, "as God is to his creation, so is the artist to his own."[140] This love of fullness and variety led to artistic individualism and

---

[138] *Ibid.*, 275.

[139] *Ibid.*, 303-304.

[140] A. E. Lussky, Tieck's *Romantic Irony* (Chapel Hill, N. C.: University of North Carolina, 1932), 69. Cf. F. Schlegel's *Gespräch über Poesie,* 1800.

emphasis on nationality, but temporalizing the Chain of Being soon destroyed the concept itself. A chain whose links are constantly shifting to new positions, the smaller becoming larger, or some links dropping out and and others coming into existence (realizing their potentiality), no longer appeals to the imagination as a chain at all. The attitudes, theories, and over-beliefs that once belonged to the concept might linger on, but the *chain* metaphor ceased to have meaning. And thus it is that Walt Whitman in the second half of the nineteenth century could still, like Robinet, talk of "germs" or, like Kant, of cosmic evolution, or like F. Schlegel try to imitate God in the poetic appreciation of fullness and variety in creation, without ever thinking of the "Chain of Being."

"Chain of Being" Assumptions in Whitman's Thought

Whitman does not treat "plenitude" specifically as an *idea,* but the influence of the doctrine of *fullness* permeates his poetry and thought from the 1855 Preface on. To a certain extent this love of plenty, size, and fecundity[141] may be typically American and nationalistic, for in 1855 the United States was *expanding* in every sense of the term, geographically, economically, politically, culturally. Whitman did not need to import from Europe youthful vigor, exuberant pleasure in the multiplicity

---

[141] Professor Oscar Cargill says, "The fear of being thought scatological has kept critics and scholars from assigning Whitman his true place in our literary history—the natural voice of breeding and prolific America, the Priapus of the new continent."—*Intellectual America:* Ideas on the March (New York: Macmillan, 1941), 541. He points out (538) that "human 'proliferation' for economic purposes began in America with the founding of the colonies"; hence "there is in American letters in the nineteenth century what might almost be termed the 'Cult of Fecundity'" (541).

of human joys, or the conviction that the United States
was destined to be the greatest nation on earth.

Yet the more we compare Whitman's ideas with those
of European romanticists who glorified the richness and
variety of life, the more astonished we are at the similarities. Like them, Whitman is not content merely to worship the fullness and variety of nature, but he must
develop this admiration into an ethical and esthetic doctrine. "Here at last is something in the doings of man
that corresponds with the broadcast doings of the day and
night. . . . The largeness of nature or the nation were
monstrous without a corresponding largeness and generosity of the spirit of the citizen."[142] And like abundance
of nature and the insatiable creativeness of God, the poet
is to be *commensurate* with this great nation of people
and to *incarnate* "its geography and natural life and
rivers and lakes." So great is the poet's delight in the
varied forms of creation that he tries to embrace the
whole range in his catalogs. But he does not stop there:

> The land and sea, the animals, fishes and birds, the
> sky of heaven and the orbs, the forests mountains and
> rivers, are not small themes . . . but folks expect of the
> poet to indicate more than the beauty and dignity which
> always attach to dumb real objects . . . they expect him
> to indicate the path between reality and their souls.[143]

The attempt *to indicate the path between reality and the
soul* very nearly sums up Whitman's whole intention in
LEAVES OF GRASS. It might, indeed, be called the "religious intention" which he so many times mentions in his
prefaces. In *A Backward Glance* he declared: "It is al-

---

[142] 1855 Preface.   [143] *Ibid.*

most as if a poetry with cosmic and dynamic features of magnitude and limitlessness suitable to the human soul, were never possible before."

But why is such poetry possible in his day more than in former times and places? Most critics have assumed that this conviction was a product of the poet's bumptious and arrogant nationalism. That he was nationalistic, there is no denying, but he also regarded himself, his country, and his age as the most perfect to date precisely because he believed, along with all those who had temporalized the Chain of Being, that all creation is constantly advancing and progressing.

We have already noticed Whitman's idea of pantheistic evolution. Let us now observe how he presents the temporalized Chain of Being, or the whole creation on its journey upward:

> We have thus far exhausted trillions of winters and
>   summers,
> There are trillions ahead, and trillions ahead of them.
> Births have brought us richness and variety,
> And other births will bring us richness and variety.
> I do not call one greater and one smaller,
> That which fills its period and place is equal to any.
>
> . . . .
>
> I am an acme of things accomplish'd, and I [am] an
>   encloser of things to be.
> My feet strike an apex of the apices of the stairs,
> On every step bunches of ages, and larger bunches be-
>   tween the steps,
> All below duly travel'd, and still I mount and mount.
> Rise after rise bow the phantoms behind me,

Afar down I see the huge first Nothing, I know I was
    even there,
I waited unseen and always, and slept through the
    lethargic mist,
And took my time, and took no hurt from the fetid
    carbon.
Long I was hugg'd close—long and long.
Immense have been the preparations for me,
Faithful and friendly the arms that have help'd me.
Cycles ferried my cradle, rowing and rowing like cheer-
    ful boatmen,
For room to me stars kept aside in their own rings,
They sent influences to look after what was to hold me.
Before I was born out of my mother, generations guided
    me,
My embryo has never been torpid, nothing could over-
    lay it.
For it the nebula cohered to an orb,
The long slow strata piled to rest it on,
Vast vegetables gave it sustenance,
Monstrous sauroids transported it in their mouths, and
    deposited it with care.[144]

It is thus that the "cosmic I" of the poem tramps a
"perpetual journey."[145] And the journey does not end with
the "identity" which the soul has achieved in Walt Whitman, the man of 1855.

This day before dawn I ascended a hill and look'd at
    the crowded heaven,
And I said to my spirit *When we become the enfolders
of those orbs, and the pleasure and knowledge of
every thing in them, shall we be fill'd and satisfied
then?*

---

[144] *Song of Myself*, sec. 44.   [145] *Ibid.*, sec. 46.

And my spirit said *No, we but level that lift to pass and continue beyond.*[146]

Whitman expressed this same conviction in many ways. In 1856 he called it "assurances":

I do not doubt I am limitless, and that the universes are limitless, . . .
I do not doubt that whatever can possibly happen anywhere at any time, is provided for in the inherences of things,
I do not think Life provides for all and for Time and Space, but I believe Heavenly Death provides for all.[147]

In 1860 he expressed these limitless possibilities in terms of "germs," which in a handful of space contain . . . "the start of each and all, the virtue, the germs of all."[148] In 1891 he named this sort of evolving plenitude "unseen buds."[149] But these germ metaphors, though interesting, are hardly worth extended illustration, for it is merely another way of expressing belief in some inner force or principle which propels the universe through its cosmic development, as in *A Song of the Rolling Earth:*

Amelioration is one of the earth's words,
The earth neither lags nor hastens,
It has all attributes, growths, effects latent in itself from the jump [*i.e.,* beginning] . . .[150]

But returning for a moment to the doctrine that the soul will "but level that lift to pass beyond": whether, like Kant, Whitman literally believed that the soul would

---

[146] *Ibid.*
[147] *Assurances.*
[148] *Germs.*

[149] *Unseen Buds.*
[150] Sec. 1.

pass to other planets after its life on earth, or whether
this is merely a poetic allegory, the idea is plainly the same
as the cosmic progression of the temporalized Chain of
Being. Life is an eternal process of births and rebirths—
"There is no stoppage and never can be stoppage."[151] And
in 1888-9, Whitman still calls life "an endless march":

> The world, the race, the soul—in space and time the
> universes,
> All bound as is befitting each—all surely going some-
> where.[152]

Thus it is a fundamental misunderstanding of Whitman to think that his fierce pride in himself, his country,
and his age is a fatuous conceit, a smug satisfaction over
his having achieved a perfect birth, life and "identity."
He and his nation are indeed "an acme of things accomplish'd," but this life, "what has come to the surface after
so many throes and convulsions," is no culmination, no
resting place. Even the American Pioneers are but a link
in the chain, who "take up the task eternal, and the burden
and the lesson."[153]

And it is also a mistake to think that Whitman's joy
in the present and his insistence that no greater perfection
has ever been reached than now are evidence of his con-
tempt for the past, as has often been asserted. He began
the 1855 Preface by saying that "America does not repel
the past or what it has produced . . .", and the whole bulk
of his thought shows how profoundly sincere he was in
this statement. He goes on to show that he thinks America
has improved on past achievements, as later in *Democratic
Vistas* he pointed out ideals still to be achieved. But these

---

[151] *Song of Myself*, sec. 45.   [153] *Pioneers! O Pioneers!*
[152] *Going Somewhere.*

beliefs should be placed in the larger framework of the perfectionist doctrine, first propounded by those thinkers who temporalized the Chain of Being.

In *Song of the Universal* the poet sings,
   In this broad earth of ours,
   Amid the measureless grossness and the slag,
   Enclosed and safe within its central heart,
   Nestles the seed perfection.[154]

Notice that the earth has not attained "perfection," but the "seed" nestles in its heart. By this time (1874) Whitman knew something of Hegel's doctrine, and the poem is obviously tinged with the Hegelian theory of evil merging with the good and disappearing—"Only the good is universal."[155] But the idea that in "mystic evolution," in "spiral routes by long detours," the cosmos, the earth, and the nation have emerged from the imperfect to a more perfect condition, is not fundamentally different from the theory of cosmic progression found in *Song of Myself* and the first Preface.

And thou America,
   For the scheme's culmination, its thought and its reality,
   For these (not for thyself) thou hast arrived.[156]
   Thou too surroundest all,
   Embracing carrying welcoming all, thou too by pathways broad and new,
   To the ideal tendest.[157]

Here, of course, "ideal" also carries the connotation of "spirit" or "Absolute," but since these likewise stand for

---

[154] Sec. 1.
[155] Sec. 2.
[156] Note that the purpose is cosmic evolution, not individualism.
[157] *Song of the Universal*, sec. 4.

the highest "good," the ordinary sense of "ideal" does not altogether miss the mark either. Presently the poet uses "immortality" in almost the same sense:

All, all for immortality,
Love like the light silently wrapping all,
Nature's amelioration blessing all,
The blossoms, fruits of ages, orchards divine and certain,
Forms, objects, growths, humanities, to spiritual images
    ripening.[158]

In other words, all creation is climbing the stairs, climbing the chain toward perfection and God, becoming more divine or God-like with the completion of each spiral. Therefore does the poet have

Belief in plan of Thee enclosed in Time and Space,
Health, peace, salvation universal.[159]

On the basis of these interpretations, the name of the section in which these poems finally came to rest takes on deeper significance. The title of the section is *Birds of Passage,* suggesting that the divine scheme of creation is accomplished by transitory flights of the soul—or souls. And the theme of *Song of the Universal,* as interpreted above, contributes to the meaning of the poem which immediately follows, *Pioneers! O Pioneers!* We are now better able to appreciate the cosmic meaning of such a stanza as this:

See my children, resolute children,
By those swarms upon our rear we must never yield
    or falter,

---

[158] *Ibid.*   [159] *Ibid.*

Ages back in ghostly millions frowning there behind
    us urging,
Pioneers! O Pioneers!

The stellar systems are also pioneers:
    Lo, the darting bowling orb!
    Lo, the brother orbs around, all clustering suns and
        planets,

. . . . . .

    All for primal needed work, while the followers there
        in embryo wait behind. . . .

As a poet Whitman was not only trying to *express* the
cosmic scheme, in which all creation was eternally evolving
into something better, but he was trying to contribute his
own effort toward achieving the divine plan. He was thus
acknowledging not only his debt to the historical past but
likewise to the immortal past when he sang in *Starting
from Paumanok*:

    Strains musical flowing through ages, now reaching
        hither,
    I take to your reckless and composite chords, add to
        them, and cheerfully pass them forward . . .[160]

And he was perhaps proclaiming an historical truth of
which he was himself only dimly aware, for the idea he
was cheerfully passing forward came, quite literally, from
previous ages—those of Robinet, Kant, Leibniz, Plotinus,
and even Plato, but especially from the age which had
temporalized the Chain of Being.

"THE ORGANIC PRINCIPLE"

The temporalizing of the Chain of Being, which resulted in the romantic delight in change and variety, pro-

---

[160] Sec. 10.

duced—first in Germany, then in France, England, and America—a doctrine which came to be known as the "Organic Principle."[161] Simply stated, it means that art is also a product of nature and cosmic processes and grows or develops like an organism. Or to consider the artist, his function is to intuit a form which will be as closely as possible analogous to organic growth. Though Whitman's organic style and versification will be discussed in a later chapter, this idea must be considered here because it is so obviously related to his cosmic ideas.

The effect on esthetics of the temporalizing of the Chain of Being can be plainly observed in Schiller's *Letters on the Aesthetic Education of Mankind*. Here we find once more the two Gods of Plato, the one immutable and self-sufficient, the other dynamic and *becoming*. This results, according to Schiller, in "two fundamental laws," the universality of God and the cosmos demanding "pure" or abstract form *(Formtrieb)* and unity, while the other demands fullness and diversity of concrete particulars *(Stofftrieb)*.[162] In both theory and practice Schiller always remained somewhat divided between these "two laws," and that is why in literary history he is still regarded as semi-classical and semi-romantic. But the trend of the romantic age was almost entirely toward a God of *becoming* and the esthetic expression of the richness, fullness, and multiplicity of nature.

As Lovejoy says, the task of the artist became "to imitate, not simply Nature's works, but her ways of work-

---

[161] For a convenient summary of the idea, see Fred W. Lorch, "Thoreau and the Organic Principle of Poetry," *Publications of Modern Language Association*, LIII, 286-302 (1938). Also discussed in Oskar Walzel, *Deutsche Romantik* (Berlin, 1923), translated by A. E. Lussky, *German Romanticism* (New York, Putnam, 1932), 51-60.

[162] See Lovejoy, *op. cit.*, 302.

ing, to enter into the spirit of the universe by aiming, as it does, at fullness and variety without end."[163] Or as another critic says:

Just as God's purpose in "the things that are made" is nothing less than to reveal "the invisible things of him, ... even his eternal power and Godhead," thus [Frederich] Schlegel thought it was the purpose of the romantic poet likewise to show in his equally objective creation his own artistic power, glory, wisdom, and love for the product of his literary genius...[164]

Hence Schlegel's comment that "as God is to his creation, so is the artist to his own." Hence also the artist's desire for "voracious participation in all life." For this reason Goethe desires to bare his bosom to every experience in order that his poetry may accurately represent cosmic reality.[165] Such poetry is unified by the attempt to convey the totality of the nature of God and Nature, but it is diversified by the attempt to imitate the details, particulars, individuals of creation.

Schleiermacher presents this problem in his *Monologen:* So there came to me what is now my highest insight. It became clear to me that every man should exemplify humanity in his own way, in a unique mixture of elements, so that humanity may be manifested in *all* ways and everything become actual which in the fullness of infinity can proceed from its womb... Yet only slowly

---

[163] *Ibid.,* 303-304.

[164] Alfred Edwin Lussky, *Tieck's Theory of Romantic Irony* (Chapel Hill: University of North Carolina Press, 1932), 78.

[165] A basic literary motif in *Wilhelm Meister,* but also Faustian. Kenneth Burke has commented, "Goethe has suggested that he was equipped as a writer by his ability to imagine himself committing every crime," *Southern Review,* II (1937), 619.

and with difficulty does man attain full consciousness
of his uniqueness. Often does he lack courage to look
upon it, turning his gaze rather upon that which is the
common possession of mankind, to which he so fondly
and gratefully holds fast; often he is in doubt whether
he should set himself apart, as a distinctive being, from
that common character ... The most characteristic urge
of Nature often goes unnoted, and even where her outlines show themselves most clearly, man's eye all too
easily passes over their sharpcut edges, and fixes itself
firmly only upon the universal.[166]

This apparent dualism is particularly obvious in Whitman's attempt to recreate or symbolize reality in his
poetry, and has led to much confused interpretation, for
at first glance the theme of particulars, of individuals—
especially the exemplification of the poet's own uniqueness
—is more easily grasped than the underlying theme of the
Unity of all creation. But in the opening lines of *Song
of Myself* he plainly says:

> I celebrate myself, and sing myself,
> And what I assume you shall assume,
> For every atom belonging to me as good belongs to you.

And not only does it belong "to you," but to all the rest
of creation, for

> ... I permit to speak at every hazard,
> Nature without check with original energy.[167]

It is because Nature speaks through him—Nature's poet—
that he can announce,

---

[166] Quoted by Lovejoy, *op. cit.*, 310, from Schiele edition (1914),
30-31.
[167] *Song of Myself*, sec. 1.

Stop this day and night with me and you shall possess
the origin of all poems,
You shall possess the good of the earth and sun, ...

You shall not look through my eyes either, nor take
things from me,
You shall listen to all sides and filter them from your
self.[168]

The object is to obtain this wisdom, insight, by filtering it
through one's self, and this is the key to the theme of
"self" in these early poems.

Man, being a part of nature—as we have seen in Whitman's pantheism—contains, like the rest of nature, the
truth in himself: "the substantial words are in the ground
and sea, ... they are in you."[169] This is Whitman's basic
"organic" doctrine. "No one can realize anything unless
he has it in him ... or has been it. It must certainly tally
with what is in him ... otherwise it is all blank to him."[170]
Therefore he thinks of the poet as growing and blooming
"like some perfect tree or flower, in Nature ... His
analogy [,] the earth[,] complete in itself[,] enfolding
in itself[,] all processes of growth[,] effusing life and
power for hidden purposes."[171] Or he thinks of himself as
a "kosmos' 'in which his own body personifies all creation,
and through which the cosmic "voices" speak:

Voices of cycles of preparation and accretion,
And of the threads that connect the stars, and of wombs
and of the father-stuff,[172]

---

[168] *Ibid.*, sec. 2.
[169] *A Song of the Rolling Earth*, sec. 1.
[170] *Workshop, op. cit.*, 46.
[171] *Uncollected Poetry and Prose*, II, 96.
[172] *Song of Myself*, sec. 24.

and of all things, peoples, and experiences. This is why he has no taboos:

> Through me forbidden voices,
> Voices of sexes and lusts, voices veil'd and I remove the veil,
> Voices indecent by me clarified and transfigur'd.[173]

Nothing is indecent to nature; therefore it is not to her spokesman. Here we have the main basis for the sex program of *Children of Adam.*

What at times may sound like mysticism in Whitman's "visions" is often a free use of the "organic" symbolism —*i.e.,* organic in the sense of the growth of the universe. In the 1855 Preface the poet's "spirit responds to his country's spirit until he spans the continent from coast to coast" and "On him rise solid growths of pine and cedar and hemlock and liveoak and locust and chestnut and cypress". . . . . etc. The catalog is an attempt to symbolize the fullness and variety of nature, and to give it "organic" expression. In this Preface the imagery is limited mainly, however, to the topography, flora, and fauna of North America, though in *Salut Au Monde!* Whitman "incarnates" not only his own country but the whole world, "Within me latitude widens, longitude lengthens";[174] and the same is of course true with *A Song of the Rolling Earth,* which also emphasizes the ethical doctrine that "there is no greatness or power that does not emulate those of the earth."[175] It is to emulate growth and completeness of God and creation that he would make his own life perfect:

---

[173] *Ibid.*
[174] Sec. 2.
[175] Sec. 3.

I swear the earth shall surely be complete to him or
to her who shall be complete,
The earth remains jagged and broken only to him or
her who remains jagged and broken.[176]

This organic theory gives the best clue to Whitman's
stylistic intentions. In order "to indicate the path between
reality" and the souls of men and women, the poet must
write like nature herself:

The rhyme and uniformity of perfect poems show the
free growth of metrical laws and bud from them as
unerringly and loosely as lilacs or roses on a bush, and
take shapes as compact as the shapes of chestnuts and
oranges and melons and pears, and shed the perfume
impalpable to form.[177]

This is why Walt Whitman tried so desperately to escape
from conventional techniques. Believing that, "All beauty
comes from beautiful blood and a beautiful brain,"[178]
he thought it more essential for the poet to have the right
kind of blood and brain and attitude ("Love the earth
and sun and the animals")[179] than education or training.
This is the kind of style he desired:

O for the voices of animals—O for the swiftness and
balance of fishes!
O for the dropping of raindrops in a song!
O for the sunshine and motion of waves in a song![180]

Since it is, after all, only by symbols and suggestions (or
as Whitman would say, by "indirections") that the poet

---

[176] *Ibid.*
[177] The 1855 Preface.
[178] *Ibid.*
[179] *Ibid.*; cf. By *Blue Ontario's Shore,* sec. 14.
[180] *Song of Joys.*

can give utterance to inarticulate nature, we might expect a great amount of "organic" imagery in LEAVES OF GRASS. Indeed, the pantheistic grass itself is an organic symbol, for the poet believes that "a leaf of grass is no less than the journey-work of the stars,"[181] which is to say that the same cosmic forces are operating in it that are forming planets from nebulae, which are the planets in embryo. Even in a nationalistic poem, like *American Feuillage*, the examples of American life are called "divine leaves" and "bouquets." The complete metaphor is not needed in the poem, but these nationalistic leaves and bouquets would have to grow on a plant or tree—something like a Tree of Life. The tree—the universal—is taken for granted, and there is nothing in Whitman's thought to deny its existence; just as procreation in *Children of Adam* is not an isolated act, but a repetition of the eternal cycle: "To the garden the world anew ascending"—[182] life entering (or re-entering) the world from immortal sources.

Without this background for Whitman's *image*, we misjudge entirely the implication which he tried to give it, as Swinburne[183] and Santayana[184] have done. On the surface the images do, indeed, appear to express the emotions of an animal or barbarian wallowing in his own

---

[181] *Song of Myself*, sec. 31.

[182] *To the Garden the World*.

[183] After greeting Whitman eulogistically in the poem "To Walt Whitman in America," Swinburne savagely attacked him in "Whitmania," calling his "Eve . . . a drunken apple-woman" and his "Venus . . . a Hottentot wench under the influence of cantharides and adulterated rum." See W. B. Cairns, "Swinburne's Opinion of Whitman," *American Literature*, III, 125-135 (May 1931).

[184] See George Santayana, "The Poetry of Barbarism," in *Interpretations of Poetry and Religion* (New York; Scribner's, 1927 [first edition, 1900]), 177-187.

sensibilia. So astute a critic as Mr. Wyndham Lewis[185] gives this misleading interpretation—probably, like many critics of Whitman, without much firsthand knowledge of the poet's works:

> [In modern thought] the thing to be stressed more than anything else is the disposition to bestow 'reality' upon the *image,* rather than upon *the thing.* The reality has definitely installed itself *inside* the contemporary mind, that is to say, as it did with the stoic and other post-socratics of the greek[186] political decadence. The external world is no longer our affair, as indeed it ceases to be ours in any civic or political sense [The year is 1928]. At first sight it is easy for the former, at least, of these tendencies to pass itself off as suggestive, of an enhanced appetite for *life.* To plunge into sensation, in the bergsonian manner, is surely a movement in the direction of 'life'?[187]

But Lewis denies that this "frenzied propaganda for sensations—for moments" is "life"; it

> is rather the experience of an aged organism than of a vigorous and fresh one. For what need has a vigorous one to be told to plunge, to immerse itself? It is immersed naturally, and without instruction, and certainly not as a cult or a philosophy. This is new with us in the West; Whitman was, I suppose, its earliest professor—*Specimen Days* one of the first characteristic utterances of what has since taken on a universal complexion.[188]

---

[185] *Time and Western Man* (New York: Harcourt, 1928).
[186] Mr. Lewis affects "lower case" for all proper adjectives.
[187] Lewis, *op. cit.,* 368.
[188] *Ibid.,* 368.

Lewis blames this "doctrinaire barbarity of the sorelian and nietzschean spirit" for the " 'blood baths' of immense wars and revolutions" of the twentieth century. With Lewis's main argument we need not deal here, for it would necessitate a long digression, and it may well be valid for the "decadence" of the twentieth century; but these somewhat lengthy quotations from Mr. Lewis will serve to emphasize what is perhaps the most crucial problem in Whitman's organic theory.

If he does bestow "reality upon the *image* rather than *things*" to the extent of withdrawing his interest from the external world, then the doctrine is truly decadent and pernicious. Whitman, however, comes much nearer to bestowing reality upon a process than either *image* or *thing,* both of which, as presented in this whole chapter, are equally symbolical of the "real" reality, which is mystical and pantheistic, but is observed in operation in living growth, in biological development, and in the evidences of life cycles.

Organic imagery is, after all, only *imagery,* and can be taken much too seriously. In specific examples Whitman's physiological images may seem individualistic, isolationist, cut off from roots imbedded in traditions and universals, but they always involve ultimately the whole plant, the organism, the Unity from which they sprout. This Unity may be ideal rather than actual, as his dream of American democracy was, or his dream of world brotherhood. But Unity always occupies a central position in his thought and intentions. Thus he sang of himself in the early poems as a symbol of universal selfhood, of his nation as an epitome of evolution to date, and in his cosmic poems of the world as a symbol of a universe in process of improving—"realizing"—itself, in the concept of the temporalized Chain of Being.

Even in the composition and arrangement of his poems Whitman was constantly striving for an organic unity— which itself grew and changed through many editions. In a passage preserved in "Notes on the Meaning and Intention of LEAVES OF GRASS" he recorded the intention: "My poems when complete should be a *unity,* in the same sense that . . . a perfect musical composition is."[189] And in 1872 he was sufficiently satisfied with the unity achieved to claim that he had fulfilled in it "an imperious conviction, and the commands of my nature as total and irresistible as those which make the sea flow, or the globe revolve."[190]

Thus the expression of organic unity was one of Whitman's major intentions in LEAVES OF GRASS, including his main ambition to symbolize in his poems the nature of the universe itself and the relation of the "self" to it, embodying this relationship in a style analogous to the processes of natural development, and permitting the work to grow with his own cumulative experiences like a plant or a tree—a miniature image of pantheistic and cosmic evolution.

PERSONALISM—THE SYNTHESIS

Although pantheism and panpsychism, the Chain of Being, and the "Organic Principle" provide analogies which illuminate and clarify Whitman's ideas, he did not, as we have noticed, adopt any of these terms and may not have been consciously aware of the extent to which they formed the background for his thought, though he

---

[189] *Notes and Fragments,* 55.
[190] Preface to *As a Strong Bird on Pinions Free* (1872).

finally came to the conclusion that German Idealism, and especially Hegelianism, epitomized his own philosophy. In 1868, however, Whitman found his own term, which he called "Personalism,"[191] using it, so far as is at present known, for the first time in the United States,[192] though it was immediately adopted by his friend Bronson Alcott, who introduced it into American philosophy.[193]

What source, if any, Whitman had for the term is unknown, though it is unlikely that he made it up and used it accidentally in the same sense that it was already known in Germany in Schleiermacher's *Discourses;* but the German form *Personalismus* was apparently not translated into English until after Whitman's death.[194] It is quite likely, however, that Whitman did encounter the word, with some indication of its philosophical meaning, somewhere in his wide and miscellaneous reading.[195]

At any rate, Whitman gave the title "Personalism" to the essay which became the nucleus of *Democratic Vistas* and used it to designate the fusion of the individual with the mass in an ideal democracy of the future. He never really defined the term, and we need considerable help in understanding what he is trying to say in a passage like this:

---

[191] The essay called "Personalism" was published in the *Galaxy,* May, 1868, pp. 540-547; but "Democracy," *Galaxy,* December, 1867, pp. 919-933, contains the same point of view.

[192] Clifton J. Furness discusses this subject in his review of Fausset's biography in *The New England Quarterly,* XV, 557-560 (1942).

[193] See Ralph T. Flewelling, "Personalism," in *Twentieth Century Philosophy,* edited by Dagobert D. Runes, (New York: Philosophical Library, 1943), 323.

[194] Albert C. Knudson, *The Philosophy of Personalism* (New York: Abingdon Press, 1927), 17-18.

[195] Professor Odell Shepard, in *Pedlar's Progress: the Life of Bronson Alcott* (Boston: Little, Brown, 1937), 494, thinks the term may have come from the St. Louis school of philosophy, but this is apparently only a guess, not confirmed by the scholars of Personalism.

The ripeness of Religion is doubtless to be looked for in this field of individuality, and is a result that no organization or church can ever achieve. As history is poorly retain'd by what the technists call history, and is not given out from their pages, except the learner has in himself the sense of the well-wrapt, never yet written, perhaps impossible to be written, history—so Religion, although casually arrested, and, after a fashion, preserv'd in the churches and creeds, does not depend at all upon them, but is a part of the identified soul, which, when greatest, knows not bibles in the old way, but in new ways—the identified soul, which can really confront Religion when it extricates itself entirely from the churches, and not before.

Personalism fuses this, and favors it. I should say, indeed, that only in the perfect uncontamination and solitariness of individuality may the spirituality of religion positively come forth at all. Only here, and on such terms, the meditation, the devout ecstasy, the soaring flight. Only here, communion with the mysteries, the eternal problems, whence? whither? Alone, and identity, and the mood—and the soul emerges, and all statements, churches, sermons, melt away like vapors. Alone, and silent thought and awe, and aspiration— and then the interior consciousness, like a hitherto unseen inscription, in magic ink, beams out its wondrous lines to the sense. Bibles may convey, and priests expound, but it is exclusively for the noiseless operation of one's isolated Self, to enter the pure ether of veneration, reach the divine levels, and commune with the unutterable.[196]

Certainly the poet cannot be praised for his lucidity in

---

[196] *Democratic Vistas,* in *Prose Works* (Philadelphia: McKay, 1892), 233-234.

prose like this, but most of the obscurity will vanish if the reader will recall our discussions of Whitman's mysticism and pantheism—or if he will remember Emerson's *Self-Reliance* and *Over-Soul.* The theme of the first paragraph is that history is not in books, or religion in churches and bibles, but that these are in the person who has an "identified soul," *i.e.,* true reality is not in externals but in the person or *self* whose soul is "identified." Only for such a person is inspiration, intuitive knowledge, and contact with the divine possible. (Which is to say that this person is both the ideal poet of the 1855 Preface and the ideal citizen of *Democratic Vistas.*) But what, then, is an "identified soul," and who has it?

We remember Whitman's doctrine that at physiological birth each body receives its "identity,"[197] meaning that a "soul" is assigned to it, so that each exists through the other. Or we might say that the soul has become individual. In other words, individuality and personality depend ultimately upon *soul* and *spirit.* Here we come to the crux of the problem of the relationship between individuality and universality, or atomic multiplicity and the pantheistic One, or man and God. Whitman says that Personalism "fuses", and as we shall see presently, he means by this that the doctrine resolves the problem, on the one hand, of individualism versus society, or on the other hand, of man versus God or "Over-Soul."

What modern writers say about Personalism will not necessarily help us to understand Whitman—for we must first make sure that they are talking about the same concept—, though after we are fairly sure of Whitman's meaning, we may use these writers to test and further

---

[197] See p. 263.

clarify his thought, and perhaps also judge to what extent Whitman anticipated (or indirectly influenced) modern Personalism.

At the present point in our examination, the most likely source for further light is Bronson Alcott, who knew Whitman as a friend and was instantly drawn to him more intimately by the receipt of the essay on "Personalism." As a matter of fact, the essay seems to have clarified Alcott's own thinking; so it is likely that he understood Whitman's doctrine if anyone did.

On April 28, 1868, Alcott wrote in his *Journal:*

> Letter from Walt Whitman, with his paper on Personalism in the *Galaxy*. [He] Is pleased with my letter of Jan. 19, last . . . if there be an ideal Personalism, so is there an actual individualism, of which Thoreau and Whitman are prodigious impersonations—Walt for institutions, Thoreau for things . . .
>
> Read 'Personalism' again after day's work. Verily, great grand doctrine, and great grand Walt, grown since I saw him in his Brooklyn garret in 185-. Greater and grown more open-eyed, as perhaps oneself, since then. Another American beside Thoreau and Emerson.[198]

Since Alcott so thoroughly approved Whitman's expression of the doctrine, what was his own conception of it? On February 12, 1858, he recorded in his *Journal:* ". . . comes Emerson and asks me to accompany him home to tea. We talk on intellect and individualism, discriminating the latter from Personality."[199] Notice that "Per-

---

[198] *The Journals of Bronson Alcott,* edited by Odell Shepard (Boston: Little, Brown, 1938), 391.

[199] *Ibid.,* 306. It is possible that Whitman's word "Personalism" is simply a form of "Personality," as Alcott here thinks of it, rather than the German *Personalismus*.

sonality" is discriminated from "individualism." Ten years later (*i.e.*, the year of Whitman's essay) Alcott explains further in a letter:

> The unity of the Personality; the difference is the Individuality. . . . We must grow into and become one with the Person dwelling in every breast, and thus come to apprehend the saying 'I and my Father are one'— that is, to perceive that all souls have a Personal identity with God and abide in him."[200]

This definition, taken by itself, sounds a good deal like Christian mysticism, and perhaps is, but the idea that "all souls have a Personal identity with God" could also be interpreted in terms of Whitman's pantheism. Alcott did, as his editor has pointed out, believe in "a personal Deity, self-conscious and purposive," whereas Emerson felt "a profound need of distinguishing the First Cause as superpersonal."[201]

But perhaps Alcott's most complete summary of this concept is the following from his *Journal*, for May 17, 1874:

> The Person is the pre-supposition of all things and beings. Nothing were without this premise. I am because God is; nor am I found save by his Presence in my consciousness, and incarnation therefrom. From my soul spring forth my senses, reflecting itself in natural images. My body is my mind's idol. From the begin-

---

[200] *Ibid.*, 306 note.

[201] *Ibid.*, 356. Emerson wrote on April 17, 1863: "Alcott defended his thesis of personality last night, but it is not quite a satisfactory use of words. . . . I see profound need of distinguishing the First Cause as superpersonal. It deluges us with power; we are filled with it; but there are skies of immensity between it and us." Ralph Waldo Emerson, *Journals* edited by E. W. Emerson and W. E. Forbes, 1856-63. Boston: Houghton Mifflin & Co., 1913), 503.

ning I was, and survive all things beside myself. Personally immortal, time deals my periods and dates me by its revolutions. I am born and die daily.

Would'st know thyself and all things see?
Become thyself, and all things be.

Now, now, thy knowing is too slow.
Thought is the knowing in the now.

Depose thyself if thou would'st be
Drest in fresh suit of deity.

Out of the chaos rose in sight
One globe's fair form in living light.

Were God not God, I were not I,
Myself in him I must descry.[202]

Here, as in Whitman's pantheism and panpsychism, the fundamental thought is that man and God are One—we might say one Personality, and that man's personality is immortal in the personality of God. We can also translate Whitman's "identified soul" into Alcott's "Become thyself, and all things be." This doctrine stresses individual self-reliance, but not as a means of becoming more individual but as a means of developing or realizing the divine personality inherent in the individual soul, so that by developing its potentiality it becomes more nearly identical with God or the pantheistic All (Hegel's Absolute, Emerson's Over-Soul, Plato's God, etc.) Thus Personalism curbs and directs Whitman's earlier extreme individualism into ethical and religiously unselfish channels. He and Alcott are in agreement:

Depose thyself if thou would'st be
Drest in fresh suit of deity.

[202] *Journals*, 450.

Although this doctrine of eliminating selfishness by merging the self with the Eternal Self resembles pantheism, as indicated above, Personalism and pantheism are by no means synonymous, and we see the distinction in the ideas of Emerson in contrast to those of Alcott and Whitman. Emerson, who rejected personal theism in favor of a "super-personal" creator or First Cause,[203] was thus more pantheistic than Whitman (in 1868). Opponents of pantheism, like Alcott himself, object to it mainly because it represents God as nonpersonal, but this does not mean that either Alcott or Whitman thought of God as anthropomorphic. In summing up Alcott's theism, Professor Shepard says:

> To [Alcott] as to George Howison and, later, to Borden P. Bowne, Personalism was the doctrine that the ultimate reality of the world is a Divine Person who sustains the universe by a continuous act of creative will. A main advantage of this doctrine is the mediation that it provides between the extreme idealistic and materialistic positions . . .
>
> Even more important to a man of Alcott's intense sociality, however, was the clear implication that all apparently separate minds are bound together, like the planets of a solar system, by their common relation to a central Mind. In the philosophic vocabulary of his later years the antonym of 'Personalism' was 'Individualism' —a term into which he crowded all human ignorance, strife, misunderstanding, and even reform. All sin and error were due, he came to think, to the effort of individual wills to act as though they were independent of all other wills human and divine."[204]

---

[203] Cf. note 201, above. [204] Shepard, *op. cit.*, 494.

Whitman adopted the term "Personalism" for his democratic and political theory in *Democratic Vistas,* and he was, especially at this time, less interested in the theological implications than Alcott was, but in his pantheism and panpsychism he had always felt the individual experience to be a part of the all-inclusive Divine Experience (or cosmic process of evolution and amelioration). For this reason, there is no great theological contradiction between Whitman's earlier, intense pantheism and his later Personalism.

But how about his agreement with Alcott that sin and error are due to the individual will acting independently "of all other wills human and divine"? Here, too, we find that he had never been as far away from Alcott's position as we might at first suspect. He had shifted his emphasis, so that in 1878 he could say that:

> It was originally my intention, after chanting in LEAVES OF GRASS the songs of the Body and Existence, to then compose a further, equally needed Volume, based on those convictions of perpetuity and conservation which, enveloping all precedents, make the unseen Soul govern absolutely at last.[205]

But although his paralysis may be given as the main reason for his not attempting this second volume, whose theme was to be almost synonymous with Alcott's Personality doctrine, actually it was perhaps less needed than Whitman thought in 1876, for this purpose had never been entirely absent in his poetry and ideas. In *Notes and Fragments* we find the thought that, "I know that Personality is divine, and gives life and identity to a man or

---

[205] Preface for 1876 edition of LEAVES OF GRASS, footnote.

woman."[206] And in another place: "behind all the faculties of the human being, as the sight, the other senses and even the emotions and the intellect stands the real power, the mystical identity, the real I or Me or You."[207] In *Carol of Occupations* (1855) he declares that the only *reality* is persons, not things,[208] and that ". . . you and your soul enclose all things."[209] This insistence that *all* reality is a pantheistic personality from which individual souls have sprung and in which they find their unity, is basically not individualistic, and never was in Whitman's thought. He had merely emphasized the potentialities of his own self—or soul—, and thereby the possible development of other individuals, as a means of stimulating them to growth, expression, and the achievement of their innate divinity. The Personalism of *Democratic Vistas,* therefore, is not a new and contradictory idea in Whitman's thought, but a synthesis of his original doctrines of the divinity of the Self, the cosmic equality of all Souls, and their complete unity in a common immortality. So long as individualism is spiritual, there can not be too much of it; but on the practical level, "the singleness of man" may endanger political democracy, and "the mass, or lump character, for imperative reasons, is to be ever carefully weigh'd, borne in mind, and provided for."[210] It is only by reconciling the individual and the mass that the development of the individual is possible.

This idea of perfect individualism it is indeed that deepest tinges and gives character to the idea of the aggregate. For it is mainly or altogether to serve inde-

---

[206] *Notes and Fragments,* 16.
[207] *Ibid.,* 60.
[208] [Sec. 5] 1855 ed.
[209] [Sec. 6] *Ibid.*
[210] *Prose Works,* 213.

pendent separatism that we favor a strong generalization, consolidation. As it is to give the best vitality
and freedom to the rights of the States, (every bit as
important as the right of nationality, the union,) that
we insist on the identity of the Union at all hazards.[211]

This analogy of the states and the Union is a perfect
illustration of the relationship between the Self and the
pantheistic All of Whitman's thought; for just as in a
spiritual sense he believes that the divine purpose is best
served by the utmost development of the individual ego,
likewise in society the good of the group is provided for
and attained by the development of individual personality and moral character. "Produce great Persons, the
rest follows."[212] Democracy itself, he warns, is not so
much a political system as a "grand experiment of development" of individuals,[213] "a training-school for making first-class men."[214]

Herein, Whitman thinks, lies the failure of American
democracy to date. As he looks about him, he still sees
everywhere meanness, vulgarity, and dishonesty in manners, character, and political life. Men have not yet
learned this lesson of "great individuals," and this is why
in *Democratic Vistas* Whitman preaches the same text
that he had first expounded in 1855: a new democratic
literature is needed to stimulate and produce the citizens
who will make a great nation: "To take expression, to
incarnate, to endow a literature with grand and archetypal
models . . ."[215] That had always been Whitman's major

---

[211] *Ibid.*, 214.
[212] *By Blue Ontario's Shore*, sec. 3.
[213] *Prose Works*, 219.
[214] *Ibid.*, 223.
[215] *Ibid.*, 238.

ambition as a poet, and he never changed it. He did shift his emphasis. In his early poems he concentrated on the primary task of arousing his readers to an appreciation of the latent potentialities of their own divinely-inherited personalities, whereas in *Democratic Vistas* he indicated the social implications of his Individualism. Here also he shows himself to be a realistic observer of American democracy in operation. No one is more keenly aware than he that this "great experiment" in human freedom, equality, and fraternity has so far been largely a failure, but he still has hopes that men can be aroused to claim their divine inheritance. Whitman's final social ideal, therefore, remains the same as that of modern Personalism:

> Since Personalism has been known as the philosophy of freedom it has at various points of its development taken on certain social and political aspects . . . To Personalism, personality is the supreme value. Society then should be so organized as to present every person the best possible opportunity for self-development, physically, mentally, and spiritually since the person is the supreme essence of democracy and hostile to totalitarianisms of every sort.[216]

THE PROBLEM OF SOURCES

In the foregoing discussion of Whitman's ideas, definitions and interpretations have been based primarily upon European philosophers, from Plato to Hegel. This procedure was necessary because the ideas presented under "Mysticism," "Pantheism" and "Panpsychism," "The Chain of Being," "The Organic Principle," and "Personalism" existed in Europe long before they did in North America, and Walt Whitman's use of these ideas was

---

[216] Flewelling, *op. cit.*, 325.

derived either directly or indirectly from these European sources. At the present time, however, it is impossible to settle the question of Whitman's philosophical sources, for they have not yet been sufficiently investigated, and many of the critical studies that have been published are contradictory. Furthermore, parallels are often as useful in the interpretation of Whitman's ideas as known sources, and this very fact indicates vital relations between the American poet and major movements in World Literature. Especially is this true of the three main fields of sources and parallels for Whitman's thought: (1) American Transcendentalism (which also drew its inspiration from both Europe and Asia[217]), (2) European philosophy, especially German Idealism,[218] and (3) Oriental mysticism, especially Hindu.[219] Each of these relationships—along with some others, such as French romanticism[220]—will be explored and evaluated in Chapter VI, "Walt Whitman and World Literature."

No attempt has been made in this chapter to analyze all the "ideas" which may be found in Whitman's writings, but only those which seem to be both fundamental and in need of interpretation. We have passed over as either philosophically unimportant or as obvious his nationalism, his championing of women's rights, his attitudes toward sex and health; and his political and social thought will receive detailed treatment in Chapter IV.

Some of the contemporary theories which Whitman attempted to assimilate are today of extremely minor importance. One of these is the pseudo-science, phren-

---

[217] Amply demonstrated by F. I. Carpenter, *Emerson and Asia* (Cambridge, Mass.: Harvard University Press, 1930) and Arthur Christy, *The Orient in American Transcendentalism* (New York: Columbia University Press, 1932).

[218] See p. 453 ff.

[219] See p. 457 ff.

[220] See p. 467 ff.

ology,[221] which furnished him, as Long has pointed out,[222] faith in himself at a time when he most needed it. From this pseudo-science Whitman adopted a jargon—like "amativeness" and "adhesiveness"[223]—which we need to translate into legitimate English; but though he often used these esoteric terms in his poems, phrenology did not provide him with any fundamental concepts, however much personal satisfaction it may have given him.

Whitman claimed also to be the poet of science, and toward the end of the century he won some recognition from men known in the scientific world.[224] It is pertinent to ask, therefore, how much he knew of scientific thought and what influence it had on him. Two interesting studies have been made of the question, one by Mrs. Alice L. Cooke on "Whitman's Indebtedness to the Scientific Thought of His Day"[225] and the other by Clarence Dugdale on "Whitman's Knowledge of Astronomy."[226] Mrs. Cooke presents evidence that the poet was acquainted, mainly through discussions in newspapers and magazines, with the popular scientific theories and discoveries of his day, especially with pre-Darwinian evolution and the nebular hypothesis in astronomy. Mr. Dugdale, supplementing Mrs. Cooke's paper, finds that "Whitman was keenly interested in astronomy, not so much from the point of view of an exact scientist as from that of a poet whose

---

[221] The fullest study is by E. Hungerford, "Walt Whitman and His Chart of Bumps," *American Literature*, II, 350-384 (January, 1931).

[222] See p. 76.

[223] These may be translated as sexual-attraction and friendship or "manly affection" (Cf. *Calamus*).

[224] E.g., William Gay, *Walt Whitman: His Relation to Science and Philosophy*, a Paper read at the Meeting of the Australasian Association for the Advancement of Science, January, 1895 (Melbourne, 1895).

[225] Published in *Studies in English (The University of Texas Bulletin)*, XIV, 89-115 (July 8, 1934).

[226] Published *Ibid.*, XVI, 124-137 (July 8, 1936).

imagination demanded a whole universe for its operation."[227] Unlike the scientist, his ambition was to give
the physical facts and theories spiritual and poetic connotations. For such a mind and for such intentions as these,
the scientific hypotheses of Newton and Darwin were
less important than the cosmic evolution of Leibniz and
Kant—which will be discussed further in Chapter VI.

Thus the background of most importance in understanding Whitman's "fundamental ideas" is in the fullest sense
of the term philosophical. Without being himself widely
read in the major works of the philosophers, he nevertheless displayed a remarkable gift—what might be called
almost an instinct—for assimilating and adapting philosophical concepts and ideas for his own artistic purposes.[228]

SELECTED BIBLIOGRAPHY

AUTHORITIES FOR BACKGROUND OF WHITMAN'S IDEAS

ALCOTT, BRONSON. *The Journals of Bronson Alcott,* edited by
    Odell Shepard. Boston: Little, Brown and Co. 1938.
    ["Personalism," and Whitman's use of, frequently discussed
    in Alcott's *Journals.*]

CARGILL, OSCAR. *Intellectual America: Ideas on the March.*
    New York: Macmillan and Co. 1941.
    [Author is interested especially in modern ideas, but his
    discussion of fecundity (p. 538 ff) is of great importance
    for Whitman's intellectual background.]

---

[227] *Ibid.,* 136.

[228] Mary Colum was essentially correct when she declared: "What was
remarkable about Whitman was that he really soaked up something of
all the ideas of his age: something of all the literary doctrines, beginning
with Lessing's idea of national and racial expression; and something of all
the political doctrines, beginning with Jefferson's Declaration of Independence; and of all the philosophic doctrines, including Hegel," *From
These Roots* (New York: Scribner's Sons, 1937), 297.

CARPENTER, FREDERIC I. *Emerson and Asia.* Cambridge, Mass.: Harvard University Press. 1930.
[Does not discuss Whitman but gives background for an appreciation of some aspects of his mysticism.]

CHRISTY, ARTHUR. *The Orient in American Transcendentalism.* New York: Columbia University Press. 1932.
[Merely mentions Whitman but provides materials for the study of his relations to Transcendentalism and to Oriental thought. A valuable background source.]

FLEWELLING, RALPH T. "Personalism," *Twentieth Century Philophy,* edited by Dagobert D. Runes. New York: Philosophical Library. 1943.
[Definition and interpretation of "Personalism" by a leading authority.]

HALLEY, EBENEZER. *The Pantheism of Germany:* A Sermon Delivered before the Synod of Albany, at Saratoga Springs, Oct. 9, 1850. Albany: Gray and Sprague. 1850.
[Of little scholarly value but of historical importance for its theological opposition to pantheism as anti-Christian and atheistic.]

HARROLD, CHARLES F. *Carlyle and German Thought, 1819-1834.* New Haven: Yale University Press. 1934.
[Gives background useful both for a study of Whitman's relations to Carlyle and to his indirect relations, partly through Carlyle, to German philosophy.]

HUNT, REV. JOHN. *An Essay on Pantheism.* London: Longmans, Green, Reader, and Dyer. 1866.
[Readable—less information than in Plumptre, *q.v.*]

JAMES, WILLIAM. "Mysticism," *Varieties of Religious Experience,* pp. 370-420. New York: Modern Library, n.d. [Longmans, Green. 1925.]
[Not only an authoritative source for the psychology of mysticism but also quotes Whitman as example.]

JONES, RUFUS M. *The Flowering of Mysticism: The Friends of God in the Fourteenth Century.* New York: Macmillan and Co. 1939.

[By one of the great authorities on mysticism, but of less immediate use in studying Whitman than James and Russell, *q.v.*]

KNUDSON, ALBERT C. *The Philosophy of Personalism.* New York: Abingdon Press. 1927.

[Primarily theological but also contains history of terms and definitions.]

LORCH, FRED W. "Thoreau and the Organic Principle of Poetry," *Publications of Modern Language Association,* LIII, 286-302 (March, 1938).

[Whitman's use of the "Organic Principle" is not entirely parallel with Thoreau's but this article is valuable for definitions and origin of the idea.]

LOVEJOY, ARTHUR O. *The Great Chain of Being: A Study of the History of an Idea.* Cambridge, Mass.: Harvard University Press. 1936.

[A great scholarly work. Whitman is not mentioned but Emerson is. Many examples also throw light on Whitman's relation to German thought.]

LUSSKY, A. E. *Tieck's Romantic Irony.* Chapel Hill: University of North Carolina Press. 1932.

[Contains general information about German ideas similar to Whitman's.]

OTTO, RUDOLF. *Mysticism East and West: A Comparative Analysis of the Nature of Mysticism.* New York: Macmillan and Co. 1932.

[Interprets Eastern mysticism as static, Western as dynamic.]

PICTON, J. ALLANSON. *Pantheism: Its Story and Significance.* London: Archibald Constable. 1905.

[A recognized authority.]

PLUMPTRE, C. E. *General Sketch of the History of Pantheism.*
London: Samuel Deacon and Co. 1878. 2 vols.
[Still chief authority in English.]

RILEY, WOODBRIDGE. *The Meaning of Mysticism.* New York:
Harper and Brothers. 1930.
[Compares "the pantheism of the Rhine region . . . with the
poetic pantheism of Walt Whitman . . ."]

RUSSELL, BERTRAND. *Mysticism and Logic and Other Essays.*
London: Longmans, Green and Co. 1921.
[One of the most useful summaries of mystical ideas.]

SHEPARD, ODELL. *Pedlar's Progress: The Life of Bronson Alcott.*
Boston: Little, Brown and Co. 1937.
[Discusses the "Personalism" of both Alcott and Whitman
and of Whitman's influence on Alcott.]

UNDERHILL, EVELYN. *Mysticism: A Study in the Nature and
Development of Man's Spiritual Consciousness.* New York:
E. P. Dutton. 11th Ed. 1926.
[A standard authority, but less useful than James and Rus-
sell, *q.v.*]

WALZEL, OSKAR. *German Romanticism,* translated by Alma
Elise Lussky, from *Deutsche Romantik* (Berlin, 1923). New
York: Putnam. 1932.
[Useful in making comparative study of Whitman and Ger-
man ideas.]

CRITICAL STUDIES OF WHITMAN'S IDEAS

ALLEN, GAY W. "Walt Whitman's 'Long Journey' Motif,"
Journal of English and Germanic Philology, XXXVIII,
76-95 (Jan., 1939).
[The "Long Journey" is the evolution of the human race.]

ARVIN, NEWTON. *Whitman.* New York: Macmillan and Co.
1938.

[Good discussions of Whitman's social and political ideas, also his relations to French rationalism and German romanticism.]

BECK, MAXIMILIAN. "Walt Whitman's Intuition of Reality." *Ethics,* LIII, 14-24 (Oct., 1942).

BERTZ, EDUARD. *Der Yankee-Heiland.* Dresden: Reissner. 1906. [Debunks Whitman as a thinker, comparing him unfavorably to Novalis and Nietzsche—especially latter—and others. Though the book is prejudiced, and now out of date, it suggests parallels for further investigation.]

BOATRIGHT, MODY C. "Whitman and Hegel." *Studies in English (The University of Texas Bulletin),* IX, 134-150 (July 8, 1929).
[On Hegel as a possible source—partly through Gostwick.]

BUCKE, RICHARD MAURICE. *Cosmic Consciousness.* New York: E. P. Dutton. 1923.
[Bucke is hardly a reliable authority on mysticism, but as an intimate friend of Whitman, what he has to say on the subject is worth considering. Gives examples of Whitman's mystical experiences.]

CARPENTER, EDWARD. *Days with Walt Whitman.* London: George Allen. 1906.
[Discusses ideas under "Whitman as Prophet," and in an appendix cites parallels between the Upanishads and *Leaves of Grass.* Book also contains good discussion of "Whitman and Emerson."]

CARPENTER, FREDERIC I. "Walt Whitman's Eidólon." *College English,* III, 534-545 (March, 1942).
[On Whitman's Idealism.]

COLUM, MRS. MARY M. "The Ideas that Have Made Modern Literature," *From These Roots,* pp. 260-311. New York: Scribner's Sons. 1937.
[Suggests interesting relationships. General.]

COOKE, MRS. ALICE LOVELACE. "Whitman's Background in the Industrial Movements of His Time." *Studies in English (The University of Texas Bulletin)*, XV, 76-91 (July 8, 1935).

————. "Whitman's Indebtedness to the Scientific Thought of His Day." *Studies in English (The University of Texas Bulletin)*, XIV, 89-115 (July 8, 1934).

DUGDALE, CLARENCE. "Whitman's Knowledge of Astronomy." *Studies in English (The University of Texas Bulletin)*, XVI, 124-137 (July 8, 1936).

[The knowledge was quite general.]

FALK, ROBERT P. "Walt Whitman and German Thought." *Journal of English and Germanic Philology*, XL, 315-330 (July, 1941).

[Parallels and possible sources; suggests general influence.]

FOERSTER, NORMAN. "Whitman," *American Criticism: A Study in Literary Theory from Poe to the Present*, pp. 157-222. Boston: Houghton Mifflin Co. 1928.

[Names all sources known at time and makes some comparison of ideas with European thought.]

FULGHUM, W. B., JR. "Whitman's Debt to Joseph Gostwick." *American Literature*, XII, 491-496 (Jan., 1941).

[Shows Whitman's extensive use of Gostwick's popularization of German thought and literature.]

FURNESS, CLIFTON J. "Walt Whitman and Reincarnation." *The Forerunner*, III, 9-20 (Aug., 1942).

[Valuable for examples and interpretations of Whitman's extensive use of the idea of reincarnation.]

GOHDES, CLARENCE. "Whitman and Emerson." *Sewanee Review*, XXXVII, 79-93 (Jan., 1929).

[Shows Whitman's indebtedness to Emerson.]

GOODALE, DAVID. "Some of Walt Whitman's Borrowings." *American Literature*, X, 202-213 (May, 1938).

[Especially important are Whitman's use of Frances Wright's *A Few Days in Athens* and *Volney's Ruins.*]

GUTHRIE, WILLIAM A. *"Walt Whitman the Camden Sage."* Cincinnati: Robert Clark Co. 1897.
[Useful especially in evaluating Whitman's Orientalism.]

HOWARD, LEON. "For a Critique of Whitman's Transcendentalism." *Modern Language Notes,* XLVII, 79-85 (Feb., 1932).
[Contrasts Whitman's "militant materialism combined with idealism in its transcendental purity."]

HUNGERFORD, EDWARD. "Walt Whitman and His Chart of Bumps." *American Literature,* II, 350-384 (Jan., 1931).
[Attempts to establish phrenology as a major source for Whitman's ideas and ambition to be a poet.]

LONG, HANIEL. *Walt Whitman and the Springs of Courage.* Sante Fe, New Mexico: Writers Editions. 1938.
[Especially good for evaluation of Whitman's indebtedness to Emerson and to phrenology.]

MATTHIESSEN, F. O. "Whitman," *American Renaissance:* Art and Expression in the Age of Emerson and Whitman, pp. 517-625. New York: Oxford University Press. 1941.
[One of the most acute modern interpretations of Whitman's art in terms of American ideas of his age. Of major importance.]

MAXWELL, WILLIAM. "Some Personalist Elements in the Poetry of Whitman." *Personalist,* XII, 190-199 (July, 1931).
[Suggestive but inconclusive.]

MOORE, JOHN B. "The Master of Whitman." *Studies in Philology,* XXIII, 77-89 (Jan., 1926).
[Emerson's influence on Whitman and Whitman's attitudes toward Emerson.]

MYERS, HENRY ALONZO. "Whitman's Conception of the Spiritual Democracy, 1855-56." *American Literature,* VI, 239-253 Nov., 1934).

[Good interpretation of Whitman's basic metaphysical assumptions.]

———. "Whitman's Consistency." *American Literature,* VIII, 243-257 (Nov., 1936).
[In terms of his Idealism, Whitman was consistent. An important contribution to Whitman criticism.]

PAINE, GREGORY. "The Literary Relations of Whitman and Carlyle with Especial Reference to their Contrasting Views of Democracy." *Studies in Philology,* XXXVI, 550-563 (July, 1939).
[Excellent study.]

PARSONS, OLIVE W. "Whitman the Non-Hegelian." *Publications of Modern Language Association,* LVIII, 1073-1093 (Dec., 1943).
[Finds little similarity in ideas of Hegel and Whitman.]

REED, H. B. "The Heraclitan Obsession of Whitman." *Personalist,* XV, 125-138 (Spring, 1934).
["The concept of endless progression and succession became . . . almost an obsession with Whitman . . ."]

SARRAZIN, GABRIEL. "Walt Whitman," translated by Harrison S. Morris, *In Re Walt Whitman,* pp. 159-194. Philadelphia: David McKay. 1893.
[One of the first critical interpretations of Whitman's pantheism. Suggests relations to European thought.]

SHIPLEY, M. "Democracy as a Religion: The Religion of Walt Whitman." *Open Court,* XXXIII, 385-393 (July, 1919).

SIXBEY, G. L. "Chanting the Square Deific—A Study in Whitman's Religion." *American Literature,* IX, 171-195 (May, 1937).
[The most complete study of Whitman's ideas for a "new religion."]

SMITH, FRED M. "Whitman's Debt to Sartor Resartus." *Modern Language Quarterly,* III, 51-65 (March, 1942).

————. "Whitman's Poet-Prophet and Carlyle's Hero." *Publications of Modern Language Association*, LV, 1146-1164 (Dec., 1940).
[Both of these articles reveal Carlyle as one of Whitman's most important sources, but the author has overlooked important examples.]

STEVENSON, ROBERT LOUIS. "Walt Whitman," *Familiar Studies of Men and Books*. New York: Scribner's Sons. 1896.
[Unfriendly—main value is historical.]

STOVALL, FLOYD. "Main Drifts in Whitman's Poetry." *American Literature*, IV, 3-21 (March, 1932).
[A survey of Whitman's shift in attitudes and thought as he matured.]

SYMONDS, JOHN ADDINGTON. *Walt Whitman: A Study*. London: George Routledge. 1893.
[Though long out-of-date, this book still contains valuable interpretations of Whitman's ideas by a qualified scholar and critic.]

CHAPTER IV

SOCIAL THOUGHT: IDEAS IN ACTION

The paths to the house I seek to make,
But leave to those to come the house itself.[1]

IDEAS AS TOOLS AND RESULTS

Whitman's major abstract "ideas" have been indicated in the preceding chapter, and many of these ideas imply theories of democracy and of society, but none of them nor any combination of them can be regarded as an integrated social philosophy. In fact, the attempt to define Whitman's ideas has necessitated the presentation of them in artificial categories, even under terms which the poet himself might not have recognized. But of course these concepts did not develop in a vacuum. Ideas, especially those of a "creative" writer like Whitman, are borrowed, re-forged, and applied in a world of physical and psychological reality. They may be accurately regarded both as implements with which the poet achieved desired results and as the results themselves. Especially is this true of such ideas as "panpsychism," the "organic principle," or "personalism."[2] At best they are formulas which solve both personal and philosophical problems; at worst they become cantrips which give the illusion of solution, like primitive magic. One of Whitman's weaknesses as a thinker is that logical contradictions did not bother him; he could too readily escape into mysticism.

---

[1] *Thou Mother With Thy Equal Brood.*
[2] See Chap. III, pp. 256, 292, 302 respectively.

325

Some critics, overly conscious of the poet's obscuritanism, would deny him any claims as a rational thinker, which is also to say as a practical and social thinker. However, though it is true that LEAVES OF GRASS and the *Prose Works* do not contain a specific "social program," Whitman was definitely interested in, and was keenly observant of, American democracy in operation; furthermore, his political opinions and social attitudes provide a valuable background for understanding and intepreting his poetic program—and the growth of his mind and art.

No one has ever made a comprehensive study of the origin and development of Whitman' ideas,[3] and until his manuscripts have been better organized and dated than they are at present, perhaps an authoritative exposition will be impossible. But meanwhile certain trends in his social thought can at least be indicated by an examination of his newspaper editorials,[4] his poetic intentions recorded in the Prefaces, and the old-age opinions preserved by Horace Traubel in *With Walt Whitman in Camden*.[5]

The student of Whitman should never forget that the poet quite literally learned to write in the newspaper office, as printer's devil, compositor, and later editor of a

---

[3] Newton Arvin's *Whitman* (New York: Macmillan Co., 1938) contains valuable criticism of the poet's social thought, but it does not pretend to be a genetic study.

[4] These have been reprinted by Cleveland Rodgers and John Black in *Gathering of the Forces* (New York: G. P. Putnam's Sons, 1920), 2 vols.; and Emory Holloway, *Uncollected Poetry and Prose* (New York: Peter Smith, 1932), 2 vols. Also: Emory Holloway and Vernolian Schwarz, *I Sit and Look Out;* editorials from the Brooklyn *Daily Times* (New York: Columbia University Press, 1932) and Emory Holloway and Ralph Adimari, *New York Dissected* [Newspaper articles] (New York: Rufus Rockwell Wilson, 1936).

[5] Vol. I (March 28-July 14, 1888), Boston: Small, Maynard and Co., 1906; Vol. II (July 16, 1888-October 31, 1888), New York: D. Appleton and Co., 1908; Vol. III (November 1, 1888-January 20, 1889), New York: Mitchell Kennerley, 1914).

fairly important metropolitan newspaper of the 1840's, the
Brooklyn *Daily Eagle*. In the latter position he had the
opportunity not only to absorb the popular thought of the
day but also to express it through his own talents and
thus to put ideas into action. This journalistic expression
is of mediocre literary quality (a fact not the least surprising); but in his democratic sympathies, his partisan
enthusiasms, and his political ambitions we can now see
in retrospect the emerging mind and character of the future author of LEAVES OF GRASS and *Democratic Vistas*.

PARTISAN IN POLITICS

During the 1840-decade Whitman was active in party
politics, attending rallies, occasionally making speeches,
and in 1846-47 writing many editorials on political issues.
As Cleveland Rodgers says, "He was a partisan in politics,
but to him Democracy and the principles of the Demo-
cratic-Republican Party were synonymous; when they
ceased to be so he ceased to be a partisan and became all
Democrat."[6] The *New Era* for July 30, 1841, reported
Whitman as having declared in a speech at a Democratic
rally for Kings County: "We are battling for great principles—for mighty and glorious truths. I would scorn to
exert even my humble efforts for the best Democratic
candidate that ever was nominated, in himself alone."[7]
This sounds like typical political ballyhoo, but that the
future poet sincerely meant what he said is borne out by
his subsequent record. The stand which he took on party
questions when he became editor of the Brooklyn *Eagle* is a
revealing chapter in the history of his intellectual develop-

[6] *Gathering of the Forces, op. cit.,* I, xxiv.
[7] *Ibid.,* II, 5.

ment. In 1846-47 the nation was already torn with dissension over two related problems: the war with Mexico and the possibility of extending slavery into whatever territory might be annexed. Whitman vigorously supported President Polk in the prosecution of the war and looked forward with great enthusiasm to the expansion of the American nation, but opposed any extension of slavery into new territory. Most biographers seem to have been embarrassed by Whitman's jingoistic "imperalism" of this period, but we should not forget, as DeVoto has pointed out: "The Americans had always devoutly believed that the superiority of their institutions, government, and mode of life would eventually spread, by inspiration and imitation, to less fortunate, less happy peoples."[8] American "democrats" of the 1840's had as strong a missionary spirit as the Russian Communists of eighty or ninety years later.

NATIONAL EXPANSION

On June 6, having heard that the people of Yucatan wanted to be annexed, the young editor of the *Eagle* exclaimed:

> We pant to see our country and its rule far-reaching, only inasmuch as it will take off the shackles that prevent men the even chance of being happy and good— as most governments are now so constituted that the tendency is very much the other way ... [But] the mere physical grandeur of this Republic ... is only desirable as an aid to reach the truer good, the good of the whole body of the people.[9]

---

[8] Bernard DeVoto, *The Year of Decision: 1846* (Boston: Little, Brown and Co., 1943), 9.
[9] *Gathering of the Forces*, I, 244.

A few days later (June 23) he thought that expansion of the United States was natural and inevitable, "And for our part, we look on that increase of territory and power . . . with the faith which the Christian has in God's mystery. —Over the rest of the world, the swelling impulse of freedom struggles, too; though *we* are ages ahead of them."[10]

July 7, 1846, on the prospect of annexing California, he asked: "What has miserable, inefficient Mexico—with her superstition, her burlesque upon freedom, her actual tyranny by the few over the many—what has she to do with the great mission of peopling the New World with a noble race?"[11] With such convictions as these he could accuse the New York *Tribune* of "abetting the enemy" by praising the Mexican cause and "leveling sarcasms at the [American] Army, the Navy, the advance of the American cause, and every successive progress of our brave fellows."[12] On January 4, 1847, he scored the Whigs for making political capital out of the war and promulgating a contemptible peace. He also desired a speedy end of the war, but asked, "how on earth are we to get peace, while our adversary . . . refuses to receive our diplomatic agents?"[13] On September 23, with no settlement yet in sight, he called impatiently for vigorous and efficient action:

> God knows we have no love for this or any other kind of war; but we know that this temporizing, delaying, negotiating, peace-begging policy with an ignorant, prejudiced, and perfectly faithless people, is not the way to end the contest. There is no middle course—

---

[10] *Ibid.*, I, 23.

[11] *Ibid.*, I, 247.

[12] *Ibid.*, I, 248.

[13] *Ibid.*, I, 255-256.

either we must back out of it entirely, or we must drive it through with a vigorous hand.[14]

On December 2 Whitman was indignant over the "Gallatin Plan" to recall American troops from Mexican territory and, in the editor's words, "act as the vanquished and weaker party instead of the victorious and powerful one."[15] Not only was he shocked to think that American lives had been spent in vain but he also believed that, "It is for the interest of mankind that its [America's] power and territory should be extended—the farther the better."[16] The latter view Whitman repeatedly expressed throughout 1846 during the Oregon dispute, displaying a consistently pugnacious attitude toward Great Britain until the treaty was finally signed, then in several editorials he rejoiced that the war had been avoided. Perhaps his most rabidly imperialistic outburst was on February 8, 1847, when he shouted that the United States "may one day put the Canadas and Russian America [Alaska] in its fob pocket!", adding, however, that this nation "will regard human life, property and rights" and will "*never* be guilty of furnishing duplicates to the Chinese war, the 'operations of the British in India,' or the 'extinguishment of Poland.' "[17] Such was the faith that Walt Whitman had in American Democracy during the 1840's.

POLITICAL ISSUES: SLAVERY, "FREE SOIL," IMMIGRATION, AND "FREE TRADE"

Despite Arvin's references to Whitman's "inglorious record in the days of the Abolitionists,"[18] as editor he was

---

[14] *Ibid.*, I, 261-262.
[15] *Ibid.*, I, 264.
[16] *Ibid.*, I, 266.

[17] *Ibid.*, I, 33.
[18] Arvin, *op. cit.*, 33.

by no means indifferent to slavery as either a moral or an economic problem. On March 18, 1846, he published an editorial on "Slavers — and the Slave Trade"[19] so strongly worded that it must have pleased even the fanatical Abolitionists. He seemed to be well acquainted with the methods of financing, building, and operating ships in the illegal trade, and he used his facts to excellent advantage. He was also no less ardent in his lecture notes on the subject, though we do not know exactly when they were written down. But on December 5, 1846, he had begun to take a sensible, moderate stand from which he never later wavered. "The mad fanaticism or ranting of the ultra 'Abolitionists' has pretty well spent its fury—and . . . has done far more harm than good to the very cause it professed to aid."[20] Though he believed firmly in the need for abolishing slavery, he wished to avoid violence, and italicized his peaceful solution: *"It is to the discoveries and suggestions of free thought, of 'public opinion,' of liberal sentiments, that we must at this age of the world look for quite all desirable reforms, in government and any thing else."*[21] Nevertheless, on December 21 he begged the Democratic Party to take a firm stand against permitting slavery in annexed territory.[22] Three weeks later (January 16, 1847) he reiterated his middle ground: "Despising and condemning the dangerous fanatical insanity of 'Abolitionism'—as impracticable as it is wild—the Brooklyn *Eagle* just as much condemns the other extreme from that."[23] He approved the Massa-

---

[19] *Gathering of the Forces*, I, 187-191; also *Uncollected Poetry and Prose, op. cit.*, I, 106-108.
[20] *Gathering of the Forces*, I, 192.
[21] *Ibid.*, I, 193.
[22] *Ibid.*, I, 194.
[23] *Ibid.*

chusetts Democrats in proposing "adherence to all constitutional rights" in solving the problem of slavery.

By February 6 he had become thoroughly alarmed by the possibility that the slavery dispute might break up the Union:

> If there is a political blessing on earth, that deserves to stand in the near neighborhood of the great common blessings vouchsafed us by God—life, light, freedom, and the beautiful and useful ordinations of nature—that blessing is involved in the UNION of these United States together into an integral Republic, "many in one."[24]

Here his attitude toward both slavery and the preservation of the Union is exactly parallel to Lincoln's, and is perhaps evidence that temperamentally the two men were much alike.[25] But fear of dissolution of the Union did not deter Whitman in his fight for "free soil."

On April 27 a new issue entered the question. Calhoun had claimed that "a large majority of both parties in the non-slave-holding States, have come to a fixed determination to appropriate all the territories of the United States now possessed, or hereafter to be acquired, to themselves, *to the entire exclusion of the slaveholding States.*"[26] Whitman pounced on the latter phrases, pointing out that with the possible exception of South Carolina, the majority of freemen in the South did not own slaves: "The only persons who will be excluded will be the *aristocracy* of the South—the men who work only with other men's

---

[24] *Ibid.*, I, 229; cf. also 234-239.
[25] Cf. T. Harry Williams' Introduction to *Selected Writings and Speeches of Abraham Lincoln* (Chicago: Packard and Co., 1943), xi-lv.
[26] *Gathering of the Forces*, I, 203.

hands."[27] Certainly the threat of slavery to free labor, especially in the industrial North, was one of the vital issues of the times. In the editor's words: "The voice of the North proclaims that *labor must not be degraded*. The young men of the free States must not be shut out from the new domain (where slavery does not exist) by the *introduction* of an institution which will render their honorable industry no longer respectable."[28]

This desire to keep the new territories "free soil," so that labor would not be degraded, intensified Whitman's idealistic enthusiasm for the West:

> The boundless democratic West! . . . The slave states are confessedly either stationary, or on a very slow progress, or in an actual decline. The Atlantic States, with a rush after wealth, and the spread among them of effeminating luxuries, need a balance wheel like that furnished by the agricultural sections of the West.[29]

During 1846 Whitman regarded as particularly undemocratic and vicious the "Nativists" or "Know-Nothing" party, which was being organized by means similar to those of the later Ku-Klux Klan to oppose immigration, and keep political control in the hands of "Native" Americans. On June 26 he sketched the wretchedness of the Old World and asked, "How, then, can any man with a heart in his breast, begrudge the coming of Europe's needy ones, to the plentiful storehouse of the New World?"[30] Funds, he thought, should be established to speed these poor people west to cheap lands.[31] On October 5, he pointed out that the course of American

[27] *Ibid.*, I, 204.
[28] *Ibid.*, I, 205-206.
[29] *Ibid.*, I, 25-26.
[30] *Ibid.*, I, 18.
[31] *Ibid.*, I, 164-165.

history had run counter to "Nativism," all presidents except John Adams having favored immigration.[32] A month later (November 24), he was still preaching immigration as the salvation of the "down-trodden of Europe" and the hope of American Democracy:

> . . . the time will surely come—that holy millenium of liberty—when the "Victory of endurance born" shall lift the masses of the down-trodden of Europe, and make them achieve something of that destiny which we may suppose God intends eligible for mankind. And this problem is to be worked out through the people, territory, and government of the United States.[33]

But the forces of demagogic-reaction could not be curbed by a few editorials. Congressman Henry I. Seaman, elected by the "Whig-Native" faction, introduced a bill in Congress ostensibly to exclude European paupers and criminals from migrating to the United States but intended to stop immigration altogether. This Whitman branded on January 22, 1847, as "The Latest Raw Head and Bloody Bones," and declared anew that, "This Republic—with its incalculable and inexhaustible resources, lying for thousands of miles back of us yet, and not possibly to be developed for ages and ages—*wants the wealth of stout poor men who will work* more than any other kind of wealth!"[34]

All his life Whitman believed unwaveringly in "free trade," and in 1846 he saw in Whig "protectionism" a social evil comparable to the introduction of slavery into the new territories or the outlawing of immigration. On July 10 he wrote:

[32] *Ibid*, I, 20.   [34] *Ibid.,* I, 163.
[33] *Ibid.,* I, 28.

When we hear of immense purchases, donations, or "movements" of our manufacturing capitalists of the North, we think ourselves how reasonable it is that they should want "protection"—and how nice a game they play in asking a high tariff "for the benefit of the working men." What a lot of cents have gone out of poor folks' pockets, to swell the dollars in the possession of owners of great steam mills! Molière, speaking of a wealthy physician, says: "He must have killed a great many people to be so rich!" Our American capitalists of the manufacturing orders, would poor a great many people to be so rich![35]

On September 3, he repeated his belief that, "Excessively high duties paralyze general trade—at least retard it immensely; and that injures enterprise and workingmen's wages."[36] December 10 he reiterated that "we can't have trade without imports."[37]

END OF PARTISANISM: "ALL DEMOCRAT"

On all these issues of "free soil," immigration, and "free trade," Whitman as editor of the Brooklyn *Eagle* was always quick to score the absurdities or the selfish policies of the Whigs or to praise the liberal principles of the Democrat-Republicans; but he had by no means sold his integrity to his party, and as a result was soon to lose both his editorial position and his party support. The Democrat-Republican Party had already split on the Wilmot Proviso, a bill introduced by Congressman David Wilmot to prohibit slavery in annexed territories. Of course the Southern Democrats were solidly opposed to

---

[35] *Ibid.*, II, 70-71.   [37] *Ibid.*, **II, 63.**
[36] *Ibid.*, II, 68.

the Proviso, and in the attempt to preserve the Party unity both the New York Legislature and the Democratic convention at Syracuse avoided a definite stand on the question. Whether this was the cause or not, the Democrats were defeated in November. Attempting to discover the cause of the failure, Whitman decided that the Party had not been "sufficiently bold, open and radical, in its avowals of sentiment."[38] He thought true Democratic principles were: minimum of government, no monopolies, free trade, and free soil. The following day, continuing his analysis of the recent defeat, he blamed his Party for not having taken a firm stand on the Wilmot Proviso, and warned:

> *We must plant ourselves firmly on the side of freedom, and openly espouse it.* The late election is a terrific warning of the folly of all half-way policy in such matters—of all compromises that neither receive or reject a great idea to which the people are once fully awakened.[39]

This outspoken criticism seems not to have pleased the owner of the *Eagle,* Isaac Van Anden, a stand-pat "regular." The split in the Party ranks widened and the "radicals" (*i.e.,* ardent Free Soilers) were read out of the Party. In Whitman's own case his open break with his "boss" did not take place until early in January, 1848.[40] The exact details are still not known, but the rupture was probably caused by Whitman's attitude toward an open letter which General Lewis Cass wrote against the Wilmot Proviso. Without printing the letter, Whitman made an editorial attack on it January 3. On January 5 the letter

[38] *Ibid.,* I, 218.   [40] Cf. *Ibid.,* I, xxxi ff.
[39] *Ibid.,* I, 222.

was published in full, and about this time the *Eagle* seems to have had a new editor. This was nearly but not quite the end of Walt Whitman's participation in political journalism. After he returned from New Orleans he founded a Free Soil weekly, the *Freeman,* which began publication on September 9, 1848. In the spring of 1849 it became a daily, but Whitman resigned his editorship on September 11 because the Free Soilers had joined the regular Party and he evidently felt that his work was no longer needed. The outstanding fact of Whitman's editor-ship of the *Eagle* and *Freeman* is the consistency of his support of "free soil" and his willingness to sacrifice his journalistic career for his political principles.

Although Whitman was perhaps too liberal and honest to prosper as a party journalist of the 1840's, he was by no means a radical or a prophet ahead of his time. In summarizing his political thought, we might begin by call-ing him a combination of Jeffersonian and Jacksonian Democrat. Like Jefferson, he believed that "the best gov-ernment is that which governs least."[41] Andrew Jackson he regarded as a *"Man of the People,* worth more than hundreds of political leaders."[42]

In fact, Whitman's whole theory of government was strongly Jeffersonian. Commenting on news of social un-rest in Europe, he remarked: "For though we are not of the school which believes that government can confer happi-ness, the signs are plain that they have sovereign potency in the prevalence of misery."[43] To this Jeffersonian Demo-crat, "all that is necessary in government [is] *to make no*

---

[41] *Ibid.,* I, 57.
[42] *Ibid.,* II, 180.
[43] *Ibid.,* I, 29.

*more laws than those useful for preventing a man or body
of men from infringing on the rights of other men."[44]*

The Whigs, he thought, exaggerated the intricacy of
Government:

> The error lies in the desire after *management,* the great
> curse of our Legislation: every thing is to be regulated
> and made straight by force of statute. And all this
> while, evils are accumulating, in very consequence of
> excessive management. The true office of government, is
> simply to preserve the rights of each citizen from spolia-
> tion: when it attempts to go beyond this, it is intrusive
> and does more harm than good.[45]

Whitman, therefore, made fun of attempts to legislate
temperance,[46] for "in his moral and mental capacity, man
is the sovereign of his individual self."[47] A "moral revolution . . . must work its way through individual minds.
It must spread from its own beauty, and melt into the
hearts of men . . .[48] Where the popular virtue is low, no
legislation can make it any higher by statute."[49] Here we
have the foundation for his theory of individual moral
development and of "Personalism"[50] in LEAVES OF GRASS
and *Democratic Vistas.*

As a Jacksonian Democrat, Whitman approved the
abolishing of the United States Bank and the establishment
of a "Sub-Treasury" (*i.e.,* a Federal treasury, such as the
American Government has had ever since 1846). This
view was not inconsistent with his theory of government
because the Treasury Law put an end to lending the people's money to " 'pet' banks, to issue and amplify on the

---

[44] *Ibid.,* II, 53.
[45] *Ibid.,* I, 54.
[46] *Ibid.,* I, 67-69.
[47] *Ibid.,* I, 70.
[48] *Ibid.,* I, 60.
[49] *Ibid.,* I, 62.
[50] See p. 302.

strength of it."[51] That he was thoroughly in favor of private enterprise is indicated by his criticism of the mismanagement of the United States Post Office Department, which he regarded as a "living oration and argument against the power of the government to compete with individual enterprise" and an illustration of "the results of the monopolizing spirit."[52] What he was evidently after, however, was more efficient management. In all matters of both economics and government he was a thoroughly orthodox Jeffersonian, believing with religious earnestness in laissez-faire and individualism.

FAITH IN THE DEMOCRATIC SPIRIT

During this period Whitman came nearest to arriving at a coherent social philosophy in his thinking about Democracy. His background was still primarily Jefferson, Paine, and the doctrines of the French and American Revolutions—doctrines which he seems to have still believed in more literally and fundamentally than most of his contemporaries did. But for this very reason he was also able to observe how far his beloved United States of America still was from achieving in actuality what her orators and apologists had so long held in ideality; thus he became a realistic critic, and eventually a disillusioned one, with faith in the future instead of the present. As early as 1842, in defending Dickens's criticism of American Democracy, Whitman wrote:

A "democratic writer," I take it, is one the tendency of whose pages is to destroy those old land-marks which pride and fashion have set up, making impassable dis-

[51] *Gathering of the Forces,* II, 77.
[52] *Ibid.,* II, 229.

tinctions between the brethren of the Great Family—to render in their deformity before us the tyranny of partial laws—to show us the practical workings of the thousand distortions engrafted by custom upon our nations of what justice is—to make us love our fellow-creatures, and own that although social distinctions place others far higher or far lower than we, yet are human beings alike, as links of the same chain; one whose lines are imbued, from preface to finis, with that philosophy which teaches to pull down the high and bring up the low. I consider Mr. Dickens to be a democratic writer.

The mere fact of a man's delineating human character in its lowest stages of degradation, and giving it unbounded scope in every species of wickedness, proves neither his "democracy" nor its opposite.[53]

Four years later he was convinced that, "The old and motheaten systems of Europe have had their day, and that evening of their existence which is nigh at hand, will be the token of a glorious dawn for the down-trodden people."[54] But when he turned his eyes on his own country, he realized that there were "Doctrines that even now are scarcely breathed" in America lest the champions of them "be scouted as worse than Robespierran revolutionists (that hacknied [sic] bug-bear theme which has never been presented in its fairness to the people of this Republic) will, in course of time, see the light here, and meet the sanction of popular favor and go into practical play."[55] Attaining the ideals of real democracy will be a slow struggle: "There must be continual additons to our great

---

[53] "Boz and Democracy," *Brother Jonathan*, February 26, 1842. Reprinted in *Uncollected Poetry and Prose, op. cit.*, I, 67-69.

[54] *Gathering of the Forces*, I, 10.

[55] *Ibid.*,I, 11 (July 28, 1846).

experiment of how much liberty society will bear . . ."[56]
Meanwhile, however, one should not be discouraged by
"the turbulence and destructiveness of the Democratic
spirit," for they are evidence of political vitality:

> They evince that the *people act;* they are the discipline
> of the young giant, getting his maturer strength . . .
> God works out his greatest results by such means [the
> means of social evolution] . . . We know, well enough,
> that the workings of Democracy are not always justi-
> fiable, in every trivial point. But the great winds that
> purify the air, and without which nature would flag into
> ruin—are they to be condemned because a tree is pros-
> trated here and there, in their course?[57]

CRITIC OF CHURCHES AND RELIGION

At the same time that Walt Whitman was emerging
from political journalism to a broad criticism of American
Democracy, and thereby laying the foundations of his
later poetic-prophetic message, he was also evolving attitudes and opinions on the churches and religion which
later profoundly affected his poetic program. On March
9, 1846, he observed that "the comfortable pews, the exquisite arrangements, and the very character of the archi-
tecture of our modern churches . . . lift a man into a com-
placent kind of self-satisfaction with himself and his own
doings."[58] In the same month (March 30) he added that
Grace Church "is a place where the world, and the world's
traits, and the little petty passions and weaknesses of
human nature, seem to be as broad blown and flush as
upon the Exchange in Wall Street, Broadway, or any
mart of trade, of a week day."[59]

---

[56] *Ibid.*, I, 12.
[57] *Ibid.*, I, 4-5 (April 20, 1847).
[58] *Ibid.*, II, 93.
[59] *Ibid.*, II, 95.

Christianity, no less than the political ideals of freedom and equality, was still more dream than reality, but it had been an important influence in the evolution of society. The birth of Christ "vitally started in manifold seeds of true good which had for ages lain dormant in humanity."[60] On December 31, 1847, he amplified this text:

> The religion of Christ is incomparably superior to all other religions—though it cannot make man essentially different. All reforms tend to the great result of freeing man's body and his mind from the dark tyranny, in some shape or other, that has been accumulating on them for centuries. They perform more the labor of hewing away than adding to.[61]

The young editor who saw in religion a means of freeing men from the tyranny of ignorance and oppression was unmistakably the disciple of Volney, Tom Paine, and the thinkers of the French Revolution; and his concept of Christianity as a method of vitalizing the good "dormant in humanity" was a religious theory of great social potentiality, supporting his faith in Democracy and justifying his patience with the slow progress of mankind.

Social Aspects of the Poetic Program

Although Whitman did not lose interest in the details of practical politics after his ambition climbed from party journalism to a poetic career, he was henceforth to turn his attention and energies to broad principles instead of strictly contemporary issues; nevertheless, we find in his great poetic program, as expressed in the 1855 Preface, an incorporation and fresh enunciation of nearly every

---

[60] *Ibid.*, II, 215 (Dec. 24, 1846).   [61] *Ibid.*, II, 212-213.

political and social conviction of the earlier editorials. In fact, with these editorials as a familiar background, the reader will find an astonishing amount of "social thought" in this Preface, much of which could not be indicated in our studies of the literary aspects of Whitman's "poetic program."

The Preface[62] begins by acknowledging that "America does not repel the past or what it has produced under its forms or amid other politics or the idea of castes or the old religions,"[63] but will build a better society on the foundations of the past, for "the life which served its requirements has passed into the new life of the new forms."[64] The United States hold forth the greatest promise and expectations in the annals of the race.

This promise resides in the democratic respect for the individual. "Other states indicate themselves in their deputies . . . but the genius of the United States is not best or most in its executives or legislatures, nor in its ambassadors or authors or colleges or churches . . . but always most in the common people."[65] It is they who have a "deathless attachment to freedom" and an "aversion to anything indecorous or soft or mean." In fact, without individual virtue no civic virtue is possible. "The largeness of nature or the nation were monstrous without a corresponding largeness and generosity of the spirit of the citizen."[66] The greatest pride and wealth of the nation is not in size or material prosperity but in "the breed of

---

[62] The 1855 Preface has been reprinted many times. For convenience Emory Holloway's "Inclusive Edition" of LEAVES OF GRASS (Garden City, N. Y.: Doubleday, Doran and Co., 1929) is used as reference.
[63] *Ibid.,* 488.
[64] *Ibid.*
[65] *Ibid.,* 488-489.
[66] *Ibid.,* 489.

fullsized men or one fullsized man unconquerable and simple."[67]

Whitman's theory that "a bard is to be commensurate with a people"[68] is social as well as literary and esthetic, for his ideal poet is to be a national leader. First of all he must be rooted not only in the geography and experience of his own nation, but also in the experience of other nations: "To him the other continents arrive as contributions."[69] Building on this foundation, he can expand with the territorial growth of his country: "When the long Atlantic coast stretches longer and the Pacific coast stretches longer he stretches with them north or south."[70] Thus the poet spiritually and imaginatively enters "the essences of the real things and past and future events."[71] Among these "things" and "events" are such vital issues as "the perpetual coming of immigrants," "free commerce," and slavery, with "the tremulous spreading of hands to protect it, and the stern opposition to it which shall never cease till it ceases or the speaking of tongues and the moving of lips cease."[72] For the right solution of these political problems Whitman looks to "the noble character of the young mechanics and of all free American workmen and workwomen."[73] That he thinks of himself as the leader of a labor party is improbable, but rather as a social guide, conscience, and patriotic inspiration.

Here comes one among the well beloved stonecutters and plans with decision and science and sees the solid and beautiful forms of the future where there are now

---

[67] *Ibid.*
[68] *Ibid.*
[69] *Ibid.*
[70] *Ibid.*

[71] *Ibid.*
[72] *Ibid.*, 491.
[73] *Ibid.*

no solid forms . . . He is the equalizer of his age and
land . . . he supplies what wants supplying and checks
what wants checking. If peace is the routine [,] out
of him speaks the spirit of peace . . . In war he is the
most deadly force of the war. Who recruits him recruits
horse and foot . . . If the time becomes slothful and
heavy he knows how to arouse it . . . Whatever stagnates in the flat of custom or obedience or legislation
he never stagnates.[74]

In this context, Whitman's seeing "eternity in men and
women" becomes a social program, and it is the democratic mass who will carry it out, for it is they who have
faith, and "Faith is the antiseptic of the soul . . . it pervades
the common people and preserves them . . . they never
give up believing and expecting and trusting."[75] Believing thus in the common people for the salvation of society,
the poet asserts that "there can be unnumbered Supremes,
and that one does not countervail another . . ." and that
"men can be good or grand only of [*i.e.,* in proportion to]
the consciousness of their supremacy within them."[76] Of
course the poet's faith in the future rests on the typical
nineteenth-century belief in cosmic melioration and social
progress: "For the eternal tendencies of all toward happiness makes the only point of sane philosophy."[77]

But even at this stage in Whitman's thought, he emphasizes the *tendency* instead of the *actuality*. Liberty is
still something to be attained—though the fact that it has
not yet been achieved should not discourage the poet-
leader:

In the make of the great masters the idea of political
liberty is indispensable. . . . The attitude of great poets

---

[74] *Ibid.*
[75] *Ibid.,* 492.

[76] *Ibid.,* 496.
[77] *Ibid.*

is to cheer up slaves and horrify despots. . . . Liberty
is poorly served by men whose good intent is quelled
from one failure or two failures or any number of failures, or from the casual indifference or ingratitude of
the people.[78]

With graphic realism Whitman describes the temporary
triumphs of "the swarms of cringers, suckers, doughfaces,
lice of politics, planners of sly involutions for their own
preferment to city offices or state legislatures or the ju-
diciary or congress or the presidency . . . when it is better
to be a bound booby and rogue in office at a high salary
than the poorest free mechanic or farmer . . ."[79] The poet
will never despair. He will persevere until he dissolves
"poverty from its need and riches from its conceit."[80]

Whitman's doctrine of "prudence" is also fundamentally social. "The prudence of the mere wealth and re-
spectability of the most esteemed life appears too faint
for the eye to observe at all when little and large alike
drop quietly aside at the thought of the prudence suitable
for immortality."[81] Stripped of all mysticism, this doctrine
is simply the belief that, "All that a person does or thinks
is of consequence."[82] Every deed has social results, now
and hereafter, both on the individual who acts and on
society itself:

> . . . not any harshness of officers to men or judges to
> prisoners or fathers to sons or sons to fathers or hus-
> bands to wives or bosses to their boys . . . not of greedy
> looks or malignant wishes . . . nor any of the wiles
> practiced by people upon themselves . . . ever is or ever
> can be stamped on the programme but it is duly realized

---

[78] *Ibid.*, 498-499.
[79] *Ibid.*, 499.
[80] *Ibid.*, 500.

[81] *Ibid.*, 502.
[82] *Ibid.*

and returned, and that returned in further performances
. . . and they returned again.[83]

In the '55 Preface we also gain further insight into
Whitman's religion—why he is opposed to institutionalized religion and what he would put in its place. The
explanation is quite simple: for a religion of super-
naturalism (with reward in a future existence) he would
substitute a religion of humanity, a social program for
life here and now.

> There will soon be no more priests. Their work is
> done. . . A new order shall arise and they shall be the
> priests of man, and every man shall be his own priest.
> The churches built under their umbrage shall be the
> churches of men and women. Through the divinity of
> themselves shall the kosmos and the new breed of poets
> be interpreters of men and women and of all events
> and things. They shall find their inspiration in real
> objects today, symptoms of the past and future.[84]

The final test of individuals and of nations is ethical
and social. "I know that what answers for me an American must answer for any individual or nation that serves
for a part of my materials."[85] We can understand now in
what sense Walt Whitman aspired to be a national poet.
"An individual is as superb as a nation when he has the
qualities which make a superb nation."[86] This is why
"The proof of a poet is that his country absorbs him as affectionately as he has absorbed it."[87] Whitman is not
thinking of literary reputation but of the poet's ethical
influence on society.

---

[83] *Ibid.*, 503.
[84] *Ibid.*, 505-506.
[85] *Ibid.*, 506.

[86] *Ibid.*, 507.
[87] *Ibid.*

LAST ATTEMPT AT PRACTICAL ACTION:
"THE EIGHTEENTH PRESIDENCY"

In 1856, after the political compromises of both parties had resulted in the nomination of those two mediocrities, Millard Fillmore and James Buchanan, for the Presidency, Walt Whitman was stirred to his final though abortive attempt at practical political action. Feeling that someone must speak out for the six million proletariat of the country ("mechanics, farmers, sailors, &c."), he wrote a political speech on "The Eighteenth Presidency,"[88] which he set up in type and apparently distributed in proof, hoping that it would attract the attention of "editors of the independent press" or "any rich person, anywhere" who might "circulate and reprint this Voice of mine for the workingmen's sake."[89] Evidently the poet had no intention of trying to organize a "labor party," and this method could hardly be called the most effective strategy to supply the political need which he so emphatically pointed out. In fact, it is not surprising that the call for action was ignored. The speech was not even formally published until long after Whitman's death.[90]

The rhetoric and form of this strange but revealing document is part stump-speech oratory, part political-science tract. The author begins by calling attention to the class distribution of the thirty million population of the nation: six million laboring men, half a million professional and business men, and 350,000 slave owners

---

[88] Printed from proof-sheets in Library of Congress by Clifton Joseph Furness, *Walt Whitman's Workshop* (Cambridge: Harvard University Press, 1928), 92-113.

[89] *Ibid.*, 87.

[90] See note 88 above. It was also printed in pamphlet form in France with an introduction by Jean Catel (Montpellier: Causse, Graille and Castelnau, 1928).

—the remainder of the population composed of non-voting women and children. Whitman's main thesis is that under the present corrupt party system in the United States, government has ceased to be representative, and the ideals of the founding fathers have not been achieved.

At present, the personnel of the government of these thirty millions, in executives and elsewhere, is drawn from limber-tongued lawyers, very fluent but empty feeble old men, professional politicians . . . rarely drawn from the solid body of the people . . .[91]

I expect to see the day when the like of the present personnel of the government, federal, state, municipal, military and naval, will be looked upon with derision, and when qualified mechanics and young men will reach Congress and other official stations, sent in their working costumes, fresh from their benches and tools, and returning to them again with dignity.[92]

Lest this be thought the romantic plea of an idealistic demagogue, let us note the almost clairvoyant demand for just such a man as the "Rail-Splitter" who came four years later.[93]

I would be much pleased to see some heroic, shrewd, fully-informed, healthy-bodied, middle-aged, beard-faced American blacksmith or boatman come down from the West across the Alleghanies, and walk into the Presidency, dressed in a clean suit of working attire, and with the tan all over his face, breast, and arms; I would certainly vote for that sort of man, possessing the due requirements, before any other candidate.[94]

---

[91] *Workshop, op. cit.,* 92.
[92] *Ibid.,* 93.
[93] Although Lincoln was in Congress in 1849, we have no evidence that Whitman was the least interested in him—or was even aware of him.
[94] *Workshop,* 93.

Notice that the mechanic-candidate for Congress must be "qualified" and the Lincolnesque-Westerner "possessing the due requirements . . ." This is no fanatical call for a class revolution in American politics. As the poet looked around him he could see that:

> To-day, of all the persons in public office in These States, not one in a thousand has been chosen by any spontaneous movement of the people, nor is attending to the interests of the people; all have been nominated and put through by great or small caucuses of the politicians, or appointed as rewards for electioneering; and all consign themselves to personal and party interests . . . The berths, the Presidency included, are bought, sold, electioneered for, prostituted, and filled with prostitutes.[95]

One part of the country was no better than the other. In the North were "office-vermin" and "kept-editors," *i.e.,* party sycophants; in the South braggarts who would dissolve the Union. "Are lawyers, dough-faces, and the three hundred and fifty thousand owners of slaves, to sponge the mastership of thirty millions?"[96]

The political power of these slave owners was really the crux of the matter. Whitman's main target was special privilege, the fact that "These States" were not ruled by the democratic majority, either North or South; but the immediate cause of this evil was slavery and the determination of a small band of Southern aristocrats to extend the institution to new territories. In order to preserve party and national unity both the Whigs and Democrats had yielded to chicanery, subterfuge, expediency, and cowardly compromise throughout the sixteenth and seven-

---

[95] *Ibid.,* 95.   [96] *Ibid.*

teentn Presidencies, which "history is to record . . . as so far our topmost warning and shame."[97] And now once more the politicians have nominated "men both patterned to follow and match the seventeenth term," men sworn to "the theories that balk and reverse the main purposes of the founders of These States."[98]

The poet was disgusted with the hypocrisy of the '56 campaign, one party flaunting "Americanism," using the "great word . . . without yet feeling the first aspiration of it," while the other party distorted the meaning of "democracy," whereas "What the so-called democracy are now sworn to perform would eat the faces off the succeeding generations of common people worse than the most horrible disease."[99]

Such conduct convinced Whitman that political parties in America were "about played out," that America had "outgrown parties; hence forth it is too large, and they too small."[100] The poet anticipated Lincoln Steffens in his perception of the almost inevitable corruption of the American political system:

> I place no reliance upon any old party, nor upon any new party. Suppose one to be formed under the noblest auspices, and getting into power with the noblest intentions, how long will it remain so? . . . As soon as it becomes successful, and there are offices to be bestowed, the politicians leave the unsuccessful parties and rush toward it, and it ripens and rots with the rest.[101]

"Platforms are of no account" either. "The right man is everything."[102] The "organic compacts of These

---

[97] *Ibid.*, 96.
[98] *Ibid.*, 98.
[99] *Ibid.*, 101.
[100] *Ibid.*, 104.
[101] *Ibid.*
[102] *Ibid.*, 105.

States"[103] are sufficient platforms. To Whitman the Constitution was not only a sacred but a prophetic document: "Like all perfect works or persons, time only is great enough to give its area."[104] Of course the Constitution can be misused, as it was being misused to protect slavery. Whitman believed the Constitution required that runaway slaves be delivered back to their masters, but he regarded the Fugitive Slave Act as a pernicious solution. The Constitution should not be corrupted and the laws disobeyed. The implication is plain: only the abolition of slavery would solve the problem. Such problems should be faced honestly and unequivocally, and Whitman still had hopes that a great leader with integrity and courage would arise. "Whenever the day comes for him to appear, the man who shall be the Redeemer President of These States, is to be the one that fullest realizes the rights of individuals, signified by the impregnable rights of These States, the substratum of the Union."[105]

Precisely what Whitman's intentions were when he wrote "The Eighteenth Presidency," we do not know. There is no evidence whatever that he had political aspirations. Quite likely a note which he dated April 24, 1857, indicates his oratorical ambitions for the preceding year also.[106] In this he thought of the desirability of being a "wander-speaker," darting "hither or thither, as some great emergency might demand—the greatest champion America ever could know, yet holding no office or emolu-

---

[103] *I.e.,* The Declaration of Independence, the Constitution, the Bill of Rights, the lives and acts of Washington, Jefferson, Madison, etc.

[104] *Ibid.,* 105.

[105] *Ibid.,* 109.

[106] *Notes and Fragments,* edited by Dr. Richard Maurice Bucke (London, Ontario: privately printed, 1899), 57. (Also printed in *The Complete Writings* [New York: G. P. Putnam's Sons, 1902], Vol. IX.)

ment whatever." To the modern biographer or critic this poet's dream of being a national orator-leader seems fantastic and pathetic, but it does record a serious desire to "keep up living interest in public questions,"[107] and to take an active part in answering these questions. Whether as poet or orator, he planned in 1856 to be the spokesman of "the great masses of the mechanics" and farmers: ". . . I shall in future have much to say to them. I perceive that the best thoughts they have wait unspoken."[108]

Despite his bitter disappointment with party politics in America during the Fillmore-Buchanan campaign, Whitman still had faith in his plan and the future of democracy because he believed the whole course of world history was against the recent anti-democratic conduct of the American politicians. "Freedom against slavery is not issuing here alone, but is issuing everywhere."[109] One practical reason for this belief was that modern inventions—steamship, locomotive, telegraph, mass production of books and newspapers, etc.—were "interlinking the inhabitants of the earth . . . as groups of one family."[110] All signs pointed to "unparalleled reforms." The oration ends:

On all sides tyrants tremble, crowns are unsteady, the human race restive, on the watch for some better era, some divine war. No man knows what will happen next, but all know that some such things are to happen as mark the greatest moral convulsions of the earth. Who shall play the hand for America in these tremendous games?[111]

---

[107] Ibid.
[108] Workshop, 112.
[109] Ibid.

[110] Ibid.
[111] Ibid.

Five years later Abraham Lincoln began playing the hand for America when one of "the greatest moral convulsions of the earth" took place, and Walt Whitman found a new patriotic and civic rôle for himself—as nurse and war correspondent.

THE SPIRITUAL DEMOCRACY

After Whitman wrote "The Eighteenth Presidency" in 1856, he made, so far as we know, no further effort to participate actively in political controversy. As we shall see later, his political convictions changed little throughout the remainder of his life, but he was henceforth ambitious to be the poetical rather than political spokesman of his time and people. Perhaps his disappointments in party journalism and his later inability to gain a hearing as either a political orator ("wander-speaker") or pamphleteer may have contributed to the shift of his interest from specific social problems to broad moral principles. But the literary rôle which he assumed in the 1855 edition of LEAVES OF GRASS and played consistently throughout all subsequent editions was that of "the caresser of life"[112] embracing all forms, good and evil alike, with a democracy that made no distinctions between persons or factions.

In 1860 Whitman played this rôle with such complete impartiality that he attained an almost Brahman serenity. *I Sit and Look Out* describes this passivity so clearly that it deserves to be quoted in its entirety:

> I sit and look out upon all the sorrows of the world,
>   and upon all oppression and shame,
> I hear secret convulsive sobs from young men at anguish
>   with themselves, remorseful after deeds done,

---

[112] *Song of Myself*, sec. 13.

I see in low life the mother misused by her children,
    dying, neglected, gaunt, desperate,
I see the wife misused by her husband, I see the treach-
    erous seducer of young women,
I mark the ranklings of jealousy and unrequited love
    attempted to be hid, I see these sights on the earth,
I see the workings of battle, pestilence, tyranny, I see
    martyrs and prisoners,
I observe a famine at sea, I observe the sailors casting
    lots who shall be kill'd to preserve the lives of the rest,
I observe the slights and degradations cast by arrogant
    persons upon laborers, the poor, and upon negroes,
    and the like;
All these—all the meanness and agony without end I
    sitting look out upon,
See, hear, and am silent.

This passivity was probably strongest in the third edition
of LEAVES OF GRASS, but it was not a temporary mood.
In fact, it was an integral part of Whitman's poetic vision,
a source of his inspiration. It was based on his panpsychism[113] and his mystical doctrine of the personality.[114] Henry Alonzo Myers, in his study of "Whitman's
Conception of the Spiritual Democracy, 1855-56,"[115] has
clearly explained the distinction between the poet's
"spiritual" and "social" democracy. The following paragraph indicates the gist of the interpretation:

Have you thought there could be but a single Supreme?
There can be any number of Supremes—one does not
    countervail another any more than one eye-sight

[113] See p. 256.
[114] See p. 302.
[115] *American Literature,* VI, 239-253 (November, 1934).

> countervails another, or one life countervails
> another.[116]

Undoubtedly this concept of equality had its origin
in the surface world of American democracy, where it
had been an ideal since the Declaration of Independence. But with Whitman equality is much more than
a political ideal; it is an *eternal fact* in the real world
of unlimited personalities; it is a great first principle.

> In all people I see myself—none more, and not one
> a barley-corn less,
>
> And the good or bad I say of myself, I say of them.[117]

Equality of this kind, a real equality between unlimited
personalities, is discovered only by piercing through
the coverings and turmoils to the insides of beings. Out
of the American democracy of 1855, Walt Whitman
constructed an inner complement to the outer world, a
spiritual democracy governed by two principles, one
the unlimited individual, the other the equality of individuals . . . Once we grasp the true nature of these
principles, realizing that they are, first and foremost,
principles of the spiritual democracy and only sec-
ondarily slogans of the social democracy, we no longer
see Walt Whitman's poems as a mere catalogue of per-
ceptions, nor as a mere satisfaction in his own sensibility; moreover, we discover that many of his themes,
which have hitherto seemed related only to his eccentricities, are direct consequents of these principles.
Why is he the poet of the body as well as of the soul?
Why is he the poet of death as well as of life? Why
is he the poet of evil as well as of good?[118]

---

[116] *By Blue Ontario's Shore*, sec. 3 (the punctuation is that of the 1856
edition, and the idea was first stated in the 1855 Preface). This doctrine
curiously anticipates William James in his *Pluralistic Universe*.

[117] *Song of Myself*, sec. 20.

[118] Myers, *op. cit.*, 246-247.

Whitman's desire to be the poet of evil as well as of good sprang not so much from his optimism (*i.e.,* denial of the existence of evil) or his failure to observe pain, cruelty, oppression, etc. in the world he lived in as from his belief in cosmic and moral evolution.[119] Thus in *A Carol of Occupations* Whitman "presents an antithesis between people as they appear in society and as they really are, an antithesis between the surface classification of people as mechanics, laborers, Presidents, drunkards, thieves, or prostitutes, and people as the equal, infinite personalities of the spiritual democracy."[120] Out of this same doctrine grew whatever social program he was henceforth to have, and his hope for its realization. In the 1856 edition he regarded his America as only "a divine true sketch."[121] In *Democratic Vistas* (1871), though admitting that "Our New World democracy . . . is, so far, an almost complete failure in its social aspects,"[122] he still believed in the "measureless wealth of latent power"[123] in the masses. The following year, in the 1872 Preface, the poet repeated that America is "a vast seething mass of *materials,* ampler, better, (worse also,) than previously known—eligible to be used to carry toward its crowning stage, and build for good the great Ideal Nationality of the future . . ."[124] The main theme of this Preface is that material prosperity of a nation is not sufficient without moral stability of its individual citizens. Finally, in 1888, Whitman states again that:

---

[119] See Chap. III.

[120] Myers, *op. cit.,* 247. The remainder of the present discussion is based only partly on Myers.

[121] *Leaves of Grass* (Brooklyn, 1856), 354.

[122] *Prose Works* (Philadelphia: David McKay, n.d. [1892]), 210-211.

[123] *Ibid.,* 216.

[124] Inclusive Edition, *op. cit.,* 509.

One main genesis-motive of the "Leaves" was my conviction (just as strong to-day as ever) that the crowning growth of the United States is to be spiritual and heroic. To help start and favor that growth—or even to call attention to it, or the need of it—is the beginning, middle and final purpose of the poems. (In fact, when really cipher'd out and summ'd to the last, plowing up in earnest the interminable average fallows of humanity —not "good government" merely, in the common sense —is the justification and main purpose of these United States.)[125]

Walt Whitman would have been the last man in the United States to regard "good government" as unimportant and not worth the struggle to attain it, but throughout his long career as a poet he wrote and prophesied not for the next presidential election but for the ages. Thus, planning for the future—proclaiming prophetically the immense spiritual possibilities of the human race in the United States, its "Vistas"—Whitman patiently accepted the temporary inequalities and injustices of contemporary American political democracy. Time and again he proclaimed his spiritual doctrine, "Produce great Persons, the rest follows."[126] If real political democracy had not yet been attained in the United States, it was because her men and women had not yet sufficiently developed their "Personalism."[127] To put this in other terms, they had not yet conquered their external selfishness by merging their egoes with the Divinity within them. Thus Walt Whitman as the prophet of a spiritual democracy was essentially a moral, not a political, leader.

---

[125] *Ibid.*, 534.
[126] E.g., *By Blue Ontario's Shore*, sec. 3.
[127] Cf. *ante*, 312.

And in the last analysis his doctrine is essentially that of
the moralists of all ages, the Christian especially. Like
Christ he taught, as the solution of all social evils, brotherly love and the Divine inheritance of mankind. All reforms must come from the soul, not from external laws
and forms of government. It would be useless to change
externals—society—without first regenerating the inner
man.

> To hold men together by paper and seal, or by com-
>   pulsion, is no account,
> That only holds men together which is living principles,
>   as the hold of the limbs of the body, or the fibres
>   of plants.[128]

An almost inevitable consequence of this doctrine was
that the poet must confine his efforts to teaching the
"principles," relinquishing to other hands the task of
practical execution; therefore he cleared only the "paths
to the house," leaving "to those to come the house itself."[129]

OLD-AGE CONFIRMATIONS

Despite Whitman's cheerful indifference to contradictions, his political attitudes and opinions changed very
little from his editorial days to his old-age in Camden,
when Horace Traubel drew him out in garrulous and uninhibited talk. We do not know positively how accurately
Traubel recorded Whitman's exact words, and it is quite
possible that the young radical may have colored (perhaps unconsciously) the old man's careless language. But

---

[128] *Chants Democratic*, 1, sec. 21, in *Leaves of Grass* (Boston: Thayer
and Eldridge, 1860-61), 115.
[129] *Thou Mother with Thy Equal Brood.*

the recorded opinions agree on the whole so closely with
the thought and expression of Whitman's published prose
and his miscellaneous manuscripts that we have no just
grounds for suspecting the essential accuracy of *With
Walt Whitman in Camden.* Assuming, then, that these
volumes are substantially reliable, we may use them as a
test of the durability and consistency of the poet's social
convictions.

Perhaps the major affirmation of these spontaneous
comments is Whitman's continued and unshakable faith
in humanity. Carlyle had long been both a challenge and
a puzzle to the American poet, both repelling and at-
tracting him. The paradox remained in 1888, for Whitman still felt that "Carlyle was a good deal of a democrat
in spite of himself," but "He did not understand humanity
—had no faith in humanity . . .: the people were not a
beautiful abstraction—they were an ugly fact: he shrank
from the people."[130] With all his disappointments and
disillusionments with the people, who had not yet given
him a hearing, Walt Whitman could still say:

> I trust humanity: its instincts are in the main right . . .
> Humanity always has to provide for the present moment
> as well as for the future: that is a tangle, however you
> look at it. Why wonder, then, that humanity falls down
> every now and then? There's one thing we have to
> remember—that the race is not free (free of its own
> ignorance)—is hardly in a position to do the best for
> itself: when we get a real democracy, as we will by
> and bye, this humanity will have its chance—give a
> fuller report of itself.[131]

---

[130] Traubel, *op. cit.,* I, 92.
[131] *Ibid.,* I, 157.

This was the old man's sustaining faith, while he still believed as strongly as in 1856, or '70, that "the American is being made but is not made: much of him is yet in the state of dough: the loaf is not yet given shape."[132] But while his faith never wavered, he was nevertheless "troubled by the merely mercenary influences that seem to be let loose in current legislation: the hog let loose: the grabber, the stealer, the arrogant honorable so and so . . ."[133] He knew that corrupt wealth, "with its sad, sad foil of extreme, degrading, damning poverty" would never make a country great,

> but the land in which there are the most homesteads, freeholds—where wealth does not show such contrasts high and low, where all men have enough—a modest living—and no man is made possessor beyond the sane and beautiful necessities of the simple body and the simple soul. The great country, in fact, is the country of free labor—of free laborers: negro, white, Chinese, or other.[134]

The theory which reconciles Whitman's crystal-clear observation of economic corruption and his almost fanatical faith in the innate goodness of the very people who make up the corrupt society is his "spiritual democracy." His descriptions of economic and social conditions may lead us at times to think that he was something of a socialist, or at least a follower of Henry George, but actually he knew little about the Single Tax theory[135] and never got far from his "beautiful abstraction" of the innate goodness of humanity. For example, he could excuse the corruption of politics with this ingenious meta-

---

[132] *Ibid.*, I, 201.
[133] *Ibid.*, III, 3.
[134] *Ibid.*, II, 84.
[135] *Ibid.*, III, 110.

phor: "Society throws off some of its ephemera, its corruption, through politics—the process is offensive—we
shudder over it—but it may be true, it is still true, that
the interior system throwing off its excreta this way is
sound, wholly sound, prepared for the proper work of
its own purification."[136]

On the basis of this theory Whitman could shrug his
shoulders over his observation that "the conventional
parties have both thrown their heritage away . . . the Republican party positively, the Democratic party negatively,
the apologists of the plutocracy."[137] Yet he was not discouraged, "for you see I am not looking to politics to
renovate politics: I am looking to forces outside—the
great moral, spiritual forces . . ."[138] He did not vote in
1884 but would have voted for Cleveland if he had gone
to the polls, because "I felt that the election of Blaine
would be a slap in the face of the South." The South was
already conquered "and why should we rub it in?"[139] Still
thinking about this election, he regarded the Negro question as serious, "but who can say the Negro is more likely
to get his due from the Republican party than from the
Democratic party?"[140] After Harned had returned from
the Chicago convention in 1888 he asked Whitman,
"Walt, you used to call yourself a Republican?" To which
the poet replied, "I suppose I don't call myself anything.
I'm no Democrat, either. Republican? with the Republican high tariff, high property principles, or no principles?
Hardly."[141]

The forthcoming election was the subject of repeated
discussions during the summer and fall of '88. On June

[136] *Ibid.*, II, 84-85.
[137] *Ibid.*, I, 14.
[138] *Ibid.*, I, 14-15.

[139] *Ibid.*, I, 147.
[140] *Ibid.*, I, 147-148.
[141] *Ibid.*, I, 373.

26 Walt found himself "inclined toward Harrison . . . prefer his personality to Cleveland's"—when the surface is scratched "the old Republican shows up." Then to Traubel: "you are too radical for me: you want the old régime all upset—but no matter—my politics don't hang heavy even on me."[142] As the election drew nearer, however, his opposition to Republican principles strengthened. On November 1 he was still not enthusiastic about either candidate, but added, "To me the condemnation of Harrison is his support—in the fact that he is the candidate of all the top-loftical conventionalisms of the North . . . of all that is commercially iniquitous, arrogant, macerating."[143] On November 4 he was still aloof: "for Cleveland personally I care nothing," have "no feelings against Harrison as a man," but "how little either Democrats or Republicans know about essential truths."[144] On November 7 he felt mildly disappointed in Harrison's election "because of the Republican attitude toward the South and on the tariff . . ." As he ruminated on the situation his disappointment rose: "I feel sore, I feel some pain, almost indignation when I think that yesterday keeps the old brutal idea of subjugation on top."[145] Then for a moment he came to grips with the real problem:

It is true there are a lot of us—like you, me, others—in whom there is developed a new cameraderie, fellowship, love: the farther truer idea of the race family, of international unity, of making one country of all countries: but the trouble is that we do not hold the whip hand.[146]

---

[142] Ibid., I, 386.
[143] Ibid., III, 4.
[144] Ibid., III, 21.

[145] Ibid., III, 43.
[146] Ibid.

On November 9 Whitman's faith in the electorate revived and he predicted that there would be a reaction to Harrison's election, and that Cleveland would "be heard from again," because "the people will realize that America means free-trade and the fartherest toleration . . ."[147] The next day he forsaw the time when political conflict would become more serious, the cleavages more desperate, for "All the real problems, the fundamentals, are yet ahead of us—will have to be tackled by us or by our children or theirs: not skin-ticklers, like the tariff, but life and death challenges which will line us up fiercely on this side or that."[148]

Whitman's comments in the above paragraphs indicate fairly accurately his political convictions in 1888. But in order to emphasize how little his attitudes and sympathies had changed since 1846, we might summarize his thought on the major questions of the day.

First there was the Negro problem. Abolition was no longer an issue, but Whitman's former attitudes toward abolition continued to influence his thinking regarding the treatment of the South by the North. As he looked back on the Civil War he still thought that the preservation of the Union was a greater problem than abolition: "The Negro was not the chief thing: the chief thing was to stick together. The South was technically right and humanly wrong."[149] He had always regarded slavery as wrong, but "I never could quite lose the sense of other evil in this evil—I saw other evils that cried to me in perhaps even a louder voice: the labor evil, now, to speak of only one, which to this day has been steadily growing

---

[147] *Ibid.*, III, 61.   [149] *Ibid.*, I, 13.
[148] *Ibid.*, III, 69.

worse . . ."[150] There was a time, around 1856, when Whitman regarded slavery as one of the greatest evils,[151] but apparently his sympathy for the South during the Reconstruction years had softened the memory of his former hatred. Sympathy, in fact, is always the key to Walt Whitman's political sensibilities.

This is especially true of his life-long belief in "free trade." To him "It is not a fiscal, it is a moral, problem— a problem of the largest humanities."[152] On another occasion he said, "While I love America, and wish to see America prosperous, I do not seem able to bring myself to love America, to desire American prosperity, at the expense of some other nation or even of all other nations." Someone asked, "But must we not take care of home first of all?," and Walt replied, "but what is home—to the humanitarian what is home?"[153] At another time he explained, "I am for free trade because I am for anything which will break down barriers between peoples: I want to see the countries all wide open."[154] American politicians are too narrow to see this problem in "its international complications." [155] In no other political opinion was Whitman's profound international sympathy more obvious than in his opposition to national tariff walls. "As for free-trade—it is greatly to be desired, not because it is good for America, but because it is good for the world."[156]

He also believed in unrestricted immigration for the same humanitarian and international reasons. All the European masses needed was a chance. Therefore:

---

[150] *Ibid.*, I, 363.
[151] Cf. "The Eighteenth Presidency."
[152] Traubel, *op. cit.*, II, 190.
[153] *Ibid.*, I, 6.
[154] *Ibid.*, I, 149; Cf. I, 359; II, 34.
[155] *Ibid.*, II, 186.
[156] *Ibid.*, III, 5; Cf. III, 19; III, 81.

> Restrict nothing—keep everything open: to Italy, to China, to anybody. I love America, I believe in America, because her belly can hold and digest all—anarchist, socialist, peace-makers, fighters, disturbers or degenerates of whatever sort—hold and digest all. If I felt that America could not do this I would be indifferent as between our institutions and any others.[157]

Here the voice is that of the 1855 edition, the poet through whom the "many long dumb voices"[158] found utterance.

On the subject of "money" Walt Whitman in 1888 often sounded socialistic, though he never got beyond generalities—or we might say ambiguities. For instance:

> We're heaping up money here in a few hands at a great rate—but our men? What's becoming of our men in the meantime? We can lose all the money and start again—but if we lose the *men?* Well, that would be disaster . . . I should feel like warning the moneyed powers in America that threaten to stand in the way: history will deal in a very drastic fashion with opposition like that should it become too stubborn.[159]

Yet in a a few days he warned as if remembering the universal sympathy of his early poems: "In the human sense I am on both sides—the side of the rich as well as the side of the poor . . ."[160] He said this, however, to defend himself against charges of sympathizing with the rich, just as he had felt compelled on another occasion to explain what he had meant by calling the German Emperor a "faithful shepherd"—"too many of the fellows forget

---

[157] *Ibid.,* I, 113; Cf. II, 54.
[158] Cf. *Song of Myself,* sec. 24.
[159] Traubel, *op. cit.,* I, 174-175.
[160] *Ibid.,* I, 199.

that I include emperors, lords, kingdoms, as well as presidents, workmen, republics."[161]

Such comments reveal not only Whitman's universal humanitarianism but also his innate conservatism. He appealed to "radicals," and the generality of his words (both his poetic symbolism and his spontaneous conversational colloquialisms) might be quoted to support diverse social programs, but his interest in radicalism scarcely went beyond personal sympathy for individuals. Traubel found him ignorant of John Weiss, Samuel Johnson, and O. B. Frothingham, and after he had been told about them, Whitman admitted, "I have neglected those remarkable men: but I hate theological, metaphysical, discussion so heartily that I run at the sight of a controversial book—always, of course, excepting Huxley and Ingersoll, as you know."[162]

Quite characteristic is the report that Whitman made to Traubel one day:

There was a kind of labor agitator here today—a socialist, or something like that: young, a rather beautiful boy—full of enthusiasm: the finest type of the man in earnest about himself and about life. I was sorry to see him come: I am somehow afraid of agitators, though I believe in agitation: but I was more sorry to see him go than come. Some people are so much sunlight to the square inch. I am still bathing in the cheer he radiated. O he was a beautiful, beautiful boy![163]

The beautiful boy's ideas—if he had any—seem to have been entirely lost on the admiring old poet. But if Whitman had listened he would probably have responded in

---

[161] Ibid., I, 22; Cf. also I, 307.   [163] Ibid., I, 166.
[162] Ibid., I, 126.

his usual way: ". . . I say to the radicals—the impatient young fellows: wait, don't be in too great a hurry: your day is near: in the meantime hold your own ground—defend what you have already won—look, listen, for the summons: it will come, sure: it can't come too soon."[164]

But he himself had no program. When Traubel inquired about his ideas on the future social order of America, Whitman could only say that he looked forward (while no doubt backward to Jefferson) "to a world of small owners."[165] When Traubel tried to get him to change this to "no owners at all," Whitman seemed uncertain and would not commit himself. His final attitude was summed up in a discussion on the anarchists: "I do not understand what they are driving at—what the anarchists want . . . I do not understand what the Henry George men want: nor do I trouble myself about it."[166] When Traubel insisted that LEAVES OF GRASS "is full of anarchism and Henry George" and that Whitman was in agreement with the socialists, the old poet was moved to an almost eloquent restatement of his social creed: "I want the people," he said, ". . . the crowd, the mass . . . to have what belongs to them: not a part of it, but all of it . . . their proper opportunities—their full life . . ."[167] The people are still "swindled, robbed, outraged, discredited, despised: I say they must assert their priority . . ."[168] With a little urging he admitted that "the people will have to fight for that they get." But he would not dispute with the anarchists, the Single Taxers, or the socialists as to "ways," for he had no definite plan of his own. At the same time, however, he insisted that he did not reject kings and million-

---

[164] *Ibid.*, III, 19.
[165] *Ibid.*, III, 315.
[166] *Ibid.*, III, 477.
[167] *Ibid.*, III, 478-479.
[168] *Ibid.*, III, 479.

aires from his all-embracing brotherhood, and mentioned especially Carnegie as a man who had done some good.

Traubel himself gave this final satisfactory comment:

All these fellows find texts in Leaves of Grass; not figures [*i.e.,* statistics or data], not names, but electrifying intimations. They don't any of them claim you as a partisan: they only claim you in a general way. We say Jesus is on our side. In the same sense we say you are on our side. With the people as against the elect few . . .[169]

That is Walt Whitman's true position from first to last: *With the people as against the elect few . . .*

A Brief Critique

Walt Whitman's weaknesses as a social thinker are no doubt obvious to anyone who has followed this discussion, or who has read the works quoted; but in order to evaluate the social aspects of his poetry and prose and the importance of his contribution to the realm of social ideas, a brief critique may be useful.

The student of Whitman cannot afford to ignore the times, conditions, and states of mind in which LEAVES OF GRASS germinated and flourished. Much that at first seems pure egotism or eccentricity in the poems turns out to be to a considerable extent the reflection of national ambitions in the time of the expansion of "The States," or the American dream that European immigrants might find new hope and freedom in the "West," or the passionate desire of simple men to achieve in this Nation—new territories and all—a living application of the great democratic

---

[169] *Ibid.,* III, 480.

ideals of liberty, equality, and fraternity. From reading Whitman's immature editorials, his pamphlets and tracts on political and national problems (like "The Eighteenth Presidency" or *Democratic Vistas*), his prefaces, and his old-age opinions, we gain a deeper respect both for his social consciousness and his social conscience. It is doubtful that anyone else in the United States was more profoundly aware of the shams, the hypocrisies, and the political treacheries in America between 1846 and '88, and surely no one else cherished a brighter dream of an ideal society of the future.

From a practical point of view, however, it is not sufficient merely to know what the social evils are, but to set about eliminating them. Here we find Walt Whitman's fundamental weakness as a constructive social force. And both his own disposition and his social theory are responsible for this weakness. Like Emerson he was an uncompromising individualist, both in nature and doctrine. As a young man he had tried to work with parties and politicians, but finding them lacking in foresight, courage, and even honesty, he decided that it was useless to expect reforms through them. To a certain extent he may have been right, for as a poet and independent thinker he almost certainly went further by going his own way. But he was wrong, as history has demonstrated, in thinking that parties, "pressure groups," and political organizations had "about played out."[170] In a free society there is no other practical means of channelling public opinion and generating social power. Either one must work through parties and organized groups or forever, like Whitman, let others "hold the whip hand."[171]

---

[170] See note 100.   [171] See note 146.

To consider the practical view further, the other fundamental weakness in Whitman's social thought is the fact that it is so abstract, and therefore ambiguous. The danger of an abstraction is that it is capable of too many applications and interpretations. Whitman himself complained in 1856 of the hypocritical use of the word "Americanism" by one party and "Democracy" by the equally-insincere rival.[172] His own social abstractions lend themselves to the same chauvinism. But fortunately this is not their final evaluation.

Perhaps the most sympathetic and yet accurate judgment of Whitman's social importance has been expressed by his friend, J. W. Wallace, a member of the "Bolton College" coterie of Manchester, England—the only organized group of "common" men ever to take up the systematic study of the American poet's social message.[173] Wallace points out that Whitman does not "advocate any particular form of society or government, and attacks no institutions . . ."[174]

> He did not attack existing institutions, for these are the natural expression of the general mentality in which they have originated, and which maintains them. His work was to transform that mentality by infusing it with his own spirit. As this spreads and grows, like leaven, it will give rise to new and nobler institutions. . .[175]

Therefore, "He simply *is* a democrat in every relationship

[172] See note 99.
[173] See Chap. VI, p. 484.
[174] J. W. Wallace, *Walt Whitman and the World Crisis* (Manchester: The National Labour Press [1920]), 10.
[175] *Ibid.*, 17. Cf. *I Hear It Was Charged Against Me:*
> I hear it was charged against me that I sought
>   to destroy institutions,
> But really I am neither for nor against institutions, . . .

of life . . . His aim throughout is the *'building up of the masses by building up grand individuals,'* and his method is that of personal comradeship with each individual reader."[176] On this "increasing spread of the love of comrades he founds his hopes for the future of America and the world. With that he 'will make the continent indissoluble,' and 'will make divine magnetic lands.' "[177]

Walt Whitman's religious faith in "the essential divinity of every human soul and of the central equality of all" is the basis of "the most absolute Democracy . . . Add to this the consciousness of the common life which all share, as Whitman says,

> Whoever degrades another degrades me,
> And whatever is done or said returns at last to me,[178]

and it becomes evident that the fullest welfare of each can only be insured by the welfare of all."[179]

SELECTED BIBLIOGRAPHY

SOME PRIMARY SOURCES FOR WHITMAN'S SOCIAL THOUGHT

[Note: only works referred to in this chapter are listed here. For a fuller list of Whitman's poetry and prose, see Bibliography for Chapter II.]

"Democratic Vistas." *Prose Works,* pp. 203-258. Philadelphia: David McKay. [1892].

[Whitman's most important treatment of social and political theory.]

"Eighteenth Presidency, The"—see *Walt Whitman's Workshop,* below.

---

[176] Wallace, *op. cit.,* 10.
[177] *Ibid.,* 18.
[178] *Song of Myself,* sec. 24.
[179] Wallace, *op. cit.,* 19. The success with which Whitman has "look'd for equals and lovers and found them ready . . . in all lands" must be judged in the light of his influence on World Literature—see Chap. VI.

Gathering of the Forces, The. Editorials, Essays, Literary and Dramatic Reviews and Other Material Written by Walt Whitman as Editor of the Brooklyn Daily Eagle in 1846 and 1847. Edited by Cleveland Rodgers and John Black. New York: G. P. Putnam's Sons. 1920. 2 vols.
[Excellent Introduction by Rodgers. This is the most valuable collection of Whitman's editorials.]

I Sit and Look Out. Editorials from the Brooklyn Daily Times. Selected and edited by Emory Holloway and Vernolian Schwarz. New York: Columbia University Press. 1932.
[Some of conjectural authenticity.]

Leaves of Grass. Inclusive Edition. Edited by Emory Holloway. Garden City, N. Y.: Doubleday, Doran and Co. 1929.
[Contains also prefaces of 1855, '72, '76, '88, and '91.]

New York Dissected. A Sheaf of Recently Discovered Newspaper Articles by the Author of *Leaves of Grass.* Edited with Introduction and Notes by Emory Holloway and Ralph Adimari. New York: Rufus Rockwell Wilson. 1936.
[Of minor importance.]

Prefaces—see *Leaves of Grass,* above.

Uncollected Poetry and Prose of Walt Whitman, The. Collected and edited by Emory Holloway. New York: Peter Smith. 1932. 2 vols. [First edition, Garden City, N. Y.: Doubleday, Page and Co., 1921; English edition, London: William Heinemann, 1922.]
[Valuable for "Notebook" material and early publications. Good Introduction by the editor on the poet's early life, writings, and ideas.]

Walt Whitman's Workshop. A Collection of Unpublished Manuscripts. Edited with an Introduction and Notes by Clifton Joseph Furness. Cambridge, Mass.: Harvard University Press. 1928.
[Contains "Notes for Lecturing and Oratory," "The Eighteenth Presidency," and valuable MS material.]

With Walt Whitman in Camden. Edited by Horace Traubel. Vol. I (March 28-July 14, 1888) : Boston: Small, Maynard and Co. 1906. Vol. II (July 16, 1888-October 31, 1888) : New York: D. Appleton and Co. 1908. Vol. III (November 1, 1888-January 20, 1889) : New York: Mitchell Kennerley. 1914.
[Record of conversations, correspondence, etc.]

CRITICAL INTERPRETATION

[Note: most of the biographies give some attention to Whitman's social thought, though none of them contains an adequate treatment. Canby is best. See bibliography for Chapter I.]

ARVIN, NEWTON. *Whitman.* New York: Macmillan Co. 1938.
[Fullest study of Whitman's social thought—with a socialistic bias.]

GABRIEL, RALPH H. "Whitman and the Civil War." *The Course of American Democratic Thought,* pp. 123-131. New York: The Ronald Press Co. 1940.
[Brief but suggestive.]

MYERS, HENRY ALONZO. "Whitman's Conception of the Spiritual Democracy." *American Literature,* VI, 230-253 (November, 1934).
[Excellent interpretation.]

WALLACE, J. W. *Walt Whitman and the World Crisis.* Manchester, Eng.: The National Labour Press. [1920].
[Wallace believes Whitman to be "the supreme prophet and exemplar of the World-Democracy." Interesting interpretation by an English socialist.]

WALLING, WILLIAM ENGLISH. *Whitman and Traubel.* New York: Albert and Charles Boni. 1916.
[Contains brief but reliable summary of Whitman's social thought, but the author's high opinion of Traubel's importance as a poet and thinker is ridiculous.]

CHAPTER V

LITERARY TECHNIQUE IN *LEAVES OF GRASS*

The words of my book nothing, the drift of it everything,
A book separate, not link'd with the rest nor felt by the
intellect,
But you ye untold latencies will thrill to every page.[1]

THE ANALOGOUS FORM

If it were possible to separate thought from form, we might say that the style of LEAVES OF GRASS has puzzled the critics, from 1855 until recent times, even more than the ideas. Certainly much of the most serious efforts of the Whitman scholars and critics has been directed toward the interpretation and rationalization of this poet's art. They have often failed, however, because they did not understand Whitman's ideas and his intentions (though it is by no means certain that he always understood them himself). But some of the ambiguity of both thought and form was implicit in his intentions—either intended or unavoidable. He was right when he claimed in 1876: "My form has strictly grown from my purports and facts, and is the analogy of them."[2] Both his successes and failures as a poet were closely analogous to his theories and literary ambitions.

---

[1] *Shut Not Your Doors, Proud Libraries.* Hermann Bahr, in his Introduction to Max Hayek's translation, *Ich Singe Das Leben* (Liepzig, Wien, Zürich: E. P. Tall & Co., 1921), 7, says: "[Grashalme] ist kunstlos, es bringt eigentlich nur das Material für ein Kunstwerk, diesen Eindruck hat man immer wieder."

[2] *Prose Works* (Philadelphia: David McKay, [1892]), 287.

When Whitman chose to mention style, or someone
nudged him into committing himself, he was likely to be
disingenuous. To Traubel's questions he replied:

> I have never given any study merely to expression: it
> has never appealed to me as a thing valuable or sig-
> nificant in itself: I have been deliberate, careful, even
> laborious: but I have never looked for finish—never
> fooled with technique more than enough to provide for
> simply getting through: after that I would not give a
> twist of my chair for all the rest.[3]

On another occasion he claimed that "What I am after
is the content not the music of words. Perhaps the music
happens—it does no harm."[4]

It is possible that Whitman's form was intuitive. De
Selincourt may have been right when he declared roman-
tically that, "His own wild music, ravishing, unseizable,
like the song of a bird, came to him, as by his own principles it should have come, when he was not searching for
it"[5]—though anyone who has studied Whitman's tor-
tured manuscripts must doubt that this miracle ever hap-
pened when the poet "was not searching for it"; he chose
the path even if he did not always know the way.

We can never know exactly what went on in Whitman's head either while he composed or while he inde-
fatigably revised and re-edited his manuscripts year after
year. As Furness says, "He was imbued more thoroughly
perhaps with the 'daemonic' theory of inspiration and

---

[3] Horace Traubel, *With Walt Whitman in Camden* (New York: Mitchell Kennerley, 1914), III, 84.

[4] *Ibid.*, I, 163.

[5] Basil De Selincourt, *Walt Whitman: A Critical Study* (London:
Martin Secker, 1914), 73.

execution than any other poet of the nineteenth century."[6] But however unconscious he may have been of technique, he was so concerned with his theory of expression that it became his favorite theme in his various prefaces. The theory has been misunderstood because it was Whitman's avowed purpose in 1855 to achieve a style which would be not only "transcendent and new" but also "indirect and not direct or descriptive or epic,"[7] and "the medium that shall well nigh express the inexpressible."[8] Certainly this is no ordinary demand to make of literary technique. Whitman had no stories to tell, no descriptions of humble life, no melody to sing like Longfellow, Whittier, or Poe. *Poetry* to him was neither words nor beautiful sounds but something within, intangible—"poetic quality . . . is in the soul,"[9] and he called "The United States themselves . . . essentially the greatest poem."[10]

Whitman's inability or unwillingness to discuss his technique in terms of craftsmanship was imbedded in his fundamental assumptions about his literary intentions. Not only must his form be capable of expressing his mystical ideas, but to admit conscious planning and moulding of the expression would have meant casting doubt on its authenticity and his own sincerity. To what extent his literary strategy was conscious, it is difficult to say: nevertheless, his very ambiguity was, for his purposes, clever strategy, as he was not entirely unaware himself:

---

[6] Clifton Joseph Furness, *Walt Whitman's Workshop* (Cambridge, Mass.: Harvard University Press, 1928), 30.

[7] Preface to 1855 edition, reprinted in Inclusive Edition of *Leaves of Grass,* edited by Emory Holloway (Garden City: Doubleday, 1929), 491.

[8] *Ibid.,* 506.

[9] *Ibid.,* 493.

[10] *Ibid.,* 488.

Without effort and without exposing in the least how it is done the greatest poet brings the spirit of any or all events and passions and scenes and persons some more and some less to bear on your individual character as you hear or read.[11]

What he is attempting, therefore, is not so much the complete "expression" or communication of a thought or an experience as exerting an influence on the reader so that he himself, by willing cooperation with the poet, may have an esthetic-religious experience of his own. It is literally true that Whitman attempts less to create a "poem," as the term is usually understood, than to present the materials of a poem for the reader to use in creating his own work of art. No doubt in a sense, as Croce has argued, this is the manner in which all esthetic experience takes place; but Whitman aims to do nothing more than "indicate," though this is on a grand, mystical scale:

The land and sea, the animals fishes and birds, the sky of heaven and the orbs, the forests mountains and rivers, are not small themes . . .[12] but folks expect of the poet to indicate more than the beauty and dignity which always attach to dumb real objects . . . they expect him to indicate the path between reality and their souls.[13]

There we have the poet's most fundamental literary intention: *to indicate the path between reality and the soul.* And this is why both the theory and the expression

---

[11] *Ibid.,* 495.

[12] The three periods spaced thus (...) do not indicate editorial omission but Whitman's own punctuation. Editorial omissions from Whitman quotations will hereafter be indicated in this chapter by four unspaced periods (....).

[13] Inclusive Edition, *op. cit.,* 493.

must always remain vague and ambiguous. It is also why Whitman attaches so much importance to gestures and "indirections." His ideal poet "is most wonderful in his last half-hidden smile or frown . . . by that flash of the moment of parting the one that sees it shall be encouraged or terrified afterwards for many years."[14] Or again in 1888, after LEAVES OF GRASS had been virtually completed:

> I round and finish little, if anything; and could not, consistently with my scheme. The reader will always have his or her part to do, just as much as I have had mine. I seek less to state or display any theme or thought, and more to bring you, reader, into the atmosphere of the theme or thought—there to pursue your own flight.[15]

Believing that his function was to hint rather than state, to initiate rather than complete, Whitman adopted and developed for his own purposes the "organic" theory of poetic expression.[16] Poetry should imitate not things but the spirit of things, not God or creation but His creativity. Hence fluency, logical structure, finish, were looked upon as artificial and useless ornamentation: "Who troubles himself about his ornaments or fluency is lost."

> The poetic quality is not marshalled in rhyme or uniformity or abstract addresses to things nor in melancholy complaints or good precepts, but is the life of these and much else and is in the soul. The profit of rhyme is that it drops seeds of a sweeter and more luxuriant rhyme, and of uniformity that it conveys it-

---

[14] *Ibid.*, 495.
[15] *A Backward Glance*, Inclusive Edition, *op. cit.*, 531.
[16] Cf. Chap. III, p. 292.

self into its own roots in the ground out of sight. The rhyme and uniformity of perfect poems show the free growth of metrical laws and bud from them as unerringly and loosely as lilacs or roses on a bush, and take shapes as compact as the shapes of chestnuts and oranges and melons and pears, and shed the perfume impalpable to form. The fluency and ornaments of the finest poems or music or orations or recitations are not independent, but dependent.[17]

Kennedy was echoing Whitman when in defending the style of LEAVES OF GRASS he declared: "it is a truism that Nature, in all her forms, avoids base mechanical regularity."[18] Perhaps Whitman began his prosody with this negative principle: to represent Nature, or the order of creation, he must avoid conventional regularity—which meant of course rime and meter as they were known in the 1850's.

One of the most curious paradoxes in Whitman's literary doctrine is his insistence upon the "simplicity" of this "organic" theory or analogy: "The art of art, the glory of expression and the sunshine of the light of letters is simplicity. Nothing is better than simplicity."[19] This, however, is his idea of stylistic simplicity: "But to speak in literature with the perfect rectitude and insousiance [sic] of the movements of animals and the unimpeachableness of the sentiment of trees in the woods and grass by the roadside is the flawless triumph of art."[20] Equally paradoxical is the added statement that, "The greatest

---

[17] Preface to 1855 Edition, Inclusive Edition, op. cit., 493.

[18] W. S. Kennedy, Reminiscences of Walt Whitman (London: Alexander Gardner, 1896), 151.

[19] The 1855 Preface, Inclusive Ed., op. cit., 495.

[20] Ibid., 495-496.

poet has less a marked style and is more the channel of thoughts and things without increase or diminution, and is the free channel of himself."[21]

This conception of the poet as a passive agent, through whom the currents of the universe flow without hindrance or his conscious direction, did not of course, in practical terms, result in a literary form either simple or unmannered. But the theory did determine what the form was not—and perhaps eventually what it was. In the first place, it was not to be restrained, disciplined.

> ....I permit to speak at every hazard, Nature without
> check with original energy.[22]

From this doctrine and the resulting uninhibited flow of confessions bubbling up from the poet's inner life came his own apparent belief that he could solve the problem of form by rejecting all conventional techniques. But if he actually did believe this, it was the greatest of all his illusions, for without conventions of some sort there can be no communication whatever. Understanding depends upon the ability of the hearer or reader to recognize some form of order in the linguistic symbols of the speaker or writer.

Of course Whitman did not evolve brand-new techniques. But he did reject and modify or readapt enough conventions to short-circuit communication for many readers for many years, and is not always intelligible even today. He is, however, more easily understood in our day than in his own because critical interpreters have sufficiently clarified his intentions for the reasonably literate reader to know at least what the poet was attempting.

---

[21] *Ibid.*, 496.   [22] *Song of Myself*, sec. 1.

For no other American poet has criticism rendered so great a service, or been so necessary.

Before attempting to discover in detail what kind of form and technique Whitman created and adapted for his purposes, we might ask ourselves, by way of summary, what he wanted the "new" style to do. It must, as we have seen, express an inner rather than an outer harmony. He is not so much concerned with things and appearances as with the "spirit" of their relationships. And these are to be suggested or implied rather than explicitly stated. The form must be "organic," though he aims not at describing or imitating external nature but at conveying the creativity of Nature, with her fecundity and variety. It must, therefore, be a democratic-pantheistic style. Never before, he thought, had "poetry with cosmic and dynamic features of magnitude and limitlessness suitable to the human soul"[23] been possible.

The Expanding Ego

All critics who have seriously tried to understand Whitman have observed that the "I" of his poems is generic: he celebrates himself as a representative man. His "soul" is but a fragment of the World-Soul, and is mystically and pantheistically related to all the souls of the universe. In asserting his own uniqueness he merely gives expression— at least philosophically and intentionally—to the creative power of the innate soul "identified" through his own personality.

This much is obvious to anyone who is familiar with Whitman's ideas and avowed poetic purposes. The almost inevitable result on his literary technique has not been

---

[23] *A Backward Glance,* Inclusive Edition, *op. cit.,* 526.

so widely recognized, though it too is obvious once we think of the relationship—the analogy to the poet's "purports and facts." His point of view (except in a few of the shorter and more truly personal lyrics) will not be finite and stationary but ubiquitous and soaring—a migrating soul transcending time and space. It is not in the least unusual for a lyric poet to identify himself with some one object or place, like Shelley in *The Cloud* or *Ode to the West Wind,* but Whitman's ego is in constant motion, flitting like a humming bird from object to object and place to place with miraculous speed.

> My ties and ballasts leave me, my elbows rest in sea-gaps
> I skirt sierras, my palms cover continents,
> I am afoot with my vision.[24]

This is his point of view not only in his spectacular cosmic visions but in nearly all his poems. Even when he is less mystical, not obviously trying to hover over the earth watching the "great round wonder rolling through space,"[25] the imagery is panoramic, unending, flowing, expanding. Whitman's description of the manner in which he "abstracts" himself from the book and stretches his mind (or poetic imagination) in all directions probably gives the best clue to the method by which he developed his style and technique. In the 1855 Preface the "bard" is not only "commensurate with a people" and attempts to "incarnate" flora, fauna, and topography, but he also "spans....from east to west and reflects what is between."[26] The point of view of the first section of *Salut au Monde!* is therefore typical of Whitman's art in general:

---

[24] *Song of Myself,* sec. 33.
[25] *Salut au Monde!* sec. 4.

[26] Inclusive Edition, *op. cit.,* 490.

O take my hand Walt Whitman!
Such gliding wonders! such sights and sounds!
Such join'd unended links, each hook'd to the next,
Each answering all, each sharing the earth with all.

Although this method results in the long catalogs, in
the piling up of image on top of image with meager
enumeration of attributes, the poet is not content with
merely photographing from an air-plane. However un-
selected the mass of images may seem to some readers, he
intended them to symbolize a pantheistic unity in himself and all creation.

What widens within you Walt Whitman?

. . . .

Within me latitude widens, longitude lengthens, . . .

The externals, the catalog of concrete details, are transcendental symbols of what he might call "spiritual
truths." Thus we have the curious paradox in Whitman's
style of snapshot imagery joined to ambiguity. Even in
his most vivid realism he is still allegorical and subjective.
The effect of this style has not been unobserved by
critics. Paul Elmer More, the late "New Humanist,"
wrote:

This sense of indiscriminate motion is . . . the impression left finally by Whitman's work as a whole . . .
Now the observer seems to be moving through clustered
objects beheld vividly for a second of time and then
lost in the mass, and, again, the observer himself is stationary while the visions throng past him in almost
dizzy rapidity; but in either case we come away with
the feeling of having been merged in unbroken processions, whose beginning and end are below the distant

horizon, and whose meaning we but faintly surmise.[27]

Reed has called this attempt to present cosmic unity in flux "The Heraclitan Obsession of Walt Whitman."[28] He finds it logically contradictory, however, because the "progressive integration" of form is not "opposed by a contrary disunity of some sort."[29] How can he blend body and soul without a dualism?

> But this logical impasse does not appear to have bothered Whitman, and criticism of his thinking need not detain us here. What is of interest . . . is the psychological effect as it is imprinted on the poems. With unification as an ideal, Whitman, one would expect, would show a fine sure insight into the oneness of the phenomenal world. Yet the reader of his poems gains no awareness of such unity. The feeling is rather of disintegration and extreme multiplicity.[30]

This criticism calls attention to the fundamental problem in Whitman's use of the expanding ego. Perhaps the effect depends largely upon the reader's own philosophy. To the Absolutist the effect is no doubt confusion, to the Relativist probably not. Perhaps this is saying that the unity is not in the poem but in the mind of the reader, as it was no doubt in the mind (or intention) of the poet —to whom these "gliding wonders" were "join'd unended links, each hook'd to the next."

This interpretation suggests Whitman's anticipation of both the modern "stream of consciousness" literary tech-

---

[27] Paul Elmer More, *Shelburne Essays,* 4th ser. (Boston: Houghton Mifflin, 1922), 203.

[28] Harry B. Reed, "The Heraclitan Obsession of Walt Whitman," *The Personalist,* XV, 125-138 (April, 1934).

[29] *Ibid.,* 132.

[30] *Ibid.,* 133.

nique and the movement known in the 1920's as "Expressionism."[31] Dahlström's characterization of this doctrine in Germany might almost be a summary of Whitman's theory and practice and indicates the need for a study of the American poet's possible influence on the movement:

> Foremost among the elements [of Expressionism] is the concept of the *Ausstrahlungen des Ichs*—the radiation, expansion, and unfolding of the ego. This is partly explained by the phrase 'stream of consciousness' which is current in our English terminology. Yet 'stream of consciousness' offers too frequently the possibility of itemization of the elements of consciousness, lingers too close to the realm of psychology. For the expressionist, consciousness is no manifoldly died punch press turning out countless items of similar or dissimilar pattern. It is rather a unifying instrument that moulds oneness of the countless items poured into it. The ego is the predominant element in our universe; it is, indeed, the very heart of the world's reality. For the artist, the ego is a magic crystal in which the absolute is in constant play. It is the subject that registers the everlasting *state of becoming* that qualifies our world; and this subject has an anti-pole *object* which is functional only in giving meaning to the subject. Conversely, the subject must give meaning to the object. It is this ego, this subject, this magic crystal that actually gathers reality in its ultimate character.[32]

The "magic crystal" accurately characterizes Whitman's technique of dynamic, creative, enumeration of the kind

---

[31] For definition and history of the term, see Carl Enoch William Leonard Dahlström's Introduction to *Strindberg's Dramatic Expressionism* (Ann Arbor: University of Michigan, 1930), 3-10; 35-38. (Also Bibliography, 221-226.)

[32] *Ibid.*, 49-50.

of pantheistic reality in which he believed, and it was his fundamental purpose to register through the eyes of his expanding ego "the everlasting state of becoming that qualifies our world." For the expression of such basic ideas as his cosmic evolution, his pantheism, and his adaptation of the "temporalized Chain of Being" concept this technique was astonishingly appropriate.

The Search for a "Democratic" Structure

In so far as the expanding ego psychology results in an enumerative style, the cataloging of a representative and symbolical succession of images, conveying the sensation of pantheistic unity and endless becoming, it is itself a literary technique. But though this psychology may be called the background or basic method of Whitman's poetic technique, the catalog itself was not chronologically the first stylistic device which he adopted. It emerged only after he had found a verse structure appropriate for expressing his cosmic inspiration and democratic sentiment. Nowhere in the universe does he recognize caste or subordination. Everything is equally perfect and equally divine. He admits no supremes, or rather insists that "There can be any number of supremes."[33]

The expression of such doctrines demands a form in which units are co-ordinate, distinctions eliminated, all flowing together in a synonymous or "democratic" structure. He needed a grammatical and rhetorical structure which would be cumulative in effect rather than logical or progressive.

Possibly, as many critics have believed, he found such a structure in the primitive rhythms of the King James

---

[33] *By Blue Ontario's Shore*, sec. 3.

Bible, though some of the resemblances may be accidental. The structure of Hebraic poetry, even in English translation, is almost lacking in subordination. The original language of the Old Testament was extremely deficient in connectives, as the numerous "ands" of the King James translation bear witness.[34] It was a language for direct assertion and the expression of emotion rather than abstract thought or intellectual subtleties. Tied to such a language, the Hebraic poet developed a rhythm of thought, repeating and balancing ideas and sentences (or independent clauses) instead of syllables or accents. He may have had other prosodic conventions also, no longer understood or easily discernible; but at least in the English translation this rhythm of thought or parallelism characterizes Biblical versification.[35]

That Walt Whitman fully understood the nature of these Biblical rhythms is doubtful, and certainly his own language did not tie him down to such a verse system. Despite the fact that he was thoroughly familiar with the Bible and was undoubtedly influenced by the scriptures in many ways, it may, therefore, have been a coincidence that in searching for a medium to express his pantheism he naturally (we might almost say atavistically) stumbled upon parallelism as his basic structure. Furthermore,

---

[34] See A. S. Cook, "The 'Authorized Version' and Its Influence," *Cambridge History of English Literature* (New York and London: G. P. Putnam's Sons, 1910), IV, 29-58.

[35] See S. R. Driver, *Introduction to the Literature of the Old Testament* (New York, Scribner's Sons, 1910), 361 ff. Also E. Kautzsch, *Die Poesie und die poetischen Bücher des Alten Testaments* (Tübingen und Leipzig, 1902), 2. Bishop Lowth first pointed out the metrical principles of parallelism in the Bible in *De sacra poesi Hebraeorum praelectiones academiae Oxoni habitae*, 1753—see Driver, *op. cit.*, 362. In the main the Lowth system is the basis for R. G. Moulton's arrangement of Biblical poetry in his *Modern Reader's Bible* (New York: Macmillan, 1922). See also note 37 below.

parallelism is found in primitive poetry other than the Biblical; in fact, seems to be typically primitive,[36] and it is perhaps not surprising that in the attempt to get rid of conventional techniques Whitman should have rediscovered a primitive one.

But whatever the sources of Whitman's verse techniques, the style of the King James Version is generally agreed to provide convenient analogies for the prosodic analysis of LEAVES OF GRASS.[37]

"The principles which governed Hebrew verse," says Gardiner, "can be recovered only in part, but fortunately the one principle which really affects the form of the English has been clearly made out, the principle of parallel structure: in the Hebrew poetry the line was the unit, and the second line balanced the first, completing or supplementing its meaning."[38]

Even the scholars of the Middle ages were aware of the parallelism of Biblical verse (*Verdoppelten Ausdruck* or "double expression,"[39] they called it) but it was first fully explained by Bishop Lowth in a Latin speech given at Oxford in 1753. Since his scheme demonstrates the single line as the unit, let us examine it.

1. *Synonymous* parallelism: This is the most frequent kind of thought rhythm in Biblical poetry. "The second line enforces the thought of the first by repeating, and,

---

[36] *E.g.,* in American Indian rhythms—Cf. Mary Austin's *The American Rhythm* (New York: Harcourt Brace, 1913).

[37] Observed by many critics and biographers, but first elaborated by Gay Wilson Allen, "Biblical Analogies for Walt Whitman's Prosody," *Revue Anglo-Americaine,* X, 490-507 (August, 1933)—basis for same author's chapter on Whitman in *American Prosody* (New York: American Book Co., 1935), 217-243.

[38] J. H. Gardiner, *The Bible as English Literature* (New York: Scribner's Sons, 1906), 107.

[39] Kautzsch, *op. cit.,* 2.

as it were, *echoing* it in a varied form, producing an effect at once grateful to the ear and satisfying to the mind."[40]

How shall I curse, whom God hath not cursed?
And how shall I defy, whom the Lord hath not defied?
—*Nu.* 23:8.

The second line, however, does not have to be identical in thought with the first. It may be merely similar or parallel to it.

Sun, stand thou still upon Gibeon;
And thou, Moon, upon the valley of Aijalon.
—*Josh.* 10:12.

2. *Antithetic* parallelism: The second line denies or contrasts the first:

A wise son maketh a glad father,
But a foolish son is the heaviness of his mother.
—*Prov.* 10:1.

For the Lord knoweth the way of the righteous;
But the way of the wicked shall perish.
—*Ps.* 1:6.

3. *Synthetic* or *constructive* parallelism: Here the second line (sometimes several consecutive lines) supplements or completes the first. (Although all Biblical poetry tends more toward the "end-stopped" than the "run-on" line, it will be noticed that synthetic parallelism does often have a certain degree of *enjambement*.)

Better is a dinner of herbs where love is,
Than a stalled ox and hatred therewith.
—*Pr.* 15:17.

---

[40] Driver, *op. cit.*, 340.

Answer not a fool according to his folly,
Lest thou also be like unto him.
—*Pr.* 26:4.
As a bird that wandereth from her nest,
So is a man that wandereth from his place.
—*Pr.* 27:8.

"A comparison, a reason, a consequence, a motive, often constitutes one of the lines in a synthetic parallelism."[41]

4. To Lowth's three kinds of parallelism Driver adds a fourth, which for convenience we may include here. It is called *climactic* parallelism—or sometimes "ascending rhythm." "Here the first line is itself incomplete, and the second line takes up words from it and completes them."[42]

Give unto the Lord, O ye sons of the mighty,
Give unto the Lord *glory and strength.*
—*Ps.* 29:1.
The voice of the Lord shaketh the wilderness;
The Lord shaketh the wilderness *of Kadesh.*
—*Ps.* 29:8.
Till thy people pass over, O Lord,
Till the people pass over *which thou hast purchased.*
—*Ex.* 15:16.

It will be noticed in these examples that parallelism is sometimes a repetition of grammatical constructions and often of words, but the main principle is the balancing of thoughts alongside or against each other. And this produces not only a rhythmical thought-pattern, but also, and consequently, a speech rhythm which we will consider later. This brief summary presents only the most elementary aspects of Biblical rhythm, but it is sufficient to

---

[41] *Ibid.*　　　　[42] *Ibid.*

establish the fact that in parallelism, or in the "rhythm of thought," *the single line must by necessity be the stylistic unit.* Before taking up other aspects of parallelism let us see if this fundamental principle is found in Whitman's poetry.

Many critics have recognized parallelism as a rhythmical principle in LEAVES OF GRASS. Perry even suggested that *The Lily and the Bee,* by Samuel Warren, published in England in 1851 and promptly reprinted in America by Harpers, may have given Whitman the model for his versification;[43] though Carpenter has pointed out that Whitman's new style had already been formed by 1851.[44] Perry's conjecture is important, however, because parallelism is unquestionably the stylistic principle of *The Lily and the Bee,* and in making the conjecture he is rightly calling attention to this principle of Whitman's style.

But if parallelism is the foundation of the rhythmical style of LEAVES OF GRASS, then, as we have already seen in the summary of the Lowth system, the verse must be the unit. Any reader can observe that this is true in LEAVES OF GRASS, and many critics have pointed it out. De Selincourt says:

> The constitution of a line in *Leaves of Grass* is such that, taken in its context, the poetic idea to be conveyed by the words is only perfectly derived from them when they are related to the line as a unit; and the equivalence of the lines is their equivalent appeal to our attention as contributors to the developing expression of the poetic idea of the whole.[45]

---

[43] Bliss Perry, *Walt Whitman* (Boston: Houghton Mifflin, 1906), 92.
[44] George Rice Carpenter, *Walt Whitman* (New York: Macmillan, 1924), 42.
[45] De Selincourt, *op. cit.,* 103-104.

And Ross adds, more concretely:

> Whitman's verse—with the exception that it is not metered—is farther removed from prose than is traditional verse itself, for the reason that the traditional verse is, like prose, composed in sentences, whereas Whitman's verse is composed in lines . . . A run-on line is rare in Whitman—so rare that it may be considered a "slip." The law of his structure is that *the unit of sense is the measure of the line.* The lines, in sense, are end-stopped. Whitman employed everywhere a system of punctuation to indicate his structure. Look down any page of *Leaves of Grass,* and you will find almost every line ending in a comma; you will find a period at the end of a group of lines or a whole poem. Syntactically, there may be many sentences in the groups of the whole poem, there may be two or three sentences in one line. But Whitman was composing by lines, not by sentences, and he punctuated accordingly.[46]

WHITMAN'S PARALLELISM

It was only after a decade or more of experimentation that Whitman definitely adopted parallelism as his basic verse structure. In a poem of 1850, *Blood-Money,*[47] he was already fumbling for this technique, but here he was paraphrasing both the thought and the prose rhythm of the New Testament (*Matthew* 26-27):

Of the olden time, when it came to pass

---

[46] E. C. Ross, "Whitman's Verse," *Modern Language Notes,* XLV, 363-364 (June, 1930). Autrey Nell Wiley demonstates this view in "Reiterative Devices in 'Leaves of Grass'," *American Literature,* I, 161-170 (May, 1929). She says: "In more than 10,500 lines in *Leaves of Grass.* there are, by my count, only twenty run-on lines," p. 161.

[47] Whitman himself misdated this poem 1843. It was published in *The Tribune,* Supplement, March 22, 1850, and the occasion of the satire was Webster's speech on March 7, 1850, regarding the Fugitive Slave Law.

That the beautiful god, Jesus, should finish his work
on earth,
Then went Judas, and sold the divine youth,
And took pay for his body.

The run-on lines show how far the poet still is from the
characteristic style of LEAVES OF GRASS. He is experimenting with phrasal or clausal units; not yet "thought
rhythm." But his arrangement of the verse is a step in
that direction.

In *Europe,* another poem of 1850, we also see the new
form slowly evolving. It begins with long lines that at
first glance look like the typical verse of the later poems,
but on closer observation we see that they are not.

Suddenly, out of the stale and drowsy lair, the lair of
slaves,
Like lightning it le'pt forth....half startled at itself,
Its feet upon the ashes and the rags....Its hands tight to
the throat of kings.

The disregard for grammatical structure suggests the
poet's mature style—the antecedent of *it* is merely implied
and the predicate is entirely lacking—, but the lines are
only vaguely synonymous.

We see the next stage of this evolving style in the
1855 Preface, which, significantly, is arranged as prose,
but the thought-units are often separated by three periods,
indicating that the author is striving for a rhythmical effect
which conventional prose punctuation can not achieve.

He sees eternity less like a play with a prologue and a
denouement. . . he sees eternity in men and women. . .
he does not see men and women as dreams or dots.
Faith is the antiseptic of the soul. . . it pervades the

common people and preserves them. . . they never give up believing and expecting and trusting.

.   .   .   .   .

The greatest poet forms the consistence of what is to be from what has been and is. He drags the dead out of their coffins and stands them again on their feet. . . he says to the past, Rise and walk before me that I may realize you. He learns the lesson. . . he places himself where the future becomes present. The greatest poet does not only dazzle his rays over character and scenes and passions. . . he finally ascends and finishes all. . . he exhibits the pinnacles that no man can tell what they are for or what is beyond. . . He glows a moment on the extremest verge. He is most wonderful in his last half-hidden smile or frown. . .[48]

Notice that the parallelism asserts without qualifications. The poet is chanting convictions about which there is to be no argument, no discusson. He develops or elaborates the theme by enumeration, eliminating so far as possible transitional and connective words. The form is rhapsodic, the tone that of inspired utterance.

In this Preface the third person is used, but the rhetorical form is that of the expanding ego, as clearly revealed in this catalog:

On him rise solid growths that offset the growths of pine and cedar and hemlock and liveoak and locust and chestnut and cypress and hickory and limetree and cottonwood and tuliptree and cactus and wildvine and tamarind and persimmon. . . and tangles as tangled as any canebreak or swamp. . . and forests coated with transparent ice and icicles hanging from the boughs and

---

[48] Inclusive Edition, *op. cit.*, 492-495.

crackling in the wind. . . and sides and peaks of mountains....[49]

The "ands" are evidently an attempt to convey the effect of endless continuity in an eternal present—the cosmic unity which the poet incarnates as he sweeps over the continent. Here in this rhapsodic Preface, both in the ideas and the manner in which they are expressed, we see the kind of literary form and style which Whitman has adopted as analogous to his "purports and facts."

And in ten of the twelve poems of the 1855 edition of LEAVES OF GRASS parallelism is the structural device, chiefly the *synonymous* variety, though the others are found also, especially the *cumulative* and *climactic*. As a matter of fact, it is often difficult to separate these three, for as Whitman asserts or repeats the same idea in different ways—like a musician playing variations on a theme—he tends to build up to an emotional, if not logical, climax. The opening lines of *Song of Myself* are obviously cumulative in effect:

> I celebrate myself, [and sing myself],
> And what I assume you shall assume,
> For every atom belonging to me as good belongs to you.

The following lines are synonymous in thought, though there is a cumulation and building up of the emotion:

> I loafe and invite my soul,
> I lean and loafe at my ease . . . . observing a spear of summer grass.

(No doubt much of this effect is due to the pronounced caesura—which we will consider later.)

___
[49] *Ibid.* 490.

In this poem, as in the following ones, the parallelism has three functions. First of all it provides the basic structure for the lines. Each line makes an independent statement, either a complete or an elliptical sentence. In the second place, this repetition of thought (with variations) produces a loose rhythmical chanting or rhapsodic style. And, finally, the parallelism binds the lines together, forming a unit something like a stanza in conventional versification.

This grass is very dark to be from the white heads of
old mothers,
Darker than the colorless beards of old men,
Dark to come from under the faint red roofs of mouths.

O I perceive after all so many uttering tongues!
And I perceive they do not come from the roofs of
mouths for nothing.

I wish I could translate the hints about the dead young
men and women,
And the hints about old men and mothers, and the offspring taken soon out of their laps.

What do you think has become of the young and old
men?
And what do you think has become of the women and
children?

They are alive and well somewhere;
The smallest sprout shows there is really no death,
And if ever there was it led forward life, and does not
wait at the end to arrest it,
And ceased the moment life appeared.

> All goes onward and outward. . . .and nothing collapses,
> And to die is different from what any one supposed, and
>   luckier.[50]

Here Whitman's characteristic structure and rhythm is completely developed and he handles it with ease and assurance. But that he does not yet completely trust it is perhaps indicated by the occasional use of a semicolon (as in next to last stanza or strophe above) and four periods to emphasize a caesura. In his later verse (including revisions of this poem) he depended upon commas in both places.

In the above extract from *Song of Myself* the similarity of the parallelism to that of Biblical poetry is probably closer than in more typical passages of Whitman's longer poems, for the couplet, triplet, and quatrain are found more often in the Bible than in LEAVES OF GRASS; and the Bible does not have either long passages of synonymous parallelism or extended catalogs. The Biblical poets were not, like Whitman, attempting to inventory the universe in order to symbolize its fluxional unity. They found unity in their monotheism, not (or seldom) in a pantheism. But when Whitman's poetic vision sweeps over the occupations of the land, as in section 15 of *Song of Myself*, he enumerates dozens of examples in more or less synonymous parallelistic form. And he repeats the performance in section 33 in a kind of omnipresent world-panorama of scenes, activities, and pictures of life, in a strophe (or sentence) of 82 lines.

Another poem in the first edition, later known as *There Was a Child Went Forth*, further amplifies both the psychology of the poet's identification of his consciousness

---
[50] *Song of Myself*, sec. 6.

with all forms of being and his expression of it through enumeration and parallelism:

There was a child went forth every day,
And the first object he looked upon and received with
wonder or pity or love or dread, that object he became,
And that object became part of him for the day or a
certain part of the day. . . . or for many years or
stretching cycles of years.

Then comes the list—early lilacs, grass, morning glories, March-born lambs, persons, streets, oceans, etc.—a veritable photomontage. The catalog and parallelism techniques arise from the same psychological impulse and achieve the same general effects of poetic identification.

The catalog, however, is most typical of the 1855-56 poems, when Whitman's cosmic inspiration found its most spontaneous and unrestrained expression. But even here we find a number of strophes arranged or organized as "envelopes" of parallelism, a device which the poet found especially useful in the shorter and more orderly poems of *Calamus, Drum-Taps,* and the old-age lyrics. It is essentially a stanzaic form, something like the quatrain of the Italian sonnet. The first line advances a thought or image, succeeding lines amplify or illustrate it by synonymous parallelism, and the final line completes the whole by reiterating the original line or concluding the thought. For example, in section 21 of *Song of Myself:*

Smile O voluptuous coolbreathed earth!
Earth of the slumbering and liquid trees!
Earth of departed sunset! Earth of the mountains misty-
topt!

Earth of the vitreous pour of the full moon just tinged
   with blue!
Earth of shine and dark mottling the tide of the river!
Earth of the limpid gray clouds brighter and clearer for
   my sake!
Far-swooping elbowed earth! Rich apple-blossomed
   earth!
Smile, for your lover comes!

Far more common, however, is the incomplete envelope, the conclusion being omitted, as in the 1860 *Song
at Sunset:*

Good in all,
In the satisfaction and aplomb of animals
In the annual return of the seasons,
In the hilarity of youth
In the strength and flush of manhood,
In the grandeur and exquisiteness of old age,
In the superb vistas of death.

But of course an "incomplete envelope" is not an envelope at all. Without a conclusion it is not a container.
And it is characteristic of Whitman, especially in 1855-56,
that he more often preferred not to finish his comparisons,
analogies, representative examples of reality, but let them
trail off into infinity. In his later poems, however, the
envelope often provides a structure and unity for the
whole composition, as in *Joy, Shipmate, Joy!:*

Joy, shipmate, joy!
(Pleas'd to my soul at death I cry)
Our life is closed, our life begins,
The long, long anchorage we leave,
The ship is clear at last, she leaps!

She swiftly courses from the shore,
Joy, shipmate, joy!

OTHER REITERATIVE DEVICES

In the above discussion parallelism was referred to as both a *structure* and a *rhythm* in Whitman's verse technique. Since rhythm means orderly or schematic repetition, a poem can have several kinds of rhythms, sometimes so coördinated in the total effect that it is difficult to isolate and evaluate the separate function of each. Thus Whitman's parallelism can give esthetic pleasure as a recognizable pattern of thought, which is to say that it is the basis of the structure of the composition. This does not necessarily result in a repetition or rhythm of sounds, cadences, music, etc. But since thoughts are expressed by means of spoken sounds (or symbols that represent spoken sounds), it is possible for the *thought rhythm* to produce, or to be accompanied by, *phonic rhythm*. The latter need not be a rhythm of accents or stressed syllables (though it often is in LEAVES OF GRASS as will be demonstrated later). Rime, or repetition of similar sounds according to a definite pattern, is another kind of phonic rhythm, and may serve several purposes, such as pleasing the ear (which has been conditioned to anticipate certain sounds at regular intervals) or grouping the lines and thereby (in many subtle ways) emphasizing the thought.

Whitman's parallelism, or thought rhythm, is so often accompanied and reinforced by parallel wording and sounds that the two techniques are often almost identical. An easy way to collect examples of his "thought rhythm" is to glance down the left-hand margin and notice the lines beginning with the same word, and usually the same grammatical construction: "I will...I will...I will..." or "Where ...Where...Where..." or "When...When...When" etc.[51]

These repetitions of words or phrases are often found in modern conventional meters. Tennyson, for example,[52] repeats consecutively the same word or phrase throughout many passages; and the refrain and repetend in Poe's versification is the same device in a somewhat different manner. In conventional meters these reiterations may even set up a rhythm of their own, either syncopating or completely distorting the regular metrical pattern. But there is this very important difference between reiteration in rime and meter and reiteration in LEAVES OF GRASS: in the former the poem has a set pattern of accents (iambic, trochaic, anapestic, etc.), whereas in Whitman's verse the pattern of sounds and musical effects is entirely dependent upon the thought and structure of the separate lines.

In every emotionally and intellectually pleasing poem in LEAVES OF GRASS these reiterations do set up a recognizable pattern of sounds.[53] Since the line is not bound by a specific number of syllables, or terminated by conventional rime, the sound patterns may seem to the untrained reader entirely free and lawless. It was part of Whitman's "organic" style to make his rhythms freer than those of classical and conventional versification, but they are no freer than those of the best musical compositions of opera and symphony. They can, of course, be too

---

[51] Cf. *Song of Myself*, sec. 33 or *Salut au Monde!*

[52] Cf. Emile Lauvriere, *Repetition and Parallelism in Tennyson* (London: Oxford University Press, 1901).

[53] Here again Emerson's theory preceded Whitman's practice. In the section on "Melody, Rhyme, and Form" in his essay on *Poetry and Imagination* Emerson wrote: "Another form of rhyme is iterations of phrases ..."

free to recognize, in which case Whitman failed as a poet—and like almost all major poets, he has many failures to his name. But in the best poems of LEAVES OF GRASS—such as *Out of Cradle Endlessly Rocking, When Lilacs Last in the Dooryard Bloom'd,* or *Passage to India,* —the combined thought and sound patterns are as definite and organized as in *Lycidas* or *Samson Agonistes.*

Several names have been given Whitman's reiterative devices in addition to the ones used here (phonic reiteration, etc.). Miss Autrey Nell Wiley, who has made the most thorough study of this subject, uses the rhetorical terms *epanaphora* and *epanalepsis.*[54] The nineteenth-century Italian scholar, Jannaccone,[55] calls these reiterations *rima psichica iniziale e terminale* (initial and terminal psychic rime) and *rima psichica media e terminale.* "Psychic rime"[56] is a suggestive term, but it probably overemphasizes the analogy with conventional rime—though it is important to notice the initial, medial, and terminal positions of Whitman's reiterations. The initial is most common, as in the "Cradle" poem:

Out of the cradle endlessly rocking,
Out of the mocking bird's throat, the musical shuttle,
Out of the Ninth-month midnight.

Although this reiteration might be regarded as "psychic rime," its most significant function is the setting up of a cadence to dominate the whole line, as the "Give me" reiteration does in *Give Me the Splendid Silent Sun,* or the "What," "I hear," "I see," etc. in *Salut au Monde!* though

---

[54] See note 46, above.

[55] P. Jannaccone, *La Poesia di Walt Whitman e L'Evoluzione delle Forme Ritmiche* (Torino, Italy, 1898), 64 ff.

[56] Cf. note 53, above.

scarcely any poem in LEAVES OF GRASS is without the combined use of parallelism and reiteration. Often a short poem is a single "envelope" of parallelism with initial reiteration, as in *I Sit and Look Out:*

> I sit and look out upon all the sorrows of the world, and upon all oppression and shame,
> I hear secret convulsive sobs from young men at anguish with themselves, remorseful after deeds done,
> I see in low life the mother misused by her children, dying, neglected, gaunt, desperate,
> I see the wife misused by her husband, I see the treacherous seducer of young women,
> I mark the ranklings of jealousy and unrequited love attempted to be hid, I see these sights on the earth,
> I see the workings of battle, pestilence, tyranny, I see martyrs and prisoners,
> I observe a famine at sea, I observe the sailors casting lots who shall be kill'd to preserve the lives of the rest,
> I observe the slights and degradations cast by arrogant persons upon laborers, the poor, and upon negroes, and the like;
> All these—all the meanness and agony without end I sitting look out upon,
> See, hear, and am silent.

Initial reiteration, as in the above passage, occurs oftener in LEAVES OF GRASS than either medial or final. Miss Wiley has estimated that 41 percent of the more than 10,500 lines in the LEAVES contain epanalepsis, or initial reiteration.[57] But words and phrases are frequently repeated in other positions. *When Lilacs Last in the Dooryard Bloom'd* contains an effective example of a word

---

[57] Wiley, *op. cit.*, 161-162.

from the first line repeated and interwoven throughout succeeding lines:

> Over the breast of the spring, the land, *amid* cities,
> *Amid* lanes and through old woods, where lately the
>   violets peep'd from the ground, spotting the gray
>   debris,
> *Amid* the grass in the fields each side of the lanes, *pass-*
>   *ing* the endless grass,
> *Passing* the yellow-spear'd wheat, every grain from its
>   shroud in the dark-brown fields uprisen,
> *Passing* the apple-tree blows of white and pink in the
>   orchards,
> Carrying a corpse to where it shall rest in the grave,
> Night and day journeys a coffin.

Here the reiterations have little to do with cadences but aid greatly in the effect of ceaseless motion—and even of *enjambment,* so rare in LEAVES OF GRASS—as the body of the assassinated president is carried "night and day" from Washington to the plains of Illinois.

Final reiteration is found, though Whitman used it sparingly, perhaps because it too closely resembles refrains and repetends in conventional versification, and also because he had little use for the kind of melody and singing lyricism which these devices produce. When he does use final reiteration, it is more for rhetorical emphasis than music, as in sec. 24 of *Song of Myself:*

> Root of wash'd sweet-flag! timorous pond-snipe! nest
>   of guarded duplicate eggs! *it shall be you!*
> Mix'd tussled hay of head, beard, brawn, *it shall be*
>   *you!*

Trickling sap of maple, fibre of manly wheat, *it shall
be you!*
Sun so generous *it shall be you!*

and so on throughout sixteen lines.

Sometimes Whitman uses reiteration through the entire
line, as in *By Blue Ontario's Shore:*

I will know if I am to be less than they,
I will see if I am not as majestic as they,
I will see if I am not as subtle and real as they,
I will see if I am to be less generous than they, . . .

C. Alphonso Smith in his study of repetitions in English
and American poetry (he does not mention Whitman,
however) has defined the difference between reiterations
in prose and poetry:

In prose, a word or group of words is repeated for emphasis; whereas in verse, repetition is chiefly employed
not for emphasis (compare the use of the refrain), but
for melody of rhythm, for continuousness or sonorous-
ness of effect, for unity of impression, for banding lines
or stanzas, and for the more indefinable though not less
important purposes of suggestiveness.[58]

Of course Smith is thinking of conventional versification, but continuousness of effect, unity of impression,
joining of lines and stanzas, and suggestiveness all apply
to Whitman's use of reiteration.

Although Whitman's reiteration is not musical in the
sense that Poe's is (*i.e.,* for melody and harmony), it is
musical in a larger sense. Many critics have developed the
analogy of music in Whitman's technique, but De Selin-

---

[58] C. Alphonso Smith, *Repetition and Parallelism in English Verse*
(New York, 1894), 9.

court's comments are especially pertinent here. "The progress of Whitman's verse," he says, "has much in common with that of musical composition. For we are carrying the sense of past effects along with us more closely and depending more intimately upon them than is possible in normal verse."[59] And he observes that:

> repetition, which the artist in language scrupulously avoids, is the foundation and substance of musical expression. Now Whitman . . . uses words and phrases more as if they were notes of music than any other writer . . . it was to him part of the virtue and essence of life that its forms and processes were endlessly reduplicated; and poetry, which was delight in life, must somehow, he thought, mirror this elemental abundance.[60]

Of course Whitman's repetition concerns not only words and phrases (Jannaccone's "psychic rime") but thought patterns as well. In fact, his favorite method of organizing a long poem like *The Sleepers, Proud Music of the Storm, Mystic Trumpeter,* or even *Song of the Red-Wood Tree* is, as remarked elsewhere, symphonic. He likes to advance a theme, develop it by enumeration and representative symbols, advance other themes and develop them in similar manners, then repeat, summarize, and emphasize. Thus Whitman's repetition of thought, of words, of cadences,—playing variations on each out of exuberance and unrestrained joy both in the thought and form—, all combine to give him the satisfaction and conviction that he has "expressed" himself, not logically or even coherently, but by suggestion and by sharing his own emo-

---

[59] De Selincourt, *op. cit.,* 104.   [60] *Ibid.,* 108.

tions with the reader. This is true even though the background of nearly every poem in LEAVES OF GRASS is "Ideas" rather than simple lyric emotion; but Whitman develops these ideas like a poet-musician, not like a philosopher or a polemical writer.

Another kind of reiteration which Whitman uses both for the thought and the musical effect is what Jannaccone calls "grammatical" and "logical rime"[61]—though *grammatical rhythm* might be a more convenient and appropriate term. Instead of repeating the same identical word or phrase, he repeats a part of speech or grammatical construction at certain places in the line. This has nearly the same effect on the rhythm and cadence as the reiteration of the same word or phrase, especially when "grammatical rime" is initial. For example, parallel verbs:

> *Flow* on, river! *flow* with the flood-tide, and *ebb* with the ebb-tide!
> *Frolic* on, crested and scallop-edg'd waves!
> Gorgeous clouds of the sunset! *drench* with your splendor me or the men and women generations after me!
> *Cross* from shore to shore, countless crowds of passengers!
> *Stand* up, tall masts of Mannahatta,

The following Jannaccone calls "logical rime":[62]
Long and long has the *grass* been *growing*,
Long and long has the *rain* been *falling*,
Long has the *globe* been rolling *round*.

Not only are *growing, falling,* and *rolling* grammatically parallel, but they are also the natural (and logical) things for the *grass,* the *rain,* and the *globe* to be doing.

---

[61] Jannaccone, *op. cit.,* 67 ff.   [62] *Ibid.,* 73.

Sometimes Whitman reiterates cognates:

The *song* is to the *singer,* and comes back most to him,
The *teaching* is to the *teacher,* and comes back most to
 him,
The *murder* is to the *murderer,* and comes back most to
 him, etc.

In all these examples the various kinds of reiterations produce also a pattern of accents which can be scanned like conventional verse.

Lóng and lóng has the grass been grówing, . . .

Parallelism gives these lines a *thought* rhythm, but this is reinforced by the phonic recurrences, giving additional rhythm which depends upon *sounds* for its effect. Of course these examples are unusually regular (or simple), whereas the same principles in other passages give a much greater variety and complexity of phonic stress. But the combined reiterations always (at least when successful) produce a composite musical pattern — a pattern more plastic than any to be found in conventional versification, but one which the ear can be trained to appreciate no less than patterns of rime and meter.

"Organic" Rhythm

As we have repeatedly emphasized, Whitman's parallelism and his phonic reiterations do not exclude accentual patterns. Anyone who examines with care the versification of Leaves of Grass will discover many lines that can be scanned with ease, but most critics have regarded such passages as sporadic and uncharacteristic. Several, in fact, have thought the style of *Drum-Taps* inferior to other periods of Whitman's poetry, and a contradiction of his professed theory, because they are much nearer to conventional patterns of verse than his earlier poems.

Sculley Bradley, however, claims accentual patterns as the "Fundamental Metrical Principle" of LEAVES OF GRASS.[63] He does not challenge the widely accepted interpretations of Whitman's basic parallelism and reiteration, but regards these as obvious—though somewhat incidental. He thinks that many lines in which these devices are not used are also rhythmical and esthetically pleasing. In other words, there must be some other—still more *fundamental*—principle in Whitman's prosody.

Such a principle would have to be an exemplification of the poet's "organic" theory, his belief that form must spring from within, that a poetic experience will find its own natural rhythm in the act of expression. Certainly this was Whitman's most fundamental literary theory, as his various analogies—and those of numerous critics—indicate. Thus he compares his rhythms to the "recurrence of lesser and larger waves on the seashore, rolling in without intermission, and fitfully rising and falling."[64]

Bradley points out the similarity of Whitman's "organic" theory to Coleridge's distinction between "mechanic" and "organic" form, as expressed in his lecture on *Shakespeare, a Poet Generally:*

> The form is mechanic, when on any given material we impress a pre-determined form, not necessarily arising out of the properties of the material;—as when to a mass of wet clay we give whatever shape we wish it to

---

[63] Sculley Bradley, "The Fundamental Metrical Principle in Whitman's Poetry," *American Literature*, X, 437-459 (January, 1939).

[64] Quoted by Perry, *op. cit.*, from unpublished preface, 207; Cf. Traubel, *op. cit.*, I, 414.

retain when hardened. The organic form, on the other hand, is innate; it shapes, as it develops, itself from within, and the fullness of its development is one and the same with the perfection of its outward form. Such as the life is, such is the form. Nature, the prime genial artist, inexhaustible in diverse powers, is equally inexhaustible in forms;—each exterior is the physiognomy of the being within,—its true image reflected and thrown out from the concave mirror;—and even such is the appropriate excellence of her chosen poet . . .[65]

It was on such a theory as this that Whitman's friend, Kennedy, defended the art of LEAVES OF GRASS as conforming to the variety and multiplicity of Nature instead of the "base mechanical regularity" of conventional poetry. De Selincourt would agree with this general interpretation, but he also insists that: "The identity of the lines in metrical poetry is an identity of pattern. The identity of the lines in LEAVES OF GRASS is an identity of substance."[66] To this statement Bradley objects:

> For in the majority of the lines of Whitman, which are not brought into equivalence by repetition of substance and phrases, there is still the equivalence of a rhythm regulated by a periodicity of stress so uniformly measured as to constitute a true "meter." It is a device capable of infinite subtlety, and we must understand it fully in order to appreciate the extent of the poet's craftsmanship.[67]

One of the principal means by which Bradley establishes his "periodicity of stress" is in the use of "hovering accent"

[65] Coleridge, *Essays and Lectures on Shakespeare and Some Other Old Poets and Dramatists* (London: Everyman Library, n.d.), 46-47.
[66] De Selincourt, *op. cit.,* 96-97.
[67] Bradley, *op. cit.,* 447.

in his scansion: "It becomes apparent to the attentive
reader of Whitman, especially when reading aloud, that
in a great many cases the stress does not fall on a single
vowel, but is distributed along the word, or a pair of
words, or even a short phrase."[68] As an example:

Which of the young men does she like the best?

Ah the homeliest of them is beautiful to her.

This is, of course, as Bradley himself would agree, a subjective interpretation, but it is undoubtedly a dramatic and
effective reading of the lines. As he himself says, without the glide or hovering accent, the second line "becomes
jocose instead of pathetic."[69]

As an extended example of both organic rhythm and a
"unified organic whole," Bradley scans the poem on *Tears*
in this manner:[70]

3   Tears! tears! tears!

3   In the night, in solitude, tears,

5   On the white shore dripping, dripping, sucked in
       by the sand,

5   Tears, not a star shining, all dark and desolate,[71]

3   Moist tears from the eyes of a muffled head.

---

[68] *Ibid.,* 444

[69] *Ibid.,* 445.

[70] *Ibid.,* 449.

[71] Would it not increase the pathos to read "all dark" and "desolate"
with hovering accent? But this scansion would not affect Bradley's accent
count.

5 O who is that ghost? that form in the dark, with
   tears,

6 What shapeless lump is that, bent, crouched there
   on the sand,

5 Streaming tears, sobbing tears, throes, choked with
   wild cries,

6 O storm, embodied, rising, careering with swift steps
   along the beach!

6 O wild and dismal night storm, with wind—
   O belching and desperate!

8 O shade so sedate and decorous by day, with calm
   countenance and regulated pace,

7 But away at night as you fly, none looking—O then
   the unloosened ocean

3 Of tears! tears! tears!

Here Bradley makes a valuable contribution to the
understanding and appreciation of Whitman's art by calling attention to the symmetry of the form. His scansion
divides the poem into three free-verse stanzas, each with
its own definite accentual pattern, and the whole with a
pyramidal structure which suggests "a large wave or
breaker with three crests."[72] And he cites several in-

_____

[72] Bradley, *op. cit.*, 449.

teresting examples to demonstrate that such structure, especially the pyramidal form, is characteristic of Whitman's more successful versification.

Without in the least denying or detracting from the value of this interpretation, we should also observe, however, that even here Whitman uses repetitions as an integral part of his organic structure. The parallelism and phonic reiteration are less obvious than in *Song of Myself* and the earlier and longer poems, but they are present in this characteristic composition of the 1860's. The word *tears* is "psychic rime" and a kind of refrain, weaving in and out and influencing both the pathos and cadences. There is also a subtle repetition of thought throughout, with the epithets for tears, the references to the "ghost" and the "storm." Furthermore, the parallelism does not entirely divide according to Bradley's stanzaic scheme, but laps over from the second to the third divisions:

(a)　O storm, embodied, rising, careering with swift
　　　　　steps along the beach!
(a)　O wild and dismal night storm, with wind—
　　　　　O belching and desperate!

The thought structure of the whole is, of course, the envelope, which was mentioned in the section on "Parallelism."

But the fact that Whitman so successfully combines thought, rhetoric, syllabic accent, and stanzaic form in an "organic" whole is sufficient evidence of expert craftsmanship and his ability to adapt technique to his literary purposes. Bradley's reading of the lines with hovering stresses also indicates that Whitman had a keener ear for sound and cadence than has been commonly supposed. Sometimes, indeed, the "subtle patterns are embroidered upon each other in a manner comparable to that of great symphonic music . . ."[73]

Every student of Whitman should read Professor Bradley's illuminating interpretation.

A careful study of Whitman's punctuation will also reveal that it was not erratic or eccentric, as many readers have thought, but that it was an accurate index to the organic rhythm, the musical effects which the poet hoped to have brought out in the reading. We have already noticed that the comma at the end of nearly every line except the last is an indication not of the usual sense-pause but of the end of a prosodic unit—usually ending in a cadenza or falling of the voice. Perhaps it might be called a final caesura—a slight pause before the voice continues with the recitative. In the first edition Whitman frequently used semicolons at the end of lines which were grammatically complete (either complete predications or elliptical sentences), but later he adopted commas. Inside the line he was still forced to punctuate somewhat according to thought, but his internal commas and dashes are also often caesural pauses.

Whitman has a great variety of caesuras, and an exhaustive study of them would reveal much about his word-music that is still little known. Only a few examples can be given here. We might begin with one of the most rudimentary effects, which may be called a catalog-caesura:

The blab of the pave,/ tires of carts,/ sluff of boot-
     soles,/ talk of the promenaders,/

---

[73] *Ibid.*, 455.

> The heavy omnibus,/ the driver with his interrogating
> thumb,/ the clank of the shod horses on the granite
> floor,/ . . .[74]

Notice the cumulative effect of the cadences, aided by the
slight caesural pauses:

$$\times \quad ' \quad \times \quad \times \quad '(\times)' \quad \times \quad '(\times)' \quad \times \quad '$$
The blab of the pave, tires of carts, sluff of boot-
soles,

the omitted unaccented syllable before "tires" and "sluff"
breaking the monotony of the pattern and emphasizing
the beat, presently giving way to longer sweeps in the
following line,

> . . . the driver with his interrogating thumb,
> the clank of the shod horses on the granite floor . . . .

A similar caesura, but with many subtle variations:

> I hear bravuras of birds,/ bustle of growing wheat,/
> gossip of flames,/ clack of sticks cooking my meals.//
> I hear the sound I love,/ the sound of the human
> voice,//
> I hear all sounds running together,/ combined, fused or
> following,/
> Sounds of the city and sounds out of the city—/sounds
> of the day and night, . . .[75]

Notice how much the shortening or lengthening of the
pause can contribute to both the rhythm and the thought.
The first line is cumulative in effect, the second balanced,
the third suggestive or illustrative, the fourth is emphatic.

---

[74] *Song of Myself*, sec. 8.
[75] *Ibid.*, sec. 26. Compare the similar idea (and "I hear . . ." reiteration) in *Salut au Monde*, sec. 3, with different caesural effect.

Sometimes the caesura divides the parallelism and is equivalent to the line-end pause:

> There is that in me—//I do not know what it is—/
> but I know it is in me.
> Wrench'd and sweaty—/ calm and cool/ then my body
> becomes,/
> I sleep—// I sleep long.//
> I do not know it—// it is without name—// it is a
> word unsaid,//
> It is not in any dictionary,/ utterance,/ symbol.[76]

Another caesural effect Jannaccone calls "thesis" and "arsis"[77] because the second half line echoes the thought of the first and receives a weaker stress and perhaps a lower pitch:

> Great are the myths—// I too delight in them;
> Great are Adam and Eve—// I too look back and ac-
> cept them. . . .[78]

This is of course also another example of Whitman's parallelism, and another indication of why he used parallelism so extensively. The employment of connectives or subordination would destroy the ring of inspired authority which he wished to give to his prophetic utterances.

Whitman's use of the parenthesis in his verse structure throws further light on his organic rhythms. Although the parenthesis in LEAVES OF GRASS has been frequently regarded as merely a mannerism without special significance so far as the versification is concerned, two critics have advanced interesting explanations. De Selincourt says:

---

[76] *Song of Myself*, sec. 50.   [78] *Great are the Myths*, sec. 1.
[77] Jannaccone, *op. cit.*, 72.

The use of parenthesis is a recurring feature of Whitman's technique, and no explanation of his form can
be adequate which does not relate this peculiarity to
the constructive principles of the whole. He frequently
begins a paragraph or ends one with a bracketed sentence . . . sometimes even begins or ends a poem paren-
thetically . . . This persistent bracketing falls well into
the scheme we have laid down of independent units
that serve an accumulating effect. The bracket, one
need not remark, secures a peculiar detachment for its
contents; it also, by placing them outside the current
and main flow of the sense, relates them to it in a
peculiar way. And although for the time being the flow
is broken, it by no means follows . . . that our sense of
the flow is broken; on the contrary, it is probably en-
hanced. We look down upon the stream from a point
of vantage and gauge its speed and direction. More
precisely, the bracket opening a poem or paragraph
gives us, of course, the idea which that whole poem or
paragraph presupposes, while the closing bracket gives
the idea by which what precedes is to be qualified and
tempered. We have thus as it were a poem within a
poem; or sometimes, when a series of brackets is used,
we have a double stream of poetry, as in *By Blue Ontario's Shore* . . .[79]

Catel argues, as one proof of his thesis that Whitman's art is that of the orator, that the parentheses indicate a change of voice or gesture. Sometimes, he points
out, the parenthetical matter is "un aveu murmuré, comme
un aparté, un à-côté personnel,"[80] as in:

---

[79] De Selincourt, *op. cit.*, 106-108.

[80] Jean Catel, Rhythme et langage dans la 1ʳᵉ édition des "Leaves of
Grass," 1855 (Paris: Rieder, 1930), 126.

The young fellow drives the express-wagon, (I love
  him, though I do not know him;)....
The canal boy trots....
The conductor beats time....
The child is baptized....
The regatta is spread....(how the white sails sparkle!)[81]

Often, as Catel says, the parenthesis is not necessary
for the thought, and unless it indicates a change in tone,
pitch, or emphasis there is no explanation for its use.

I do not trouble my spirit to vindicate itself or be
  understood,
I see that the elementary laws never apologize,
(I reckon I behave no prouder than the level I plant
  my house by, after all.)[82]

Or in the following:

All truths wait in all things,
They neither hasten their own delivery nor resist it,....
The insignificant is as big to me as any,
(What is less or more than a touch?)[83]
I hear all sounds running together....
The steam-whistle....
The slow march play'd at the head of the association
  marching two and two,
(They go to guard some corpse, the flag-tops are draped
  with black muslin.)[84]

As both a summary and supplement to these interpretations, we can say that almost invariably Whitman's
parentheses indicate a break or change in the organic
rhythm. Often, as in the first example above, the general

---

[81] *Song of Myself*, sec. 15.
[82] *Ibid.*, sec. 20.
[83] *Ibid.*, sec. 30.
[84] *Ibid.*, sec. 26.

rhythmical pattern for the passage seems to be suspended momentarily by the bracketed comment: "The young fellow drives . . . (I love him though I do not know him) . . . The canal boy trots . . . The conductor beats time . . . The child is baptized . . . The regatta is spread . . . (how the white sails sparkle!)," etc.

But in some passages Catel's theory of a change of voice or gesture applies only as a thin analogy. In the following example the bracketed passage seems fully as emphatic as the preceding and succeeding lines, although it does not have quite the same cadence as the "to the" reiterations and also presents a specific image in a passage of panoramic and symbolical details:

> To the leaven'd soil they trod calling I sing for the last,
> (Forth from my tent emerging for good, loosing, untying the tent ropes,)
> In the freshness of the forenoon air, in the far-stretching circuits and vistas again to peace restored,
> To the fiery fields emanative and the endless vistas beyond, to the South and the North,
> To the leaven'd soil of the general Western world to attest my songs,
> To the Alleghanian hills and the tireless Mississippi,....
> To the plains....etc.[85]

Such uses of the parenthesis add further proof that Whitman's rhythm is in actuality as well as in theory formed from within, and also controlled and shaped to harmonize with both his thought and emotion. The very fact that so many analogies occur to the critics is evidence both of an "organic form" and at the same time of Whitman's success in subordinating his technique to his "pur-

---

[85] *To the Leaven'd Soil They Trod.*

ports and facts." Thus De Selincourt thinks of the punctuation as indicating the ebb and flow of musical composition and Catel as stage directions for an orator. In attempting to explain Whitman's form, Matthiessen uses
three analogies—oratory, opera, and the ocean.[86] No
poet ever tried more conscientiously to wed sound and
sense. As Matthiessen says:

> When he spoke of his 'liquid-flowing syllables,' he
> was hoping for the same effect in his work as when he
> jotted down as the possible genesis for a poem: 'Sound
> of walking barefoot ankle deep in the edge of the water
> by the sea.' He tried again and again to describe what
> he wanted from this primal force, and put it most
> briefly when he said that if he had the choice of equal-
> ling the greatest poets in theme or in metre or in perfect
> rhyme,
>
>> These, these, O sea, all these I'd gladly barter,
>> Would you the undulation of one wave, its trick
>>   to me transfer,
>> Or breathe one breath of yours upon my verse,
>> And leave its odor there.[87]

This ambition, however, should not lead the reader to
expect pronounced onomatopoeia in Whitman's verse.
Not even in *When Lilacs Last in the Dooryard Bloom'd*
does the vicarious bird-singing sound convincingly like
the notes of the "gray-brown bird." What the poet does
is to convey the spirit, the lyric feeling, of the time and
place of his allegory. What he makes is music of the soul,
not a literal mimicry of lapping waves or bird-chirping.

---

[86] F. O. Matthiessen, *American Renaissance* (New York: Oxford University Press, 1941), 549-577.

[87] *Ibid.*, 565. (Poem quoted: *Had I the Choice.*)

The song, wondrous chant of the gray-brown bird,
And the tallying chant, the echo arous'd in my soul,

.   .   .   .

For the sweetest, wisest soul of all my days and lands—
    and this for his dear sake,
Lilac and star and bird twined with the chant of my soul,
There in the fragrant pines and the cedars dusk and dim.

Here the esthetic problem is quite similar to that of
"program" *vs.* abstract music—except for the fact that
music depends entirely upon sound, whereas in poetry
the *words* convey ideas and images in addition to rhythms
and tones. Many imaginative listeners think they hear
in the marvelous symphonies of Sibelius the pine-tree
whisperings of Finlandia, but it is doubtful that Sibelius
has attempted any literal imitation of these sounds. And
seldom is there any indication that Whitman's object is
the phonographic reproduction of rustling or splashing
water. What he wants in his verse is the "breath" and
the "odor" of the sea (abstractions), and "the echo
arous'd in my soul." Freneau might capture the rhythms
of the "katy-did" or Emerson of the "humble-bee," but
Walt Whitman's "organic" rhythms are those of the spirit
of Nature "twined with the chant of my soul." This is why
he anticipated Expressionism in modern art and was
adopted by the French Symbolists as one of their own,
though he was neither Expressionist nor Symbolist, but
Walt Whitman, poet of a "spiritual democracy."

CONVENTIONAL TECHNIQUES IN LEAVES OF GRASS

Although Whitman's "organic" theory of poetic style
is commonly assumed to be completely antithetical to

conventional techniques, there is no logical reason why the poet might not occasionally have an experience or an emotion which would find natural expression in rime and meter. According to the organic principle, the form must be shaped from within, not from external conventions. But who can say that the inner experience can never find a conventional outlet? At any rate, it is true, as Miss Ware has said, that Whitman "exemplified at some point or other virtually all of the conventions that he professed to eschew, and that he employed some of these conventions on a large scale."[88]

The most obvious conventions against which Whitman was supposedly revolting were rime and meter. Yet we find him using rime in several of his mature poems, all written after the adoption of his "organic" style. The earliest of these is in the first section (or strophe) of *Song of the Broad Axe*, which was apparently written in 1856. The rhythm is "organic" in the sense that it varies from line to line, and the lines themselves are often of different lengths, but the accents are surprisingly metrical and the final syllables are so nearly rimed that the pattern is trochaic tetrameter couplets:[89]

Weapon shapely, naked, wan,
Head from the mother's bowels drawn,
Wooded flesh and metal bone, limb only one and lip
  only one,
Gray-blue leaf by red-heat grown, helve produced from
  a little seed sown,

---

[88] Lois Ware, "Poetic Conventions in Leaves of Grass," *Studies in Philology*, XXVI, 47 (January, 1929).

[89] Since *bone—one* and *grown—sown* are at least approximate rimes, he third and fourth lines are also tetrameter couplets.

Resting the grass amid and upon,
To be lean'd and to lean on.

Curiously enough, this effective trochaic movement survives from an early manuscript, in which the poet was apparently trying to imitate the sound of rain drops:

> The irregular tapping of rain off my house-eaves at night
> after the storm has lulled, [probably the subject, not
> a line for a poem],
> Gray-blue sprout so hardened grown
> Head from the mother's bowels drawn
> Body shapely naked and wan
> Fibre produced from a little seed sown.[90]

In this case it would seem, then, that the rhythm was salvaged from a manuscript poem having nothing to do with the subject-matter of the *Broad-Axe;* it did not grow from within but was adapted—not however, inappropriately.

The first section of *By Blue Ontario's Shore* also rimes in almost the same manner, being *aabbcb.* The main part of this poem was also published in 1856, but the version including these rimes was not added until 1867. The conventionality of *O Captain! My Captain!,* 1865, has probably been observed by all students of Whitman. The stanza is composed of four long lines and four short ones, the latter being used as a refrain. The meter is iambic and the stanzaic pattern is approximately as follows: $a_5a_7b_7b_7c_3d_3e_4d_3$. But one of the most conventional of all poems in LEAVES OF GRASS is the prisoner's song in *The*

---

[90] See Variorum Readings, Inclusive Edition, *op. cit.,* 614. Perhaps it is not certain that these four lines were intended to exemplify the "irregular tapping of rain," but they at least indicate the organic growth of plants after receiving moisture—a very different subject from the forging of the axe.

Singer in Prison, 1869. The first stanza is almost com- pletely regular:

A soul confined by bars and bands,
Cries, help!, O help, and wrings her hands,
Blinded her eyes, bleeding her breast,
Nor pardon finds, nor balm of rest,

Still another poem with a definite rime-scheme is *Ethiopia Saluting the Colors,* 1871. The scheme is approximately $(a)a_6bb_7$ (the first being an internal rime).

In addition to the above poems in more or less conventional stanzas, Whitman also used stanza forms in the following poems: *A Noiseless Patient Spider,* 1862-3, a five-line stanza in irregular meter but recognizably metrical; *For You O Democracy,* 1860, in a five-line and four-line stanza with a refrain, ending with a free-verse couplet (of parallelism); *Pioneers! O Pioneers!,* 1865, in four-line trochaic stanzas, the first line being mainly three-stress and the fourth line being the refrain of the title; *Dirge for Two Veterans,* 1865-6, in four-line stanzas, the scheme being mainly 3-4-3-6; *Old War Dreams,* 1865-6, in a four-line stanza, the fourth being a refrain; *Gods,* 1870, in short unrimed strophe (mainly triplets) with refrain; *In Cabin'd Ships at Sea,* 1871, in iambic eight-line stanzas, each first and last line being shorter than the others; and *Eidólons,* 1876, in four-line stanzas, the first and fourth lines being dimeters and trimeters and the second and third being longer, of indefinite length.

Nearly half of these poems are, as indicated, in conventional meters. Especially interesting is the anapestic-iambic *Beat! Beat! Drums!*

Beat! beat! drums! —blow bugles! blow!
Over the traffic of cities—over the rumble of wheels
    in the streets;
Are beds prepared for sleepers at night in the houses?
    no sleepers must sleep in those beds,
No bargainers bargain by day—no brokers or spec-
    ulators—would they continue?

One of the most metrical poems in LEAVES OF GRASS
is the trochaic *Pioneers! O Pioneers!*, 1865. The number of stresses in the second and third lines varies from
seven to ten, and occasionally an iamb is substituted for
a trochee, but the pattern is almost as regular as in conventional verse.

For we cannot tarry here,
We must march my darlings, we must bear the brunt
    of danger,
We the youthful sinewy races, all the rest on us
    depend,
Pioneers! O Pioneers!

Most of Whitman's poems contain occasional lines
that scan easily as iambic, trochaic, anapestic, or—very
rarely — dactyllic. The poems mentioned above are
nearly all that adhere closely to a definite conventional
metrical pattern—though most of the LEAVES can be
scanned by Bradley's method.

But it will be observed that most of these examples were first published in the 1860's. Both *Drum-Taps* and *Sequel to Drum-Taps* are a great deal more conventional in form and style than earlier poems in the LEAVES. Apparently the poet found more conventional metrics either convenient or necessary for the expression of his experiences and emotions connected with the war. Even *Pioneers! O Pioneers!* is a marching poem. But what is more natural than that the poet's heart-beat would throb to the rhythms of marching feet—especially a poet who aspired to give organic expression to his own age and country?

Throughout most of his poems, of all periods, Whitman made extensive us of other conventional devices such as alliteration, both vowel and consonantal, and assonance, but these are rather embellishments (perhaps often unconscious) than fundamental techniques. They are interesting in view of Whitman's determination in the '55 Preface not to use any ornamentation in his verse, but they have so long been taken for granted in English poetry that they can hardly be called a contradiction of the poet's doctrines. In a poem like *Tears* they are almost inevitable, and it is not surprising to find them in the more onomatopoetic description of sea-shore experiences and memories. Although Miss Ware probably attaches too much importance to these particular conventions, her conclusion is no doubt sound:

A comparison of the results found by a study of *Leaves of Grass* and the *Uncollected Poetry and Prose* of Walt would seem to indicate that when Whitman discarded the more obvious poetic devices—like regular stanza forms, meter, and rhyme,—he unconsciously adopted the less obvious conventions, such as alliteration, assonance, repetition, refrain, parallelism, and end-stopped lines.[91]

Whether these survive in Whitman's versification unconsciously or not, it is difficult to say, but it is quite certain that he could not very well write intelligible poetry without retaining some conventions—and adapting or creating some basic prosodic techniques not altogether "transcendent and new." But they were sufficiently new to puzzle his own generation, and as the many critics have demonstrated, need to be explained and interpreted even today.

THE ORGANIC THEORY OF WORDS

Since the publication of the first edition of LEAVES OF GRASS, critics have been interested in Whitman's bold use of words and have tried to discover the secret of his large but indiscriminate vocabulary. Wordsworth's poetic reform, as set forth in the Preface to *Lyrical Ballads,* was mainly concerned with diction, with the rejection of artificial "poetic diction" of neo-classicism and the adoption of living speech of ordinary people (though pruned of the grossest crudities). Many critics have assumed that Whitman was completing the reform begun by Wordsworth. Catel says, "Whitman a retrouvé, par un instinct très sûr de poète, la source vive du langage qui est le style oral, ce qu'il a appelé lui-même 'a vocal style'."[92]

Whitman himself anticipated modern linguistic theory by declaring in his *American Primer* that "Pronunciation is the stamina of language,—it is language,"[93] and there

---

[91] Ware, *op. cit.,* 53.

[92] Catel, *op. cit.,* 84.

[93] *An American Primer,* edited by Horace Traubel (Boston: Small, Maynard and Co., 1904), 12.

is no doubt that he tried to make extensive use of the vernacular in his poems. Perhaps it would not have been inconsistent with his other literary theories for him to have cultivated almost exclusively a vernacular vocabulary. But it is a notorious fact that he did not do so. True, he greets the earth as "top-knot"[94] and he likes to close his poems with a "so long"[95] to the reader, but he practically ransacks the dictionaries for literary words like "chyle," "recusant," and "circumambient,"[96] and he is almost childlishly fond of foreign words, especially French[97] and Spanish ones, which he sometimes uses with a reckless disregard for correct spelling or meaning.[98] English biographers and critics, especially,[99] still cringe at the democratic "mélange" which often resulted from Whitman's indiscriminate mixture of all levels of linguistic usage. No one with literary taste can deny that this self-styled poet of democracy often brewed a linguistic concoction as strange as the barbaric rituals of Melville's Quequeg. Possibly, too, many of his philological indiscretions were due to ignorance or primitive delight in verbal displays; but his theory of language was more fully de-

[94] *Song of Myself*, sec. 40.

[95] Closing poem in third edition—see p. 160, *ante*.

[96] See Matthiessen, *op. cit.*, 517-532. In the first edition of LEAVES OF GRASS Whitman was especially fond of such rare or obsolete words as *exurge* (p. 60), *caoutchouc* (p. 83), and *albescent* (p. 84).

[97] See Louise Pound, "Walt Whitman and the French Language," *American Speech*, I, 421-430 (May, 1926).

[98] Cf. Louise Pound. "Walt Whitman's Neologisms," *American Mercury*, IV, 199-201 (Feb., 1925). Louis Untermeyer, in "Whitman and the American Language," New York *Evening Post*, May 31, 1919, calls Whitman "the father of the American language."

[99] Cf. John Bailey, *Walt Whitman* (New York: Macmillan, 1926), 87 ff. Hugh I'Anson Fausset, in *Walt Whitman: Poet of Democracy* (New Haven: Yale University Press, 1942) shares Bailey's lack of sympathy and understanding of the principles on which Whitman chose his diction and form. He simply regards the poet as ignorant and careless.

veloped than some critics have realized, and it harmonizes surprisingly well with his "organic" conception of poetic form.

And nowhere do we find evidence of Whitman's indebtedness to Emerson and Transcendentalism more than in his theory of words. In *The Poet* Emerson says that,

> Things admit of being used as symbols because nature is a symbol, in the whole, and in every part. Every line we can draw in the sand has expression; and there is no body without its spirit or genius. All form is an effect of character; all condition, of the quality of the life; all harmony, of health; and for this reason a perception of beauty should be sympathetic, or proper only to the good.

From this Neo-platonic point of view, "the world is a temple whose walls are covered with emblems, pictures and commandments of the Deity," and it is also interesting to see that here, as in Whitman's cosmic equalitarianism, "the distinctions which we make in events and in affairs, of low and high, honest and base, disappear when nature is used as a symbol."

The poet is the man, above all others, who has the power to use symbols, and thus to indicate men's relationships to nature, God, and the universe they inhabit. "We are symbols and inhabit symbols; workmen, work, tools, words and things, birth and death, all are emblems . . ." But the poet gives to words and things "a power which makes their old use forgotten, and put eyes and a tongue into every dumb and inanimate object." Thus to Emerson, words are symbols of symbols. Above all they are images with spiritual significance. Even more to him than to the philologist, "Every word was once a poem," and language itself "is fossil poetry."

On the basis of this theory Emerson declares that:

The vocabulary of an omniscent man would embrace words and images excluded from polite conversation. What would be base, or even obscene, to the obscene, becomes illustrious, spoken in a new connection of thought. The piety of the Hebrew prophets purges their grossness. The circumcision is an example of the power of poetry to raise the low and offensive. Small and mean things serve as well as great symbols. The meaner the type by which a law is expressed, the more pungent it is, and the more lasting in the memories of men . . . Bare lists of words are found suggestive to an imaginative and excited mind . . .

There we have Whitman's complete theory and attitude toward words. He added little if anything to it, but it was he, not Emerson, who made the broadest application of the theory. Here we find the foundation of Whitman's doctrine in the 1855 Preface that words reveal the character and the inner harmony of the speaker, and that "All beauty comes from beautiful blood and a beautiful brain. If the greatnesses are in conjunction in a man or woman it is enough."[100] Or as he later expressed it in *An American Primer*, "Words follow character."[101] And thus in his great faith in the future of the Democratic Republic he envisions a nation of people who will be "the most fluent and melodious voiced people in the world . . . the

[100] The 1855 Preface, Inclusive Edition, *op. cit.*, 493. Cf. Jean Gorely, "Emerson's Theory of Poetry," *Poetry Review*, XXII, 263-273 (August, 1931); and Emerson Grant Sutcliffe, "Emerson's Theories of Literary Expression," *University of Illinois Studies in Language and Literature*, VIII, 9-143 (1923).

[101] *American Primer, op. cit.*, 2. Cf. Inclusive Edition, *op. cit.*, 488.

most perfect users of words."[102]   Some critics have thought
Whitman an atavistic savage who believed in the magic
of words. Actually, however, he worships neither words
nor images, but the mystic powers and relationships which
they feebly signify. If the meaning is not in the user of
words, it cannot be in the verbal symbols which he em-
ploys. As Matthiessen comments, "Whitman's excitement [in naming things] carries weight because he realized
that a man cannot use words so [as Whitman did] unless
he has experienced the facts that they express, unless he
has grasped them with his senses."[103]

Whitman's propensity for inventorying the universe is,
therefore, evidence of his desire to know life—*being*—
in all its details, the small and the mean as well as the
great and the good. Locked in the words is the vicarious
experience of the poet, to whom even bare lists are suggestive and exciting.

A perfect writer would make words sing, dance, kiss,
do the male and female act, bear children, weep, bleed,
rage, stab, steal, fire cannon, steer ships, sack cities,
charge with cavalry or infantry, or do anything, that
man or woman or the natural powers can do.

Latent, in a great user of words, must actually be all
passions, crimes, trades, animals, stars, God, sex, the
past, might, space, metals, and the like—because these
are the words, and he who is not these, plays with a
foreign tongue, turning helplessly to dictionaries and
authorities.—How can I tell you?—I put many things
on record that you will not understand at first—perhaps
not in a year—but they must be (are to be) understood.—The earth, I see, writes with prodigal clear

---

[102] *Ibid.*   [103] Matthiessen, *op. cit.*, 518.

hands all summer, forever, and all winter also, content, and certain to be understood in time—as, doubtless, only the greatest user of words himself fully enjoys and understands himself.[104]

Although Whitman's poetic form and technique throughout LEAVES OF GRASS exemplify both his theory and attitude toward words, he treated the problem specifically in the 1856 *Poem of the Sayers of the Words of the Earth.*[105]

> Earth, round, rolling, compact—suns, moons, animals
> —all these are words,
> Watery, vegetable, sauroid advances—beings, premonitions, lispings of the future,
> Behold! these are vast words to be said.
>
> Were you thinking that those were the words—those upright lines? those curves, angles, dots?
> No, those are not the words—the substantial words are in the ground and sea,
> They are in the air—they are in you.[106]

Though this doctrine is mystical and transcendental, it is also *semantic.* What Whitman is trying to get at is "meaning," and meaning, he says, is in cosmic processes (evolution: "sauroid advances" and "lispings of the future"), in things, and "in you." Language is conduct and words are merely gestures:

> A healthy presence, a friendly or commanding gesture, are words, sayings, meanings,

---

[104] *American Primer, op. cit.,* 16.

[105] Renamed in 1881 *Song of the Rolling Earth.*

[106] Version of 1856 edition; first three lines in this passage were dropped in 1881. See also *Song of Myself,* sec. 25.

The charms that go with the mere looks of some men
and women are sayings and meanings also.[107]

But though the meaning of words is subjective, it must
tally with objective fact. Whitman anticipated modern
semantic doctrine in his insistence on this harmony between the inner and outer meaning:

> I swear the earth shall surely be complete to him or
> her who shall be complete!
> I swear the earth remains broken and jagged only to
> him or her who remains broken and jagged!
>
> I swear there is no greatness or power that does not
> emulate those of the earth!
> I swear there can be no theory of any account, unless
> it corroborate the theory of the earth![108]

Far from worshipping words or mistaking them for
reality, Whitman sees their inadequacy and searches for
the meaning behind words:

> I swear I begin to see little or nothing in audible words!
> I swear I think all merges toward the presentation of
> the unspoken meanings of the earth!
> Toward him who sings the songs of the body, and of
> the truths of the earth,
> Toward him who makes the dictionaries of words that
> print cannot touch.[109]

As a poet Whitman must make carols of words, but
he knows that these are only "hints of meanings" which

---

[107] *Poem of the Sayers of the Words of the Earth* (1856); *Song of the
Rolling Earth*, sec. 1.
[108] *Ibid.*, sec. 3.
[109] *Poem of the Sayers of the Words of the Earth* (1856); *Song of the
Rolling Earth*, Sec. 3.

"echo the tones of Souls, and the phrases of Souls." This attitude toward words and the form of his poems he never renounced, but continued to regard his poems as mere hints and "indirections," and, as Hermann Bahr says, to present and arrange the materials of poems instead of finished products.[110] In 1855 he liked to think of the poet (or himself as a poet) as a "kosmos,"[111] or a kind of microcosm symbolizing the macrocosm. But it is just as accurate to say that he thought of a poem itself as a mirror-like monad (to use Leibniz's term) which reflected in itself the form, structure, and spiritual laws of the universe.

In a manuscript dating from around 1850 Holloway has discovered[112] a great deal about the nature of Whitman's inspiration and the manner in which he composed his poetry. The poem, only a fragment of which was included in LEAVES OF GRASS, was called "Pictures." Bucke printed four lines in *Notes and Fragments:*

O Walt Whitman, show us some pictures;
America always Pictorial! And you Walt Whitman to name them
Yes, in a little house I keep suspended many pictures—it is not a fixed house.
It is round—Behold! it has room for America, north and south, seaboard and inland, persons . . .[113]

This crude picture-gallery allegory was not published as

[110] See note 1, above.

[111] See Inclusive Edition, *op. cit.,* 497; also *Song of Myself,* sec. 12.

[112] First published in "Whitman's Embryonic Verse," *Southwest Review,* X, 28-40 (July, 1925), later in *Pictures: An Unpublished Poem by Walt Whitman,* Introduction and Notes by Emory Holloway (London: Faber and Gwyer, 1927).

[113] Richard Maurice Bucke, *Notes and Fragments* (London, Ontario, printed for the editor, 1899), 27.

a single poem because the various images and catalogs
which it contained were expanded into a number of
separate poems—in fact, might be thought of as the
genesis of the first editions of LEAVES OF GRASS. In an
outline for the original "Pictures," we glimpse the poet's
method:

> Poem of pictures. Each verse presenting a picture of
> some characteristic scene, event, group or personage—
> old or new, other countries or our own country. Picture
> of one of the Greek games—wrestling, or the chariot
> race, or running. Spanish bull fight.[114]

Of the finished "Pictures" Holloway says:

> Each is a microcosm of the whole "Leaves of Grass,"
> which the author looked upon less as a book than as a
> picture of himself in all his cosmopolitan diversity.
> And the more we learn of the facts of Whitman's com-
> prehensive life, whether experience, reading, or medi-
> tation, the more we realize that before each thumb-nail
> picture was set down on paper it had really been hung,
> as a personal possession, on the walls of his "Picture-
> Gallery."[115]

Thus in his desire to explore life, personality, and the
inner meaning of Being, Whitman turned to Emerson's
theory of symbols for guidance in the development of a
literary technique. By imaginative identification of his
own ego with the creative processes of nature, and by the
vicarious exploration of all forms of existence, he evolved
the technique of panoramic imagery, "organically" echoing a subjective harmony and rhythm of his own "Soul,"

---

[114] *Ibid.*, 177.
[115] Holloway, *Pictures, op. cit.*, 10-11.

and revealing by "hints" and "indirections" the spiritual truths of the universe. Both in form and content LEAVES OF GRASS is primarily cosmic, pantheistic, and democratic, and Walt Whitman's literary technique is admirably adapted for his "purports and facts and is the analogy of them."

SELECTED BIBLIOGRAPHY

[See also bibliographies for texts (Chap. II) and ideas (Chap. III). Most biographers (Chap. I) also have something to say about Whitman's literary techniques.]

AUTHORITIES FOR BACKGROUND OF WHITMAN'S STYLE

COOK, A. S. "The 'Authorized Version' and Its Influence." *Cambridge History of English Literature,* IV, 29-58. New York and London: G. P. Putnam's Sons. 1910.

DAHLSTRÖM, C. E. W. L. [Definition and history of "Expressionism."] *Strindberg's Dramatic Expressionism,* pp. 3-82. Ann Arbor: University of Michigan. 1930.

DRIVER, S. R. *Introduction to the Literature of the Old Testament.* New York: Scribner's Sons. 1910.
[Parallelism or "thought-rhythm" in Biblical poetry.]

GARDINER, J. H. *The Bible as English Literature.* New York: Scribner's Sons. 1906.
[Parallelism in Biblical poetry.]

KAUTZSCH, EMIL FRIEDRICH. *Die Poesie und die Poetischen Bücher des Alten Testaments.* Tübingen: J. C. B. Mohr, 1902. [Based on Bishop Lowth's discovery of parallelism as the metrical principle of Biblical verse—*De sacra poesi Hebraeorum praelectiones academiae oxonii habitae,* 1753.]

MOULTON, R.G. *The Literary Study of the Bible.* Boston: D. C. Heath and Co. 1895.

[Parallelism. Moulton's *Modern Reader's Bible* (New York: Macmillan, 1922) arranges the Biblical poetry in accordance with the principles of "thought-rhythm."]

SMITH, C. ALPHONSO. *Repetition and Parallelism in English Verse.* New York: University Publishing Co. 1894.
[Shows use of repetition and parallelism in conventional verse—does not mention Whitman.]

SUTCLIFFE, EMERSON GRANT. "Emerson's Theories of Literary Expression." *University of Illinois Studies in Language and Literature,* VIII, 9-143 (1923).
[Provides background for a study of the influence of Transcendentalism on Whitman's theories and practices.]

TEXTS OF SPECIAL IMPORTANCE

An American Primer. Edited by Horace Traubel. Boston: Small, Maynard and Co. 1904.
[Printed from unpublished MSS which the poet wrote in preparation for a lecture and treatise on "words" and linguistic theory. A significant document.]

Notes and Fragments. Edited by Richard Maurice Bucke. London, Ontario: printed for the editor. 1899.
[Collection of unpublished MSS, many of which reveal Whitman's stylistic intentions and preliminary experiments.]

Pictures. Edited by Emory Holloway, from unpublished manuscript. London: Faber and Gwyer. 1927.
[Poem shows Whitman's style in its embryonic growth. Editor's critical introduction stresses the symbolical importance of the image in the poet's style. Important.]

Prefaces—reprinted in the Inclusive Edition of *Leaves of Grass,* edited by Emory Holloway, pp. 488-538. Garden City: Doubleday, Doran and Co. 1929.

CRITICAL INTERPRETATION

ALLEN, GAY WILSON. "Biblical Analogies for Walt Whitman's Prosody." *Revue Anglo-Américaine*, X, 490-507 (August, 1933).

[First detailed study of subject.]

——. "Walt Whitman." *American Prosody*, pp. 217-242. New York: American Book Co. 1935.

[Presents "parallelism" as Whitman's main prosodic technique—an interpretation modified by Bradley (see below).]

BAHR, HERMANN. Introduction to Max Hayek's translation, *Ich Singe Das Leben*. Leipzig, Wien, Zürich: E. P. Tall and Co. 1921.

[Point of view indicated by quotation in note 1, at beginning of this chapter.]

BRADLEY, SCULLEY. "The Fundamental Metrical Principle in Whitman's poetry." *American Literature*, X, 437-459 (January, 1939).

[Argues that Whitman's "organic rhythms" are fundamentally metrical. Interesting and important.]

CATEL, JEAN. *Rhythme et langage dans la 1er édition des "Leaves of Grass," 1855.* Paris: Les Editions Rieder. [1930].

[Regards oratory as greatest influence on formation of Whitman's poetic style.]

COX, REBECCA. "A Study of Whitman's Diction." *University of Texas Studies in English*, XVI, 115-124 (July, 1936).

DE SELINCOURT, BASIL. *Walt Whitman: A Critical Study.* London: Martin Secker. 1914. P. 73 ff.

[Inclined to idealize Whitman's "organic" style, but especially useful for the stress on analogies with music.]

ERSKINE, JOHN. "A Note on Whitman's Prosody." *Studies in Philology*, XX, 336-344 (July, 1923).

[Shows importance of Whitman's line as verse-unit.]

FURNESS, CLIFTON JOSEPH. *Walt Whitman's Workshop.* Cambridge, Mass.: Harvard University Press. 1928.

[Many acute critical interpretations of style in the lengthy editorial notes.]

JANNACCONE, P. *La Poesia di Walt Whitman e L'Evoluzione delle Forme Ritmiche.* Torino. 1898.

[Demonstrates Whitman's use of primitive techniques. Calls his reiterations "psychic rime."]

KENNEDY, W. S. "The Style of Leaves of Grass." *Reminiscences of Walt Whitman,* pp. 149-190. London: Alexander Gardner. 1896.

[Sympathetic interpretation of the "organic principle" in Whitman's style is of special historical value: for date and point of view of an intimate friend of the poet.]

MATTHIESSEN, F. O. "Only a Language Experiment." *American Renaissance,* pp. 517-625. New York: Oxford University Press. 1941.

[Interprets the style of *Leaves of Grass* as above all else a major experiment in the use of language.]

MORE, PAUL ELMER. "Walt Whitman." *Shelburne Essays,* 4th ed., new ser., pp. 180-211. Boston: Houghton Mifflin. 1922.

POUND, LOUISE. "Walt Whitman and the French Language." *American Speech,* I, 421-430 (May, 1926).

[Whitman's use and knowledge of French words.]

―――. "Walt Whitman and Italian Music." *American Mercury,* VI, 58-63 (September, 1925).

[Influence of Italian opera on Whitman's style.]

―――. "Walt Whitman's Neologisms." *American Mercury,* IV, 199-201 (February, 1925).

[Examples and analysis of the poet's coinages.]

REED, HARRY B. "The Heraclitan Obsession of Walt Whitman." *The Personalist,* XV, 125-138 (April, 1934).

[On the flux and endless progression in Whitman's style.]

Ross, E. C. "Whitman's Verse." *Modern Language Notes,* XLV, 363-364 (June, 1930).
[Points out the importance of Whitman's punctuation—end-stopped lines.]

SCHUMANN, DETLEV W. "Enumerative Style and Its Significance in Whitman, Rilke, Werfel." *Modern Language Quarterly,* III, 171-204 (June, 1942).
[". . . three characteristically different variations of a mysticism whose central article of faith is the oneness of existence."]

SCOTT, FRED NEWTON. "A Note on Whitman's Prosody." *Journal of English and Germanic Philology,* VII, 134-153 (1908).

SWAYNE, MATTIE. "Whitman's Catalog Rhetoric." *University of Texas Studies in English,* No. 412, pp. 162-178 (July, 1941).

WARE, LOIS. "Poetic Conventions in Leaves of Grass." *Studies in Philology,* XXVI, 47-57 (January, 1929).
[Rime, stanza, alliteration, and other conventions.]

WEEKS, RUTH M. "Phrasal Prosody" [with special reference to Whitman]. *English Journal,* X, 11-19 (January, 1921).

WILEY, AUTREY NELL. "Reiterative Devices in 'Leaves of Grass'." *American Literature,* I, 161-170 (May, 1929).
[Rhetorical devices of epanaphora and epanalepsis in Whitman's poetic style.]

CHAPTER VI

WALT WHITMAN AND WORLD LITERATURE

*My spirit has pass'd in compassion and determination
around the whole earth,
I have look'd for equals and lovers and found them
ready for me in all lands . . .*[1]

WHITMAN AS WORLD POET[2]

In the United States Walt Whitman is commonly regarded as the most nationalistic poet of American Democracy because in his first edition (1855) he announced
a nationalistic program: "The United States themselves
are essentially the greatest poem...Of them a bard is
to be commensurate with a people...His spirit responds
to his country's spirit . . . he incarnates its geography and
natural life and rivers and lakes."[3] Whitman's emphasis
on these ambitions has resulted in the failure of many
readers, from 1855 to the present day, to observe that he
also declares in this same Preface that, "American poets
are to enclose old and new." In fact, he begins the mani-
festo by acknowledging that, "America does not repel
the past or what it has produced" but "accepts the lesson

---

[1] *Salut au Monde!,* sec. 13.

[2] John Burroughs declared with accurate prophecy in his *Whitman:
A Study* (Boston: Houghton Mifflin and Co., 1896), 19-20, that "the next
age and the next will make more of Whitman, and the next still more,
because he is in the great world-current..."

[3] *Leaves of Grass,* Inclusive Edition edited by Emory Holloway (Garden
City, N. Y.: Doubleday, Doran and Co., 1929), 489-490 (in the 1855
Preface). In quotations from Whitman's works, editorial omissions are
indicated by unspaced periods (...).

with calmness." Even in this stage of patriotism he is not unaware of Europe and the past as the cultural progenitors of the new nation and the young dream of future greatness. His nationalism rests on the conviction that the creative impulse, in poetry as well as politics, has been handed down to his own time and country: "the life which served its requirements has passed into the new life of the new forms...its action has descended to the stalwart and wellshaped heir who approaches . . . and... he shall be fittest for his days."[4] Here in this consciousness of an inheritance from the past was the germ of an internationalism to match the cosmic themes of his first great lyric poems.

After the financial disappointment of the first three editions of LEAVES OF GRASS, this germ of internationalism was psychologically stimulated until in 1868 Whitman's poetic program embraced the whole earth:

> All these separations and gaps shall be taken up and
>   hook'd and link'd together,
> The whole earth, this cold, impassive, voiceless earth,
>   shall be completely justified, . . .
> Nature and Man shall be disjoin'd and diffused no
>   more,
> The true son of God [the poet] shall absolutely fuse
>   them.[5]

After his poems had won recognition in Europe, and were being translated into foreign tongues, Whitman became convinced that he was the poet of mankind. In a letter to T. W. Rolleston, his German translator, he wrote:

---

[4] *Ibid.*, 489.   [5] *Passage to India*, sec. 5.

...I had more than my own native land in view when I was composing Leaves of Grass. I wished to take the first step toward calling into existence a cycle of international poems. The chief reason for being of the United States of America is to bring about the common goodwill of all mankind, the solidarity of the world.[6]

Probably neglect by his country did increase Whitman's pleasure in his fame abroad, but that this latent internationalism actually was inherent in his thought and literary ambitions from the beginning is obvious to anyone who will examine the unpublished experiments preserved in *Notes and Fragments,* in which the young poet recorded his desire to write "A volume...running in idea and description through the whole range of recorded time...,"[7] and an experimental poem was called "The march of the human race across the earth."[8] The frequent references in the manuscripts to "those stages all over the world...leaving their memories and inheritances in all the continents," and the reverence with which the poet stands "before the movements of the great soul of man"[9] leave no doubt that Walt Whitman's special theme is to be the journey of the human spirit through all lands and all ages.[10]

With this background in mind, the reader will discover that the central theme of *Song of Myself,* and the basic

---

[6] Quoted by W. S. Kennedy, *The Fight of a Book for the World* (West Yarmouth, Mass.: Stonecroft Press, 1926), 249-250.

[7] *Notes and Fragments,* edited by Dr. R. M. Bucke (London, Ontario: privately printed, 1899), 124.

[8] *Ibid.,* 13, note. Cf. also pp. 10, 21, 140-144, 175, *et passim.*

[9] *Ibid.,* 140-141.

[10] For further discussion of this point see Gay Wilson Allen, "Walt Whitman's 'Long Journey' Motif," *Journal of English and Germanic Philology,* XXXVIII, 76-77 (January, 1939).

motif of LEAVES OF GRASS as a whole, is cosmic and human development. The poet, using the now-famous "generic I", calls himself and his nation "an acme of things accomplish'd," but this life, "what has come to the surface after so many throes and convulsions,"[11] is no culmination, no resting-place. Even the American "pioneers" are but a link in the chain, who "take up the task eternal, and the burden and the lesson."[12]

Not only was Whitman consistent with his own doctrines when he sang in *Starting from Paumanok,*

> Strains musical flowing through ages, now reaching hither,
> I take to your reckless and composite chords, add to them, and cheerfully pass them forward,[13]

but he was actually proclaiming an historical truth of which he himself may have been only dimly aware. For in his literary theory, his poetic technique, even in many of his personal mannerisms, he reveals himself to the student of comparative literature not as the unique original which he and most of his biographers thought him to be, but as an apostle of a literary movement which linked the continents, like the cable which he celebrated in *Passage to India.* To recognize this fact is not to minimize his genius but to understand it and to explain in part why he has been a more powerful inspiration to European than to American poets.

The history of this literary movement, which for lack of a better name we may call "Whitmanism", has never

---

[11] *Starting from Paumanok,* sec. 2.
[12] *Pioneers! O Pioneers!*
[13] Sec. 10.

been traced in detail, and Schyberg[14] in Denmark is the only scholar who has called special attention to it, though numerous comparative studies have vaguely indicated the outlines. It is a phenomenon inside the general Romantic Movement, from which come such ideas as the pantheism of Spinoza; the cosmic evolution of Leibniz, Kant, and Hegel; the "organic theory" of German Romanticism; the "primitivism" of Rousseau; the egoism of Fichte, etc.—in fact, all the "fundamental ideas" which have been presented in Chapter III.

These "ideas", however, are also found in Goethe, Shelley, Hugo, and the whole romantic school. They are of the utmost importance as the background or matrix of Whitman's theory and expression, but they are communal characteristics of the school. Likewise all the romantics are revolutionary in both style and thought and are inclined to be mystical. But what especially distinguishes Whitmanism is the international-nationalism mentioned above and the preaching of an "ethical democracy." The utterance of these doctrines seems even to result in similar prophetic poses, attempts to formulate a new religion, worshipping the simple and the common, and a rhapsodic style which invariably annoys the critics of the day. "Bibles" of Democracy and Humanity are common among these Whitmanesque poets and writers.

Perhaps the most important aspect of this movement is that it is not a question of literary sources and influences so much as common origins and similar ambitions. Often the poets who most resemble each other did not

---

[14] Frederik Schyberg, "Whitman i Verdenslitteraturen," *Walt Whitman* (København: Gyldendalske Boghandel, 1933), 273-338.

know of each other's existence—further evidence of the international scope of the movement. Contrary to the belief of Whitman's early friends and critics that he had no literary sources whatever, we now know beyond any doubt that he borrowed and adapted from many books. And on the other hand, many poets in foreign lands have acknowledged their indebtedness to him. But even Whitman's astonishing influence abroad is at least partly due to the fact that he lived and moved in a cultural and literary stream whose sources and confluences were intercontinental. At times he was prophetically aware of this fact, too, for in 1888, in handing over some letters and documents to Traubel, he remarked: "they are not records of my life—of my personal life—of Walt Whitman—but scripture material applying to a movement in which I am only an episode."[15]

Thus Walt Whitman's relations to World Literature are of three kinds, often difficult if not impossible to separate: (1) foreign sources for his own ideas and inspiration, (2) parallels revealing literary movements which influenced him indirectly, or in which he was "only an episode," and (3) direct influences of the American poet on major writers of nearly every civilized country. Subsequent history has completely verified the accuracy of John Burroughs's belief that Walt Whitman was "in the great world-current."

WHITMAN AND AMERICAN TRANSCENDENTALISM

One reason both for the many striking parallels to Whitman's thought and expression in World Literature

---

[15] *With Walt Whitman in Camden*, edited by Horace Traubel (New York: Mitchell Kennerly, 1914), III, 425.

and for his dynamic influence on later writers is that his own major literary sources were international in origin. The first and most important of these was ostensibly American, being the "transcendentalism" of Emerson, Thoreau, Alcott, Margaret Fuller, Channing, Hedge, etc., that group of congenial minds which came together informally in the 1830's and 40's and generated not a school but a fermentation of ideas and attitudes which became the major stimulation of literary activity in the United States during the "American Renaissance."[16] This group followed no single master, creed, or even philosophy, but all members were profoundly interested in speculative thinking and in the great minds of the past. Most of them read and translated writings from Plato to Goethe and George Sand. They were especially interested in German Idealism, which came to them directly from the study and discussion of the Kantian school and indirectly through Coleridge and Carlyle, who were also reading and interpreting the poetry and philosophy of the German Romantic School.

To complete the international cycle, the Germans were, in turn, influenced by the mysticism both of Neo-Platonism and of the Orient. In fact, many of the leaders of the Romantic School in Germany, like the Schlegels, were philologists and Orientalists. The American Transcendentalists, however, became sufficiently interested in the literature and religion of Asia, especially of the Hindus, to make some explorations of their own. Sanskrit was taught at Harvard, and India was frequently discussed in newspapers and popular magazines—to judge by the large

---

[16] The phrase is used by F. O. Matthiessen in one of the best interpretations of the period, *The American Renaissance:* Art and Expression in the Age of Emerson and Whitman (New York: Oxford, 1941).

number of clippings which Whitman amassed in his own scrap-books.[17] American Transcendentalism was not a creed, a "school", or a systematic philosophy, but its basic assumptions came simultaneously from East and West, modified, of course, by American experience and Yankee character.[18]

One of the first Transcendentalist assumptions was the Rousseauistic belief in the innate goodness of human nature. The Emersonian absolute moral and intellectual self-reliance might also be regarded as the ultimate in Protestantism, the last phase of the Reformation, and a reaction against Calvinism. The greatest single philosophical influence on this group of American thinkers was probably the "transcendentalism" of Immanuel Kant, or at least the interpretations which they (partly following Coleridge and Carlyle) made of the *Critique of Pure Reason* (1781). In this work Kant, attempting to establish the limits of human reason, concluded that the finite mind could deal reliably only with phenomena. He did not deny the reality or existence of *something* behind appearances or phenomena, but insisted that it was unknowable. Kant admitted, however, the human need for belief in such ultra-rational ideas as God, Immortality, Freedom, etc., and the result was that, especially in Great Britain and the United States, speculative minds were stimulated to explore the realm of the unknowable, the hypothetical "world-beyond-phenomena." W. F. Taylor has summarized the result in this manner:

---

[17] See *Notes and Fragments, op. cit.,* Part IV, 193-554—especially items No. 210-236, 332-339, and 395.

[18] This is essentially Arthur Christy's attitude toward the Orientalism of Emerson and Thoreau in *The Orient in American Transcendentalism* (New York: Columbia University Press, 1932).

The transcendentalists, then, were mystics. They hoped to "transcend" the realm of phenomena, and receive their inspirations toward truth at first hand from the Deity, unsullied by any contact with matter. Spiritual verities alone were of great importance to the transcendentalists; and, like the "divine and supernatural light" of Jonathan Edwards, these were immediately imparted to the soul from God. Yet God, the Over-Soul, was revealed also in nature, which was a beautiful web of appearances veiling the spirituality of the universe, a living garment, half concealing, half revealing, the Deity within.[19]

Some of the close parallels between Whitman's thought and the ideas of the Transcendentalists may be due to the fact that he also wrote as a mystic; but it would have been impossible for him to escape some direct influence from such members of the group as Channing, Hedge, Parker, Margaret Fuller, Thoreau, and Emerson, who wrote for the very magazines and newspapers which Whitman read and to which he also contributed during the 1840's. In fact, nearly all scholars now agree that Emerson himself was the one single greatest influence on Whitman during the years when he was planning and writing the first two or three editions of LEAVES OF GRASS. Arvin was probably right when he declared that Emerson was for Whitman what Epicurus was for Lucretius or Spinoza for Goethe.[20] Another critic, who made a special investigation of the relationship, decided that, "Whitman was more indebted to Emerson than to any other for fundamental

---

[19] Walter F. Taylor, *A History of American Letters* (New York: American Book Co., 1936), 145-146.

[20] Newton Arvin, *Whitman* (New York: Macmillan and Co., 1938), 190.

ideas in even his earliest LEAVES OF GRASS."[21] Despite the fact that "on certain occasions [he] endeavored to minimize his debt to Emerson . . . Whitman ultimately arrived at an open, almost undeviating, allegiance both to Emerson as a person and to Emersonian ideas in general."[22]

A later critic, however, has pointed out what he regards as a significant difference between the thought of Emerson and Whitman. This difference, as presented by Leon Howard,[23] is parallel to the contrast which we have already mentioned between true Kantian transcendentalism and Coleridge and Carlyle's interpretation of Kant. It is the old question of the *reality* of phenomena, "appearances," matter, etc. Howard regards transcendentalism as monist, the true *reality* being spirit or Soul: "Running through Whitman's poetry is the constantly iterated idea of equalitarianism, one aspect of which is the avowal of equality between body and soul."[24] From this point of view the famous argument which Emerson gave Whitman on the Boston Commons against the inclusion of the sex poems in the third edition was a struggle "between militant materialism combined with idealism and idealism in its transcendental purity."[25] However, it is still a moot question whether Emerson was a monist, a pure idealist, or a dualist. The humanistic critics argue that Emerson placed neither mind nor matter over the other. This argu-

---

[21] John B. Moore, "The Master of Whitman," *Studies in Philology,* XXIII, 77 (January, 1926). See also Clarence Gohdes, "Whitman and Emerson," *Sewanee Review,* XXXVII, 79-93 (January, 1929).

[22] Moore, *op. cit.,* 77.

[23] Leon Howard, "For a Critique of Whitman's Transcendentalism," *Modern Language Notes,* XLVII, 79-85 (February, 1932).

[24] *Ibid.,* 83.

[25] *Ibid.,* 85.

ment merely indicates the close parallels between Emerson and Whitman's mystical pantheism. As F. I. Carpenter says, Emerson always "expressed his mystical belief in 'the eternal ONE.' By religion, rather than by philosophy, he was a monist, as 'The Over-Soul' and 'Brahma' bear witness."[26]

We see these tendencies further in two more of Emerson's theories which are also parallel to Whitman's ideas. One is the Plotinian theory of *emanation,* and the other is cosmic evolution:

Emanation may be described as an idealistic monism; evolution as a materialistic monism. The first readily adapted itself to the theory (then merely a suggestion, but now well established), of the identity of energy and matter—energy continually "emanating" from God, and condensing itself, as it were, in the forms of the material world. The second, describing the gradual evolution of life from inanimate to animate matter, and from lower to higher forms until it issues at last in the intelligence of man, also seemed to furnish such a satisfactory monistic theory, and recommended itself especially to Emerson as confirming his idea of progress, or melioration.[27]

Perhaps all that we can say, finally, is that Whitman emphasized the physical with more gusto and lack of restraint than Emerson. Since neither developed his theories with clear logic or explicit definition, it is almost impossible to settle the argument of the monism or dualism of either Emerson or Whitman; but this very confusion is symptomatic of a common philosophical foundation.

[26] F. I. Carpenter, *Emerson: Representative Selections* (New York: American Book Co., 1934), xxxiii.
[27] *Ibid.,* xxxiii.

Whitman, Carlyle, and German Idealism

In the case of Carlyle, however, it is easier to differentiate. Whitman's interest in Carlyle was perhaps second only to his interest in Emerson, but he usually found himself combatting Carlyle's ideas, though he finally came around to a grudging admiration of the dour Scotchman who was so critical of American democracy. In fact, almost all Whitman knew about German philosophy he got either from American popularizations or from Carlyle. Thus Carlyle was one of Whitman's main sources. But the following differences should be clearly borne in mind: (1) For Whitman *things* are real (even though they may be symbolized by pantheistic metaphors); for Carlyle nature is illusory and dream-like. (2) To Whitman, the poet of democracy, every man is a hero; whereas to Carlyle the average are merely "hodmen", whom the "heroes" have the divine right to rule. (3) Though Whitman believes that all symbols are in a sense religious, he does not, like Carlyle, think that the highest symbol is the Church. (4) There is in Whitman, unlike Carlyle, no renunciation, no hatred of evil, no need for expiation for sins.[28]

Yet despite these contrasts, Whitman undoubtedly owed a great debt to Carlyle—especially, as remarked above, for arousing his curiosity in German philosophy. It is difficult to assess this debt, for Carlyle was only one of Whitman's sources of information about German Idealism, others being Gostwick's popular handbook on *German Literature,* Hedge's *Prose Writers of Germany,*

---

[28] For a good summary of Carlyle's ideas see Charles Frederick Harrold, *Carlyle and German Thought* (New Haven: Yale University Press, 1934), especially Chap. IV: "Carlyle's Universe."

and of course to some extent Emerson himself. But Whitman's manuscript notes on Kant, Fichte, Schlegel, Hegel, etc. show considerable knowledge of Carlyle's discussion of these men.[29]

John Burroughs declared (undoubtedly with Whitman's approval) that LEAVES OF GRASS "tallies . . . the development of the Great System of Idealistic Philosophy in Germany,"[30] and in 1884 Whitman called himself "the greatest *poetical* representative of German philosophy."[31] Although these pretentious claims may amuse the scholars, there is no reason to doubt the poet's sincerity, and there is even considerable truth in the claim. Arvin remarks that,

> At some indeterminate period—though the chances are that it was after two editions of *Leaves of Grass* had appeared and perhaps mainly during the sixties—Whitman began looking more closely and more curiously into the significance of certain stupendous names that had recurred invitingly in so much that he had heard and read, in Coleridge, in Carlyle, in Emerson too; and these were the names of the great German metaphysicians of idealism, Leibniz, Kant, Fichte, Schelling, Hegel . . .[32]

Probably he actually read little of the "Critiques", "Systems", and "Encyclopaedias"; however, though Whitman "was certainly neither a professional nor a formal thinker,

---

[29] See *Notes and Fragments, op. cit.,* 132-141. In his notes on Goethe and Schiller (*Ibid.,* 105-106) Whitman mentions Carlyle several times, as if he were taking notes from Carlyle's books.

[30] R. M. Bucke, *Walt Whitman* (Philadelphia: David McKay, 1883), 211—Bucke attributes the quotation to Burroughs.

[31] Clifton Joseph Furness, *Walt Whitman's Workshop* (Cambridge: Harvard University Press, 1928), 236, note 138.

[32] Arvin, *op. cit.,* 191.

[he] was responsive enough to these activities of the ideologues to go into the subject at his own leisure and in his own way."[33]

What the poet got primarily from Leibniz, Kant, and Hegel seems to have been, in his own words, "the religious tone,...the recognition of the future, of the unknown, of Deity over and under all, and of the divine purpose, [which] are never absent, but indirectly give tone to all."[34] Though this "tone" may be vague, it is important because it indicates not only Whitman's assumptions and attitudes but also the scope and application of his ideas. However general his borrowings, the German names and theories gave him confidence in the ideas which he had already adapted for his "message." As Riethmuller puts it, "His comprehensive mind affectionately absorbed the great literary ideas of the Germanic countries and rejected or moulded them to fit his compass of a national American literature."[35] The route by which Whitman derived these ideas cannot be clearly traced, and is perhaps best indicated by the figurative language of Woodbridge Riley: "The migrations of the Germanic mysticism form a strange story. It began with what has been called the pantheism of the Rhine region; it ended, if it has ever ended, with the poetic pantheism of Walt Whitman, for in this modern American may be found traces of a remote past, and echoes of a distant land."[36]

As for specific authors, Hegel has often been cited as both source and parallel for Whitman's ideas. Boatright

---

[33] *Ibid.*

[34] *Prose Works,* (Philadelphia: David McKay, [1892]), 250, note.

[35] Richard Riethmuller, "Walt Whitman and the Germans," *German American Annals,* New Ser., IV (1906), 126.

[36] Woodbridge Riley, *The Meaning of Mysticism* (New York: Richard R. Smith, 1930), 64.

made the first extensive investigation of the subject, and
he came to the conclusion that Hegel at least "strengthened Whitman's convictions"[37]—especially in his cosmic
evolution, his pantheistic "unity," and his synthesis of
Good in which the antithesis, Evil, merges and disappears.
But he thought that the poet's knowledge of Hegelianism
came more from Gostwick than Hegel's own writings, a
deduction which Fulghum has since then amplified and
further demonstrated.[38] Falk has also studied the relationship and decided that:

> In the case of Hegel, Whitman certainly buttressed, and
> possibly largely derived, his evolutionary conception of
> a universe, exhibiting conflict and struggle, yet tending
> toward a vague divine culmination in the return of the
> individual souls to the Absolute. But most of all, he
> saw in the Hegelian metaphysic a logical rationalization
> of the New World Democracy which he aimed to
> glorify.[39]

The latest investigator of this subject, however, Miss
Parsons, believes that "many of the likenesses [between
Whitman and Hegel] cited from time to time are misleading, if not fallacious, or are too general to be of significance."[40] Her argument is based mainly on Whitman's
failure, or perhaps inability, to understand the Hegelian
dialectic. In this contention she is probably quite correct,

---

[37] Mody C. Boatright, "Whitman and Hegel," *Studies in English*, No.
9, University of Texas Bulletin, July 8, 1929, p. 150.

[38] W. B. Fulghum, Jr., Whitman's Debt to Joseph Gostwick," *American Literature*, XII, 491-496 (January, 1941).

[39] Robert P. Falk, "Walt Whitman and German Thought," *Journal of
English and Germanic Philology*, XL, 329 (July, 1941).

[40] Olive Wrenchel Parsons, "Whitman the Non-Hegelian," *Publications of the Modern Language Association*, LVIII, 1073 (December,
1943).

but this admission does not contradict the popularized
Hegelianism which the American poet derived indirectly,
through Gostwick and others. At any rate, Whitman's
relations to Hegel seem closer than those with other philosophers of the Rhineland. Falk says,

> In the case of the other German metaphysicians, we
> can ascribe no certain influence; yet, it is true that Whit-
> man reveals parallels in thought and even phrase with
> most of the transcendental philosophers from Kant on
> down. In all of them Whitman sees lessons for Ameri-
> can Democracy.[41]

There we have the significant relationship: we cannot be
sure what part German Idealism played in the origin of
Whitman's ideas (though he could have read Gostwick
in 1854, and Carlyle earlier), but he found there con-
firmations of his own metaphysics—and "lessons for
American Democracy."

WHITMAN AND INDIA

Whitman's indebtedness to Oriental literature and
mysticism is even more difficult to trace than his relations
to German philosophy, and yet almost from the first edition students of Oriental thought have recognized in
LEAVES OF GRASS such striking parallels to the *Bhagavad
Gita* and other Hindu poems that they have speculated on
Whitman's use of translations as primary sources for his
poems. In 1856 Thoreau, an amateur but ardent Oriental-
ist, called LEAVES OF GRASS "Wonderfully like the
Orientals . . . considering that when I asked [Whitman]
if he had read them, he answered, 'No: Tell me about

---

[41] Falk, *op. cit.,* 330.

them.' "[42] Later, on numerous occasions, Whitman evinced some knowledge of Hindu and other Oriental translations. In *A Backward Glance*, for example, he claims to have read "the ancient Hindoo poems"[43] in preparation for LEAVES OF GRASS—*i.e.*, apparently before publishing the first edition. Whether in his reply to Thoreau's question he was trying to conceal this source, or whether Thoreau's question directed his attention to this field and stimulated his curiosity to explore it, we can at present only guess. But as with the German influence, this Orientalism was very much in the American intellectual atmosphere of the 1840's and 50's,[44] and it would have been impossible for Whitman to escape at least some indirect influence. Indeed, American Transcendentalism, as we have seen, got it from two directions: German Idealism and Romanticism were strongly indebted to Oriental mysticism,[45] and American Transcendentalism might be called the offspring of a German father and a Hindu mother.

In 1866 Viscount Strangford, an Oriental scholar, observed the similarity of Whitman's rhythms to those of

---

[42] Henry Thoreau, *Familiar Letters* (Boston: Houghton Mifflin Co., 1894), 347. Quoted by Bliss Perry, *Walt Whitman* (Boston: Houghton Mifflin and Co., 1906), 121-122.

[43] Preface to *November Boughs*, 1888, reprinted in Holloway's Inclusive Edition, *op. cit.*, 530.

[44] Cf. Christy, *op. cit.*, and F. I. Carpenter, *Emerson and Asia* (Cambridge: Harvard University Press, 1930). See also O. B. Frothingham, *Transcendentalism in New England* (New York: Putnam's Sons, 1876), Chaps. I-III; and H. C. Goddard, *Studies in New England Transcendentalism*, (New York: Columbia University Press, 1908).

[45] Cf. Friederich von Schlegel, "The Indian Language, Literature, and Philosophy," reprinted in *Aesthetic and Miscellaneous Works* (London: George Bell and Sons, 1900), 425-526. Edwyn C. Vaughn says, in *The Romantic Revolt* (New York: Scribner's, 1907), that this work "forms nothing short of an epoch in the history of European learning, and even of letters and philosophy." See also Arthur F. J. Remy, *The Influence of India and Persia in the Poetry of Germany* (New York: Columbia University Press, 1910).

Persian poets,[46] and in the same year Moncure D. Conway found Asia the key to both Whitman and the Transcendentalists.[47] In 1889 Gabriel Sarrazin declared that "Walt Whitman in his confident and lofty piety, is the direct inheritor of the great Oriental mystics, Brahma, Proclus, Abou Saïd."[48] In 1906 Edward Carpenter cited interesting parallels (which he did not claim as sources) between the Upanishads and LEAVES OF GRASS.[49] But the only extensive investigation that has so far been completed is an unpublished dissertation by Dorothy Frederica Mercer, of the University of California, *Leaves of Grass and the Bhagavad Gita: A Comparative Study* (1933).[50] Dr. Mercer does not claim definitely that the *Bhagavad Gita* was one of Whitman's actual sources—though she suggests that it may have been—, but she quotes an Indian scholar who does believe that the poet "must have studied *The Bhagavad Gita,* for in his *Leaves of Grass* one finds the teachings of Vedanta; the Song of Myself is but an echo of the sayings of Krishna."[51]

It is probably impossible in brief space even to define the Vedantic terms, let alone illustrate and compare the religious and philosophical concepts with Whitman's ideas; but perhaps it will be sufficient to mention the ideas which

---

[46] Lord Strangford, "Walt Whitman," *The Pall Mall Gazette,* February 16, 1866. See note 103 below.

[47] Moncure D. Conway, "Walt Whitman," *The Fortnightly Review,* VI, 538-548 (October 15, 1866).

[48] Gabriel Sarrazin, "Walt Whitman," translated by Harrison B. Morris from *La Renaissance de la Poèsie Anglaise, 1798-1889, In Re Walt Whitman* (Philadelphia: David McKay, 1893), 161.

[49] Edward Carpenter, *Days with Walt Whitman* (London: George Allen, 1906), 94-102.

[50] The author is indebted to the University of California Library for the privilege of reading Dr. Mercer's valuable work, and to Dr. Mercer herself for kind permission to quote from her thesis.

[51] Mercer, *op. cit.,* 25.

can be most closely paralleled in Hindu literature and to quote some generalizations from Dr. Mercer, who is at present the only authority on the subject.

The first striking parallel between Whitman's ideas and the Vedantic teaching is the doctrine of the *self*. "Whitman's soul, like the self of the *Bhagavad Gita*, is the unifying energy."[52] This self is not material, but spiritual; "it is a passive spectator; it is Brahma incarnate in the body; and it is permanent, indestructible, eternal, all-pervading, unmanifest." In the same way Whitman's "Me, Myself" is immortal, and through his cosmic "I" he merges with all creation, feeling himself to be the spirit of the universe. Out of this conception of the relation of the self to the cosmos arises the doctrine that good and evil are mere appearances (*maya*). Like all mysticisms, the Vedanta teaches that Love unifies all existence and that knowledge is obtained not through reason but in-tuition.

There are two Brahmans, the Higher Brahman and the Lower Brahman. The former is absolute identity with the "Over-Soul" and is unspeakable, indescribable—"any attempt to describe it indicates that one has not realized it."[53] Dr. Mercer finds little or none of the Higher Brahman in LEAVES OF GRASS; it is the Lower which is sig-nificant for the interpretation of Whitman's mysticism. "The Lower Brahman is the great *mayin,* who, for sport, creates spontaneously this 'seeming' world out of Itself ... Through all the *kalpos,* or cycles of worlds, Brahman remembers the word, and creates anew in accordance with Its eternally existent memory."[54] The potential God-

---

[52] *Ibid.,* 110.   [54] *Ibid.,* 93.
[53] *Ibid.,* 88.

head cannot be realized in one life, "and therefore the evolutionary immortality which depends on *karma* and *reincarnation* as well as the subtle body are necessary for liberation."[55]

Whitman did not, as we have previously noticed, regard the world as illusion, and the visible universe is too sacred for him to think of it as having been created for sport; but, as Dr. Mercer says:

All the ideas he advances are consistent with the fundamental notion of oneness. Men who have realized oneness realize equality; they are joyous; they have no fear; they have prophetic vision; they are creators; they are self-sufficient; they are imperturbable; their life transcends the life of the senses; they are free from a sense of duty [Whitmanesque?]; they realize a harmony of relations, a unity of subject and object, a sameness of time and space, an identity of the individual spirit and the universal spirit; and they are immortal because all is One and they are It.[56]

It seems to me that Whitman has realized for himself the self from which emanates the beauty which brings freedom, that he has realized the creating Brahman in himself; that in this knowledge he is joyous, for whoever thinks himself different from Brahman is subject to sorrow, to tragedy, to the ugly. And although Whitman is impelled by cosmic will to create an eternally existent Word, he is in no wise cast down, for he is a great lover, an all powerful creator, and the strength of his knowledge is such that it impels the substance of things hoped for to become manifest, the evidence of things not seen to become visible, for were they not Existent in the beginning?[57]

---

[55] *Ibid.*, 61.
[56] *Ibid.*, 183.
[57] *Ibid.*, 191.

Whether these parallels are direct or indirect sources or merely analogies for LEAVES OF GRASS, they are illuminating. So long ago as 1897, William N. Guthrie declared that Walt Whitman "is steadily misunderstood by most readers for years unless they have chanced to study the idealistic philosophy of Germany, the mystics of Christian centuries, the neoplatonists, or better yet, for interpreting Emerson and Whitman, *The Bhagavad Gita*."[58]

THE FRENCH BACKGROUND

These American, English, German, and Indian parallels —and possible origins—provide clues and analogues for Whitman's mysticism and philosophical idealism. But there was also another side of his thought and expression, which Arvin refers to as "a kind of Transcendental atheism."[59] This is the Whitman of French rationalism, skepticism, and "free thought," who declares in the '55 Preface that, "There will soon be no more priests. Their work is done....A new order shall arise and they shall be the priests of man, and every man shall be his own priest."[60] This is partly Emersonian "self-reliance" and the ultimate result of the Reformation, but it is also the offspring of the French Revolution, and of Thomas Jefferson and Tom Paine in America.

As the heir of this tradition Whitman wrote such early poems as *Europe, Boston Ballad,* and *To a Foil'd Euro-*

---

[58] William N. Guthrie, *Walt Whitman, Camden Sage* (Cincinnati: Robert Clark Co., 1897), 25. "Vedantic views are at times expressed [in *Leaves of Grass*] with such originality and energy as to have brought a smile of delight to the serene immobile countenance of a Hindu friend, to whom I read them," *Ibid.*

[59] Arvin, *op. cit.*, 201.

[60] Holloway, Inclusive Edition, *op. cit.*, 505.

pean Revolutionaire, and felt great sympathy for the defeated revolutionists of France (and other European countries) of 1848. He too shouts "Equality!" and "Liberty!" At this time the "headsman"[61] is a symbol to him of reactionary Europe, where the oppressors of mankind are "hangman, priest, tax-gatherer."[62] Whitman's realization that the ideals of the American and French Revolutions had been thwarted in Europe intensified his own nationalism and increased his conviction that, politically, the United States was the only hope of the world for freedom and equality.[63]

Even his Christ-rôle, his vicarious sympathy, was to some extent the product of these times and influences.

> Through me many long dumb voices,
> Voices of the interminable generations of slaves,
> Voices of prostitutes, and of deformed persons . . .[64]

The above interpretation is strengthened by the fact that he was more exercised over abstract political slavery than the concrete example of racial slavery in his own nation.[65]

Whitman's interest in comparative religion and his attempt to construct a theology which would fuse and extract the best of all religions probably also came to a considerable degree from French deism and rationalism, both directly and indirectly.

> Magnifying and applying come I,
> Outbidding at the start the old cautious hucksters,
> [*i.e.,* priests of historical religions].[66]

---

[61] *Song of the Broad-Axe,* sec. 8.
[62] *Europe.*
[63] Cf. *By Blue Ontario's Shore,* sec. 10.
[64] *Song of Myself,* sec. 24 (1855 edition).
[65] See p. 364.
[66] *Song of Myself,* sec. 41.

He will accept only "the rough deific sketches to fill out better in myself." Bibles and religions "have all grown out of you...It is not they who give the life....it is you who give the life."[67] Institutionalized religion is dead and ought to be buried:

> Allons! From all formulas!
> From your formulas, O bat-eyed and materialistic priests!
> The stale cadaver blocks up the passage—the burial waits no longer.[68]

And the only guide is each person's own conscience:

> I only am he who places over you no master, owner, better, God, beyond what waits intrinsically in yourself.[69]

Of course there are many posible sources for Whitman's "free thought" and "natural religion." According to Arvin, his father was a great admirer of the deistic Jefferson, "had some sort of acquaintance with Thomas Paine as an old man,"[70] and *The Age of Reason* was one of the prized books in the Whitman home. But Walt's father also subscribed to the *Free Enquirer,* published by Frances Wright, the radical Scotch-woman and intimate of Lafayette, and the English socialist, Robert Dale Owen. Intellectually, all three of these minds were as much French as, or more than, British, for in this period England was far more conservative than France, from whence emanated the theories of socialism, women's rights, co-

---

[67] *Carol of Occupations* [sec. 4], (1855 ed.)
[68] *Poem of the Road* (1856 ed.)
[69] *To You* (1856).
[70] Arvin, *op. cit.,* 162.

öperative communities (like Fourier's *phalanges*—model for Brook Farm in America).

Precisely how much Whitman owed to each of these influences, it is unwise to estimate, but there is another source, of primary importance, which is unmistakably French and can actually be documented. This is *The Ruins,* by the French radical, C. F. Volney,[71] who was also a friend of Jefferson and a famous visitor to America. Whitman himself regarded this as one of the important books of his youth, and David Goodale has demonstrated that the poet drew upon it extensively for both "concepts and phrases."[72]

The theme of Volney's *Ruins* is the cause of the rise and fall of civilizations. While traveling "in the empire of the Ottomans, and through those provinces which were anciently the kingdoms of Egypt and Syria," the author broods over the wreck of empires and the transitory glory of man's greatest achievements. Plunged into melancholy, he decides that "a blind fatality" sports with the destiny of man; but an Apparition then appears before him, as in a vision, to deny this explanation:

How long will man importune heaven with unjust complaint? How long, with vain clamors, will he accuse FATE as the author of his calamities? Will he then never open his eyes to the light, and his heart to the insinuations of truth and reason?[73] . . . . The source of his calamities is not in the distant heavens, it is beside him on the earth; it is not concealed in the bosom of

---

[71] C. F. Volney, *The Ruins,* or Meditation on the Revolutions of Empires, to which is appended *The Law of Nature* (New York: Calvin Blanchard, n.d. [1st French Ed., 1791]).

[72] David Goodale, "Some of Walt Whitman's Borrowings," *American Literature,* X, 202-213 (May, 1938).

[73] Volney, *op. cit.,* 26.

the divinity; it resides in man himself, he bears it in his own heart.[74]

The Apparition (also called Phantom or Genius) then carries the author high up in the aerial regions, where, like Whitman in one of his cosmic flights of inspiration, he looks down upon the revolving globe, while the Genius points out to him oceans, continents, rivers in a veritable *Salut au Monde!*

From this point on Volney's book becomes a treatise and a survey of the history of the human race, from "The Primitive State of Man" through all the stages of social development. This is at least one source for Whitman's own desire to write "A volume...running in idea and description through the whole range of recorded time— Egyptian, Hindustanee, Assyrian, Greek, Roman, Alb, Gallic, Teutonic—and so on down to the present day."[75] He attempted one poem on "The march of the human race across the earth," in which he tried to celebrate the "procession without halt," and he never lost interest in the subject of "processions," "journeys," and cosmic cycles.

Volney's account of the origins and developments of the religions of the world was also an important source for Whitman's interest in, and knowledge of, comparative religion, as his own notes plainly indicate.[76] His ambition to incorporate the best of all religions without accepting the creed of any may have been suggested by Volney's doctrine that the object of all religions is identical. But here we also see the difference between Whit-

---

[74] *Ibid.*, 28.
[75] See note 7, above.
[76] *Notes and Fragments, op. cit.*, 152-154. See Goodale, *op. cit.*, 208-210.

man and Volney and can estimate the limits of his influence on the American poet. The lesson which Volney draws from the history of religions is that in all ages priests and kings have taken advantage of the religious credulity and superstition of the people to contrive and maintain their own political tyranny. Whitman never denied this typical doctrine of the philosophers of the French Revolution, but his "free thought" attitudes were considerably modified, and perhaps even superseded, by the mysticism of German Romanticism. And in the end the mysticism seems to have outweighed the rationalism in his thought and poetic expression.

Whitman's own statements and his verbal borrowings sufficiently establish Volney as one of his sources—though a source for only one aspect of his thought, a distinctly limited aspect which does not entirely harmonize with his larger pattern of ideas. But when we come to the romantic as distinguished from the rationalistic French authors, it is more difficult to separate source from parallel. Bliss Perry regarded Whitman as an heir of Rousseau,[77] but what romantic poet in Europe or America was not? No one can deny the influence of the doctrines of innate goodness of human nature and "primitivism" on LEAVES OF GRASS. Of course Whitman was well acquainted with Rousseauism, but it is not an influence which can be weighed objectively.

Of the French Romantic School, George Sand has been claimed not only as a major but even as Whitman's main source. Mrs. Esther Shephard thinks[78] that in the wandering carpenter poet of the *Countess of Rudolstadt* Whit-

---

[77] Perry, *op. cit.*, 277-280.
[78] Esther Shephard, *Walt Whitman's Pose* (New York: Harcourt, Brace and Co., 1936).

man found the literary rôle (she calls it a "pose") which he was thereafter to adopt as his own through all the editions of LEAVES OF GRASS. That he read and admired this and other novels by George Sand, there can be no doubt. It is even possible that George Sand's carpenter poet aroused in Walt Whitman the literary ambitions which he sought to achieve in LEAVES OF GRASS, but Mrs. Shephard's claims for this source lose much of their strength when we discover equally striking parallels in the works of other French romanticists.

One of these is Victor Hugo—though Whitman seems not to have admired him as much as he admired George Sand.[79] However, they had much in common, as Kennedy has pointed out:

> Walt Whitman continually suggests another great humanitarian poet,—Victor Hugo. That which chiefly affines them is sympathy, compassion. To redeem our erring brothers by love, and not inflexible savage justice, is the message of each. Who is worthy to be placed beside these two as promulgators of the distinctive democratic ideas of these times,—the thirst for individual growth, space for the expansion of one's own soul, and equal rights before the law? . . . They had the same love of the sea and the immensities, and the same ingrained love of freedom.[80]

More specifically, one might compare Hugo's assertion that everything has a soul with Whitman's panpsychism, or his including the ugly as a necessary part of his esthetic[81] with Whitman's complete equalitarianism, or his belief

---

[79] *Uncollected Poetry and Prose, op. cit.,* II, 53.
[80] W. S. Kennedy, *Reminiscences of Walt Whitman* (London: Alexander Gardner, 1896), 106.
[81] *Cf.* Hugo's Preface to *Cromwell.*

that the spirit is always advancing toward something better with Whitman's cosmic meliorism.[82] Although these
parallels indicate not so much sources or direct influences
as a general literary movement to which both belonged,
the very fact that the American poet shared these fundamental resemblances with one of the major poets of nineteenth-century France indicates that the ground was already partly prepared for Whitman's later reception in
France.[83]

Another French writer of the period whose thought and
expression parallel Whitman's to an astonishing degree is
the historian, Jules Michelet. In 1847 Whitman reviewed
his *History of France*[84] and in 1876 he paraphrased (one
might almost say plagiarized) a passage from Michelet's
The Bird in his poem, *To the Man-of-War Bird.*[85] Before
he published the first edition of LEAVES OF GRASS Whitman probably also read Michelet's *The People,*[86] but there
is no conclusive evidence. Nevertheless, the literary theory
on which Michelet wrote this book is completely analogous
to Whitman's poetic program. In his preface Michelet
says, "This book is more than a book; it is myself, therefore it belongs to you . . . Receive, then, this book of *The
People,* because it is you, because it is I . . ."[87] Compare:

[82] *Cf. Ce que Dit la Bouché D'Ombre; Le Satyre; La Lapidé; La
Chouette; Je Lisais, Que, Lisais-Je?; Abîme; Paroles dans l'Epreuve;
Voyage de Nuit; Plein Ciel;* and *Ibo.*

[83] The author is indebted to Dr. O. F. Pucciani for the privilege of
reading his valuable dissertation (Harvard, 1943) on *French Criticism
of Walt Whitman.*

[84] See *Uncollected Poetry and Prose, op. cit.,* I, 134.

[85] First pointed out by Adeline Knapp, "Walt Whitman and Jules
Michelet, Identical Passages," *Critic,* XLIV (1907), 467-468. Discussed
by Gay Wilson Allen, "Walt Whitman and Jules Michelet," *Études
Anglaises,* I, 230-237 (May, 1937).

[86] Jules Michelet, *The People,* translated by G. H. Smith (New York:
Appleton, 1846).

[87] *Ibid.,* 6.

Camerado, this is no book,
Who touches this touches a man,[88]

"Son of the people," says Michelet, "I have lived with
them, I know them, they are myself . . . I unite them all
in my own person."[89] Whitman:

In all people I see myself, none more and not one a
barley-corn less,
And the good or bad I say of myself I say of them.[90]

Through Michelet's historian and Whitman's poet "the
people" find their voice:

The people, in the highest sense of the word, is seldom
to be found in the people . . . it exists in its truth, and
at its highest power in the man of genius; in him resides
the great soul . . . the whole world [vibrates] at the
least word he utters . . . That voice is the voice of the
people; mute of itself, it speaks in this man, and God
in him.[91]

This "genius" is Whitman's ideal poet, who "is to be
commensurate with a people...He is a seer...he is
individual...he is complete in himself...the others are
as good as he, only he sees it and they do not."[92] Throughout the 1855 Preface Whitman insists that only the poet,
who is the true man of genius, can express the heart of
the people; only through the poet can the people become
articulate.

Michelet also anticipates Whitman in the cult of the
barbarian:

[88] *So Long*, lines 53-54.
[89] *The People*, 25.
[90] *Song of Myself*, sec. 20.
[91] *The People*, 135.
[92] Holloway, Inclusive Edition, *op. cit.*, 489-492.

The rise of the people, the progress, is often nowadays compared to the invasion of the *Barbarians!* yes! that is to say, full of sap, fresh, vigorous, and for ever springing up . . . travellers toward the Rome of the future.[93]

As one of the barbarians, he glories in their crude, un-tutored, natural strength of expression,

> striving to give everything at once—leaves, fruit, and flowers—till it breaks or distorts the branches. But those who start up thus with the sap of the people in them, do not the less introduce into art a new burst of life and principle of youth; or at least leave on it the impress of a great result.[94]

We could easily imagine that they are Whitman's words, he who sounds his "barbaric yawp over the roofs of the world,"[95] and would have his verse break forth loosely like lilacs on a bush. Even more than Michelet he strives "to give everything at once . . . till it breaks or distorts the branches."

Whether or not *The People* was a literary source for LEAVES OF GRASS, Michelet and Whitman had a common heritage as sons of the French Revolution and brothers of nineteenth-century romantic nationalism. Whitman's theory of ethical democracy is one of the corner stones of his whole philosophy of art. Michelet speaks of "Faith in my native land, as a religious faith"; and he believes that "The native land, my native land, alone can save the world."[96] The dogma of this religion of patriotism is "the dogma of love, God made man . . . and love . . . was in-

---

[93] *The People,* 24.
[94] *Ibid.*
[95] *Song of Myself,* sec. 52.
[96] *The People,* 185.

scribed, in the laws of the Revolution, so that the God within man might be made manifest."[97] To Frenchmen he preaches, "You are not a nation only, you are a principle . . . As principle you must live. Live for the salvation of the world." Whitman has the similar faith that,

> Sole among nationalities, these States have assumed the task to put in forms of lasting power and practicality, on areas of amplitude rivaling the operations of the physical kosmos, the moral political speculations of ages..., the democratic republican principle, and the theory of development and perfection by voluntary standards, and self-reliance.[98]

These parallels are important, if for no other reason, because they reveal close nineteenth-century cultural and literary relations between the two countries which had been so intimately associated in their respective revolutions. Even in his rôle of untutored American barbarian, Walt Whitman was merely embodying (perhaps unconsciously) Jules Michelet's ideal of the literary genius of the people who would be the articulate voice of the masses.

WHITMAN IN ENGLAND:
RECEPTION AND INFLUENCE

In beginning a survey of Whitman's reception, reputation, and influence in foreign countries, we inevitably start with the British Isles, where he was first appreciated and first recognized as a major poet. The story need not be told in complete detail, however, for it is familiar to most students of American literature, and much of it has already been covered in this book in the account of the

---

[97] *Ibid.*   [98] *Prose Works, op. cit.,* 203.

biographies.[99] Furthermore, it is largely the story of Whitman's reputation in Great Britain (and the poet's reflected fame at home), for even to the present time he has had less actual literary influence in England than in France or Germany.[100]

The introduction of LEAVES OF GRASS to the British Isles began more or less by accident. Several months after the almost complete failure of the first edition to gain sales or recognition in America, Thomas Dixon, a cork cutter of Sunderland, bought a copy from a peddler, James Grinrod, a veteran of the American Civil War. Dixon sent this copy to his friend William Bell Scott, a minor poet and sculptor. Scott gave a copy to William Rossetti for a Christmas present in 1856, and Rossetti was so pleased with the work that he immediately began telling his friends about it.[101] In the same year Emerson sent a copy, with an apologetic note, to Carlyle, but until his death Carlyle remained either indifferent or merely irritated by Whitman's poems.[102]

English criticism of Whitman did not get under way, however, until about 1866. Lord Strangford published a critical essay in *The Pall Mall Gazette,* February 16, 1866,[103] in which he recognized the American poet's Oriental style without approving his use of it. Whitman, he says, "has managed to acquire or imbue himself with not only the spirit, but with the veriest mannerism, the

---

[99] See p. 15, *passim.*

[100] The subject has been admirably presented by Harold Blodgett, *Walt Whitman in England* (Ithaca, N. Y.: Cornell University Press, 1934).

[101] *Ibid.,* 14 ff.

[102] *Ibid.,* 163-166.

[103] Reprinted in *A Selection from the Writings of Viscount Strangford* (London, 1869), II, 297 ff. See Blodgett, *op. cit.,* 198.

most absolute trick and accent of Persian poetry."[104]
Instead of wasting his gifts on LEAVES OF GRASS, he
should have translated Rumi. This observation might have
started interesting and fruitful discoveries in comparative literature, but no one at the time, not even Lord
Strangford, pursued the comparison any further. In
October of the same year, Moncure Conway, who had
visited Whitman in America, wrote a personal sketch of
the poet for the October *Fortnightly Review.*

Over ten years after his introduction to LEAVES OF
GRASS, Rossetti published his first article on Whitman in
the *Chronicle,* July 6, 1867. He attempted to enlarge the
theory of poetry by declaring that, "Only a very restricted
and literal use of the word, rhythm, could deny the claim
of these writings to being both poetic and rhythmical."
He called LEAVES OF GRASS "incomparably the largest
poetic work of our period."[105] But in the introduction to
his edition of *Selections*[106] published the next year, he was
cautious and judicious, perhaps the best strategy for increasing Whitman's reputation in England. Also the fact
that his poems were edited in England at this time by
Rossetti, a man known and respected by the literary profession, who carefully eliminated the most daring sex
poems, accounts to a considerable extent for Whitman's
greater fame in Britain than at home.

It was this edition of selected poems which Mrs. Anne
Gilchrist read in 1869, having borrowed a copy from
Madox Brown. She was not satisfied, however, with a
censored edition and borrowed the complete LEAVES from
Rossetti himself. So profoundly affected was she that she

---

[104] *Ibid.*
[105] Quoted from *Chronicle* article by Blodgett, *op. cit.,* 22.
[106] See *Ante,* p. 16.

wrote the famous "An Englishwoman's Estimate of Walt Whitman," published in the *Boston Radical,* May, 1870. To her LEAVES OF GRASS was not only sacred literature but also a personal plea for love. It is doubtful that anywhere else in the whole range of Whitman criticism any other person ever responded to the poet's message with such absolute sympathy and understanding—such sympathy, in fact, that she fell in love with the man through the book, and after this one article the story belongs to biography rather than to criticism.[107]

Ironically, one of Whitman's most ardent and impetuous friends and critics in England at this same time was that eccentric enemy of the Rossetti-Swinburne circle, Robert Buchanan. This son of socialist and "infidel" parents was the first in Great Britain to accept Whitman unreservedly as a prophet and a modern Socrates. Blodgett calls his first criticism, published in *The Broadway Magazine* (1868) and reprinted the same year in the book *David Gray,* "the most exhilarating that had yet appeared on Whitman in England."[108] But Buchanan worked himself into an embarrassing position in 1871 in an attack on the sensuality of Swinburne, Dante Gabriel Rossetti, Baudelaire, and others, which he called "The Fleshly School of Poetry."[109] When Swinburne inquired why Buchanan "despised so much the Fleshly School of Poetry in England and admired so much the poetry which is widely considered unclean and animal in America,"[110] he was hard pressed for a defence of *Children of Adam,* and even admitted that LEAVES OF GRASS contained about

---

[107] See Chap. I, pp. 17-18.
[108] Blodgett, *op. cit.,* 78.
[109] Published in *The Contemporary Review,* October, **1871,** and reissued in an expanded pamphlet, London, 1872.
[110] Quoted by Blodgett, *op. cit.,* 79.

"fifty lines of a thoroughly indecent kind."[111] But the controversy only intensified his loyalty to Whitman, whose cause he did at least two good services. In the first place, he was one of the earliest foreign critics to recognize the literary quality of Whitman's "wonderful poetic prose, or prose-poetry";[112] and in the second place, in 1876 he started a storm of controversy over Whitman's neglect which stimulated the sale of his books and raised a substantial sum of money for him. Hearing that the poet, "old, poor, and paralyzed,"[113] was shamefully neglected in America, Buchanan wrote a letter to *The London Daily News* hotly denouncing the poet's unappreciative countrymen. Naturally many Americans resented the charge and Whitman's cause thereby became entangled with Anglo-American antagonisms which lingered on for years. After visiting the United States in 1885, Buchanan poured more oil on the fire with a satirical poem against the Bostonians for their indifference to Whitman, and in 1887 he added that in his native land Whitman was "simply *outlawed*":

> In a land of millionaires, in a land of which he will one day be known as the chief literary glory, he is almost utterly neglected. Let there be no question about this; all denial of it is disingenuous and dishonest. The literary class fights shy of him.[114]

Swinburne's criticism of Whitman illustrates anew the fortuitous and erratic reception of LEAVES OF GRASS in

---

[111] *Ibid.*

[112] *The Fleshly School of Poetry* (London: Strahan, 1872), 97.

[113] Article in *The Athenaeum*, March 11, 1876, partly reprinted from the *West Jersey Press*, January 26, 1876. The original article on the American neglect of Whitman may have been written by the poet himself—see Furness, *op. cit.*, 245.

[114] Robert Buchanan, "The American Socrates," *A Look Round Literature* (London: Ward and Downey, 1887), 344.

Great Britain. A copy of the 1855 edition found its way into the hands of George Howard, the ninth Earl of Carlyle, who passed it on to Swinburne.[115] It interested Swinburne so much that he ordered a copy for himself, and then later procured a copy of the 1860 edition. In the latter volume he greatly admired *Out of the Cradle Endlessly Rocking* (then called "A Word Out of the Sea").[116] In his biography of Blake (1860) he compared the Universal Republic and the spiritual democracy of the two poets. Their writings seemed to him like "fragments . . . of the Pantheistic poetry of the East."[117] After *Drum-Taps* was published, Swinburne declared the threnody on Lincoln to be "the most sweet and sonorous nocturne ever chanted in the church of the world." The height of his admiration for Whitman was reached in 1871 when in *Songs Before Sunrise,* dedicated to Mazzini, he addressed a poem "To Walt Whitman in America." Whitman and his friends took the poem as a personal greeting, but as Blodgett points out, Swinburne's "interest in political freedom, never realistic, took the form of a passionately expressed idealism in which Walt Whitman appeared as the prophet of liberty, the 'strong-winged soul with prophetic lips hot with the blood-beats of song.' " Whitman and his country were "apostrophized as symbols of the freedom which with Swinburne was a seductive abstraction . . ."[118]

The following year (1872), in *Under the Microscope,* Swinburne's admiration for Whitman's poetry became

---

[115] Blodgett, *op. cit.,* 105.

[116] Swinburne incorrectly called it "A Voice Out of the Sea."

[117] Algernon Charles Swinburne, *William Blake* (London: Hotten, 1868), 335.

[118] Blodgett, *op. cit.,* 108.

more restrained and judicial. While still accepting the American poet's democracy, he began to find fault with his style and his lapses from good taste. *Under the Microscope* was directed especially at Buchanan, and it is understandable that Swinburne would begin to have his doubts about the poet so noisily praised by the enemy of Swinburne's circle.

Edmund Gosse thought Watts-Dunton was responsible for the cooling of Swinburne's enthusiasm for the American poet,[119] but recent investigators[120] find nothing either remarkable or treacherous in his increasing impatience with Whitman as formalist and thinker, the two special deficiencies mentioned in *Under the Microscope*. Even the notorious "Whitmania," published first in *The Fortnightly Review,* August, 1887, and reprinted in *Studies in Poetry and Prose* (1894), is, as Cairns says, "directed primarily against those enthusiasts who give Whitman a place 'a little beneath Shakespeare, a little above Dante, or cheek by jowl with Homer.'"[121] It was no outright "recantation," for Swinburne still admired Whitman's "genuine passion of patriotic and imaginative sympathy" and his "earnest faith in freedom,"[122] but he objected to the weakness of thought, the unpoetic style, and the manner of treating sex. It is not surprising that a poet of Swinburne's temperament and culture would eventually find the self-appointed poet of American Democracy uncongenial, and his objections are essentially those of the

---

[119] *Ibid.,* 115.

[120] See especially W. B. Cairns, "Swinburne's Opinion of Whitman," *American Literature,* III, 125-135 (May, 1931). Also W. S. Monroe, "Swinburne's Recantation of Walt Whitman," *Revue Anglo-Américaine,* IX, 347-351 (March, 1931).

[121] Cairns, *op. cit.,* 131.

[122] *Ibid.* (Quoted from *Fortnightly Review,*) 131-132.

later British biographers, such as John Bailey and Hugh I'Anson Fausset.[123]

The biographical and critical contributions of John Addington Symonds to Whitman literature in England have been treated in a previous chapter,[124] but we may note here that he became acquainted with Whitman's writings in 1865 at Trinity College, Cambridge, through his friend Frederic Myers. Young university men in Great Britain seem to have been especially attracted by Whitman at this time. Other bookish men drawn to him were Lionel Johnson, Robert Louis Stevenson, and Edward Dowden.

Edward Dowden, Professor of English Literature and Oratory at Trinity College, Dublin, was one of the most gifted and remarkable critic-admirers of Whitman in the British Isles. What especially attracted him to LEAVES OF GRASS were the spiritual values. In his first book on Shakespeare (1879) he ranked Whitman with the "spiritual teachers": Wordsworth, Coleridge, Shelley, Carlyle, Browning, and others.[125] Whitman's form, however, was a challenge to his powers of analysis and he attempted to rationalize it.

Dowden's essay, "The Poetry of Democracy: Walt Whitman," was rejected in 1869, as too dangerous to print, by *Macmillan's Magazine* and *The Contemporary Review* but was finally published by *The Westminster Review* in July, 1871 (reprinted in *Studies in Literature,* London, 1878). In this essay Dowden accepted the view that America lacked native literature before Whitman

---

[123] See pp. 54, 83.

[124] See pp. 19, 31.

[125] Edward Dowden, *Shakespere: A Critical Study of His Mind and Art* (London: C. Kegan Paul and Co., 1879), 40. Mentioned by Blodgett, *op. cit.,* 43.

and regarded LEAVES OF GRASS as democratic art, which must reject aristocratic form and make its own rules and techniques. However, he regarded Whitman as a poet despite his unconventional form, not because of it. Though he admitted guardedly that Whitman might not have been sufficiently reserved in the treatment of sex, he did not think that the poet exalted the body over the soul. On the whole, Dowden accepted Whitman on his own terms, but brought to his interpretations a literary skill and critical background which greatly advanced the American poet's reputation abroad—and even influenced the course of his reception at home. The distinguished Dublin professor found himself embarrassed and repulsed by Whitman's American disciples, but this did not affect his critical opinions or published support. He reviewed *Specimen Days* in *The Academy,* November 18, 1882, and arranged for an English edition of Dr. Bucke's biography, for which he collected and arranged an appendix, "English Critics on Walt Whitman."

Despite Dowden's championship of Whitman, however, LEAVES OF GRASS was removed from the Trinity College library after Boston banned the 1881-82 edition. But meanwhile other Irish scholars were also active in spreading Whitman's fame in the British Isles. Standish O'Grady ("Arthur Clive") published "Walt Whitman: the Poet of Joy" in the December, 1875, *Gentleman's Magazine.* With Irish exuberance he elaborated in the vein of O'Connor and Bucke: "Often we think one of the elements of nature has found a voice, and thunders great syllables in our ears."[126] O'Grady's friend, Thomas W.

---

[126] Reprinted in part in Traubel, Bucke, and Harned, *In Re Walt Whitman* (Philadelphia: David McKay, 1893), 284.

Rolleston, discovered Whitman in 1877. After four years
in Germany, he published at Dresden a study called *Über
Wordsworth und Walt Whitman* (1883). Rolleston was
one of the first critics to perceive Whitman's connection
with German philosophy and to interpret him not as a
"primitive" but in terms of comparative literature—an important step toward the recognition of Whitman as a
"world poet." However, like the American disciples, he
thought that criticizing Whitman was like criticizing
Nature. Rolleston also translated a book of "selections"
from LEAVES OF GRASS into German (1884), but it was
not published until Dr. Karl Knortz, a German-American
scholar, revised it and finally got J. Schabelitz, of Zurich,
to bring it out in Switzerland in 1889.

Scotland was slow in accepting Whitman. John Nichol,
Professor of English Literature at the University of Glas-
gow, discussed him in an article on "American Literature"
in the ninth edition of the *Encyclopedia Britannica* (1875)
in the following tone:

> . . . although this author on various occasions displays
> an uncouth power, his success is in the main owing to
> the love of novelty, wildness, and even of absurdity,
> which has infected a considerable class of critics and
> readers on both sides of the Atlantic. . . . he discards
> not only rhyme, but all ordinary rhythm. . . . "The
> Leaves of Grass" is redeemed by a few grand descriptive
> passages from absolute barbarism both of manner and
> matter. It is a glorification of nature in her most un-
> abashed forms, an audacious protest against all that
> civilization has done to raise men above the savage state.

These views were amplified in Nichol's book, *American
Literature* (1882), in which he decided that "If Shakes-

peare, Keats, and Goethe are poets, Whitman is not."[127]
He regretted Swinburne's favorable comparisons of Blake
and Whitman. The Earl of Lytton and Sir Leslie Stephen
also, as Blodgett says, "felt the need of British austerity
toward American literary bumptiousness,"[128] and many
Scotchmen seem to have shared their attitudes. One of
these was Peter Bayne, a prominent editor of the day, who
in the December, 1875, *Contemporary Review* "pounced
upon Whitman like a Sunday school superintendent upon
a bad boy, and he plainly intimates, in doing so, that he
is exposing the hoax that Dowden, Rossetti, and Buchanan
had been playing off on the British public." Blodgett also
rightly calls this "A very plausible Tory attack," stating
"the formidable case that all respectable persons have
against *Leaves of Grass.*"[129] But another Scotchman, John
Robertson, published a kind and sympathetic though undistinguished pamphlet on *Walt Whitman: Poet and
Democrat* at Edinburgh in 1884.

Despite the Tory opposition, Whitman made steady
progress in England, partly, as Blodgett suggests, because,
"In the seventies or eighties a young critic or journalist,
trying to get a foothold in the London literary world,
would be quite likely to seize upon Whitman for 'material'."[130] Among these young critics were H. Buxton
Forman, Ernest Rhys, and Edmund Gosse. Forman observed similarities between Whitman and Shelley and
tried, without much success, to interest Whitman in Shelley. At the age of twenty-five Rhys turned from mining
engineering to literature in order to advance the cause of

---

[127] Quoted by Blodgett, *op. cit.,* 185.
[128] *Ibid.,* 186.
[129] *Ibid.,* 199.
[130] *Ibid.,* 190.

labor, and he thought he saw in Whitman the enemy of
"the stronghold of caste and aristocracy and all selfishness
between rich and poor."[131] Consequently Rhys gave popular lectures on Whitman and edited, with a good critical
introduction, a pocket edition of selected poems. It was
Rhys's intention to make Whitman known to the common
people, the very kind of audience which the poet had
originally attempted to address in his own country. Gosse,
like Swinburne, passed from ardent admiration to cool ob-
jectivity in his criticism of Whitman and was regarded
with increasing hostility by the Camden circle. But he
was one of the most competent critics that Whitman had
in Great Britain.

There were, however, other distinguished critics. One
was George Saintsbury, who reviewed LEAVES OF GRASS
in *The Academy,* October 10, 1874. He admired Whitman
as poet and artist, though demurring somewhat at his
idealization of the animal. He found Whitman's rhythm
"singularly fresh, light, and vigorous," and praised his
technique in the great *History of Prosody* (1910). Another critic, George C. Macaulay, gave a more philosophical analysis in *The Nineteenth Century,* December, 1882,
describing Whitman's religion as pantheistic, his ethics as
Greek, and his sympathy as universal. Still earlier William
Kingdon Clifford, Professor of Mathematics at the University College, London, had made one of the first contributions to the understanding of Whitman's mysticism by
citing him as an illustration of "Cosmic Emotion" in *The
Nineteenth Century,* October, 1877. In 1886 even the
staid *Quarterly Review* (in a review of Stedman's *Poets
of America,* published in the October number) called

---

[131] *Ibid.,* 193.

Whitman "a lyric genius of the highest order," praising especially his cosmic qualities.

Though Walt Whitman was befriended by such famous men in England as William Rossetti, John Addington Symonds, and Lord Tennyson (who remained a steadfast friend and correspondent though not a public critic), and had what might be called a strong personal following his actual literary influence in the British Isles was negligible. In fact, it included only one well-known writer and a small group of left-wing socialists and reformers in Lancashire. The one writer was Edward Carpenter, a young poet, socialist, and idealistic reformer who, in Blodgett's words, "felt himself dedicated, heart and soul, to the life work of interpreting and expanding Whitman's dream of democratic brotherhood."[132] *Toward Democracy* is such an expansion, and *My Days and Dreams* outlines in detail a social program inspired by LEAVES OF GRASS, though it probably goes far beyond anything Whitman ever dreamed.

The one group of ordinary folk who organized a club to study and apply Whitman's doctrines was known as "Bolton College," a satirical name adopted by the members, middle-class Lancashire business men, professional men, and artisans. Two of the members visited Whitman and wrote books about the meeting.[133] The group had no great influence on the course of Whitman criticism, but, as Blodgett remarks, "it is strangely interesting that the story of Whitman's English following should begin with the effort of Thomas Dixon, cork-cutter, to call attention

---

[132] Blodgett, *op. cit.*, 201.

[133] John Johnston and J. W. Wallace, *Visits to Walt Whitman in 1890-1891 by Two Lancashire Friends* (London, 1917; New York, 1918).

to him, and end with the homage of a middle-class coterie in the cotton-manufacturing town of Bolton."[134]

What pleased and encouraged Walt Whitman most about his reception in Great Britain was the friendly praise and the personal comradeship of both the professional writers and the disciples. This recognition sustained him during the dark hours of his neglect in America. But it can not be said that many of these critics made permanent contributions to Whitman criticism, except for some psychological interpretations which the poet could never appreciate.

It was the British who first tried to penetrate the mystery of the "Calamus" emotions, first Symonds, then Carpenter, and finally Havelock Ellis. Carpenter, like Symonds, seems to have felt in himself something of the same emotion and he never gave up the attempt to understand both himself and Whitman, and to discover the social value of "manly love." He did not shrink from the analysis of "sexual inversion,"[135] but he also thought that "The comradeship on which Whitman founds a large portion of his message may in course of time become a general enthusiasm . . ."[136] It was Ellis, however, who came nearest getting to the bottom of this question and who analyzed Whitman's psychology with the most penetrating insight. But he also warned that:

> It is as [a prophet-poet] that Whitman should be approached, and I would desire to protest against the tendency, now marked in many quarters, to treat him

---

[134] Blodgett, *op. cit.,* 215.

[135] Cf. *Homogenic Love* (1894), *Love's Coming of Age* (1896), *An Unknown People* (1897), *Some Friends of Walt Whitman* (1904), *The Intermediate Sex* (1908).

[136] *The Intermediate Sex* (London: Sonnenschein, 1908), 117.

merely as an invert, and to vilify him or glorify him accordingly. However important inversion may be as a psychological key to Whitman's personality, it plays but a small part in Whitman's work, and for many who care for that work a negligible part.[137]

Out of Whitman's emotional sensitivity came a more sane and wholesome attitude toward the physical basis of life: "Whitman represents, for the first time since Christianity swept over the world, the reintegration, in a sane and whole-hearted form, of the instincts of the entire man, and therefore he has a significance which we can scarcely over-estimate."[138] Here we have the foundation for the later growth of reputation and understanding of the message of Walt Whitman in both Europe and America.

Finally, it was also the English critics who first suggested—though they did not develop—Whitman's relations to other poets and literatures: to Blake, to Shelley, to Eastern pantheism. It is doubtful that many of these critics ever fully understood Whitman's literary technique, but out of this cosmopolitan approach would eventually come a deeper appreciation of both the form and the matter of LEAVES OF GRASS.

WHITMAN IN FRANCE: RECEPTION AND INFLUENCE

The first critics of Walt Whitman in France used him as a horrible example of the cultural chaos to be ex-

---

[137] Havelock Ellis, *Sexual Inversion* (Philadelphia: Davis, 1915, 3rd ed.), 51.

[138] Havelock Ellis, *The New Spirit* (New York: Modern Library, 1921), 31.

pected of rampant "democracy" and "republicanism" in
a semi-civilized country like the United States of America.
This was the opinion, during the reign of Emperor Na-
poleon III, of Louis Etienne in his "Walt Whitman,
poète, philosophe et 'rowdy'," *Revue Européenne,* November, 1861, adding, however, "mais gardons-nous de con-
fondre la nation de Washington et de Franklin avec les
héros de ce nouveau Tyrtée."

In 1872, soon after the founding of the Third Republic, Mme Blanc (Thérèse Bentzon) still held essentially
the same view:

> *Soi-même et en masse,* l'égoïsme et la démocratie, voilà
> les sujets favoris des chants de Whitman; à ce titre, ils
> sont essentiellement modernes. Certes aucun écrivain
> européen, poète ni prosateur, n'est tombé dans les excès
> d'énergique mauvais goût que voudraient inaugurer sur
> les ruines de l'idéal Walt Whitman et ses sectaires;
> mais enfin il existe malheureusement chez nous, depuis
> quelque années, une tendance marquée vers ce réalisme
> qui est le contraire du naturel et de la vérité, une dis-
> position à confondre les muscles avec le génie.[139]

But despite the fact that she associated Whitman's
"muscle and pluck" with the school of realism, Bentzon
was fully aware of Whitman's mystic identification of
himself with the universe—though she regarded this as
a "pretension":

> Une des prétentions de Walt Whitman est non-seule-
> ment de représenter un citoyen de l'univers, comme il
> nous le fait entendre en déclarant qu'il est un vrai Paris-
> ien, un habitant de Vienne, de Pétersbourg, de Londres

---

[139] "Un poète américain, Walt Whitman: 'Muscle and Pluck Forever,'" *Revue des Deux Mondes,* Année XLII, 566-567 (June 1, 1872).

(tant de villes sont énumérées dans son hymne *Salut au monde* qu'on croirait lire une leçon de géographie ancienne et moderne), mais encore de contenir en lui-même l'univers tout entier.[140]

In such comments as these Bentzon did not misunderstand or misrepresent Whitman; she was merely unsympathetic and afraid of the "tendencies" which he represented in literature. Immediately Émile Blémont, a Parnassian poet, replied to Bentzon in a series of articles on "La Poésie en Angleterre et aux États-Unis," published in *Renaissance littéraire et artistique*. He understood and approved Whitman's new "ensemble" of body and soul and the significance of his *one's-self* and *en-masse*, accurately summarizing the thought in this concise manner:

> Il est biblique, mais comme Hegel, il admet le principe de l'identité dans les contraires. Il est réaliste et optimiste, il est spiritualiste aussi; pour lui le mal n'existe pas, ou s'il existe, il est utile. Il a les vigoureuses conceptions d'une forte santé, chaste et sobre. Il est le champion sans honte de la sainteté de la chair, et des instincts charnels.[141]

Following the poet's own clues, Blémont idealized him as a man of the people, a prophet, and an original genius. This of course prevented the critic from a full comprehension of Whitman's literary antecedents and his relations to other writers. It is significant, though, that Blémont did understand fairly well the "organic style," for it was Whitman's form perhaps more than anything else that

---

[140] *Ibid.*, 572.
[141] Quoted by Pucciani, *op. cit.*, 70-71, from Émile Blémont, "La Poésie en Angleterre et aux États-Unis, III, Walt Whitman," *Renaissance littéraire et artistique*, 1872. The article ran in three numbers: No. 7, June 8, No. 11, July 6; No. 12, July 13, 1872.

for many years prevented most French critics from appreciating LEAVES OF GRASS.

Five years later Henri Cochin, in "Un poète américain, Walt Whitman," *Le Correspondant*, November 25, 1877, still thought that Whitman's democracy and friendship degraded society and threatened the safety of all nations. He saw in LEAVES OF GRASS "democracy run wild, a form of insanity and megalomania."[142] Whitman, he thought, had no moral code at all, advocating chaos and license; and his form was equally contradictory and incoherent. But even in the attacks of Etienne, Bentzon, and Cochin on Whitman as a materialist, vulgarian, and political menace, "they recognized," as Pucciani says, "his growing stature in world literature, and that he was at all events a figure to be coped with."[143]

By 1884 Whitman was no longer feared in France. The violent opposition had spent itself, but his form was still a major difficulty. Léo Quesnel thought that Whitman fooled himself in believing that poetic sentiment intuitively generated artistic form: "N'est-ce pas une naïveté que de croire que parce qu'un poète aura le coeur plein de beaux sentiments, l'esprit rempli de hautes pensées, la rime et la césure viedront d'elles-mêmes se ranger sous sa plume?"[144] Quesnel predicted that Whitman would be slow in winning the recognition in France that he had already received in Great Britain. In the first place, his "langue riche et libre" is difficult to translate; in fact, "Whitman traduit n'est plus Whitman." And in the sec-

---

[142] Quoted by F. Baldensperger, "Walt Whitman and France," *Columbia University Quarterly*, October 1919, p. 302.

[143] Pucciani, *op. cit.*, 58.

[144] Léo Quesnel, "Poètes américains: Walt Whitman," *Revue politique et littéraire*, February 16, 1884, p. 215.

ond place, the French are still children of Greece, from whence they have inherited a sense of delicacy and elegance in language. He regards Whitman as a great poet for Americans (who are not "children of Greece"!), but not for Frenchmen.

Still, discussions such as Quesnel's brought Whitman to the attention of French men of letters and prepared the way for appreciation of him. This appreciation came during the period of Symbolism, during the 80's and 90's. Whitman's influence on the movement—if any—is still extremely controversial; nevertheless, it was the Symbolists "who brought Whitman to France, who espoused him, translated him, and to some extent recognized in him a literary parent,"[145] and he is still associated with the "decadents," as Rockwell Kent's illustrations bear witness.[146] Catel thinks Whitman a forerunner of Symbolism, but Pucciani points out, for example, Whitman's dissimilarities to Mallarmé.[147] It seems, in fact, to have been mainly the "decadent" aspect of Whitman which the Symbolists adopted. In the broader aspects he and they are quite different, for Whitman's symbols were universal, theirs specialized and often so subjective that they had little meaning for anyone except the author.

Although the early critics translated fragments of LEAVES OF GRASS in their articles, it was the Symbolist poet, Jules Laforgue, who in 1886 published three numbers of translations in *La Vogue* and thus stimulated interest in Whitman among the young poets of France. The following year the American expatriate, Francis

---

[145] Pucciani, *op. cit.,* 94.

[146] *Leaves of Grass,* with one hundred drawings by Rockwell Kent (New York: Heritage Press, 1936).

[147] *Ibid.,* 141.

Viélé-Griffin, translated the entire *Song of the Broad-Axe* for *La Revue indépendante*. It was through Laforgue, however, that Whitman most strongly influenced the *vers-librists*.[148]

In 1888 a comprehensive, scholarly critique of Whitman was published by Gabriel Sarrazin, first in the *Nouvelle Revue,* May 1, 1888, and a year later in his book, *La Renaissance de la poésie anglaise.* Especially valuable for the assimilation of Whitman in France was Sarrazin's comprehension of the poet's pantheism, which revealed an inheritance from the mysticism of the East and linked him in modern times to German Idealism, especially Hegel. Unlike most of Whitman's contemporary admirers in America, this learned French critic did not regard him as an untutored "original genius" but as a man who knew his way around Parnassus. "Non seulement il n'était point un illettré, mais il avait lu tout ce que nous avons lu nous-mêmes. Il avait vu aussi beaucoup plus que

---

[148] Édouard Dujardin, in "Les premiers poètes du vers libre," *Mercure de France,* March 15, 1921 (vol. 146, pp. 577-621), denies that Whitman had any influence on "free verse" in France, pointing out: "Exactement parlant, le vers de Walt Whitman, du moins celui des *Brins d'Herbe,* n'est pas le vers libre, mais le verset . . . Nous avons vu que le vers libre et le verset sont de la même famille, et qu'on pouvait considérer le verset comme un vers libre élargi, le plus souvent composé lui-même de plusieurs vers libres étroitement associés," p. 606. It would seem significant, however, that Laforgue was experimenting with the new form at the same time that he was translating Whitman (see *La Vogue,* II, No. 7; III, Nos. 1, 3, 8, 1886) ; and the following year Gustave Kahn, editor of *La Vogue,* published "La Belle au château rêvant" in *Revue indépendante,* Sept., 1887. And even Dujardin admits that "le vers libre et le verset sont de la même famille." It seems likely, therefore, that Whitman's form had some effect on the French experiments. See also P. M. Jones, "Influence of Walt Whitman on the 'Vers Libre'," *Modern Language Review,* XI, 186-194 (April, 1916). "Perhaps it would be safest to say that in the days when the first *vers libres* were being written, the poets who knew Whitman—and they were few, though important—were attracted mainly through the appeal made by his brusque originality to their pronounced taste for literary novelties," p. 194.

nous, et bien plus distinctement . . ."[149] Pucciani thinks Sarrazin's special virtue the fact that he sees Whitman as "an event in world literature that has already been operative for some time."[150]

The Symbolists, themselves influenced by the free verse of the Bible, were the first critics fully to appreciate the Biblical style of LEAVES OF GRASS. Rémy de Gourmont mentions it in 1890: "en Whitman, le grand poète américain, se régénère l'esprit ancien de simplicité, l'esprit biblique . . ."[151] This "Biblical spirit" has a curious international relationship to the Symbolists because they were also influenced, especially through Gustave Kahn, the editor of *La Vogue,* by the style of the German Bible, as Rémy de Gourmont has pointed out in *Le Problème du style* (1902)[152] and *Promenades littéraires* (1904).

Walt Whitman was sufficiently known in France in 1892 for news of his death to arouse a new flurry of critical activity. We are thus enabled to see that Sarrazin's effort had been only partly successful. For example, Paul Desjardins, in "Walt Whitman," *Journal des Débats,* April 4, 1892, still regards the American poet as "a kind of beautiful primitive,"[153] to use Pucciani's phrase, lack-

---

[149] Gabriel Sarrazin, *La Renaissance de la poésie anglaise, 1798-1889* (Paris: Perrin, 1889), 236-237. Also in *In Re Walt Whitman, op. cit.,* 160.

[150] Pucciani, *op. cit.,* 103.

[151] In review of Havelock Ellis's *New Spirit, Mercure de France,* June, 1890, tome 1, p. 220.

[152] "Le vers libre, tel que le comprend ce dernier poète [Francis Viélé-Griffin], vient en partie de Whitman; mais Whitman était lui-même un fils de la Bible et ainsi le vers libre, ce n'est peut-être, au fond, que le verset hébraïque des prophètes: c'est bien également de la Bible, mais de la Bible allemande, cette fois, que semble nous venir une autre nuance du vers libre, celle qui a valu sa réputation à M. Gustave Kahn," *Le Problème du style* (Paris: Mercure de France, 1924 [first ed., 1902]), p. 159.

[153] Pucciani, *op. cit.,* 118.

ing in restraint and self-control—and this amoral interpretation was also repeated by Théodor de Wyzewa[154] and B. H. Gausseron,[155] the latter thinking that Whitman had rejected all laws and all traditions. But Desjardins admires Whitman's patriotism, understands his doctrine of good and evil, and thinks the poet a *précurseur* of future popular literature.

At this time Henri Bérenger, who had quoted Whitman as early as 1873 in his novel, *L'Effort,* and had shown an interest in his themes—though not his forms—in *L'Ame moderne* (1890), translated Havelock Ellis's essay on Whitman (*L'Ermitage,* June, 1892). Thus the course of French criticism was influenced by this English psychologist, whose brilliant and sensible interpretation has seldom been equalled in Whitman scholarship. Ellis understood even better than Sarrazin Whitman's mysticism, his cosmic philosophy, his doctrine of the equality of matter and spirit, and the immortality of the Ego. It is safe to say that no previous critic had been so well prepared to appreciate the sanity of the poet's attitude toward sex. He saw also the similarity between Whitman and Millet. On the subject of Whitman's reading he struck a happy medium, somewhere near the real truth. Without being either a blind admirer or a skeptical detractor, Ellis fully appreciated Whitman's personality. This essay did a great deal for the American poet's reputation on the continent.

It was also in *L'Ermitage* (December, 1902) that Henri Davray undertook to present Whitman to French readers through faithful, accurate translations, with little or no

---

[154] Théodor de Wyzewa, "Walt Whitman," *Revue politique et littéraire,* XLIX, 513-519 (April, 1892).

[155] B. H. Gausseron, "Walt Whitman," *Revue encyclopédique,* May 15, 1892, pp. 721-726.

interpretation. Before Whitman could be widely known in France, such translations as these were needed, and they prepared the way for others.

During the next two decades Walt Whitman became almost a major force in French literature. But he continued to be identified with special groups and movements, each finding some special doctrines, attitudes, or tricks of style to admire or to confirm its own theories. Whitman's importance in World Literature is in great measure due to his astonishing adaptability. Just as the Symbolists found much in him to support their own program, so also did two of the three movements of reaction against Symbolism: *naturisme* and *unanimisme*. The *romanisme* of Moréas and Maurras, with its attempt to restore classicism, had of course no use for Whitman. But the whole generation of *naturisme* poets and critics adopted the pantheism, the glorification of physical joy and health, and the anti-art-for-art's sake attitude of the American poet. The Unanimist school, led by Jules Romains, was interested especially in Whitman's mystic and cosmic *ensemble*. The influence is particularly evident in the section of Romains' *La Vie unanime* which he entitled, significantly, "L'Individu."[156] Baldensperger is authority for the statement that, "The movement known as *l'unanimisme*, aiming at a sort of pantheistic and pan-social vision where the poor individual is more or less absorbed, claimed [Whitman] as a master."[157]

The Unanimist who did most for Whitman in France was Léon Bazalgette,[158] whose first biography, *Walt Whit-*

---

[156] Jules Romains, *La Vie unanime: poème* (Paris: "L'Abbaye", 1908), 121-236.

[157] Baldensperger, *op. cit.*, 307.

[158] See Dominique Braga, "Walt Whitman," *Europe nouvelle*, année 5, No. 35 (Aug. 19, 1922), 1042.

man: l'homme et son oeuvre appeared in 1908, followed in 1909 by his complete translation, *Feuilles d'herbe*. Both the biography and the translation highly idealized Whitman and his language, but they influenced a whole generation of young writers, among them the Abbaye group, which included Georges Duhamel, a later Whitmanesque poet. During this period, however, it is difficult to separate influence from parallels, for as Pierre de Lanux has emphasized,[159] Whitman's point of view exactly suited the new twentieth century, especially his mysticism, his humanism, his belief in the present, and his functional style without ornamentation.

On June 1, 1912 a critic in *Nouvelle Revue française* mentioned *le Whitmanisme* as a real force in French poetry. About the same time Henri Ghéon declared, "Il a nourri notre jeunesse."[160] Jean-Richard Bloch, in *L'Anthologie de l'Effort* (1912) praised Whitman as "the prophet from whom Vildrac and Duhamel, André Spire and Jules Romains, have learned most."[161] Duhamel himself said in *Les Poètes et la poésie* (1912), "J'ai dit que Walt Whitman fut et demeure un grand introducteur à la vie poétique."[162]

In 1914 Valéry Larbaud traced the history of Whitman criticism in France, giving a factual and sensible account up to that date. In 1918 this essay was used as the preface to a book of translations called *Walt Whitman: Oeuvres*

---

[159] Pierre de Lanux, *Young France and New America* (New York: Macmillan, 1917).

[160] Baldensperger, *op. cit.*, 307.

[161] *Ibid.*

[162] Georges Duhamel, *Les Poètes et la poésie, 1912-1914* (Paris: Mercure de France, 1912) [fourth ed.], 141. Duhamel continues: "En fait il a dévoué tous ses chants à l'éducation des hommes. Il a voulu, naïvement, prouver que le vie n'était pas une chose impossible et qu'il n'y avait pas que de la honte à vivre."

choisies, composed of poetry and prose rendered into French by Jules Laforgue, Louis Fabulet, André Gide, and Francis Viélé-Griffin. André Gide himself had been highly displeased by Bazalgette's "prettified" version and had spent much time during the first World War on a translation of his own, which finally appeared in 1919 in the "Important World Literature" series of *Nouvelle Revue française.* In 1918 Eugène Figuière also gave a series of lectures on Whitman, accompanied by recitations by various people, at the Odéon Theatre in Paris; and the following year, June 10, 1919, John Erskine lectured on him at Dijon. There was no longer any doubt in France about Whitman's being a poet. An interesting side-light on his reputation was provided in January, 1919, by Jean Guehenno in an article in *Revue de Paris* entitled "Whitman, Wilson et l'esprit moderne," in which the author accused President Wilson of having borrowed his "Fourteen Points" from Walt Whitman—a charge repeated in Germany several months later.[163]

The culmination of outright Whitman worship in France was reached in 1921 when Bazalgette published the last of his studies, *Le Poème-Évangile de Walt Whitman.* Although the attitude had been anticipated in Bazalgette's earlier biography, it is difficult to imagine how any one could go further in deifying the poet-prophet and his evangel-poem. As Schyberg remarks, this latest "idealization of the Whitman figure was too much even for the disciples in America."[164] Both this new interpretation and the re-publication of Bazalgette's translation of LEAVES OF GRASS in 1922 raised a fresh protest from Gide and his friends.

---

[163] See Note 230 below.   [164] Schyberg, *op. cit.,* 313.

Throughout these years the name of the American poet was frequently mentioned in Baldensperger's *Revue de littérature comparée,* and in 1929 Baldensperger's former student, Jean Catel, published his great study, *Walt Whitman: La Naissance du poète* (discussed in Chap. I),[165] followed in 1930 by a penetrating analysis of style, *Rythme et langage dans la première édition des "Leaves of Grass."* Both are interesting contributions to Whitman scholarship—and testify anew to the fact that this scholarship has become truly international.

In his critical biography Catel attempted to discover the reality hidden beneath Whitman's imagery, or poetic symbols. His basic theory is that here we have a poet isolated from humanity by his genius. LEAVES OF GRASS is a plea for love, an attempt to solve the personal problem. Failing to identify himself with humanity or nature, the poet tried *identité* exclusively (*i.e.,* he attempted to pierce to the soul of things, to understand the phenomenon of being). Whether or not later critics would accept this psycho-analytical interpretation, they could hardly ignore it. In subtlety and suggestiveness the French criticism of Whitman had thus surpassed the English or American— but after Catel it is mainly academic.

In the above rapid survey of Whitman's reception in France several references have been made to his influence on French literature. No one has yet made a thorough investigation of this influence, but some idea of its extent and importance (and the need for further study of the subject) may be gained by a brief discussion of a few key examples.

---

[165] See p. 59.

The Unanimist lyric socialism closely parallels Whitman's "adhesiveness" and "comradeship," and was at least in part inspired by *Calamus.* Schyberg refers to Jules Romains' novel of brotherly love, *Les Copains* (1913) as "the half glorification of the 'manly friendship' which is at once Calamus-sentimentality and devil-may-care swaggering"; but Romains' lyric poetry shows a greater Whitman influence, "with its deeply religious worship of life, its bursting fullness and democratic variety."[166] The four prophets and masters of the Unanimists were Hugo, Whitman, Verhaeren, and Claudel, "and usually all the Unanimist lyricism can be traced to the influence of one of these four."[167] Bazalgette was mainly responsible for the group's admiration for Whitman. Other Unanimists who used Whitman themes were Georges Duhamel, Pierre Jean Jouve, and Charles Vildrac. Duhamel's *Vie des martyrs* (1917), written from his experiences as a doctor in the first World War, is reminiscent of Whitman's *Drum Taps* and Civil War diaries. Both Jouve and Vildrac adopted the loose verse-form of LEAVES OF GRASS, as Vildrac plainly indicated in *Verslibrism* (1902) and *La Technique poétique* (1910).

Closely related to the Unanimists was another group of writers who were united through their internationalist sympathy and Gide's *Nouvelle Revue française,* the organ of a number of French intellectuals during World War I. Two of these who were especially affected by Whitman's influence were Panaït Istrati and Valéry Larbaud.[168] Istrati, who wrote romances of an Oriental nature —Cf. *Dyra Kyraline* and *Mikail*—used the vagabond

---

[166] Schyberg, *op. cit.,* 319.   [168] Cf. *Ibid.,* 322.
[167] *Ibid.*

friendship motifs in the Whitman manner, even to the length of phrase and cadence. Larbaud, whose preface has already been mentioned, was one of the revolutionary leaders of his literary generation, a champion in France of D. H. Lawrence and James Joyce in addition to Walt Whitman.

Most revealingly Whitmanesque is Larbaud's *Les Poésies de A. O. Barnabooth* (definitive edition, 1923). The irony and satire in the character of Barnabooth is un-Whitmanesque—or perhaps rather like a parody on Whitman—, but the vicarious desire to cover continents, to share every human experience, to embrace all knowledge, and to live in his verses after his death are extremely close in theme and spirit to many poems in LEAVES OF GRASS. Schyberg calls "Europe" a "re-worked Whitman poem" in which the poet greets in turn the great cities, the seas, and the rivers of Europe, all of which he wished to embrace simultaneously in one grand panoramic vision. "That is 'Salut au Monde' in modern French. A fastidious artist fell in love with the Whitman poetry to such an extent that he imitated it, not merely the contents, but the forms—with catalogues, participles, exclamations and acclamations, parentheses, and everything."[169]

For this brief period of post-war internationalism in France, Larbaud's Whitmanism appealed to a small coterie of intellectuals. But for a more deep and sustained influence we turn back to André Gide, who first became interested in the American poet in 1893 through Marcel Schwob, a distinguished Symbolist critic, poet, romancer, etc., who had discovered consolation in Whitman after

---

[169] *Ibid.*

deep personal bereavement. Like Symonds in England, these men found LEAVES OF GRASS a spiritual tonic. According to Rhodes, who has made a close study of the influence of Whitman on André Gide,[170] in 1893 Gide was struggling to emancipate himself from two great handicaps, puritanism and the sort of physical *anomalie* which Whitman expressed in *Pent-up Aching Rivers* and other poems in *Calamus* and *Children of Adam*. These poems "gave Gide the assurance he needed that 'la perversion de [son] instinct était naturelle . . .' Morally as well as spiritually, he felt that he had been saved; he felt that he was a new man, reborn to life as well as to art."[171]

This experience turned Gide from Symbolism, his nihilistic cynicism, and his earlier "Christian concept of the duality of human passion." In *Les Nourritures terrestres* (1897),

> He turned away from reading and dreaming to desiring and living. His emotions blossomed out; he felt every sensation with the fervor of a religious experience. He hungered for a fresh awareness of the world about him to be apprehended not only by his reason but also by his senses. "Il ne me suffit pas de *lire* que les sables des plages sont doux; je veux que mes pieds nus les sentent." To be alive, merely to be, had become a voluptous and intense satisfaction to him.[172]

In addition to the emancipation of his senses, Gide also found in Whitman "an attachment similar to that

---

[170] S. A. Rhodes, "The Influence of Walt Whitman on André Gide," *Romanic Review*, XXXI, 156-171 (April, 1940). See also Huberta F. Randall, "Whitman and Verhaeren—Priests of Human Brotherhood," *French Review*, XVI, 36-43 (1942).

[171] Rhodes, *op. cit.*, 159.

[172] *Ibid.*, 161.

he was finding in Dostoievsky 'for the precious image of Christ before us,' who 'worked His first miracle to help men's gladness . . .' "[173] Thus he could share the religious joy of life and love of all things of Whitman's *Song of Joys* or *Song of the Rolling Earth*. "Je n'ai jamais rien vu de doucement beau dans ce monde, sans désirer aussitôt que toute ma tendresse le touche. Amoureuse beauté de la terre, l'effloraison de ta surface est merveilleuse. O paysage où mon désir s'est enfoncé!"[174] Whitman's doctrine of the inseparability of good and evil healed Gide's divided spirit and convinced him of the goodness and unity of all creation. Freed from "the metaphysics of symbolist ideologies 'en dehors du temps et des contingences,' uttering the shadows of words instead of their substance," Gide "took up and lived the life of *Les Nourritures terrestres*, and sang it subsequently."[175]

Whitman was of course not solely responsible for Gide's spiritual and literary growth:

He had started moving in the same direction from the beginning. His moral and social preoccupations have become not less but more intense with the passing of time . . . The ideal both he and Whitman have pursued has been the same: the salvation of the individual soul in the modern world. The course Gide has followed describes thus a spiritual curve that runs somewhat parallel to that of Whitman. Having discovered him at the start of his career, and felt his influence, he meets him again at its close.[176]

Here we have not only the clue to the growth of Whitman's reputation in France from Etienne to Gide, but

---

[173] *Ibid.*, 162.
[174] *Ibid.*, 163.
[175] *Ibid.*, 170.
[176] *Ibid.*, 170-171.

also a clue to his importance in the modern world. The American poet was in the strong currents of a world stream of social and artistic change. Like André Gide, the twentieth century mind and spirit might have arrived at the same conclusions without Whitman, but he has quickened the human sympathy and strengthened the social conscience of democratic writers in all countries—and in none more than France.[177]

In the great socialistic Belgian poet, Émile Verhaeren, we find a literary artist so like Whitman in temperament, in lyric inspiration, and in oratorical style (with its catalogues, parallelisms, and reiterations), that it is hard to believe he was not an adoring disciple; yet he apparently had no direct knowledge of the American poet, and in the words of his biographer, "independently and unconsciously arrived at the same goal from the same starting-point."[178] But as Schyberg remarks, "Jules Laforgue provides a connecting link between them. Like the whole group of 'The Younger Belgians,' Verhaeren was definitely influenced by Laforgue's 'free form,' 'ce vers libre, si adéquat à l'âme contemporaine . . .' "[179]

Verhaeren's first poems, written under the inspiration of Symbolism, were not Whitmanesque, being protests against modern life, against industrialism and the city. But he soon threw off the shackles of Symbolism, or at least its "décadence," and in *Les Visages de la Vie* (1899), *Les Forces tumulteuses* (1902), *La Multiple Splendeur*

---

[177] This conclusion is supported by the recent biography of Klaus Mann, *André Gide and the Modern Spirit* (New York: Creative Age Press, 1944).

[178] Stefan Zweig, *Emile Verhaeren* (Boston: Houghton Mifflin Co., 1914), 108.

[179] Schyberg, *op. cit.*, 316.

(1906), and *Les Poèmes ardents* (1913) he celebrated
the joy of existence in the modern world.

> The poet wished to include the whole rhythm of life
> in his verse, the winds, the woods, the waters, 'the
> thunder's loud shout,' the whole earth as it unfolds
> itself from North to South, from East to West, from
> the cities of India and China to the 'shining cities'
> along the shores of America and Africa! He wished
> to be allowed to enter into every single person, priest,
> philosopher, soldier, money-changer, swindler, or sailor.

> Il faut admirer tout pour s'exalter soi-même . . .
>   (*Les Forces tumulteuses*)

> Je ne distingue plus le monde de moi-même . . .
>   (*La Multiple Splendeur*)[180]

In *Le Multiple Splendeur* he writes "to the winds which
go over the earth so full of love, to the grass which has
fallen down in an excess of joy, to the enthusiasms which
shall inspire the poets of today and bring forth 'the new
form for the new time!', to the joys which he, like Whitman, finds in all parts of his own body . . ."[181]

Professor P. M. Jones, who has made a penetrating
analysis of this relationship between Whitman and Verhaeren, summarizes the Belgian poet's major points of
view in three of his most important works:

> In *Les Forces tumulteuses* he has sung the mysterious
> union which pervades all forms of reality; in *La Mul-
> tiple Splendeur* the ethical role of admiration; while
> *Les Rythmes souverains* gives the world its most august
> ideal of the struggle of man to reach divinity and free

---

[180] *Ibid.*, 317.
[181] *Ibid.*

himself from the sway of chance and the supernatural.[182]

Jones finally decides, however, that Verhaeren went far beyond Whitman, though in a way that fulfilled and developed Whitman's program:

> Broadly speaking, Whitman theorizes, Verhaeren achieves. In spite of all the former has said on the subject of science and industry, he has written no poems like "La Science" or "Les Usines." Many themes which have received full treatment from Verhaeren exist as hints or indications in Whitman's works. And although Emile Verhaeren is considered one of the most original of living Continental poets, his work so often appears to realize the ideals of the American prophet-poet that he seems, all unconsciously, to be the first to have answered Whitman's appeal to the "poets to come."
>
> *I myself but write one or two indicative words for the future . . .*[183]

Another Belgian poet who also reflects the reputation and influence of Whitman is Charles van Lerbherge (1861-1907). His *Chanson d'Eve* (1904) has the themes and sentiments of *Children of Adam* and a verse form that reminds one of LEAVES OF GRASS. This is especially apparent in Eve's discovery of the beautiful earth, her pantheistic feeling about God, and her yearning for death, "which is released like a word, a note in the whistling and roaring of the universe."[184] It is, however, Whitman's "decadent" aspects which suggest the com-

---

[182] P. M. Jones, "Whitman and Verhaeren," *Aberystwyth Studies* (University College of Wales), II, 82-83 (1914).

[183] *Ibid.*, 106.

[184] Schyberg, *op. cit.*, 319.

parison. As Schyberg says, "There is a continual and peculiar interlocking between Whitman and the *Fin de Sièclists* which is remarkable."[185] But it is not the whole of Whitman, and to an English reader LEAVES OF GRASS is more unlike than like Symbolist and "decadent" poetry. The most remarkable thing about Walt Whitman's influence abroad, however, is his adaptability. He could provide inspiration for Symbolists, *Fin de Sièclists,* Unanimists, and democratic humanitarians like Verhaeren and Gide (in their "redeemed" phases). Each group found something to admire or adopt from the American poet, thus testifying to his fertility and his perennially dynamic vision of life and its meaning.

WHITMAN IN GERMANY: RECEPTION AND INFLUENCE

In no other country in the world has Walt Whitman been so extravagantly admired and even worshipped as in Germany. But from England came the initial impetus, for while a political exile in Great Britain Ferdinand Freiligrath read the Rossetti edition of Whitman's poems[186] and felt moved, as one critic has expressed it, "to contribute toward the realization of Goethe's ideal of 'Welt-Literatur' "[187] by publishing an appreciative account in a German newspaper, April 24, 1868.[188] This enthusiastic essay aroused little interest, but it is significant that in the "ego" of LEAVES OF GRASS Freiligrath found a "part of

---

[185] *Ibid.*

[186] See p. 16.

[187] O. E. Lessing, "Walt Whitman and His German Critics prior to 1910," *American Collector,* III, 7 (October, 1926).

[188] *Augsburger Allgemeine Zeitung,* reprinted in Freiligrath's *Gesammelte Dichtungen* (Stuttgart: Goschen'sche, 1877), IV, 86-87.

America, a part of the earth, of humanity, of the universe."[189] The structure of the poems reminded him of the "Northern Magus," of Hamann, of Carlyle, and, above all, of the Bible, and he thought they might, like Wagner's music, shatter "all our canons and theories." It was thus as a world poet that Walt Whitman gained his first, though obscure, recognition in Germany. Freiligrath followed up this article with some undistinguished and inaccurate translations from the Rossetti edition, which seems to have been the only one he knew; and when he returned to Germany in 1869 he encouraged his friend, Adolf Strodtmann, who had also been exiled and had spent 1852-56 in the United States, to undertake other translations from LEAVES OF GRASS.[190] These translations, however, attracted almost no attention.

For two decades after this unpromising beginning, Whitman was almost completely ignored in Germany— perhaps not surprising when one considers the period, which was a time of intense nationalism, of scientific interest, and of social agitation. Meanwhile in 1882 a German-American, Karl Knortz published an essay on the American poet in a German language newspaper in New York, later reprinted as a monograph, *Walt Whitman, der Dichter der Demokratie*.[191] His biographical interpretation was based on Bucke and O'Connor, and he himself wrote like a member of the "inner circle."

---

[189] Lessing, *op. cit.*, 7.

[190] These were published in 1870 in *Amerikanische Anthologie*. See Harry Law-Robertson, *Walt Whitman in Deutschland* (Giessen, 1935), 13-14.

[191] The paper was *New Yorker Staatszeitung*. The essay was translated for *In Re Walt Whitman* (Philadelphia: David McKay, 1893), 215-230. *Walt Whitman, der Dichter der Demokratie* appeared in several German editions, 1882, 1886, 1889, and 1899.

Thus Knortz helped to lay the foundation for the Whitman cult in Germany. But he, too, did not stop with criticism. After T. W. Rolleston was unable to get his translations of LEAVES OF GRASS published in Germany,[192] Knortz revised the manuscript and found a publisher in Switzerland in 1889. Knortz's contribution to this book seems to have been mainly editorial, but he added some translations of his own to a third edition of his *Walt Whitman, der Dichter der Demokratie* (1889). Not only were these versions superior to Freiligrath's, though still literal and crude, but German readers also got for the first time such long, characteristic, poems as *Song of Myself, Starting from Paumanok,* and *Out of the Cradle.*

As early as 1883 Rolleston had tried to call attention to Whitman's embodiment of democratic ideals,[193] but the time was not yet ripe for the appreciation in Germany of a "democratic" poet. By the time the Rolleston-Knortz edition appeared, however, the ground had been prepared. Especially among the young socialists and revolutionaries there was a great desire to break with the traditions of the past and to find new forms and expression for art and society. Both the ideas and the style of LEAVES OF GRASS quickly became vitalizing symbols for many of the young writers. Eduard Bertz felt that the high point of his visit to the United States was making the acquaintance of Whitman's poetry, which he considered naturally religious, with a gnarled originality and strength.[194] J. V. Widmann

---

[192] Rolleston wrote Whitman that he had been advised that there would be difficulties with the police if he tried to publish his translations in Germany. See *With Walt Whitman in Camden* (Boston: Small, Maynard, 1906), I, 18.

[193] *Über Wordsworth und Walt Whitman* (Dresden, 1883), written in collaboration with C. W. Cotterill.

[194] Quoted by Law-Robertson, *op. cit.,* 39, from *Deutsche Presse,* Jg. II, No. 23 (1889).

declared in the same tone: "Walt Whitman is to be understood as a Jacob Boehme, an Angelus Silesius. In him the basic principle of his ideas and creations is always an overwhelmingly strong feeling of the sacredness and innate nobility of all existence."[195] This complete acceptance of Whitman as a prophet of a new natural religion, or ontological monism, was the central faith of the Whitman cult in Germany—and "cult" is not too strong a term.[196]

The most ardent disciple of this cult was Johannes Schlaf, who, much like Carpenter in England—though more uncritical—was to make the promotion of Whitman the great work of his life. The American poet's doctrine of the unity of all creation, of man and nature, of spirit and matter, strongly influenced Schlaf's volume of poems, *Der Frühling* (1896). Among his many publications on Whitman, the best known are his monograph, *Walt Whitman*, first published in 1896 and reissued in 1904,[197] and his translation, *Grashalme, in Auswahl* [selection], 1907, 1919. He also adapted or improvised upon O'Connor's work in his essay, *Vom Guten Grauen Dichter*, 1904, and made an attempt to translate the English biography of Binns. But unfortunately Schlaf knew English so

---

[195] *Ibid.*, from *Magazin für Literatur des In- und Auslandes,* Nr. 37, S. 584 (1889).

[196] "Most of the references to Whitman [1889-1909] are characterized by a supreme admiration which, in some instances, rises in intensity even to the point of fanaticism or deification. It is this extravagant admiration for the poet which justifies the term cult as a name for the agitation as a whole," Edward Thorstenberg, "The Walt Whitman Cult in Germany," *Sewanee Review,* XIX, 77 (January, 1911).

[197] Lessing, *op. cit.,* 10, says: "This little book is an unparalleled example of high-handed arrogance, cowardly imposition, and utter ignorance." Lessing claims (following Bertz—see note 198 below) that Schlaf had read no more than 15% of Whitman's writings, and those in German translations.

imperfectly that he botched all his translations, both prose
and poetry, and drew down upon his head scathing de-
nunciations, especially from Eduard Bertz, who attempted
to expose Schlaf's ignorance and pretence.[198] But this
infatuated disciple was undaunted by such attacks and
was still "promoting" Whitman as late as 1933.[199]

There would have been a "Whitman movement" in
Germany without Schlaf's efforts, though it might not
have been so fanatical. In 1904 Karl Federn published a
collection of selected poems in translation,[200] using as
Introduction an essay which he had written twenty-five
years before.[201] He called the poems "simple and crude"
like the Psalms or the Eddas. Goethe and Whitman were
said to be alike in that "the man and his work are inseparably united." Here we find also an observation which
explains not only Whitman's appeal to these German
admirers but also his astonishing world-wide reception:
he "possessed one secret, which is the profoundest secret
of the real poet, namely that of calling forth in the reader
his own mood." Certainly this was true in Germany, and
how many of the critics interpreted the poet out of their
own moods it would be difficult to say.

Federn's translations are more poetic than those of
Knortz and vastly superior to Schlaf's, though Law-Robertson has pointed out serious inaccuracies.[202] Especially note-
worthy is the fact that Federn arranges the poems chronologically. His text is based on the 1881 edition. The same

---

[198] In *Jahrbuch für sexuelle Zwischenstufen*, IX, 551-564 (Jg. 1908).
Law-Robertson, *op. cit.*, 51, discusses the controversy.

[199] See Law-Robertson, 85.

[200] *Grashalme, Eine Auswahl*, Minden, 1904.

[201] Written for *Aus Amerikanischen Kriegszeiten*—see Lessing, *op.
cit.*, 10.

[202] Law-Robertson, *op. cit.*, 20.

year (1904) Wilhelm Schölermann published still another translation, but in his attempt to make his version
poetic he resorted to rhyme and omitted some of the repetitions from *Song of Myself*. Needless to say, the result
was not characteristic of the original. But in his introductory essay Schölermann provides an interesting illustration of the German deification of Whitman during
this period:

> Whitman belongs to a class of individuals who are
> more than life size, who spring into existence in a mo-
> ment of lavish exuberance on the part of procreative
> nature . . . Beethoven and Bismarck are men of similar
> calibre; Whitman also betrays a number of traits in
> common with that awe-inspiring man-of-men (*Ganz-
> menschen*) Jesus of Nazareth, for example, his exalted,
> tender, kindness, his heroic love . . . The healing
> power of this kindness and goodness, that ancient
> miracle-performing gift which causes the blind to see
> and the lame to walk, that gift Whitman also pos-
> sessed.[203]

Less exalted but no less ardent was the declaration in
1905 of O. E. Lessing, who had spent a year on the faculty
at the University of Illinois, that Whitman "is the center,
summit, and fountain-head of a first great epoch in the
intellectual life of the new world."[204] He called Whitman "the greatest poet since Goethe . . . He is the embodiment, the representative, and the illuminator of
American Literature in the same sense that Dante is of
the Italian, Shakespeare of the English, and Goethe of

---

[203] Translated by Thornstenberg, *op. cit.*, 79, from Schölermann's
Grashalme, p. xiv.
[204] *Walt Whitman: Prosaschriften*, Auswahl übersetzt (Münden und
Leipzig: R. Piper and Co., 1905), p. xxvi.

the German." Several years later in his retraction Lessing could truthfully say that he had "made Whitman *only* a superman instead of a God as my predecessors had done."[205] But in 1905 his prose translations, in the main accurate and competent, were a great boon to the Whitman movement in Germany. In his sound introduction he quoted from Whitman's notebooks, especially, as Law-Robertson remarks, "those which show his cosmic world outlook as well as his personal opinions about personal and human relationships."[206]

From about 1895 to 1905 or 1907, Whitman's name was a convenient literary and social symbol for many of the more revolutionary German writers, but aside from Schlaf, his actual influence is difficult to assess. Schlaf eagerly adopted Whitman's religious and cosmic ideas and attempted to re-express them in his own lyrics. *Frühling* was written under the direct inspiration of Schlaf's second-hand knowledge of LEAVES OF GRASS. *Sommerlied* (1903), though more conventional in form, showed strong influence of *Children of Adam,* while *Das Gottlied* (1922), an attempt to treat the theme of the origin of the world, was consciously Whitmanesque in manner. Like Whitman, Schlaf expected a new poetic language to emerge from the age of science and materialism, a view which he shared with his friend, Arno Holz, who deliberately tried to establish a modern theory and technique in his *Revolution der Lyrik* (1899). Because Holz was friendly both to Schlaf and Whitman at the time he was experimenting with free (Whitman's "organic")[207] rhythms, he has often been accused of indebtedness to the

---

[205] Lessing in *American Collector, op. cit.,* 11.
[206] Law-Robertson, *op. cit.,* 21.
[207] See Chap. V, pp. 409-422.

American poet. But Holz admired Whitman as a personality and ethical leader, not as a poet. In a letter he explained:

Quite a different man from Goethe or Heine was Whitman. I shall never write the name without taking off my hat to this American. He is one of the names dearest to me in the literature of the world. He wanted the change which has now taken place. But although he broke the old forms, he did not give us new ones.[208]

Amelia von Ende, in the best article on the subject in English, says of Whitman:

His aim was to give us new values of life, not new forms of art. This he has accomplished; he has given us a view of life, which it will take generations to accept, to assimilate and to put into practice. Whitman is a man among men, a poet for mankind. Holz is a poet among poets, a poet for poets.[209]

To the present writer, the chief link between Whitman and Holz seems to be their cosmic mysticism and evolutionary transmigration. Holz projects himself backward and forward in time, identifying himself with various objects in Whitman's manner, but decidedly not in his poetic form.[210]

---

[208] Quoted by Amelia von Ende, "Walt Whitman and Arno Holz," *Poet Lore*, XVI, 65 (Summer, 1905).

[209] *Ibid.*

[210] For example, one of the poems quoted by Amelia Von Ende, p. 65:
Seven billions of years before my birth
    I was an iris.
        My roots
    Were imbedded
        In a star.
    Upon its dark waters floated
    My large blue blossom.

Law-Robertson thinks that in the impressionistic school, which regarded Schlaf's *Frühling* as something of a "program," Whitman did influence the form of certain German lyricists.[211] He mentions especially Alfons Paquet's *Auf Erden* (1904-05). "Paquet's impressionistic sketches are compressed into compact pictures and therefore lack the strong exuberance of the cosmic breadth of Whitman's verse. Otherwise he uses the same stylistic methods —repetitions, enumerations, participle constructions."[212] In a letter to Law-Robertson Paquet acknowledged his indebtedness to Whitman, whom he regarded as the "Great American poet, the great prototype . . . and as often as I read his poetry, there always streams out something of the infinite space, of the simplicity and brave goodness of humanity, such as I felt in a few unforgettable happy days [in the United States], especially in the wilderness of Colorado."[213] But other impressionists, like Karl Röttger, found the basis for their "free rhythms" in older German literature, and some members of the group broke with conventional rules without knowing Whitman.[214]

The reaction against Whitman began as early as 1900 when Knut Hamsun's savage attack in a Danish paper was translated into German,[215] though the editor felt compelled to insert a footnote saying, "We who love Whitman prefer to learn about him from Johannes Schlaf."[216]

---

[211] Law-Robertson, *op. cit.*, 65-66.

[212] *Ibid.*, 65.

[213] *Ibid.*, 66-67.

[214] Cf. *Ibid.*, 68.

[215] "Walt Whitman," translated by Rudolf Komadina, for *Die Gesellschaft Halbmonatschrift für Litteratur, Kunst, und Sozialpolitik*, XVI, Bd. I, pp. 24-35 (Jg. 1900).

[216] *Ibid.*, 24.

Hamsun's argument was simply that of the literary conservatives of all countries, not least of Whitman's own contemporary Americans: he is not a poet, but an uncouth fraud. He is modern only in his brutality. In short, Hamsun attempted with heavy irony to demolish every one of the poet's literary pretentions.

Eduard Bertz was first an admirer but later a disillusioned critic of Whitman. In 1881-83 he lived in Tennessee (in one of the numerous American social experiments similar to Brook Farm) and later settled in London. He was thus better prepared than most of the German critics for genuine understanding of Whitman. In 1889 he wrote: "As the greatest benefit which I derived from my sojourn in America, nay as one of the happiest events of my life, I regard the acquaintance with the writings of the most original and deepest of all American poets."[217] Bertz sent this article to Whitman, who responded so eagerly—bombarding the author with material for future articles—that Bertz was shocked and wrote a reserved account of the poet for Spemann's *Goldenes Buch der Weltliteratur* (1900). Now suspicious, he re-examined Whitman's claims—and the claims made in his name by his over-zealous disciples—to being the founder of a new religion. In 1905 he attempted to reveal what he now regarded as Whitman's sex pathology,[218] agreeing with Edward Carpenter in the verdict. In *Der Yankee-Heiland* Bertz attempted further to destroy the "prophet myth," though he still regarded Whitman as a great lyric poet.[219] Schlaf replied to these at-

---

[217] "Walt Whitman zu seinem siebzigsten Geburtstag," *Deutsche Presse*, II, No. 23. Quoted by Lessing, *op. cit.*, 8.
[218] See note 198 above.
[219] See Chap I, p. 40.

tacks upon his "saint", and it was as a result of this quarrel that Bertz so mercilessly exposed Schlaf's pretentions as a translator and scholar.

O. E. Lessing was likewise drawn into the controversy, against Schlaf. In 1910 he confessed "to the guilt of a serious attack of Whitman"—as previously mentioned.[220] Many critics had tried to couple Whitman's name with Nietzsche's, partly, no doubt, because Nietzsche was a great name to conjure with in the late nineteenth and early twentieth century, but also because these Germans could think of no one else who had created a literary form so daring and impressive. Lessing, however, now used this comparison to "debunk" Whitman:

> As artists [Nietzsche and Whitman] have fallen below many a less famous poet. Neither *Zarathustra* nor *Leaves of Grass* are, strictly speaking, poetical compositions. They contain a wealth of esthetic material . . . . Accepting Sainte-Beuve's view [Cf. Diary of 1882 and *Democratic Vistas*] that a work of art should rather suggest emotions than give definite form to an esthetic experience, Whitman, in true romantic fashion, meets the critic's objection to the hazy vagueness of the majority of his poems.[221]

But Whitman's poetry in "its final effect is enervating rather than invigorating. In this Whitman resembles a vastly superior artist: Richard Wagner, whom Nietzsche justly calls the great sorcerer."[222] Both "possessed . . . an

---

[220] See note 205 above.

[221] Lessing, *op. cit.*, 14. Lessing first published his essay on "Walt Whitman and the German Critics" in the *Journal of English and Germanic Philology*, IX, 85-98 (1910), but to avoid confusion references are given here only to the *American Collector* version.

[222] *Ibid.*, 14-15.

indomitable sensuality, the magnetism of which, vibrating through all their compositions, causes an ecstatic intoxication invariably followed by utter exhaustion."[223]

Although the first great wave of Whitman enthusiasm in Germany had ebbed by 1910, he was not forgotten. In 1906 the Alsatian, Friedrich Lienhardt, considered the American poet the successor of Goethe.[224] A year later the proletarian poet of Austria, M. R. von Stern, hailed him as an Hegelian conditioned by a "strong autochthonic democratic instinct. There is no other poet who is so consistently permeated by democratic ideas."[225] In 1911 Knortz entered the controversy over Whitman's abnormality by publishing *Walt Whitman und seine Nachahmer, Ein Beitrag zur Literatur der Edelurninge.* He agreed in the main with Carpenter and Bertz on the subject, which he said he deliberately ignored in his *Dichter der Demokratie* in order to secure a favorable response to Whitman in Germany. This admission was an indication of the passing of the "cult".

In only a few years, however, the second Whitman movement in Germany began when the labor press discovered him at the beginning of the first World War. He was hailed by the people as he had never been in America. As Jacobson remarks, *Drum-Taps* and *Whispers of Heavenly Death* "struck upon the ear and heart of an era that experienced a similar disaster."[226] These writers were interested not so much in the poet as in the "wound-

---

[223] *Ibid.,* 15.

[224] Quoted by Law-Robertson, *op. cit.,* 69, from *Wege nach Weimar* Bd. 1, S. 279 (1906).

[225] *Ibid.,* from "Der Kollektivismus Whitmans," *Berliner Tageblatt. Beil. Zeitgeist,* No. 7, 1907.

[226] Anna Jacobson, "Walt Whitman in Germany since 1914," *Germanic Review,* I, 133 (April, 1926).

dresser" and social prophet. He became, in fact, a kind of official spokesman for the Social Democrats. Franz Diedrich thought the poet of *Drum-Taps* could be "consoler, physician, pathfinder" to the enslaved and oppressed,[227] and Max Hayek praised him in the same way in the *Sozialistische Monatshefte,* in which he frequently published translations from LEAVES OF GRASS between 1914-1931. In emphasizing this aspect of Whitman, the Social Democrats were also strongly influenced by Schlaf—thus to some extent reviving the "cult".

Of the World War I poets who were influenced by Whitman, one of the most interesting was Gerrit Engelke, a young German poet who read Whitman in the trenches and was killed in battle. His posthumous book, *Rhythmus des neuen Europa* (1923) shows us, as Jacobson remarks, "how Whitman's message became his gospel,"[228] though "his racing through all continents is not a mere imitation of Whitman, but an inevitable outcome of his inner feeling."[229] Karl Otten's song *An die Besiegten* is also reminiscent of *Drum-Taps.* And though the poems of Heinrich Lersch are more conventional in form than Whitman's, we find in them many of the themes and sentiments of LEAVES OF GRASS, especially significant being the eternal now, embracing past, present, and future.

When the war ended, Whitman became in Germany the poet of peace, and also more than ever the symbol of Democracy. Hugo Wolf, reviewing Hayek's translation, *Ich Singe das Leben,* in *Der Friede,* July, 1919, declared that President Wilson's "fourteen points" had been

---

[227] Quoted, *Ibid.,* from "Ein Beispiel Kriegsdichtung," *Die Neue Zeit,* Dez., 1914. pp. 373-382.
[228] Jacobson, *op. cit.,* 136.
[229] *Ibid.,* 136-137.

plagiarized from Whitman.[230]   Many celebrations were held in honour of the poet's centenary. Schlaf hailed him again as the perfect social and religious leader.[231]   The Socialists of the November Revolution considered him as a comrade, and the Communist poet, Johannes Becher, wrote a poem to *Bruder Whitman*. Max Hayek called LEAVES OF GRASS "in fact the Bible of Democracy. . . . Walt Whitman's time has only now arrived. He is the poet of the modern day . . . of the year that now unfolds [1919]."[232]   Whitman not only wrote of Democracy, but he lived it himself; therefore, he is a perfect example for "Social Democracy" in Germany. The working men were summoned to study Whitman.[233]   But in Austria and Hungary, translations of Whitman's works were suppressed[234]—the proletariat had found in him the power of the masses. *Freie Jugend,* a very radical paper, published a translation of Whitman's *To a Foil'd European Revolutionaire.* "Here," as Jacobson says, "Whitman is celebrated as the enemy of the state because of his love for order among men, as the enemy of the church because of his religion and conscience."[235]

This new cult led to Whitman evenings, "with slides and recitations, as for instance, in Vienna, where an actor makes out of Whitman's 'Mystic Trumpeter' a symphony

---

[230] The same charge had previously been made in France—see note 163 above.

[231] See Law-Robertson, *op. cit.,* 71.

[232] "Whitman der Dichter der Demokratische, zu seinem 100. Geburtstag, 31 Mai 1919," *Der Kampf, Sozialdemokratische Wochenschrift,* May 31, 1919, pp. 342-344.

[233] Cf. Erich Grisar, "Walt Whitman," *Leipziger Volkszeitung,* March 24-26, 1923.

[234] According to Associated Press dispatches in the *New York Times* for January 1 and March 11, 1922.

[235] Jacobson, *op. cit.,* 134.

of drama and lyricism, or in Munich, in Frankfort, and in Berlin, where Hans Reisiger and a great Reinhardt actress try to introduce Whitman into larger circles, the actress even over the radio."[236] Meanwhile the "expressionists" had also taken up Whitman,[237] and René Schickele included three of his poems (in Landauer's translation)[238] in *Menschliche Gedichte im Kriege* (1918). In fact, during the turbulent years in Germany from about 1918 to 1922 the American poet of Democracy seems to have been all things to all men.

Despite the great critical excitement over Whitman, however, no really good translations of his poems existed in Germany until the gifted Munich poet, Hans Reisiger, undertook the task. His first small volume of selections appeared in 1919, and was followed in 1922 with a greatly expanded translation in two volumes, with an eloquent Introduction.[239] This work is now regarded as a classic. Herman Stehr declared: "it is as if the great American had written not in English, but in German."[240] And Law-Robertson, who has pointed out serious faults in all previous attempts to turn Whitman's poems into German, is almost lyrical in praise of this one. In his now-famous Introduction Reisiger idealized Whitman almost as much as Schlaf had done, but he wrote from full knowledge of the poet and his work and his eloquence is due not to subjective fictionizing but to his deep, intelligent conviction of Walt Whitman's importance. In his psychological

---

[236] *Ibid.*

[237] *Ibid.*, 136.

[238] Gustav Landauer—see Law-Robertson, *op. cit.*, 78.

[239] *Walt Whitmans Werk*, Ausgewählt, übertragen und eingeleitet von Hans Reisiger (Berlin: S. Fischer, 1922). 2 vols.

[240] Quoted by Law-Robertson, *op. cit.*, 30, from *Vossiche Zeitung*, 17 Nov. 1919 (review of first edition in one volume).

approach he also anticipated Catel, Schyberg, and Canby: "Walt Whitman was one of the fortunate people who, even in ripe old age, remained wrapped in a strong and warm mother-world...."[241] At the heart of Walt Whitman's being was the fact that he had never lost the miraculous twilight gleam of childhood, the gleam of the first delightful surprise in mere existence."[242] Like many of his contemporaries in Germany, Reisiger appreciated more deeply than most Americans what the Civil War had meant to the author of LEAVES OF GRASS, and he thought that *Democratic Vistas* had a special meaning for the post-war generation in Germany.

Had political history in this nation followed a different road from the one the people were already unconsciously choosing even in 1922, Reisiger's great work might have been the beginning of a long and fruitful Whitman epoch in Germany rather than the crest of the interest which would soon recede. With unconscious irony Reisiger declared at this time:

The quick success of my first selected translation in 1919 and the fact that I can now bring out this larger work are proofs of the ever-growing interest taken by the German speaking intellectuals of Europe in this man who is being recognized with increasing certainty as the most powerful, purest, and most virile embodiment of a truly cosmo-democrat.

In the developing democracy of Germany—I use the word democracy in its political as well as its social sense—Walt Whitman will be more and more regarded as *the* poet of a new community of mankind, who has, by his truly magnetic personality, succeeded

---

[241] Reisiger, *op. cit.*, I, p. xiii.   [242] *Ibid.*, p. xix.

in blending most completely the contrast between individuality and the mass; who, fully conscious of the
wonder of his existence in the midst of the universe,
the wonder of Now and Here, expresses it with
the highest power of love, and, dwelling thus in his
Self, embraces All; whose work is nothing less than
the natural, wild, and sweet language of an exalted
type of future humanity, totally liberated in himself,
lovingly housed in the Seen and Unseen; in a word, a
Columbus of the Soul, who truly leads on God's seas
to a New World.[243]

The irony of these optimistic hopes first appears in the
use which the renowned novelist, Thomas Mann, made
of the American poet in 1922. Mann seems to have discovered Whitman in the early 1920's at a time when he
despaired of his own negative inheritance from Schopenhauer, Nietzsche, and Wagner. In thanking Reisiger for
a copy of his two-volume translation Mann called it a
"holy gift" and declared it to be of special benefit "to us
Germans who are old and unripe at one and the same
time, to whom contact with this powerful member of
humanity, the humanity of the future, can prove a very
blessing if we are able to receive his message."[244] But could
Germany receive the message? No one was more fearful
than Mann himself, for in the same year he saw the tragic
necessity of beginning a personal fight to prolong the life
of the young Republic. In his historic speech, *Von Deut-*

[243] Quoted by Theodore Stanton, in a review of Reisiger's work, "Walt
Whitman in Germany," *The Literary Review* formerly the Literary Supplement of the *New York Evening Post,* September 30, 1922, p. 68. Most
of this article is devoted to printing valuable letters from Reisiger and
Thomas Mann.

[244] Quoted, *Ibid.* Same letter also quoted by Law-Robertson, *op. cit.,*
73-74, from *Frankfurter Zeitung,* V. 16, April, 1922.

scher Republik,[245] delivered in 1922 to strengthen popular approval of the new democratic experiment in Germany, he hailed the identity of American Democracy with German Humanity, and cited Whitman and Novalis as the arch-types of each, as in his letter to Reisiger he had cited Whitman and Goethe. Mann also tried to contribute to this *rapprochement* by extoling Whitman's "athletic" Democracy, an appeal which even a National Socialist might understand; but from this time on Whitman's influence in Germany rapidly faded. The American poet was still loved by Stefan Zweig,[246] Franz Werfel,[247] and the Mann family[248]—but they were soon writing in exile, like the first German critic and translator three-quarters of a century before, Ferdinand Freiligrath. Whether the "poet of the future" which so many Germans admired between 1868 and 1922 still has a rôle to play in that unhappy land remains for the inscrutable future to disclose.

WHITMAN IN OTHER COUNTRIES

Even to outline the complete story of Whitman's reception and influence as a World Poet is obviously a task too great for the confines of this chapter. Moreover, in many countries, such as India, China, Japan, and to a large

---

[245] Republished in *Bemühungen, Neue Folge Gesammelten Abhandlungen und kleinen Aufsätze* (Berlin: Fischer, 1925), 141-190.

[246] His biography of Verhaeren (see note 178 above) is often Whitmanesque in style. Zweig is also quoted on Whitman by Stanton, *op. cit.* The influence of Whitman on Zweig's work needs to be investigated.

[247] Cf. Law-Robertson, *op. cit.,* 78. Actual influence of Whitman on Werfel is a matter of dispute. See also Detlev W. Schumann, "Enumerative Style and Its Significance in Whitman, Rilke, Werfel," *Modern Language Quarterly,* III, 171-204 (June, 1942).

[248] See especially the interesting article by Thomas Mann's son, Klaus Mann, "The Present Greatness of Walt Whitman," *Decision,* I, 14-30 (April, 1941). Klaus Mann's biography of André Gide (see note 177 above) shows great admiration for Whitman.

extent even Russia, scholars have not yet done sufficient research for an evaluation of Whitman's importance in these lands—though it is known that he has had some influence. Until this story can be told in greater detail, perhaps a rapid survey of Whitman's reception in some of these other countries will serve to emphasize his world-importance.

In 1926 Anna Jacobson began her study of Whitman in Germany by saying:

> This essay is a chapter in comparative literature, since it is the portrait of an American poet drawn, seen and interpreted from a German point of view. As this portrait has parallels of rather striking resemblance in nearly all countries of the European continent, of North and South America, and even in Asia (Japan),[249] it is also a chapter in world literature. But more than both it is a part of the great American cultural wave that is sweeping over the old Continent carrying American tendencies and ideas to other shores.[250]

The last sentence gives the key to Whitman's reception abroad, at least in recent years. His own strong personality and his dynamic art have often attracted the attention of foreign critics, but his reputation has been greatest in those times and places where American prestige was also felt.[251] This prestige was very high in Germany around 1919-20, but by 1926 it was fast ebbing away. Future studies of Whitman abroad may, therefore, il-

---

[249] Little is known about Whitman in Japan, though parts of *Leaves of Grass* and *Specimen Days* were translated and printed at Tokyo in 1920 and 1931 by S. Naganumma and Kataro Takamura. Apparently the military authorities disapproved even then.

[250] Jacobson, *op. cit.*, 132.

[251] An exception to this generalization might be the British enthusiasm for the American poet in the 1870's and '80's.

luminate the history of the cultural influence of the United States.

Denmark, as Schyberg has pointed out with some pride,[252] discovered Whitman almost as soon as England and Germany, and contemporaneously with France. In 1872 Rudolf Schmidt began writing articles on him in Copenhagen[253] and two years later he published a translation of *Democratic Vistas*. His "Walt Whitman, the Poet of American Democracy" is a sympathetic but fair summary and analysis of the poet's ideas and art, well worth reading today.[254] In 1888 Niels Møller translated *Autumn Rivulets*, but Schyberg says that "because of its remarkably complicated rhythmic diction, it did not contribute to the future understanding of Whitman's poetic art."[255] However, the fact that Whitman had no influence on Danish writers of the late nineteenth century is probably attributable to the complete indifference to him of Georg Brandes,[256] the critical dictator of the period; and Knut Hamsun, of Norway, was openly hostile.[257] Johannes V. Jensen counteracted this indifference and hostility when he published his novel, *Hjulet* (*The Wheel*), in 1905. This is a very unusual contribution to Whitman criticism, for both the hero and the villain represent the American poet's doctrines on two planes, that of a social idealist and

---

[252] Schyberg, *op. cit.*, 325.

[253] Notably, "Walt Whitman, det amerikanske Demokratis Digter," *Ide og Virkelighed*, I, 152-216 (1872); and "Walt Whitman," *Buster og Masker*, 1882, pp. 123-192.

[254] This essay translated and reprinted in part in *In Re Walt Whitman, op. cit.*, 231-248.

[255] Schyberg, *op. cit.*, 325.

[256] *Ibid.*, 15, note.

[257] See note 215 above. The German translator says, "Die Studie Hamsuns, die einen Teil einer Reihe von Vorträgen bildet, die er im Studentenverein zu Kopenhagen gehalten, stammt aus dem Jahr 1889," p. 26, note.

of a charlatan "prophet." The book contains long translated passages from LEAVES OF GRASS, which Jensen and
Otto Gelsted edited in an enlarged edition in 1918, with
a critical Introduction by Gelsted. This collection is said
to have had considerable influence on the generation of
World War I lyricists in Denmark.[258]

In 1929 Børge Houmann translated *Song of Myself*
and some other poems, with a highly romantic Introduction. And in 1933 Frederik Schyberg published his biographical and critical study, which has been mentioned so
frequently in this *Handbook* that little more need be said
about it.[259] In the same year he also published another
little book of translations.[260] There were at this time, according to this competent witness, several Whitmanesque
Danish poets, notably Harald Bergstedt, " a kindred spirit
of Whitman's—not only in his great democratic declama-
tions" but also in his lyric style. Bergstedt denies the influence, though admits that he has known Whitman since
he began writing.

In Norway Whitman has not been translated, but in
Sweden an interesting selected edition of his poems appeared in 1935, with a mediocre Introduction by the translator, K. A. Svensson. In neither of these countries, however, has the American poet had any appreciable influence.

Whitman's reception in Russia is a subject of major
importance still awaiting adequate investigation, but a
few of the more important details can be stated here. In

---

[258] Cf. Schyberg, *op.cit.,* 325. Whitman's influence on Jensen himself
is found mainly in his series of novels finally published as *The Long
Journey*—see G. W. Allen, "Walt Whitman's 'Long Journey' Motif,"
Journal of English and Germanic Philology, XXXVIII, 76-95 (January,
1939).

[259] See especially Chap. I, p. 63.

[260] *Walt Whitman, Digte* (København: Gyldendal, 1933), 126 pp.

one of the few articles on the subject,[261] we learn that while in Paris in 1872 Turgenev studied Whitman, whom he called "an amazing American poet."[262] He claimed to have undertaken some translations, though in a few months his enthusiasm cooled, and the translations have never come to light. Roman I. Zubof claimed in 1892 that LEAVES OF GRASS was known to some Russian writers, "parts of the book having already been published in the periodicals of the Russian émigrés in Switzerland."[263] The Russian decadents, like the French Symbolists, were especially attracted to Whitman. Konstantin Balmont translated LEAVES OF GRASS in 1903-05, but Parry calls the version "sickly, coquettish, aesthetic jabberwock."[264] It was denounced by Chukovsky for its inaccuracy and incompetency. He himself began translating the poems and was tried in 1905 by the Tsar's courts for publishing *Pioneers! O Pioneers!* In 1909 Maxim Gorky, who had become a champion of the American poet, declared that "Walt, having begun with individualism, had eventually reached Socialism," though Chukovsky disagreed. Many of Whitman's Russian friends tried to interest Tolstoi in him, but without success. The Socialists and Marxists, however, steadily appropriated him and he became very popular in Russia between 1917-1920. In 1918 "a poem by Walt Whitman extolling struggle [*To a European Revolutionaire?*] was distributed to Red troops fighting White Russians and American Expeditionary Forces."[265] The Soviet Government published LEAVES OF GRASS and

---

[261] Albert Parry, "Walt Whitman in Russia," *American Mercury,* XXXIII, 100-107 (September, 1934).
[262] *Ibid.,* 101.
[263] *Ibid.,* 103.
[264] *Ibid.,* 107.
[265] *Ibid.,* 100.

it became a best seller. Chukovsky's translation went through many editions. In 1922 university students in Petrograd formed a literary society in Whitman's name. Parry reports that, "By the middle nineteen-twenties, the influence of Walt Whitman could be definitely traced in the work of a score of recognized Soviet poets, and how proud they were to affirm their debt to the American!"[266]

The Russian revolutionists, therefore, accepted Whitman as one of them, but the professional Marxist critics were more discriminating. One of the outstanding Marxist studies of the American poet is that of D. S. Mirsky.[267] He sees Whitman not as the prophet of a new society but as "the last great poet of the bourgeoise epoch of humanity, the last poet of the line which begins with Dante."[268] He "is the poet of the American democracy of the fifties and sixties, with all its strength and all its limitations . . . the poet of its illusions about a new humanity already born and having only to grow and develop normally."[269] Whitman's faith in the eventual triumph of democracy is, of course, the stumbling block for the Marxists, who believe that society must first be remade before the individual can improve. Thus Mirsky thinks that Whitman is important today not for his thought but for his artistry, especially because he "brought into poetry a new concreteness, a new appreciation for the material object."[270] A later critic, Leonard Spier, writing in the English language magazine published in Moscow, *International*

---

[266] *Ibid.*
[267] D. S. Mirsky, "Walt Whitman: Poet of American Democracy," translated by B. G. Guerney, *Dialectics* (Critics Group), No. 1, 1937, pp. 11-29.
[268] *Ibid.*, 11.
[269] *Ibid.*, 14.
[270] *Ibid.*, 28.

many imagined amours; which needs, above all else, breadth of vision."[279] A third article in 1883 aroused the interest of Gabriele D'Annunzio, and in a fourth (1884) he compared Whitman to Mazzini. His essay on the "Poet of the American War," published in 1891 in *Nuova Antologia*, was translated and reprinted in America in *The Literary Digest*.[280] Here we are told that, "The humanitarian and democratic idea had already had powerful and efficacious interpreters in Burns, Schiller, Shelley, Mazzini, Victor Hugo, and a few others; but the largest, the cosmopolitan understanding of the idea is that of Whitman."[281] The names which the critic associates with Whitman are most interesting. He says further: "To me it appears that the greatest poetical imaginations in our age have been four in number: Carlyle, Michelet, Victor Hugo, Walt Whitman."[282] He thinks the reading of Browning, Tolstoi, and Whitman would be "a salutary tonic for the contemporary pessimism and fatalism of Europe."[283]

This Italian interest in Whitman led Pasquale Jannaccone to write the first acute critical analysis of his poetic technique, *La Poesia di Walt Whitman* (1898)—which still deserves to be translated into English. A scholar well acquainted with primitive Greek and Latin poetry, Jannaccone recognized that Whitman had not so much evolved new techniques as revived old ones. He thus pro-

---

[279] McCain, *op. cit.*, 7.

[280] *Literary Digest*, IV, 317-318 (January 23, 1892).

[281] *Ibid.*, 317. Nencioni apparently knew almost nothing about Whitman biography, for he wrote of the poet: "His father was a naval engineer of rigid manners . . ." and his son, after many occupations, was "like his father, a naval engineer." *Ibid.*

[282] *Ibid.*, 318.

[283] *Ibid.*

vided a rationale and an esthetics for the poet's "organic" strophic rhythms and his "psychic" rimes.[284]

As early as 1887 Luigi Gamberale began translating Whitman's poems, first publishing a collection of forty-eight as *Canti Scelti*. In 1890 he added seventy-one more poems and the 1855 Preface. This edition was reprinted in 1932 and 1934.[285] His complete translation, *Foglie di Erba*, appeared in 1907 and was reprinted in 1923. Kennedy says that Giovanni Papini, who reviewed the book, "finds Gamberale's version is by no means perfect, but 'decent and readable',"[286] but McCain reports that in Italy it is regarded as definitive.

Apropos this translation, Papini wrote a long essay on "Walt Whitman" which he later reprinted in *Four and Twenty Minds*.[287] Here he confesses that "the sage of Manhattan . . . is intimately related in my mind to one of the most important discoveries of my early youth: the discovery of poetry."[288] He compares Whitman to Nietzsche in his pride and Dionysiac emotion, but also thinks that "on other grounds" he was "a precursor of Dostoevsky and Tolstoi."[289] Papini also believes that the Italians are too polite, too gentlemanly. "If we would find again the poetry we have lost, we must go back a little toward barbarism—even toward savagery."[290] And he knows no better teacher than the American poet.

In 1920 H. Nelson Gay, an American living in Rome,

---

[284] See discussion in Chap. V, p. 403.

[285] See McCain, *op. cit.*, 10.

[286] W. S. Kennedy, *The Fight of a Book for the World* (West Yarmouth, Mass.: Stonecroft Press, 1926), 97.

[287] *Four and Twenty Minds*, translated by Ernest Hatch Wilkins, (London: George C. Harrap and Co., 1923), 130-168.

[288] *Ibid.*, 130.

[289] *Ibid.*, 154.

[290] *Ibid.*, 168.

decided "to place before the Italians an interpretation of Western thinking through a series of biographies of Americans."[291] The Americans chosen were Jefferson, Lincoln, Grant, Whittier, and Whitman. For the Whitman biography Gay selected the charming little account of Harrison S. Morris.[292] Possibly it was written expressly for this purpose, for it was not published in English until 1929.[293] No doubt the style and the size made it especially appropriate for Gay's purpose, and perhaps Italian readers would not have been interested in a longer, fuller life of Whitman, such as Bliss Perry's. Despite the eminence of some of the critics, there was never in Italy anything comparable to the French or German enthusiasm for Whitman, though he was still being discussed in critical magazines as late as 1933.[294]

Walt Whitman has never, in fact, appealed strongly to the Latin mind. This fact is emphasized by the kind of reception which Spain and Latin America accorded him. The only study of Whitman in Spain is long out of date, being the section of De Lancey Ferguson's *American Literature in Spain* (1916) devoted to the subject.[295] The very absence of later studies, however, is probably significant. And Ferguson's summary will at least indicate the nature of the Spanish reaction. He found that Whitman was "more talked about than read."[296] There was no

---

[291] McCain, *op. cit.*, 14.

[292] *Walt Whitman, poeta della democrazia* (Florence: Bemporad & Figli, 1920).

[293] *Walt Whitman, a Brief Biography with Reminiscences* (Cambridge, Mass.: Harvard University Press, 1929).

[294] See Cesare Pavese, "Interpretazione di Walt Whitman, poeta," *La Cultura*, XII, 584-604 (September, 1933). McCain, *op. cit.*, 16, also mentions an article by Mario Praz in *Enciclopedia Italiana*, 1937.

[295] John De Lancey Ferguson, "Walt Whitman," *American Literature in Spain* (New York: Columbia University Press, 1916), 170-201.

[296] *Ibid.*, 170.

translation of LEAVES OF GRASS until 1912 (a Catalan version in 1909).[297]

The Spanish critics had of course heard of Whitman through the French, but Enrique Gómez Carillo (1895) had also read the sonnet which the Nicaraguan poet, Rubén Darío, had addressed to the North American poet. Carillo's opinion of Whitman was that, "Rather than a poet of this century he seems a bard anterior to the time of Jesus; rather than a companion of Swinburne he seems a brother of Isaiah."[298]

The second Peninsular study was published in Barcelona in 1900 by J. Pérez Jorba.[299] It is mainly an exposition of Whitman's intentions and doctrines on his own terms, but we also find here one of the earliest comparisons of Whitman and Verhaeren. In 1909 Jaime Brossa, after reading Bazalgette's studies and translations, discussed the American poet as an incarnation of the spirit of the age.[300] A year later Ángel Guerra[301] decided that Whitman was not suited to the Latin temperament, though in 1911, in a second article,[302] he regarded him as the only American poet and the poet of the future. In 1912 D. Armando Vasseur published his selected translations in Valencia.[303] The next year the Catalan author, Cebriá Montoliu published the fullest study to date in Spain.[304] He had read

---

[297] *Fulles d'herba*, traducció de Cebriá Montoliu (Barcelona, 1909), 103 pp. *Walt Whitman, Poemas*, versión de Armando Vasseur (Valencia, n. d. [?1912]), 220 pp.

[298] Quoted by Ferguson, *op. cit.*, 172.

[299] J. Pérez Jorba, "Walt Whitman," *Catalonia*, February 10, 1900.

[300] Jaime Brossa, "Walt Whitman en Francia," *La Lectura*, December, 1909.

[301] Ángel Guerra, "La lírica de Walt Whitman," *La Ilustracion española y americana*, April 8, 1910.

[302] *La España moderna*, June, 1911.

[303] See note 297 above.

[304] Cebriá Montoliu, *Walt Whitman, l'home i sa tasca* (Barcelona: Societat Catalana d'Edicions, n.d. [1913]), 214 pp.

the works of the Camden "circle" and consequently gave an idealized account, though the book is important because Montoliu also traced the history of Whitman's followers, and even indicated the contours of a European movement. He had read Jannaccone and was thus prepared to understand Whitman's form. This is probably a more intelligent discussion of "the poet of the future," his intentions and his significance, than had yet appeared in English.

To judge from the representative examples which Ferguson has provided, Spanish criticism of Walt Whitman has been as intelligent and perceptive as that of any other foreign country—more intelligent, in fact, than that of most of the infatuated disciples in France, Germany, or even the United States. But there was no "cult", no "movement", and little evidence of influence.

In Spanish America Walt Whitman has aroused more excited comment, and even at times would-be idolatry, than in Spain; but once again we become convinced that the Latin mind does not readily find him congenial, or even understandable. It must be confessed, however, that no one has yet sufficiently investigated the subject, but the evidence available bears out this conclusion. The best discussion on the subject in English is the short but excellent article by John E. Englekirk.[305] The field is also being investigated by the brilliant young Chilean novelist and critic Fernando Alegría, now teaching at the University of California, who has kindly made his notes available for the following summary.

---

[305] John E. Englekirk, "Notes on Whitman in Spanish America," *Hispanic Review*, VI, 133-138 (1938).

Alegría describes the problem in this way:

To study Whitman in Spanish American poetry is to trace the wanderings of a ghost that is felt everywhere and seen in no place. His verses are quoted with doubtful accuracy by all kinds of critics; poets of practically all tendencies have been inspired by his message and have either written sonnets celebrating his genius or repeated his very words with a somewhat candid self-denial.[306]

The three main literary movements of modern times in Latin America, have, according to Alegría, responded in different ways to the North American poet. First the *Modernista* period: in 1887 José Martí, the Cuban poet, wrote an article on Whitman, after hearing him read his Lincoln poem in New York. The Nicaraguan poet, Rubén Darío addressed a sonnet to Whitman in his book, *Azul* (1888), and Armando Vasseur translated the bulk of LEAVES OF GRASS (1912?).[307] But most of these writers knew Whitman very superficially, even Darío. Alegría says, "Whitman's voice is present throughout the modernistic movement, but not his spirit." Alegría thinks the Chilean poet, Pablo de Rokha, comes nearest matching the genius and expression of Whitman.

The post-war (World War I) *Vanguardismo* movement was mainly French in origin and had little use for Walt Whitman, though in the transition from "dadaism", "surrealism", etc., some of these poets became interested in social revolution and developed enthusiasm for Whitman, among them the Peruvian César Vallejo, the Colom-

---

[306] From unpublished manuscript.

[307] See note 297 above. Later edition: *Walt Whitman, Poemas,* traducción y prólogo de A. Vasseur con un juicio de A. Guerra (Montevideo: Claudio García y Cía., 1939).

bian Sabat Ercasty, and in Argentina, E. Martínez Estrada, Parra del Riego, and Luis Franco.

The generation of the civil war in Spain, however, sings, as Alegría says, "with a civic accent, with a love of man and democracy that can only be traced back to the author of *Song of Myself*." Among these is Franco,[308] but, like the Russian Marxists, he thinks that there can be no democracy without the socialized state.

In 1938 Englekirk, finding Poe still the most popular of all North American authors in Spanish America, decided that, "The 'good grey poet,' though universal in spirit and in theme, lacks the universal appeal of 'el gran Edgardo,' and this is especially true in Spanish America where the true democratic spirit is wanting, where the prevailing note is essentially romantic, and where the Gallic influence is still all too strong."[309] But Englekirk seemed to feel in 1938 that Whitman still had a future in Latin America, and the publication of several pamphlets and books on him in the last three years supports his optimism.[310]

If space permitted, this survey might be extended to cover other countries.[311] Perhaps it would be most appropriate to complete the circle by raising the question of the effect of Whitman's increasing world-wide fame on

---

[308] Luis Franco has published two recent articles: "Walt Whitman, el pioneer," *Babel* (Santiago, Chile), Sept.-Oct., 1940; and "Vida Política de Walt Whitman," *Repertorio Americano*, No. 963, June 26, 1943.

[309] Englekirk, *op. cit.*, 133.

[310] For example: a translation of Cameron Rogers' fictionized life (*The Magnificent Idler*, London, 1926), *Vida de Walt Whitman* (La Plata, Argentine: Cayetano Calomino, 1942); C. Montolici, *Walt Whitman, el Hombre y su Obra* (Buenos Aires: Poseidon, 1943); Turina Pepita, *Walt Whitman, Cotidiano y Eterno* (Santiago: University of Chile Press, 1943).

[311] Cf. Joseph Remenyi, "Walt Whitman in Hungarian Literature," *American Literature*, XVI, 181-185 (November, 1944).

the English speaking countries. But to our surprise we discover that, despite the abundance of recent publications on Whitman in English, this subject has never been investigated. Indeed, no information is available on the reception of our poet in Canada, Australia, or New Zealand—though he was the subject in the 1890's of some lectures in the latter countries by William Gay,[312] and Mr. and Mrs. W. H. Trimble compiled a concordance of LEAVES OF GRASS in New Zealand.[313]

From South Africa, however, comes one of the most interesting of all examples of Whitman's influence. While a student at Cambridge University in England, Jan Christian Smuts wrote a book on the American poet in 1894-95.[314] He submitted the manuscript, entitled simply *Walt Whitman,* to several publishers, including Chapman and Hall, for whom George Meredith was a reader. Meredith rejected the manuscript because at that time Whitman was "so little considered in this country" that he thought the book would not sell.[315] After several other unsuccessful attempts at publication, Smuts put the book away and did not re-read it for a number of years. When he did re-examine it, he found that what he now had to say must be expressed in a philosophical work, which he has since published as *Holism and Evolution,*[316] but in his Preface he gave his *Walt Whitman* credit for the origin of this more ambitious, philosophical book. "Holism"

---

[312] See Chap. III, note 224.

[313] See Annie E. Trimble, "Concordance Making in New Zealand," *Atlantic Monthly,* CIV, 364-367 (September, 1909). This manuscript, still unpublished, is now owned by Brown University.

[314] See Sarah Gertrude Millin, *General Smuts* (Boston: Little, Brown, and Co., 1936), I, 35 ff.

[315] *Ibid.,* 36.

[316] J. C. Smuts, *Holism and Evolution* (New York: Macmillan Co., 1926).

(*i.e.,* philosophy of the "whole") cannot be explained in a few words, but to the present writer it seems to be mainly a scientific view of what is more commonly known as Whitman's "organic" doctrine[317]—especially the "organic" theory applied to Personality and Society, though Smuts does not neglect the cosmic aspects.[318] In her account of the relations between Smuts and President Wilson, the General's recent biographer also reveals that Smuts was at least in part the author of the famous "fourteen points."[319] In view of his interest in Whitman, the French and German critics who claimed that the "fourteen points" originated with the American poet may not have been entirely wrong.[320]

When we return to Whitman's own land, we meet what seems at first a paradox. No other native poet is more often quoted by press or radio, or more highly admired by present-day critics and historians of literature. Yet among the writers themselves he apparently has no followers. No poet, from Amy Lowell to Carl Sandburg,[321] has confessed indebtedness to him. Moreover, there is no evidence that they are wrong. But "influence" is a difficult word to define. The fact that Whitman has no imitators or "disciples" (like Horace Traubel or Edward Carpenter) does not mean that his example of literary pioneering and his democratic ideas have not permeated the heart and spirit of writers like Sherwood Anderson and Thomas Wolf, to mention only two. These two, in fact, help to

---

[317] See discussion of Whitman's "organic" doctrine, Chap. III, p. 292.
[318] *Ibid.,* Chap. XII, "The Holistic Universe," 317-345.
[319] Millin, *op. cit.,* II, 159 ff.
[320] See notes 163 and 230, above.
[321] Sandburg admires Whitman, however, and wrote a warmly appreciative Introduction for the Modern Library edition of LEAVES OF GRASS in 1921.

explain the nature of Whitman's influence in modern American literature, for they were both obviously influenced by such European authors as Proust and Joyce. The latter probably owed little, if anything, to LEAVES OF GRASS but the literary technique of Whitman's "expanding ego", for example, was a forerunner of the "stream-of-consciousness" style; and his democratic idealism is in the life-blood of every social-minded writer of contemporary America. Walt Whitman's influence, even in his own beloved States, is difficult to trace today because he was, as Burroughs said, "in the great world-current."

SELECTED BIBLIOGRAPHY

[Note: additional references to criticism in various languages will be found in the footnotes of this chapter. See also the Whitman bibliography in *The Cambridge History of American Literature*, Vol. II, and G. W. Allen, *Twenty-Five Years of Walt Whitman Bibliography* (Boston, 1943).]

AMERICAN TRANSCENDENTALISM

FROTHINGHAM, O. B. *Transcendentalism in New England*. New York: Putnam's Sons. 1876.
[Gives some attention to German sources.]
GODDARD, H. C. *Studies in New England Transcendentalism*. New York: Columbia University Press. 1908.
[Standard work.]
GOHDES, CLARENCE C. "Whitman and Emerson." *Sewanee Review*, XXXVII, 79-93 (January, 1929).
[Study of the relationship.]
HOWARD, LEON. "For a Critique of Whitman's Transcendentalism." *Modern Language Notes*, XLVII, 79-85 (February, 1932).
[Differentiates between Emerson and Whitman.]

MOORE, JOHN B. "The Master of Whitman." *Studies in Philology,* XXIII, 77-89 (January, 1926).
[Influence of Emerson on Whitman.]

ORIENTALISM

CARPENTER, EDWARD. "The Upanishads and *Leaves of Grass.*" *Days With Walt Whitman,* pp. 94-102. London: George Allen. 1906.
[Interesting parallels quoted.]
CARPENTER, F. I. *Emerson and Asia.* Cambridge, Mass.: Harvard University Press. 1930.
[For background—more superficial than Christy, *q. v.*]
CHRISTY, ARTHUR E. *The Orient in American Transcendentalism.* New York: Columbia University Press. 1932.
[Discussion of Orientalism of Emerson and Thoreau provides valuable background for Whitman.]
GUTHRIE, WILLIAM N. *Walt Whitman, Camden Sage.* Cincinnati: Robert Clark Co. 1897.
["Vedantic views" in *Leaves of Grass,* p. 25 ff.]
MERCER, DOROTHY FREDERICA. *Leaves of Grass and Bhagavad Gita.* University of California. 1933.
[Unpublished doctoral dissertation. Critical rather than source study.]

GERMANY[322]

BOATRIGHT, MODY C. "Whitman and Hegel." *Studies in English,* No. 9, *University of Texas Bulletin,* July 8, 1929, 134-150.
CLARK, GRACE DELANO. "Walt Whitman in Germany." *Texas Review,* VI, 123-137 (January, 1921).
FALK, ROBERT P. "Walt Whitman and German Thought." *Journal of English and Germanic Philology,* XL, 315-330 (July, 1941).
FULGHUM, W. B., JR. "Whitman's Debt to Joseph Gostwick." *American Literature,* XII, 491-496 (January, 1941).
[Supplements Boatright.]

---

[322] For additional bibliography see references in Clark, Jacobson, Law-Robertson (best), Riethmueller, and Thorstenberg.

JACOBSON, ANNA. "Walt Whitman in Germany since 1914."
Germanic Review, I, 132-141 (April, 1926).

LAW-ROBERTSON, HARRY. *Walt Whitman in Deutschland.* Giessen: Münchowsche Universitäts. 1935.
[The fullest account of Whitman's reception in Germany.]

LESSING, OTTO EDUARD. "Walt Whitman and His German Critics prior to 1910." *American Collector,* III, 7-15 (October, 1926).

PARSONS, OLIVE W. "Whitman the Non-Hegelian." *Publications of Modern Language Association,* LVIII, 1073-1093 (December, 1943).
[Claims that Whitman did not understand the Hegelian dialectic.]

RIETHMUELLER, RICHARD. "Walt Whitman and the Germans." *The German American Annals,* n. s., IV, Nos. 1-3 (January-March, 1906).
[Some of the comparisons are far-fetched.]

SPRINGER, OTTO. "Walt Whitman and Ferdinand Freiligrath." *The American-German Review,* XI, 22-25 (December, 1944).
[On Whitman's first German critic and translator.]

THORNSTENBERG, EDWARD. "The Walt Whitman Cult in Germany." *Sewanee Review,* XIX, 71-86, (January, 1911).

VON ENDE, AMELIA. "Walt Whitman and Arno Holz." *Poet Lore,* XVI, 61-65 (Summer, 1905).
[Holz admired Whitman's ideas, not form.]

ZAREK, OTTO. "Walt Whitman and German Poetry." *Living Age,* CCCXVI (Vol. XXIX in 8th ser.), 334-337 (February 10, 1923).

Translation:

Walt Whitmans Werk. Ausgewählt, übertragen und eingeleitet von Hans Reisiger. Berlin: S. Fischer. 1922. 2 vols.
[The only successful translation into German.]

ENGLAND[323]

BLODGETT, HAROLD. *Walt Whitman in England*. Ithaca: Cornell University Press. 1934.
[A definitive study; contains bibliography.]

CAIRNS, W. B. "Swinburne's Opinion of Whitman." *American Literature*, III, 125-135 (May, 1931).

MONROE, W. S. "Swinburne's Recantation of Walt Whitman." *Revue Anglo-Américaine*, VIII, 347-351 (March, 1931).

PAINE, GREGORY. "The Literary Relations of Whitman and Carlyle, with Especial Reference to their Contrasting Views of Democracy." *Studies in Philology*, XXXVI, 550-563 (July, 1939).

SMITH, FRED M. "Whitman's Debt to Sartor Resartus." *Modern Language Quarterly*, III, 51-65 (March, 1942).

————. "Whitman's Poet-Prophet and Carlyle's Hero." *Publications of Modern Language Association*, LV, 1146-1164 (December, 1940).

FRANCE

ALLEN, GAY W. "Walt Whitman and Jules Michelet." *Etudes Anglaises*, I, 230-237 (May, 1937).
[Parallels between *Leaves of Grass* and *The People*.]

BALDENSPERGER, F. "Walt Whitman and France." *Columbia University Quarterly*, XXI, 298-309 (October, 1919).
[Whitman's reception and influence.]

GOODALE, DAVID. "Some of Whitman's Borrowings." *American Literature*, X, 202-213 (May, 1938).
[Shows especially Whitman's indebtedness to Volney's *Ruins*.]

JONES, P. M. "On the Track of an Influence in 1913." *Comparative Literature Studies*, VI-VII, 20-22 (1942).
[Notes on Whitman's influence in France before First World War.]

---

[323] For primary sources—too many to list here—, see bibliography in Blodgett, *q. v.*

————. "Whitman and Verhaeren." *Aberystwyth Studies* (University College, Wales), II, 71-106 (1914). [Invaluable comparative study.]

KNAPP, ADELINE. "Walt Whitman and Jules Michelet, Identical Passages." *Critic*, XLIV, 467-468 (1907). [Whitman's "The Man-of-War-Bird" based on passages in Michelet's *The Bird*—see also Allen.]

LANUX, PIERRE DE. *Young France and New America*. New York: Macmillan and Co. 1917. [Whitman frequently mentioned.]

RANDALL, HUBERTA F. "Whitman and Verhaeren—Priests of Human Brotherhood." *French Review*, XVI, 36-43 (1942).

RHODES, S. A. "The Influence of Walt Whitman on André Gide." *Romanic Review*, XXXI, 156-171 (April, 1940).

SARRAZIN, GABRIEL. *La Renaissance de la Poésie Anglaise, 1798-1889*. Paris: Perrin. 1889. [Discussion of Whitman translated in Traubel, Harned, Bucke, *In Re Walt Whitman*. Philadelphia: David McKay. 1893. Pp. 159-194.]

SHEPHARD, ESTHER. *Walt Whitman's Pose*. New York: Harcourt, Brace and Co. 1938. [On George Sand as Whitman's major source. Valuable information, doubtful conclusions.]

STARR, WILLIAM T. "Jean Giono and Walt Whitman." *French Review*, XVI, 118-129 (December, 1940).

Translations:

Feuilles d'herbe. Traduction intégrale d'après l'édition définitive par Léon Bazalgette. Paris: Mercure de France. 1909. 2 vols. [The standard translation, though strongly criticized by André Gide and others.]

Oeuvres choisies, poèmes et proses. Traduits par Jules Laforgue, Louis Fabulet, André Gide [et autres] . . ., précédes d'une étude par Valéry Larbaud. 6 éd. Paris: Gallimard, Éditions de la Nouvelle revue française. 1930. [Perhaps the best translation of selections.]

SCANDINAVIA

ALLEN, GAY W. "Walt Whitman's 'Long Journey' Motif."
Journal of English and Germanic Philology, XXXVIII, 76-95 (January, 1939).
[Compares the evolution-of-the-race motif of Wergeland, Jensen, and Whitman.]

BENSON, ADOLPH B. "Walt Whitman's Interest in Swedish Writers." *Journal of English and Germanic Philology*, XXXI, 332-345 (July, 1932).
[Interest too late to affect Whitman's poetry.]

SCHYBERG, FREDERIK. "Whitman i Verdenslitteraturen." *Walt Whitman*, pp. 273-338. København: Gyldendal. 1933.
[Most complete and valuable study in print on "Whitman in World Literature."]

Translations:

Walt Whitman, Digte. Translated by Johannes V. Jensen and Otto Gelsted: Introduction by Jensen. København and Kristiania: Nyt Nordisk Forlag. 1919. 143 pp.
[Revision and expansion of Jensen's translations in *Hjulet*, 1905.]

Walt Whitman, Digte. Translated by Frederik Schyberg. København: Gyldendal. 1933. 126 pp.

Strån av Gräs. Selected translations with an Introduction, by K. A. Svensson. Stockholm: A. B. Seelig. 1935. 207 pp.

RUSSIA

MIRSKY, D. S. "Walt Whitman: Poet of American Democracy." Translated by B. G. Guerney. *Dialectics* (Critics Group), No. 1, 1937, pp. 11-29.
[Perhaps the outstanding Marxist study of Whitman.]

PARRY, ALBERT. "Walt Whitman in Russia." *American Mercury*, XXXIII, 100-107 (September, 1934).

SPIER, LEONARD. "Walt Whitman." *International Literature* (Moscow, Russia), No. 9, 1935, 72-89.

Translation:

CHUKOVSKII, KORNEI IVANOVICH. Vot Vitmen i ego "List' ia travy." Izdanie shestoe, dopol. [Walt Whitman and his Leaves of Grass. 6th ed., enl.] Moskva: Gosudarstv. izd. 1923. 165 pp.

ITALY

McCAIN, REA. "Walt Whitman in Italy: a Bibliography." *Bulletin of Bibliography,* XVII, 66-67; 92-93 (Jan.-Apr., May-Aug., 1941).

————. "Walt Whitman in Italy." *Italica,* XX, 4-16 (March, 1943).

NENCIONI, ENRICO. "Poet of the American War." *The Literary Digest* (anonymous translator), IV, 317-318 (January 23, 1892).

[Published in 1885 in *Nuova Antologia.*]

PAPINI, GIOVANNI. "Walt Whitman." *Four and Twenty Minds,* 130-168. Translated by Ernest Hatch Wilkins. London: Harrap. 1923.

Translation:

Foglie di erba. Translated by Luigi Gamberale. Palermo: Remo Sandron. 1907. Revised, 1923. 2 vols.

[Accepted as complete and definitive.]

SPAIN AND LATIN AMERICA[324]

DONOSO, ARMANDO. "The Free Spirit of Walt Whitman." *Inter-America,* III, 340-346 (August, 1920).

ENGLEKIRK, JOHN E. "Notes on Whitman in Spanish America." *Hispanic Review,* VI, 133-138 (1938).

[Brief but best in print.]

FERGUSON, JOHN DE LANCEY. "Walt Whitman." *American Literature in Spain,* pp. 170-201. New York: Columbia University Press. 1916.

[Contains short but useful bibliography.]

---

[324] Additional bibliographical items in footnotes, No. 295 ff. Fernando Alegría of the University of California has in preparation critical and bibliographical articles on this subject.

Torres-Rioseco, A. *Rubén Dario.* Cambridge, Mass.: Harvard University Press. 1931. [Discusses Whitman and Darío.]

Translation:

Walt Whitman, Poemas. Traducción y Prólogo de A. Vasseur con un juicio de A. Guerra. Montevideo: Claudio García y Cía. 1939. [Vasseur's first translation was published in Valencia in 1912.]

INDEX

Abbreviations: *n* indicates footnote; *b*, bibliography.